The Irish
Labor Movement in the
Nineteenth Century

The Irish
Labor Movement in the
Nineteenth Century

John W. Boyle

The Catholic University of America Press
Washington, D.C.

Copyright © 1988
The Catholic University of America Press
All rights reserved
Printed in the United States of America

Library of Congress Cataloging-in-Publication Data

Boyle, John William, 1914–
    The Irish labor movement in the nineteenth century / John W.
Boyle.
        p.   cm.
    Bibliography: p.
    Includes index.
    ISBN 0-8132-0637-5
    1. Trade-unions—Ireland—History—19th century.   2. Labor and
laboring classes—Ireland—History—19th century.   I. Title.
HD6670.3.B69   1987
331.88'09415—dc19   87-27983
                                                            CIP

John W. Boyle
The Irish Labor Movement in the Nineteenth Century

ERRATUM

p. 9, line 32 should read:

· · ·; he was granted 20 pounds, to be · · · ·

instead of:

· · ·; he was granted 201 pounds, to be · · · ·

I gcuimhne
Chonchúir
1945 – 1958

Contents

Preface

NOTE. *I have chosen to regard the nineteenth century as beginning in 1825 and ending in 1906. The repeal of the combination laws in 1824, and the amending legislation in 1825, not only gave trade unions a legal existence but also brought Irish trade union law into conformity with that prevailing in the rest of the United Kingdom. Such events as the election of a Liberal government that made Irish Home Rule a distinct possibility, the passing of a long-awaited Trades Disputes Act, and the inconclusive debates on highly contentious issues at the Athlone meeting of the Irish Trades Union Congress suggest 1906 as a terminal date, but the primary justification is the arrival in January 1907 of James Larkin, for in due course his campaign to organize general workers altered the character of the Irish labor movement by transferring its leadership from the old to the new unionism.*

Many historians of Irish labor have written on the lives and times of Larkin and Connolly, the two leaders who grew up in British cities before beginning their careers in Ireland. The choice is understandable but, at a time when much remains to be done in Irish labor history, it has left not a few students with an impression of the Irish labor movement before the two men's arrival as a confused, indistinct canvas, a backdrop already in place. How it came to be there, or how the canvas acquired the scenes and colors on it, are questions that, at least until relatively recently, have excited but moderate interest. Yet these are not negligible questions; the answers to them can provide a clearer realization of the obstacles faced by the two men and, of greater importance, some understanding of the conditions that determined the fortunes of urban labor in a country primarily agricultural, which, by virtue of its political and economic subordination to the first fully industrialized nation, exhibited some of the features associated with colonial rule. I have attempted to answer these questions in this account of the Irish labor movement in the nineteenth century.

In 1925 the Columbia University Press published Professor Jesse Dunsmore Clarkson's *Labour and Nationalism in Ireland*. The present volume differs from Clarkson's pioneer study in a number of respects. My object has been to describe the growth in Ireland during the nineteenth century of labor, socialist, and kindred organizations, but I have not excluded consideration of the pervasive and continuous influ-

ence of nationalism or of the relations between Irish and British labor.
The importance of Belfast, both as an industrial center and as the
headquarters of Ulster Unionism, has justified a fuller treatment of its
labor movement, which should not be treated in isolation but requires
that, in any serious study of labor in Ireland, its role be recognized. I
have made use of the minutes and related documents of the two most
important trades councils in Ireland, those of Belfast and Dublin,
because the annual reports of the Irish Trades Union Congress, which
the councils antedate and later dominate, inadequately reflect developments in the two cities. In addition, the records are crucial to an
understanding of the sharply differing milieux in which the councils
worked and of the pressures that helped to determine their actions.

It is my pleasant duty to acknowledge the assistance given me since I
began the study of Irish labor history some three decades ago. My major
debt is to the late Professor T. W. Moody, who was the supervisor of my
thesis, part of which I have used in this work, for the degree of Ph.D.
from the University of Dublin (Trinity College). I remember gratefully
his encouragement and patient counsel during the research and writing, and his continued interest in an erstwhile pupil. Dr. Henry Pelling of St. John's College, Cambridge, who aided me in divers ways,
prompted me to trace the early growth of British general unions in
Ireland.

My debt to Professor Emmet Larkin of the University of Chicago is
not to be measured by references to his writings. From the earliest days
of our acquaintance I have benefited by his advice and open-handed
generosity, shown not least in his entrusting me with unpublished
work and research. To Dr. A. G. Donaldson I owe the elucidation of
some legal questions, notably the history of Irish election deposits. My
particular thanks go to Messrs. F. A. D'Arcy, R. P. Davis, and F. J.
Whitford, who lent me the theses listed in the bibliography.

For ready access to libraries and archives I am indebted to officials of
the following institutions: Queen's University Library and the Linen-
hall Library (Belfast), the Irish State Paper Office, the Library of
Trinity College (Dublin), the National Library of Ireland, the British
Museum Newspaper Library (Colindale), the British Library of Po-
litical and Economic Science, Instituto Feltrinelli (Milan), Institut
Français d'Histoire Sociale (Paris), International Instituut voor Sociale
Geschiedenis (Amsterdam), La Maison du Peuple (Brussels), and the
State Historical Society of Wisconsin (Madison). I must thank es-
pecially Mr. James Vitty (Linenhall Library), Mr. Patrick Henchy
(N.L.I.), Professor Tom O'Neill and Mr. Ailfrid MacLoichlainn (for-
merly of N.L.I. and latterly of University College, Galway), who have

earned the gratitude of many students by allowing them to draw upon
their special knowledge and by endeavoring to maintain the services of
two indispensable repositories in the face of difficulties long aggravated
by official indifference.

I have been greatly aided over the years by permission to consult,
borrow, or microfilm original records, documents, and correspondence; by gifts of trade union histories, pamphlets, election addresses,
periodicals, and other ephemeral material; and, especially in the earlier
years, by interviews with veteran members of labor organizations, their
relations, or contemporaries, some, alas, now dead. I owe thanks to
Mr. Ruadhri Roberts and Mr. Donal Nevin of the Irish Congress of
Trade Unions (formerly the Irish Trades Union Congress), to the former
secretaries of the Belfast and Dublin Trades Councils (Miss Betty Sin-
clair and Mr. John Collins), to Belfast district officers of the Amalgamated Society of Woodworkers and of the Typographical Association,
to Professor Chimen Abramsky, Professor François Bédarida, Mr.
D. W. Bleakley, Mr. R. R. Bowman, Mr. Andrew Boyd, Mr. William
Boyd, Mr. R. H. Campbell, Mr. Fred Carson and Mrs. Carson, Mr.
Joseph Cooper, Miss Morna Crawford, Mr. Samuel Hazlitt, Mr.
Bulmer Hobson and his sister Mrs. F. F. Patterson, Mr. John Jamison,
Mr. Thomas R. Johnson and Mrs. Marie Johnson, Mr. Jack Mac-
gougan, Mr. D. J. McDevitt, Mrs. Kathleen T. McCloy, Mrs. Mar-
garet McCoubrey, Mr. Sean McKeown, Mr. Robert McClung, Mr.
William McMullen, Mr. Robert Matchett, Mr. William O'Brien, and
Mrs. Walker, widow of William Walker. I remember with gratitude
Bob McClung, whose wry complaint during an election campaign in
the 1940s that his subagents would not send him "the scrape of a pen"
made me realize how easily lost are the sources of labor history; Fred
Carson, who was unwearying in his search for documents and for
veterans of the labor movement; and Danny McDevitt, whose memories of events and persons around the turn of the century were remarkably detailed and vivid even in his nineties.

The late Dr. F. S. L. Lyons, in the introduction to his *Ireland since the
Famine* (1971), pointed out that much of the research on the nineteenth
century carried out during the previous forty years was concerned with
political history to the serious neglect of other kinds. To attempt a
history of Irish labor is to realize the uncomfortable truth of Professor
Lyons's statement and to be all the more grateful to those who have
made contributions to it. Accordingly I have tried to be scrupulous in
acknowledging the work of others while endeavoring to fill, however
imperfectly, some of the gaps that remain. I hope it will not be invid-
ious to single out as particularly helpful the work of Andrew Boyd,
J. D. Clarkson, Fergus D'Arcy, Desmond Greaves, Emmet Larkin,

Rachel O'Higgins, Desmond Ryan, and John Swift. Elizabeth Boyle, in addition to providing general support, advice, and comment, assisted in the discovery of some source material and in the preparation of sections of the manuscript. To sum up, while I cannot follow the pavement artist and claim that what I present is all my own work, I must still claim all responsibility for errors and omissions.

I have to thank Mrs. Helen Brown (Sackville, New Brunswick) for typing large portions of the manuscript, Mrs. Patricia Law (Guelph) for typing the appendixes, and Dr. David and Mrs. Gisela Schweitzer (Guelph) for deciphering my revisions.

These acknowledgements would be incomplete if I did not express my appreciation of yet other kinds of assistance. I am grateful to the Warden and Fellows of New College, Oxford, who at an early stage of this work elected me to a schoolmaster studentship, and to the Governors of the Royal Belfast Academical Institution who enabled me to accept it by granting me a sabbatical term. At a later period, when it was imperative that I investigate newly available primary sources, I was signally helped by the Canada Council (now the Social Sciences and Humanities Research Council) and the University of Guelph with travel grants. Finally, to Ms. Peggy Leonard, staff editor, and others who have prepared the manuscript for publication I owe my sincere thanks.

Department of History   JOHN W. BOYLE
University of Guelph

Abbreviations

A.O.H.	Ancient Order of Hibernians
A.S.C.J.	Amalgamated Society of Carpenters and Joiners
A.S.E.	Amalgamated Society of Engineers
A.S.L.E.F.	Amalgamated Society of Locomotive Engineers and Firemen
A.S.R.S.	Amalgamated Society of Railway Servants
A.S.T.	Amalgamated Society of Tailors
B.E.T.	*Belfast Evening Telegraph*
B.N.-L.	*Belfast News-Letter*
B.P.A.	Belfast Protestant Association
B.T.C.	Belfast Trades Council
B.T.U.C.	[British] Trades Union Congress
B.W.S.	*Belfast Weekly Star*
Clarkson	J. D. Clarkson, *Labour and Nationalism in Ireland*
D.F.I.	*Documents of the First International*
D.N.B.	*Dictionary of National Biography*
D.S.U.	Dublin Socialist Union
D.T.C.	Dublin Trades Council
D.T.P.S.	Dublin Typographical Provident Society
F.J.	*Freeman's Journal*
G.S.W.R.	Great Southern and Western Railway
H.C.	House of Commons
I.D.A.	Irish Drapers' Assistants
I.F.U.	Irish Federal Union of Bakers
I.H.S.	*Irish Historical Studies*
I.I.S.G.	International Instituut voor Sociale Geschiedenis
I.L.P.	Independent Labour Party
I.N.	*Irish News*
I.N.L.U.	Irish National Labour Union
I.R.B.	Irish Republican Brotherhood
I.O.O.	Independent Orange Order
I.S.R.P.	Irish Socialist Republican Party

I.T.	*Irish Times*
I.T.U.C.	Irish Trades Union Congress
I.W.M.A.	International Working Men's Association
J.P.	Justice of the Peace
L.E.A.	Labour Electoral Association
L.R.C.	Labour Representation Committee
M.-E.N.	Marx–Engels Nachlass
M.N.	[Belfast] *Morning News*
M.P.	Member of Parliament
N.A.U.L.	National Amalgamated Union of Labour
N.A.U.S.A.W.C.	National Amalgamated Union of Shop Assistants, Warehousemen and Clerks
N.L.I.	National Library of Ireland
N.U.D.L.	National Union of Dock Labourers
N.U.R.	National Union of Railwaymen
N.W.	*Northern Whig*
S.D.F.	Social-Democratic Federation
S.L.	Socialist League
S.L.P.	Socialist Labour Party
S.P.I.	Socialist Party of Ireland
S.S.F.	Scottish Socialist Federation
T.A.	Typographical Association
T.U.C.	Trades Union Congress
U.T.A.	/Dublin/United Trades' Association

Introduction

The town was not indigenous to early Ireland. Those in existence before the Anglo-Norman invasion of the late twelfth century were Ostman seaport towns and their citizens the descendants of Vikings who had turned from piracy to trade. Under Angevin rule they received charters modeled on those of Bristol or Breteuil, but their subsequent growth was slow until the Tudors ended the recurrent threats to Dublin and other towns by subduing Norman or Gaelic overmighty subjects and extending the royal writ throughout Ireland. English legislation governing certain trades was dutifully adopted by the colonial Irish parliament. In the sixteenth century regulation of wages, first decreed by the 1388 Statute of Artificers, was entrusted to justices of the peace, who were still determining the pay of masters, journeymen, and apprentices in the late seventeenth century. When the widening gap between master and man gave rise to combinations of journeymen is uncertain, but their legal, or rather illegal, existence was officially acknowledged in 1729 by an act, the first of many, that punished with imprisonment workmen guilty of combining to secure higher wages or fewer hours of work.

In the late eighteenth century there was no marked difference in organization, objectives, and activities between Irish and British trade clubs and societies, which were local in character, composed of skilled craftsmen, and hampered by broadly similar repressive legislation. In some trades, clubs in both islands exchanged information on wage and price lists, and afforded relief to members "on the tramp" in search of work. What changes the new century brought appeared to herald an even closer relationship. Efforts were made, especially after 1825, to form federations or United Kingdom—wide trade unions, and where they failed the causes were geographical or financial, not political: societies were reluctant or unable to pay the expenses of delegates sent to distant meeting places. In the second half of the century a united labor movement in the British Isles seemed assured; British amalgamated unions, aided by greater ease of travel and improved communications, increased their Irish membership by opening new branches or absorbing existing Irish societies until they included the great majority of organized Irish workers, while the participation, however irregular, of Irish trade unionists in the British Trades Union Congress (T.U.C.) seemed a further indication of where their allegiance lay. Even the formation of a separate Irish Trades Union Congress (T.U.C.) in 1894 was not a declaration of independence by its founders, who took pains to deny any charge of promoting disunity and saw its role as supplementary to that of the larger body.

Yet the unity of organized labor in the British Isles was more apparent than real and rested on a basis scarcely more solid than that of the United Kingdom itself. The eighteenth-century Irish parliament was not unrepresentative merely because, like the British model, it was unreformed, but because it was a Protestant ascendancy parliament in a colonial country where the majority of the population was Catholic. A concession was made in 1793 when Catholics were allowed to vote on the same basis as Protestants, though they could not become Members of Parliament. The Act of Union abolished the Irish parliament, giving representation in the United Kingdom parliament, but left in Dublin an administration subject to a Westminster-appointed executive. From 1829, however, the adjective "colonial" requires qualification if it is to be accurate. The Catholic emancipation bill passed in that year, allowing Catholics to be elected to parliament, marks an important step in the erosion of Protestant ascendancy, a process continued throughout the century. Successive extensions of the parliamentary and local government franchises, the disestablishment of the Protestant episcopalian Church of Ireland, and a series of agrarian reforms were changes that placed more power in the hands of those who represented what politicians delighted to call "the plain people of Ireland." And yet "colonial" is not an inapposite description as long as Westminster rejected the demand of a majority of the Irish population for some form of self-government.

British legislators had attempted to dissipate Irish political discontents by including Ireland in the larger polity of the United Kingdom, but did little to ease its economic difficulties. Even before 1800 the two economies differed markedly, for Great Britain, with its abundant supplies of coal and iron, was undergoing those changes that were to make it the first industrialized nation in the world. Except in the northeast, and then at a later date, Ireland underwent no industrial revolution. Its economy remained primarily agricultural and its manufactures, with few exceptions, were small-scale, rural, or even domestic in character. Rapid population growth was common to both islands, but whereas in Great Britain much of it was accommodated in the new industrial towns, in Ireland the greatest increases were in the rural areas where population pressure added greatly to the difficulties of an inefficient agricultural system. There was no British equivalent of the Irish Great Famine of the 1840s, which savagely reversed demographic trends by death and emigration. At the end of the century the fall in the number of rural inhabitants had reduced the population total to little more than half of the pre-Famine figure. The small urban population, on the other hand, had risen by 22 percent, thanks mainly to the growth of Belfast.[1]

Though the depopulation caused by the Great Famine contributed to the decline in rural trades, the fundamental reason for the decay of Irish manufactures was Ireland's failure to undergo an industrial revolution. Even before the Famine large quantities of English-made goods were appearing on the Irish market, and every increase in the efficiency of English industry through the adoption of new processes, improved machinery, and large-scale production made Irish manufacturers less able to withstand competition from the workshop of the world. There was no recovery in the second half of the century. The food and drink trades managed to do more than hold their own, but elsewhere the tale was a dismal one. By the end of the century most consumer goods except food were imported, as were premanufactured supplies for the building trade—even to the extent of whole shop fronts in some instances. Only in the northeast, dominated politically by Protestant Ulster Unionists[2] and economically by flourishing textile, shipbuilding, and engineering industries, was there little cause for complaint. It is therefore not surprising that elsewhere in Ireland perennial items in the addresses, manifestoes, and agendas issued by the skilled trades from the 1820s onward should be appeals to the public to support Irish manufactures, coupled increasingly with denunciations of the evils of importation.

The contrast between the economic conditions in which the British and Irish labor movements developed could hardly have been greater. British urban workers were part of an expanding economy, while most of their Irish brethren were imprisoned in a contracting, or at best stagnant, one. Their appeals to buy Irish goods were met by charges that they had injured trade by their demands and restrictive practices, and by assertions that if there were to be an Irish industrial renaissance they must be prepared to accept lower wages and poorer working

1. The total population in Ireland amounted to 8,175,124 in 1841 and 4,458,775 in 1901. The corresponding figures for the urban population (i.e., in towns with a population over 2,000) were 1,135,465 and 1,384,897, an increase of 249,432. Belfast's increase in the same period was 272,880 from 75,300 to 348,180.

2. I have spelled the words "Unionist" and "Unionism" with a capital "U" to denote support for the Act of Union and to distinguish them from "trade unionist" and "trade unionism."

conditions and to submit to the dilution of the work force with greater numbers of apprentices, nonunionists, and the semiskilled. These arguments were not accepted by Dublin tradesmen, who were remarkably successful in maintaining wage rates on a parity with those in the larger English towns. The semiskilled and unskilled were less fortunate. The organization of general workers could be difficult even in a healthy economy, and it was peculiarly so in most Irish towns, where the influx of rural laborers provided a constant supply of reserves willing to accept inferior wages and conditions. The new unionism of 1889 had some notable successes in Ireland, but they were short-lived and followed by defeats, amounting in the case of the Gasworkers to utter annihilation. In the economically more favorable climate of Belfast, difficulties were compounded by easily aroused politico-sectarian passions. The well-organized skilled trades were almost a Protestant preserve, but general unions catering to the unskilled had to contend with sectarian rivalries over jobs that were either better paid or less vulnerable to trade fluctuations.

The English working class was free of Bernard Shaw's "agonising symptom of a suppressed natural function"—a nationalist movement. Irish workers could not ignore the claims of nationality, and when the political temperature rose they rallied in support of national causes or organizations. If on occasion they pressed their own claims too vigorously for the comfort of nationalist leaders, they were reminded that the cause of Ireland was higher and holier than any sectional or partisan interest and were assured that when Ireland was her own again, then, and only then, could all her children's wrongs be righted. Nationalist politicians did take up social and economic as well as political questions, but they were primarily agrarian and denominationally religious in character—e.g., support for the ownership of their holdings by tenant farmers and support for a separate, Catholic-controlled system of education, which were questions of greater electoral weight than urban labor grievances. Not until the Irish T.U.C. emerged as a pressure group did labor spokesmen command a hearing from Irish parliamentary leaders, who finally became alarmed at the possibility of independent labor representation and argued that the Irish party was itself a labor party.

British trade unionists, slow to break their dependence on the older parties, did not form the Labour Representation Committee until 1900. In 1906, at the thirteenth annual meeting of the Irish T.U.C., efforts to decide on a policy for labor representation ended in stalemate when partisans of the Irish party, the British Labour Party, and a proposed Irish Labour Party were all defeated. The debates on this and other questions—the control of education and a scheme for an Irish, as opposed to a British, Federation of Trade Unions designed to give mutual support during industrial disputes—exposed the conflicting interests that had hitherto been held in check by the Irish T.U.C. leadership's desire to preserve political neutrality. Political and even religious allegiances were debated. Northern trade unionists, for the most part against Home Rule in politics and Protestant in religion, were unalterably opposed to any development that might imperil the British connection. While not all of them agreed that secular or non-denominational control of education was feasible or desirable, they were convinced that any strengthening of clerical control combined with Home Rule would, in the words of the Belfast labor leader William Walker, place Irish trade unionism "under the upas tree of Rome's priesthood." It was a far cry from the euphoric declaration, made by a president of the Belfast Trades Council in 1889 during an early attempt to form an Irish T.U.C., that there was "only an imaginary difference between the men of Belfast and those of the rest of Ireland." A united labor movement in the United Kingdom was no longer possible when the Irish T.U.C., disappointed in its fruitless role of slighted auxiliary to the British T.U.C., rejected a peremptory invitation in 1901 to return to the British fold and ended relations with it.

Provincial boundaries

• Towns where the I.T.U.C. met

ULSTER

Derry

Belfast

Sligo

Newry

CONNAUGHT

Athlone

Dublin

LEINSTER

Kilkenny

Limerick

Wexford

MUNSTER

Waterford

Cork

0   80
      Km

I

The Beginnings to 1825

Labor Under the Combination Acts

The Legal Framework

The early history of urban labor in Ireland is, not surprisingly, similar to that of English labor if allowance is made for the smaller number and size of the towns and their more recent origin. Shortly after the Anglo-Norman invasion of the twelfth century the principal Irish towns had received charters modeled on that of Bristol and soon possessed the usual medieval complement of town government and merchant and craft guilds. There seems, however, to have been no development of journeymen guilds, possibly because the numbers involved were too small to allow separate organization; certainly there was nothing to correspond to the thirteenth century journeymen's associations to be found in such English centers as York, Coventry, London and Bristol.[1]

As in England, combinations of workmen were made illegal in the sixteenth century.[2] By acts of Henry VIII (1542) and Elizabeth (1569),[3] justices of the peace were authorized to fix maximum wages twice yearly, at Easter and Michaelmas. Thus the commons of the assembly of Dublin decreed in 1563 that any craftsman (master as well as journeyman and apprentice) who refused to work at his trade within the city except at a daily wage higher than that authorized should be fined ten shillings for every offense, half going to the informer and half to the city funds.[4] Again, in 1602, when complaints were made that artificers withdrew into the country during the summer, the aggrieved inhabitants were given permission to engage country workmen, whose wages were to be regulated by the mayor or recorder, acting as justices of

1. E. Lipson, *The Economic History of England,* 7th ed. (1937), i. 392–411.
2. 2 and 3 Edward VI, c. 15.
3. 33 Henry VIII, c. 9; 11 Elizabeth, c. 5, sess. i.
4. J. T. Gilbert, ed., *Calendar of the Ancient Records of Dublin,* ii. 30.

laborers.[5] Nearly a century later, in 1689, when Dublin was still in Jacobite hands, the deputy lord mayor issued an ordinance fixing maximum wages: 2s. a day for master workmen, 1s. 2d. for journeymen, and 8d. for common laborers.[6]

During the eighteenth century the power of guilds to control trades weakened as manufactures grew and the gap between master and journeyman widened. Official regulation of wages declined and journeymen came to rely increasingly on combination for their protection. The Irish parliament, true to mercantile principles, made repeated efforts to retain the direction of economic activities by passing a series of enactments aimed at regulating the working conditions and wages of craftsmen. Early eighteenth century statutes (in 1715, 1729, and 1743) provided for the judicial recovery of unpaid wages and stipulated that they should be paid in money, without deductions, thus anticipating nineteenth-century truck acts. Later acts repeated these provisions; one, that of 1792, forbade the payment of wages in public houses (a practice common on quaysides a century later) under penalty of a ten-shilling fine. The parliament also attempted to maintain regulation of wages; as late as 1772 it charged justices of the peace in Cork with the duty of ascertaining at Easter sessions the current wages of artificers and enforcing adherence to them—workmen receiving higher wages were to forfeit them and be sent to prison for three months, employers paying lower wages could be forced to pay double by way of fine. Another act of the same year fixed wages and hours for tailors and shipwrights in Dublin, and silk and provision trade workers were similarly provided for by a 1780 act.[7]

Though the Irish legislature disapproved of combinations of employers as well as of journeymen, its statutes were aimed principally at suppressing associations among workmen and servants. The series of early eighteenth-century statutes denouncing their formation and prescribing penalties is proof of their growth during this period. Workers could combine to petition parliament for relief, but any attempt to meet for the purpose of altering wages and hours of labor, or of fixing the number of apprentices, was expressly forbidden. A penalty of three months' hard labor was provided by the 1729 act, and when this proved ineffective, parliament had recourse to stronger measures. In 1743 it declared that assemblies of three or more persons (not legally incorporated) meeting to make regulations regarding journeymen, appren-

---

5. Ibid., ii. 396.   6. Ibid., v. 612.

7. This account of the legal position of Irish workmen is, unless otherwise indicated, based on that given by J. D. Clarkson in *Labour and Nationalism in Ireland* (hereinafter referred to as Clarkson), pp. 33–57.

tices, or servants were unlawful; that they were forbidden to collect funds even for unemployment relief; and that the owners of public houses where they met were to be treated on the same legal footing as "those who keep common bawdy houses." When character assassination failed to check combinations parliament passed new enactments.

It would be tedious to list the successive anticombination acts passed by the Irish legislature, some of which were directed against workers in particular trades, but their general intent was to provide increasingly stiff penalties. Thus a 1757 act punished by six months' hard labor and whipping any attempt to administer or take oaths, or to dissuade or hinder men from working for an agreed price. Proof of combination could be of the slenderest nature; a 1780 act provided that a workman leaving his master before the end of the agreed term, being absent for three days or returning work unfinished without his master's consent, constituted evidence sufficient to convict. Certain acts of violence attracted the death penalty.

Evidence of the activities of combinations of journeymen is abundant in the second half of the eighteenth century. Workers in the textile trades were apparently peculiarly susceptible to temptation. In 1752 three journeymen woolcombers of Dublin were charged with riotous assembly and with "unlawfully forcing away from their work such as would not come into their illegal combination,"[8] and were sent to Newgate prison. In the following year three workmen were "justly" ordered by the court to be fined five shillings each and receive two months' imprisonment for "unlawful assemblies and combinations"; in July they pleaded to the city assembly that they were starving and asked for a remission of their fine. The assembly agreed on condition that they undertook to be of good behavior for three years.[9] The same assembly shortly afterwards listened sympathetically to the plea of one James Lacey who had spent much time and money in prosecuting and securing the conviction of journeymen hosiers guilty of combining to raise wages and reduce hours of work; he was granted 201 pounds, to be paid from fines levied on offenders.[10] In 1770 two weavers guilty of combining were whipped from Newgate to College Green under the eyes of the high sheriffs.[11] Some days later the same officers, accompanied by master tailors, raided a number of houses where journeymen tailors met to plan "their most dark and pernicious schemes," and removed books, boxes, and money; two of the combinators were subse-

8. *Faulkner's Journal*, 1 Aug. 1752, quoted in J. Swift, *History of the Dublin Bakers and Others*, p. 168.

9. Gilbert, *Calendar*, x. 104.   10. Ibid., x. 134.

11. *Freeman's Journal*, 3 Jan. 1770, quoted in Swift, *Dublin Bakers*, p. 169.

quently arrested.[12] The landlords of houses (usually public houses) where combining workmen met were punished in accordance with their legal status as keepers of common bawdy houses, one Thomas Tennant, for instance, a publican of Winetavern Street, was pilloried at the Tholsel (City Hall) in 1770 for keeping a house of resort for combining journeymen tailors.[13]

The last decade of the century was marked by growing unrest among the urban working class. The outbreak of the French revolution, the spread of democratic ideas and of such reform societies as the United Irishmen, and consequent governmental fears for public order brought increasingly harsh measures to deal with combinations and associations in Ireland as well as in England. But they could not banish economic distress. In 1792, a year of severe unemployment and rising prices, combinations and "turn-outs" (strikes) were frequent in Dublin, not only among textile workers, but also among corn porters, ship carpenters (and apprentices), shoemakers, paper workers, and bricklayers.[14] Punishments were not passively accepted; when four combinators were whipped through the Liberties (that part of the city, outside the lord mayor's jurisdiction, where most trades were carried on), soldiers guarding the cart carrying the prisoners were stoned by the populace and were ordered to charge their firearms.[15] Weavers thrown out of work by competition from Yorkshire woolens and Lancashire cottons attacked shops selling the imported cloth; John Conway, a cotton weaver, who with others had destroyed cotton goods belonging to a Mr. Grey of Francis Street, was sentenced to death, but reprieved in December "as there was something honourable to this unfortunate man."[16] In the same month the Dublin journeymen bakers felt sufficiently strong to make public their existence by authorizing their secretary (John Strong) to write to *Faulkner's Journal* a letter attacking the master bakers. He charged them with bringing in country bakers, although some city men were idle, because the journeymen would not join in measures aimed at exploiting the consumers.[17] Six months later, in July 1793, the same journeymen demanded an increase of two shillings in their weekly wages of six shillings with board and lodging.[18]

12. *F.J.*, 10 Mar. 1770, quoted in Swift, *Dublin Bakers*, pp. 169–70.
13. *F.J.*, 18 Mar. 1770, quoted in Swift, *Dublin Bakers*, p. 170.
14. Swift, *Dublin Bakers*, pp. 170–72.
15. *Dublin Chronicle*, 15 Nov. 1792, quoted in Swift, *Dublin Bakers*, p. 172.
16. *Hibernian Chronicle*, 13 Dec. 1792, quoted in Swift, *Dublin Bakers*, p. 170.
17. *Faulkner's Journal*, 18 Dec. 1792, quoted in Swift, *Dublin Bakers*, p. 173.
18. *Dublin Chronicle*, 18 July 1793, quoted in Swift, *Dublin Bakers*, p. 173.

Structure and Methods

Our knowledge of the structure and workings of early trades organizations is in the main derived from such sources as memoirs, petitions, minutes of evidence of royal commissions, information derived from court cases, and newspaper reports. The minute book of the journeymen cabinet makers of Belfast, the oldest surviving building trade union document in the British Isles, is therefore of peculiar interest. The union was founded in May 1788 with twenty members who, to judge from their names, seem to have included Catholics, in accordance with the nonsectarian and democratic spirit that characterized Belfast at that time. Its organization was equally democratic, for its rules provided for the election of a president, secretary, treasurer, and two stewards every three months. A committee consisting of the officers and three other members were charged with the general direction of the society's affairs, were liable to be fined 6½d. each if they failed to meet monthly at 7 o'clock, and were allowed a maximum of 1s. for drink out of the chest if they met for special business. The Cabinet Club (the name adopted) met on the first Monday of each month with the president in the chair. Members had to stand uncovered when addressing the chair and could be fined up to 6d. for a breach of standing orders; they contributed 3½d. monthly to the common chest, 3d. of which was spent on ale. Nonattendance for three months resulted in a fine of 1s. 7½d. in addition to monthly dues. The club admitted only those men who had served a regular apprenticeship of seven years, limited apprentices to two per employer, drew up a book of prices to be adhered to by members, and decreed that the book was to be available only to those employers paying for a copy. One resolution declared that "the interest of our meetings is for the better encouragement of other travelling journeymen and by no means meant to be detrimental to our employers but for the good of the trade." Other resolutions made it clear that "the good of the trade" involved members agreeing that they would not work for any except those who agreed to the prices already determined and that no more "colts" (i.e., men who had not served a regular apprenticeship) were to be admitted to any regular shop.[19]

The essentially local character of the club, and as such representative of the kind of organization prevailing among craftsmen in the British Isles at this period, is shown by the regulations governing the admission of members. "Strangers" (i.e., those from outside Belfast) were admitted on payment of £1 14s. 1½d. for their "ticket," as against 16s.

19. S. Higenbotham, *Our Society's History*, pp. 2–5, and reproduction facing p. 32.

3*d*. from those who had served an apprenticeship in the town; in both cases payment was to be made within two months, or, for an additional charge of 1*s*. 1*d*., within three. The larger entrance fee for "strangers" was designed to control the total number of journeymen in the locality rather than exclude newcomers. Traveling and subsistence money was paid to members going to take up jobs as far away as London, the scale depending on the distance and on whether members were married or single. Benefits were paid to members who were sick or otherwise incapacitated, but the club was primarily a trade union, not a friendly society.

The early history of combinations is not as well documented for Ireland as for England, but as they were both affected by much the same legal restrictions and their members worked, at least until the early nineteenth century, in not dissimilar economic and technical conditions, their evolution differed little. Outside Dublin, Cork, and one or two lesser towns, however, the number of craftsmen in any one trade was small and did not offer the same basis for organization as the rapidly growing English centers of industry. Under the combination acts they existed ostensibly as mortality clubs or friendly societies, though in practice they also concerned themselves with wages and working conditions. The inquiries by parliamentary committees preceding the repeal or modification of the combination laws in 1824 and 1825 provide some valuable evidence on the workings of the combinations, Irish as well as English. Three Dublin societies, the saddlers, the cabinet-makers, and the carpenters, may be regarded as typical examples of early Irish trade unionism.

The general tenor of the evidence given by Charles Graham was to stress the friendly society nature of his organization, the Dublin saddlers, known as the Halifax Society. It had been founded as a mortality society in 1791 and registered according to act of parliament; the greater part of the dues of 1*s*. 1½*d*. per week went for this purpose, only 2*d*. going to assist members in distress or out of work. Graham, who had been deputed to appear before the select committee by delegates from forty-two Dublin trades supporting the repeal of the combination acts, said that the Dublin associations were either mortality societies like his own or met only "to protect their trade," that is, "to protect themselves from the encroachments of their masters." [20] Further questioning showed that his own society combined both functions and even that until recently each member on admission swore on a prayer book that he would not divulge the transactions of the society, that he

---

20. *First Report from the Select Committee appointed to Inquire into the State of the Law Regarding Artizans and Machinery*, pp. 448–54, H.C. 1824 (51).

would not work with any nonmember, and that he would endeavor to enroll any journeymen saddlers who were not members. He admitted that his society did meet to consider wages and to control the number of apprentices engaged by the employers, but defended his society's actions on the grounds that the masters had acted treacherously. The masters had invited the men's delegates to meet them to discuss a reduction in wages, but when the men asked for a lesser reduction the masters locked out a large number, replacing them with a number of nonsociety men and charging the delegates under the combination acts. Though the men were enabled to have the charges dropped after they had countercharged the employers with combination, Graham declared that until the laws were repealed they would refuse to meet the masters again. The history of the society, as presented by Graham, is one of initial moderation, but the emphasis on its benefit functions diminished as greater militancy developed.

The Dublin cabinetmakers were organized in the Samaritan Society. Despite their name they were made of sterner stuff than the saddlers and their society seemed more concerned with preventing wounds than binding them up: they frankly admitted that they assembled for the purpose of trade and were not a benefit society.[21] According to their representative, Christopher Leahy, they were, like their Belfast brethren, adamant in preventing the employment of nonsociety men, in limiting the number of apprentices to two per master, and in not allowing their members to work for less than the prevailing wage rates in the town.

If the evidence of Patrick Farrell, journeyman carpenter, and Acheson Moore, a working employer, before the same committee is correct, a carpenters' society had been in existence in Dublin since 1764. It had friendly society functions, but it also laid down the scale of wages members could accept within a ten-mile radius of Dublin, as well as the conditions under which apprentices might be taken. New members had to swear an oath on a prayer book to obey the rules and not reveal business transacted at meetings. The society, at least by 1824, seems to have extended its influence over the whole island. It met four times a year outside the city to escape the vigilance of the authorities and have sufficient room for those attending. At these quarterly meetings a council of five—one each for the provinces of Ulster, Munster, and Connaught and two for Leinster—was appointed to conduct the society's affairs in the interim period.[22]

The rules of the Belfast cabinetmakers' club show that the club's first

21. Ibid., pp. 454–9. Four of their members, imprisoned in 1822 for combination, were allowed £1 5s. a week.

22. Ibid., pp. 428–39.

duty was to local journeymen, but they also recognize, by their provisions for accepting "strangers," some duties to those outside the locality. Generally speaking, even in the absence of a loose association, clubs accepted a system whereby journeymen "on the tramp" were given, on producing their "ticket" (trade union card) or "pass," brief hospitality and, if no work was available in the town, assistance in getting to a more promising area. Dues varied from club to club and trade to trade, depending on the benefits given for sickness, unemployment, or hardship resulting from imprisonment for trade union activities. Some club dues were one shilling a week or more, others less, though in such cases levies to meet exceptional needs were common; in the long term dues tended to rise. Entrance fees also differed considerably and, as in the case of the Dublin carpenters, might be raised sharply in years of depression to repel "strangers." Some standardization of dues and benefits took place when clubs were linked in an association.

No organization that embraced different trade societies existed. As in England, it was not uncommon for a society to lend or borrow from another trade when the need arose. Some of these loans could be substantial. The Dublin paper workers, for instance, lent woolen operatives one hundred pounds during a strike. Patrick Farrell of the Dublin carpenters put the matter succinctly to the 1824 committee: "When we are short of money we are obliged to borrow from other trades, they lend us ten or twenty pounds and we pay them again punctually." Cooperation of this kind was not necessarily confined to the trades in a single area: London hatters facing a prosecution were loaned money by their fellow hatters in Dublin, but they in turn had borrowed it from the Dublin cabinetmakers. If two other witnesses, a chief constable and a solicitor, may be deemed credible, assistance went further than loans, for at times an aggrieved trade society employed out-of-work members of another trade to use more than moral suasion on recalcitrant employers, "colts" (i.e., nonsociety men), and other offenders.[23]

An interesting example of what appears to be the efficacy of moral suasion is given by James Gandon, the architect of several of the more imposing public buildings of Dublin, in his account of the construction of the Custom House in the 1780s. To hasten the work Gandon employed workmen from outside Dublin. The Dublin masons agreed only if the strangers would take an oath of secrecy, pay one guinea

---

23. Ibid., pp. 289, 292, 426, 436, 456, 461–2. See also *Report from the Select Committee* to inquire into the effects of 5 Geo. 4, c. 95, Apps. 1–4, pp. 15–19, Minutes of Evidence, pp. 8–26, 205–7, H. C. 1825 (437, 417); Clarkson, pp. 116–9.

entrance fee, and obey the rules of the combination. Gandon, to his disgust, found that these "aliens," though some were reluctant at first, accepted these conditions, and "subsequently exhibited a zeal more turbulent and refractory than the others." English stonecutters and carpenters, who were also employed, forsook their English sobriety and became "more refractory than the natives, more exorbitant in their demands for wages, and worse by far as to drunkenness." Gandon, himself of English origin, was particularly distressed by the combinators, whether Irish or English, devoting their fund to non–friendly society functions, "unlike English combinators"; instead they used it to pay what in effect were full-time shop stewards.

It was given to a few idle vagabonds as a stipend enabling them to live without daily labour. These fellows were called 'orators', and were attached to each of the fraternities, attending the clubs of the various artificers in order to keep up a perpetual ferment, rendering the men dissatisfied with their employers. Whenever an order for any great work was given, particularly if much expedition and exertion were required, then there was a 'strike' or 'turn-out' for more wages; as long as this lasted they were supported in idleness, and if any were sent to prison, they fared best of all, being deemed martyrs.[24]

A more turbulent method of wage negotiations was noted by the young French émigré De Latocnaye during his walking tour of Ireland in 1797. The normally somnolent town of Cork was enlivened by bands of journeymen shoemakers who had by common accord withdrawn their labor. They ran shouting through the streets, pausing to argue hotly with their masters in front of workshops. A city magistrate at the head of some soldiers pursued them, but they played hide-and-seek with him until nightfall put an end to it.[25]

Two charges were frequently brought against Irish trade unionists of this period, that they were more than ordinarily addicted to violence and that the decay of Irish industries can be attributed to the evil effects of combinations. Acts of violence indeed occurred. The Dublin carpenters resented the importation of "colts" and "strangers" at a time when their trade was steadily declining and the intruders were frequently attacked. Lisburn weavers in 1811 formed a combination and seized and destroyed webs of cloth. In 1816 an attempt was made to blow up the house of a Belfast muslin manufacturer involved in a dispute with his workmen, and two men found guilty of taking part were hanged. But violence was not confined to one side; the president of the Muslin Weavers' Society, one Gordon Maxwell of Lisburn, was shot on the

---

24. T. J. Mulvany, *The Life of James Gandon,* p. 63.
25. De Latocnaye, *Promenade d'un Français dans l'Irlande* (1797), pp. 95–6.

outskirts of Belfast and before he died he accused his employer, John McCann, of being responsible. McCann was, however, acquitted.[26]

In an age when constitutional processes were virtually denied to workers, it is not surprising that they occasionally resorted to illegal means. There seems no sound basis for alleging that violence was peculiarly an Irish characteristic or that trade unionism elsewhere (i.e., in England) during this period was free of it. As for the allegation that combinations brought about the decline of Irish industries, an examination of the evidence shows that they were engaged in a defensive operation, vainly trying to protect their standard of living against worsening economic conditions over which they had no control.[27]

The assertion of Sidney and Beatrice Webb that the Dublin trades formed a joint committee, the "Board of Green Cloth," which became the terror of Dublin employers, has been challenged by Clarkson and others; the committee in question was a joint committee representing the men in woolen factories.[28] The Dublin trades did assemble, but only on rare occasions. Under the combination acts they were allowed to do so in order to petition parliament, and aggregate meetings had been held—according to Acheson Moore, the working employer, and Charles Graham, the saddler—about 1789, 1814 and 1824. The 1789 meeting had been accompanied by a demonstration of fifteen to twenty thousand men who had marched, carrying white wands, from the Phoenix Park to the Irish parliament in College Green, where they successfully petitioned the speaker for the rejection of a bill designed, they thought, to lower wages and make workmen produce evidence of good character from previous employers.[29]

Such public demonstrations, well-ordered and peaceful, do not make up the whole picture of popular protest. A proposal for a union with England was discussed in the Irish parliament during December 1759, with the result that a crowd entered the House of Lords and mockingly placed an old woman on the viceroy's throne. Occasionally the populace voiced their political feelings from the gallery of the House of Commons or in theaters.[30] A later viceroy, Lord Fitzwilliam,

26. E. R. R. Green, *The Lagan Valley, 1800–1850*, p. 101.

27. See Clarkson, pp. 105–8, and G. O'Brien, *The Economic History of Ireland from the Union to the Famine*, pp. 338–402.

28. Sidney and Beatrice Webb, *History of Trade Unionism*, 1920 ed., p. 104; Clarkson, pp. 99, 110–11. According to Swift (*Dublin Bakers*, p. 221) "going before the green cloth" is still used in the Dublin Bakers' Union when a member is summoned to appear before the committee of the union. The phrase may be a tribute to the woollen trade procedure rather than evidence of the existence of a joint trades committee.

29. *Report Regarding Artizans and Machinery*, pp. 431–2, 542.

30. Constantia Maxwell, *Dublin under the Georges*, p. 123.

was treated differently in 1795. He had favored Catholic emancipation and the day of his departure after his forced resignation was marked as a day of mourning in Dublin. Several high officials in the Irish administration were held responsible and their houses attacked; that of the Lord Chancellor of Ireland, John Fitzgibbon, earl of Clare, was assailed by a crowd of some six thousand men armed with various weapons and crowbars, and several hundred women who had filled their aprons with paving stones. Fitzgibbon's coach was stoned and he himself would have been killed had not his sister, hurriedly disguised as one of the female assistants, spread a false rumour that dragoons were approaching.[31]

Industrial depression traceable to competition was a signal for rioting, as has already been noted in the case of Dublin cotton weavers in 1792,[32] but perhaps the most extreme example occurred over a half century earlier. In May 1734 weavers in the Liberties attacked the shops of woolen drapers who had imported English goods. Though they failed to carry off any notable amount before they were stopped by the sheriff and his bailiffs and several were imprisoned, they threatened to pull down several houses if the prisoners were not released. Troops were brought in and clashes between them and the weavers continued for several days, during which seven were killed and nine wounded.[33]

Visitors to Dublin, and to Irish provincial towns, were struck by the glaring contrast between luxury and misery, and especially by the large number of the poor, whether unemployed artisans, beggars, itinerant hawkers and pedlars, or casual laborers. This reservoir of discontent found an outlet during times of scarcity in food riots. The failure of the harvests in 1739 and 1740 resulted in severe famine conditions. The more unscrupulous suppliers of corn, flour, and bread indulged in the cardinal medieval economic sins of forestalling and regrating. In Dublin the bakers, who had kept the supply of household bread low, had their shops broken open on two successive days in June 1740. Some of the rioters paid for the bread at normal prices, others paraded through the city with it, and yet others unloaded a barrel of beef from a ship moored in the river Liffey and distributed its contents. Though the lord mayor and sheriffs arrested some, the rioters resumed their attacks the following day and peace was restored only by a proclamation forbidding hoarding.[34]

It would be wrong to assume that those taking part in such affairs

31. Ibid., p. 30.　　　　　　　　　　32. Ibid., p. 5.

33. *Dublin Evening Post*, 17 May 1734, quoted in Maxwell, *Dublin under the Georges*, pp. 123–4.

34. *Dublin Daily Post*, 3, 7 June 1740, quoted in Swift, *Dublin Bakers*, p. 117.

were merely the unorganized spontaneous "mobs" of popular imagination, intent simply on looting. Looting did occur, but not infrequently the rioters were in effect enforcing a "just price." John Wesley, normally strong on law and order, nevertheless gives an account that is almost approving of the action of a mob in Jamestown, County Leitrim, a small town on the banks of the river Shannon, during his tour of that area in May 1758:

[they] had been in motion all the day; but their business was only with the forestallers of the market, who had bought up all the corn far and wide, to starve the poor, and load a Dutch ship, which lay at the quay; but the mob brought it all out into the market, and sold it for the owners for the common price. And thus they did with all the calmness and composure imaginable, and without striking or hurting anyone.[35]

The times of scarcity and depression that occurred during the American war of independence, the revolutionary and Napoleonic wars, and the postwar period were marked by further outbreaks. The high price of food in Limerick in April 1791 caused an attack on a ship laden with meal and the crowd then proceeded to break open several stores; they were finally pacified and dispersed by the mayor and magistrates.[36] During the century from 1745 to 1845, bread in Dublin reached its highest price in 1817 when the quartern loaf cost 1s. 9½ d.[37] Rioting broke out in June, first with the seizure of potatoes and then with the stopping of bakers' men: "the bread [was] taken from them, which was greedily devoured by the hungry mob, mostly consisting of women and children."[38] Joined by men, the crowd then ransacked shops and stores, and though some were dispersed by police cavalry, the magistrates "still conceived it necessary (however reluctant they might feel) to apply for military aid"; they called in squadrons of Dragoon Guards and British Lancers to patrol the city and placed infantry guards at markets and stores. The lord mayor imposed a curfew on the city, but raids on bakeries continued. The rioting was effective in stimulating a sudden rush of philanthropy, a distress fund was increased, a public bakery was opened to supply bread at a more reasonable price and the master bakers decided to consider applying to parliament to permit open trade as it existed in London.[39] But lest

35. *Journals*, ed. N. Curnock, London, 1909–16, vol. 4, p. 268, entry of 27 May 1758.

36. *Hibernian Magazine*, April 1791, quoted in Constantia Maxwell, *Country and Town in Ireland under the Georges*, pp. 263–64.

37. Swift, *Dublin Bakers*, pp. 370–71.

38. *Saunders' News-Letter*, 20 June 1817, quoted in Swift, *Dublin Bakers*, pp. 203–4.

39. Swift, *Dublin Bakers*, pp. 204–5.

charity be abused, the lord mayor and his committee of the poor fund had, in December of the previous year, sent a letter to the minister and church wardens of each parish instructing parish committees not to grant relief to unemployed applicants unable to produce a certificate from their former employers; these applicants might include trades- men and others who had combined in order to refuse work at reduced wages.[40]

A further outbreak of bread rioting, documented in police reports, that occurred some nine years later is worth noting. Heavy unemploy- ment in 1826 produced widespread distress, the weavers being par- ticularly affected. A relief association put some of them to work at 1s. a day mending roads, but subsequently reduced pay to 6d. a day. The weavers issued handbills asking the citizens if they had approved of the reduction and ended this appeal on a threatening note: "Give us bread for our families: so, of the two evils, choose the least; for, rely on it, we will billet our children where is [sic] something for them to eat."[41] The threat was not idle, for on August 7 and 8 they attacked bakeries. The police report of those charged shows that while weavers were in the majority, other trades were represented among those arrested: four weavers, one silk weaver, five cotton weavers, one cloth weaver, three cotton printers, one cotton dyer, two wool spinners, three bricklayers, one shipwright, one carter, one hatter, one carpenter, three glass- blowers, one servant, and five laborers. The variety of trades repre- sented among those arrested after a single day's rioting is proof of how widespread the distress was and is an indication of a continuing pro- cess—the decay of small-scale handicrafts unable to withstand the growing competition of British manufactures as the removal of protec- tive duties made the whole of the British Isles a free trade area.

The Political Setting

The various rebellions, confiscations, wars, and plantations of the six- teenth and seventeenth centuries laid waste portions of the country- side, put an end to the old Gaelic order, and disrupted economic life, even though in some areas planters introduced more efficient agricul- tural techniques. The effect of these events on urban life is difficult to gauge, though it is obvious that frequent interruptions to trade must have brought hardship to the towns and slowed the growth of industry; it is a matter for speculation how the urban population would have fared had settled political conditions allowed the development of a prosperous hinterland and commerce unhampered by restrictions dic-

---

40. Ibid., pp. 205–6.   41. Ibid., pp. 206–7.

tated by English fears. A Protestant ascendancy in the guilds barred
Catholics from full membership until 1793 (as quarter-brothers they
could not be freemen of their towns) so that they tended to be more
numerous in the provision and retail trades than in the highly skilled
manufactures; as a consequence the number of Catholic journeymen
was less than it otherwise might have been. The part played by the
Dublin populace in political demonstrations in the earlier eighteenth
century has already been noted; it would be unwise, however, given the
small number of inhabitants that comprised the political nation, in a
century when rotten and pocket boroughs returned so much of the
parliamentary representation, to assume that artisans could constitute
a really important political pressure group.

The later years of the eighteenth century are of greater importance.
How far the urban working class, or for that matter the peasants, were
stirred by the agitation that led to the removal of restrictions on Irish
trade and to a qualified legislative independence is doubtful. The
original Volunteers of 1779 were, in Henry Grattan's words, "the
armed property of the nation," and they and their political leaders in
the patriot party in the Irish House of Commons represented the
landed, commercial, and professional classes; the years 1782 to 1800
were the heyday of the Protestant nation. A more democratic flavor was
added by the subsequent appearance of Volunteer companies composed
of merchants and shopkeepers in the early 1780s, but the only working-class element seems to have been the Liberty Corps, drawn from
skilled workers, mainly weavers and for the most part Catholics, in the
Liberties of Dublin, men whose goal was parliamentary reform, including Catholic emancipation. The Liberty Corps found no favor with the
other Volunteer companies, who disapproved of them for both their
admission of Catholics and their social composition, and who, therefore, refused to join with them in exercises. Grattan in 1785 treated
them with aristocratic disdain in a speech in parliament, in which he
drew the attention of the House to "the alarming measure of drilling
the lowest classes of the populace," adding that the Volunteers "had
originally been the armed property; were they to become the armed
beggary?" That "the armed beggary" were more formidable in the eyes
of the Irish administration was proved in 1793, after the passing of an
arms act, for the government had little difficulty inducing the other
two Dublin corps, the Merchants and the Lawyers, to give up their
artillery for safekeeping, but seized that of the Liberty Corps.[42]

Modern democratic nationalism, as opposed to Protestant ascendancy autonomy, made its appearance in Ireland with the founding of

42. Rosamund Jacob, *The Rise of the United Irishmen*, pp. 40, 41, 153.

the Society of United Irishmen in 1791. As a political reform society it shared many of the aims of contemporary English reformers and the enthusiasm generated by the French declaration of the rights of man. In an Irish context the rights of man and the citizen meant the attainment of national government, free of English executive influence, to be achieved by the abolition of religious disabilities that still prevented Catholics (and to a lesser degree Protestant Dissenters) from becoming full citizens and by "an equal representation of all the people in parliament." A third goal, the establishment of a republic, was adopted only at a later stage when repression made constitutional methods impossible and the less timid members revolutionaries.

It is difficult to ascertain to what extent the urban working class and the peasantry were represented in the United Irishmen. During the three years of the society's legal existence the Dublin branch's membership was, it would appear, exclusively drawn from merchants, manufacturers, shopkeepers, professional men, and country gentlemen, though the latter were few in number.[43] One member, Abraham Creighton, a tailor, had been denounced in 1784 by his journeymen for making them work on Sundays and for discharging them because they belonged to a friendly society. The Belfast membership also seems to have been predominantly middle-class, to judge by the names that have survived, though our information is by no means as complete as in the case of the Dublin branch. But any generalization about United Irish membership must be qualified; the semisecret nature of the society, the scarcity of information about branches outside Dublin and Belfast, the reorganization of the society on conspiratorial, military lines after its suppression in 1794—these are some of the reasons that make any firm conclusion dubious. But it is reasonable to deduce from the evidence available about those who took part in the 1798 rising that, at least in the post-1794 years, a growing proportion of the rank-and-file membership and sympathizers belonged to the "lower orders"—urban workers and peasantry.

Despite their bourgeois origins, United Irish leaders carried their democratic ideas very far indeed. The Dublin society issued a plan of reform in 1794 that called for universal male franchise (over age twenty-one), equal electoral districts, the abolition of all property qualifications whether for voters or candidates, payment for Members of Parliament (M.P.s), who should declare on oath that they had not

43. See R. B. McDowell, "The Personnel of the Dublin Society of United Irishmen, 1791–4," in *Irish Historical Studies*, ii, pp. 12–33. The material consists in the main of reports supplied by an informer to the government. The subscription was a guinea (£1. 1s.) a year in addition to a guinea entrance fee, in itself an indication of the economic status of the members (see Jacob, *Rise of the United Irishmen*, p. 72).

resorted to bribery, and annual parliaments. Its preface concluded with an appeal to "you, the poorer classes of the community, for whose welfare we have peculiarly laboured" and asserted that their many social and economic disabilities could be removed only by these reforms.[44] It is not surprising that such an anticipation of Chartist demands, passed by 11 votes to 9 in committee, led to a considerable number of resignations,[45] or that it provoked from Grattan comments worthy of Edmund Burke: "a monstrous constitution, whose frenzy, folly and wickedness must excite at once your scorn and your horror," since it would rob the individual and the community of the fruit of their industry, destroy the representation of property, and give the vote to "the beggar on the bridge and the scavenger in the kennel."[46]

Grattan's horror of this document embodying the leveling principles of French fraternity arose from his fears of social revolution. It is clear that some of the United Irish leaders contemplated such a prospect with equanimity. Wolfe Tone concluded that if the men of property refused to take part in the fight for liberty, they would fall, since it would be the men of no property who would win it, and that merchants did not make good revolutionaries. His friend Thomas Russell was of a like opinion: "I can see the men of property all through Ireland, whether landed or commercial, are decidedly against a struggle . . . the people are beginning to see this and in time when they feel their strength and injuries will do it themselves and then *adieu* property—*tant mieux.*"[47] Russell's prophecy was prompted by a similar observation made by the watchmaker Thomas McCabe, a Belfast United Irishman who in 1786 had almost single-handedly prevented merchants of his town from engaging in the African slave trade.

Nor is it difficult to cite passages from the writings of other United Irishmen to show their conviction that, to quote Russell, property was

44. Jacob, *Rise of the United Irishmen,* pp. 212–3.

45. McDowell, "Personnel of the Dublin Society of United Irishmen," p. 18, and D. A. Chart, ed., *The Drennan Letters,* p. 122. William Drennan, then resident in Dublin and a member of the committee, stated in one of his letters that the plan was carried chiefly by the eloquence of Thomas Addis Emmet (a brother of Robert Emmet); he himself disapproved of the removal of a voting property qualification as "premature, impolitic and impracticable in the present state of this country."

46. Jacob, *Rise of the United Irishmen,* pp. 213–4.

47. Journals of Thomas Russell, 9 Sept. (?) 1793. I am indebted to Dr. R. B. McDowell, who lent me his transcript of Russell's journals, which are in the Irish State Paper Office, Dublin. If we use Russell's definition of men of property (which includes commercial as well as landed property) as a gloss on Wolfe Tone's better-known quotation about "that large and respectable class, the men of no property," we are justified in extending the denotation of the latter term to include small manufacturers and journeymen as well as tenant farmers.

being put before life and must be altered in some measure.[48] The brothers Henry and John Sheares, the Templepatrick (County Antrim) weaver, James Hope, and Robert Emmet are but some. Emmet's proclamation on the occasion of the tiny, ill-fated conspiracy of 1803 decreed not only the nationalization of church property but forbade the transfer of all landed property, bonds, debentures, and public securities until a national government had been established and the national will declared. And it is not irrelevant that his followers were drawn mainly from the Liberties and the Dublin docks, or that he was in touch with Colonel Despard and his English fellow revolutionaries who, like Emmet, were radical republicans. We cannot know what proportion of urban workers might have taken part in the 1798 insurrection, since repeated arrests of leaders and a policy of repression sustained over many months from the autumn of 1796 aborted plans for a general rising, Dublin and other large towns being heavily garrisoned. But it is a reasonable conjecture that, in the absence of the very efficient government secret service and its many informers, it would have been high, judging from the temper of the Irish immigrants, most of them artisans and laborers, in England. In that country they made their presence felt in radical societies and conspiracies, not only in the more shadowy groups of United Irishmen and United Englishmen, but in the London Corresponding Society, where, armed with the traditional shillelagh, they formed an important proportion of the guard that beat off the attack on its shoemaker secretary, Thomas Hardy, in October 1797.[49] And their roles included the suborning of soldiers, mutinies in the fleet and participation in Despard's conspiracy and Luddite activities. There is little doubt that the Irish "lower orders" easily reconciled social with political revolutionary ideas, or a fight for Irish independence with a struggle for "the rights of long downtrodden man."

On any realistic assessment, the United Irish movement was a failure. The common name of Irishman did not replace those of Protestant, Catholic, and Dissenter; instead, the formation of the Orange Order in 1795 was a guarantee that a powerful mass organization of Protestants, patronized by the men of property, was henceforth dedicated to maintaining Protestant ascendancy and intensifying sectarian rivalries. Hopes of reform of parliament disappeared in the White Terror that followed the insurrection, for even the more liberally minded of the men of property drew back appalled at the *jacquerie* in County Wexford

48. Ibid., 8 July 1793.
49. For the part played by Irish immigrants in English radical and revolutionary activities see E. P. Thompson, *The Making of the English Working Class* (Penguin edition, 1968), especially pp. 82, 146, 183–8, 469–85, 523–6, 556–8, 650–55, 771.

and the prospect of the lower orders being admitted to any share in government. As for any increase in self-governing powers, let alone a republic, the 1798 rising determined Pitt to abolish a separate Irish parliament and led directly to the Act of Union in 1800. Normal emigration was increased by the addition of political exiles, not only leaders but humbler refugees, thus depriving the country of the most radical elements of its population.

But if many middle-class supporters of Irish independence and radical reform made their peace with government, turned to philanthropy, or simply retired to cultivate their gardens, United Irish ideals, however simplified, were still cherished. The names of Tone, McCracken, Russell, Emmet, and other leaders were preserved in the book of the people, to be recalled in popular songs, ballads, and stories and to embody a vision of Irish nationality that was demotic, nonsectarian and, at its best, free from xenophobia. The very failure of the United Irish movement became in due course an asset and the names of its leaders who died on the gallows emotional dynamite to be used in a renewed struggle for Irish independence.

Pitt's motive in abolishing the Irish parliament, which he considered dangerously incompetent, was to pacify a discontented and deeply divided country that seemed open to French invasion; he decided that this could best be done by a legislative union that would exercise tighter control and by Catholic emancipation. The union was resisted strongly by groups in the Irish parliament for a variety of reasons: regret at the disappearance of a symbol of nationality, fear of losing the spoils of office, possible weakening of Protestant ascendancy and patronage. Orange lodges opposed the union while Catholic bishops supported it since Pitt had committed himself, at least morally, to Catholic emancipation as a *quid pro quo*. The measure did not follow the Act of Union as Pitt, unable to carry George III and some of the Cabinet with him, resigned. Ireland started the new century with the great majority of her population still politically disabled and a minority trusting to the union to preserve Protestant ascendancy.[50]

Unlike Scotland after 1707, Ireland after 1800 continued to have what was apparently a separate government. A lord lieutenant and a chief secretary headed a separate executive in Dublin Castle, the center of continuing ascendancy rule; though it was but a branch of the central

50. No accurate figures are available, since the first Irish census to be carried out on accurate lines was that of 1841, when the population was just over 8 million. Tone's statement on the situation in Ireland, prepared for the Rev. William Jackson, a French emissary, in 1794, gives the following estimate: population, 4,500,000, consisting of 450,000 members of the established Church of Ireland, 900,000 Protestant Dissenters and 3,150,000 Catholics (*The Life of Theobald Wolfe Tone*, ed. W. T. Wolfe Tone,

British executive its civil service was separately organized. The Act of Union provided for a United Church of England and Ireland (unlike the established Presbyterian Church of Scotland, the established episcopal church in Ireland was not the church of the majority) but the ecclesiastical establishment, like the executive, was separate in Ireland.

In other ways, too, the United Kingdom of Great Britain and Ireland was less than united. The exchequers of the two countries did not become one until 1817, when the Irish debt, swollen by wartime demands, had increased by 250 percent, as against 50 percent for Great Britain; the debt burden was now shared, but already the Irish economy had been weakened by the need to service war loans raised outside the country. Increased landlord absenteeism produced a further drain on capital, which was not replaced by British investment, and a constant shortage of "risk" capital continued to stunt economic growth, save in the Belfast region, throughout the nineteenth century. With the removal of a number of protective tariffs in the 1820s (some minor tariffs and duties were maintained until the 1840s) financial and fiscal unity was substantially achieved. But even if political factors are ignored it is clear that the forced marriage came too late; the two economies, already markedly different, continued to diverge at an even more rapid pace.

Legal uniformity, so far as combinations were concerned, did not come about with the Act of Union. Several post-Union acts were passed, usually providing stiffer penalties than those inflicted on British workmen, applying specifically to Ireland. Finally British and Irish workers, whether craftsmen or factory workers, were placed on the same footing by the 1824 and 1825 acts, which repealed previous legislation and applied to both countries.[51]

Washington, 1826, vol. 1, p. 278). The population in 1800 was probably about 5 million, of which at least two-thirds were Catholics. See W. E. Vaughan and A. J. Fitzpatrick, *Irish Historical Statistics*, pp. xi–xxii, 1–2.

51. Clarkson, pp. 55–7.

2

In Defense of Trade Unionism

A Quarter-Century's Efforts

Factories and Printing Houses

Francis Place, a former member of a Breechmakers' Benefit Society and one-time president of the London Corresponding Society, was the moving spirit behind the reform of the combination laws. By 1824 a master tailor, he had ceased to believe in the efficacy of combinations to influence wages, which he saw as determined by the laws of supply and demand; he was of the opinion that combinations were kept in existence only because of repressive legislation and that they would disappear once the ban was removed.

At first glance the evidence of a master cotton and flax spinner and power loom weaver, James Campbell of Belfast, before a select committee on combinations of workmen in 1838, would appear to support Place's belief. Campbell agreed, in reply to a question by Daniel O'Connell, who was responsible for the committee being appointed, that "human labour [was] perfectly free in the cotton-spinning trade in Belfast."[1] This "freedom" had existed only since 1825 as previous to that date combinations had ruled. But the extinction of combinations was to be explained not by Place's hypothesis but by an unsuccessful strike in 1825 and a long-continued depression in the Belfast cotton trade that led to its decline and replacement by a revived linen industry.[2] It is noteworthy that when a slight advance in wages in 1836, made during a short period of recovery, was cancelled in 1837, Campbell's employees refused to take the advice of Glasgow cotton trade union delegates, accepted the reduction, and did not form a combination.

---

1. *First Report from the Select Committee on Combinations of Workmen: Minutes of Evidence*, p. 229, H.C. 1838 (488), viii.
2. For the fortunes of the Belfast cotton industry see J. J. Monaghan, "The rise and fall of the Belfast cotton industry," in *I.H.S.*, iii, pp. 1−17.

The male cotton spinners in Belfast worked a twelve-hour day (nine hours on Saturday) exclusive of meal times and were paid 30s. to 32s. 6d. for their sixty-nine-hour week; out of their wages they had to pay three juvenile assistants an estimated amount of 10s. These children also worked sixty-nine hours, but Campbell asserted that he employed none below the age of thirteen, though he could not offer proof apart from his own statement. He did not deny that what was not good for the workers was good for the masters: if there was no formal employers' association there was general agreement on wages and prices, as, for instance, the reduction of wages in 1837. In the hackling and carding of the flax fiber, processes carried out by men preparatory to the actual spinning, which was done by female labor, he employed little machinery, unlike other manufacturers; he admitted candidly that at present he found it as economical to employ labor as machinery, in view of the saving on capital costs, but if hacklers were to demand an increase in wages he would have the work done mechanically. Further questioning showed that the "very respectful and proper" behavior of Campbell's employees was ensured by the knowledge that any "uneasy spirits among them" would be blacklisted by other mill owners.[3]

This glimpse of factory conditions in Belfast, which was to become the center of the linen trade in the United Kingdom, an industry notorious for low wages, occupational diseases, and lack of trade union organization (unionization did not begin until the 1870s among the men), would be incomplete without some reference to two other branches of the Belfast textile industry. Thomas Grimshaw, a cotton printer whose factory was in Whitehouse, on the outskirts of Belfast, had a different story to tell. His employees' combination, the Journeymen Calico Printers of the North of Ireland, had refused Grimshaw's proposal to raise the number of apprentices "to increase the quantity of work, to get it done at the cheapest rate."[4] They insisted on a five-pound apprenticeship fee, but offered to pay the fee themselves if the boys were bound to them rather than to their employers; Grimshaw refused to allow them to do this, as it would mean they would choose the apprentices. The men also refused to allow women to do the work, as in Dublin, Scotland, and Lancashire, and when some were brought over from Scotland they met them, entertained them, and paid their passage back. Grimshaw then closed his works, throwing some three hundred out of work. He added that though many of them had been driven to break stones for road-mending at 5s. to 6s. a week instead of the 18s. to 20s. they would have earned as cotton printers, the union

3. *First Report on Combinations of Workmen,* 1838, pp. 230–5.
4. Ibid., p. 235.

was nevertheless still in existence. Despite the tendentious nature of O'Connell's questions, Grimshaw was doubtful if "free labour" would restore prosperity to the Belfast cotton trade and saw combination among workmen as only one factor in its decline.

The pitiful history of the handloom weavers in England is well-known. Their gradual loss of independence and the steady decline in their earnings in the early nineteenth century had reduced them by the 1830s to a hopeless position as they strove to compete with the power loom. A similar fate overtook the weavers in the north of Ireland. In 1835 Emerson Tennant, an M.P. for Belfast, gave a picture of the homes of linen weavers in his constituency: "A quarter once remarkable for its neatness and order; he remembered their whitewashed houses, and their flower gardens, and the decent appearance they made with their families at markets, or at public worship. These houses were now a mass of filth and misery."[5] The cotton handloom weavers had also enjoyed prosperity in earlier years, when a man could earn as much as one pound per week and an observer in the Ards district of County Down could note disapprovingly the "dressy appearance" of young women weavers;[6] like their fellows in linen they were losing the long drawn-out technological battle of the late thirties.

Unlike Grimshaw's cotton printers the muslin handloom weavers had no combination. According to a Belfast employer, James McConnell, none had existed for some fourteen or fifteen years before 1838. His weavers and tambour needlewomen were outworkers, the men usually supplementing their piecework wages by cultivating patches of ground.[7] He was unable to hazard a guess at their earnings, but they must have been pitiably small, judging from other evidence. James Boyd, a Belfast weaver, stated that the handloom weavers in his district worked fourteen to eighteen hours a day and earned from 6s. to 3s. 6d. a week.[8] Weavers elsewhere in Ireland were if anything more distressed.[9] So low were earnings in the Lagan valley compared with those in Great Britain that Scottish employers found it worth their while to start business in Belfast. Alexander Moncrieffe, himself a Belfast manufacturer, explained that Catholic and Orange rivalries made trade

5. Speech in the House of Commons, 28 July 1835, quoted in Thompson, *The Making of the English Working Class,* p. 197.

6. R. B. McDowell, "Ireland on the Eve of the Famine," in R. Dudley Edwards and T. Desmond Williams, eds., *The Great Famine,* p. 14.

7. *First Report on Combinations of Workmen,* 1838, p. 240.

8. *Report from the Select Committee on Handloom Weavers' Petitions: Minutes of Evidence,* 1835 (341) (492), xiii, pp. 88–9.

9. Ibid., p. 192; *Third Report from the Commissioners for inquiring into the Condition of the Poorer Classes in Ireland,* App. C, Pt. I, pp. 28, 85, 87, H.C. 1836, xxx.

union organization impossible and ensured a supply of cheap labor.[10] The possession of some land enabled the handloom weavers to prolong the unequal struggle, but at best it only postponed their absorption into the linen factories of Belfast.

But factory workers represented a minority of Irish industrial workers in the early nineteenth century and trade unions were for long to be confined to craftsmen and the semiskilled. We have seen that a tenuous relationship had already been established between local societies in a trade. In small crafts it might be minimal,[11] in others it might embrace the whole island, as in the case of the carpenters, or even extend to Great Britain. A few were more closely linked, notably the printers, who set up an Irish Typographical Union that lasted from 1836 to 1844. How strongly its local societies were connected is shown by the 1837 edition of the Belfast Typographical Society's rule book, which insisted on membership of the union as well as the society. The union drew up rules and regulations for the whole of the Irish printing trade, and its Dublin headquarters gave aid to striking provincial printers. In 1836 it sent substantial amounts to printers in Belfast, where the redoubtable F. D. Finlay of the *Northern Whig* was determined to crush opposition, and Newry.[12] The Dublin society had a paid secretary and in four years spent over £1200 on assistance to its members.[13] The secretary of the all-Ireland union accounted for the strength of the Dublin society by rehearsing its history: an earlier society collapsed during the depression year of 1825 because it had fixed dues at a rate too low and its members, humiliated by having to beg relief from the public, determined to form a properly financed society.[14]

Irish journeymen printers labored under notable difficulties. Many Irish newspapers, insufficiently capitalized and with tiny circulations, had little more than a mayfly's life; between 1824 and 1838 ninety-four perished.[15] Master printers in most provincial towns employed an excessively high ratio of apprentices to journeymen,[16] though not all went so far as Finlay who, after giving notice to one of his compositors over a dispute involving the employment of a nonunion man, staffed a printing office secretly with ten-year old children from country free schools; these he exercised at night and, despite the Sabbath, on Sundays at his

---

10. *Report on Handloom Weavers' Petitions*, pp. 120–1.

11. *Third Report inquiring into the Condition of the Poorer Classes (Ireland)*, App. C, Pt. II, p. 51c, H.C. 1836.

12. *Second Report on Combinations of Workmen*, pp. 236–7, H.C., 1838 (646), viii.

13. Ibid., p. 97.   14. Ibid., pp. 105–6.

15. Ibid., p. 236–7. See also Brian Inglis, *The Freedom of the Press in Ireland, 1784–1841*, pp. 206, 213–7, 232–4.

16. *Second Report on Combinations of Workmen*, p. 106.

country cottage. He was proud of setting at defiance "the threats of these mighty combinators" and of feeding and clothing the children, whom he proposed in due course to bind apprentice.[17] He was driven to this ingenious scheme by an earlier unhappy experience in endeavoring to recruit "free labour" from Glasgow, Edinburgh, and Dublin. Some men were dissuaded by societies in Great Britain, and though others from Dublin did come and reach his office through a hostile crowd of some two thousand, thanks to police protection, they were sufficiently ungrateful to join the union at a later stage.[18] He claimed that by his advice and example he had enabled several newspaper offices to suppress combinations. He was unable to see that he himself had engaged in a combination when he pointed out that the master printers of Belfast, irrespective of political differences, had agreed on this course of action. This early union of hearts among Belfast employers, whether Catholic or Protestant, conservative, liberal, or nationalist, was to be duplicated frequently in later years; it occurred but rarely among Belfast workers, whose divisions were actively encouraged by those whose own economic interests prompted them to pursue a *divide et impera* policy where their employees were concerned.

The strength and high degree of organization over the whole island that distinguished the Irish Typographical Union were atypical of other trades; in general Dublin did not attempt to lay down wages and prices, but left them to be determined by the local societies. Information regarding wages, apprentices, and working conditions were exchanged, and some general agreement was thought desirable on assistance to those members traveling in search of work; mutual aid in disputes was a well-established tradition in a number of trades. A high degree of local autonomy, or indeed independence, was still the rule at this period.

Irish and British Unions

Relations between British and Irish unions were restricted, not because of any nationalist or separatist feeling, but because communication before the days of steam and the penny post was slow and costly. In some trades the Irish societies corresponded with their English counterparts and had a system of passes in both islands entitling bearers "on the tramp" to assistance.[19] The shoemakers' representative before an 1836 commission made the astonishing claim that Irish journeymen were in communication with no fewer than thirty-nine different trades

---

17. Ibid., pp. 87, 93.   18. Ibid., pp. 84–5.
19. *Report Regarding Artizans and Machinery*, pp. 72, 295–6.

extending throughout Great Britain, France, and Germany.[20] The hatters had a benefit union in operation throughout the British Isles and its London headquarters supplied up-to-date lists of prices and wages prevailing in different areas and sent aid during strikes.[21]

A United Kingdom-wide trade union was scarcely feasible, though the experiment was tried for a while by the cabinetmakers. The Liverpool cabinetmakers started such a union in 1833 with its "seat of management" in their town. The 1835 annual delegate meeting, held in Manchester, was attended by representatives from Dublin and Londonderry, and ten of the thirty societies affiliated were Irish. But the president's report was not encouraging, for it announced that strikes had been so numerous and irregular that claims for assistance could not be met from the special levy raised earlier. In 1837 the Liverpool society withdrew from the union, complaining that the other societies were in arrears. Manchester then became the headquarters, but the next year saw the end of Irish participation, for the corresponding secretary announced that the union was withdrawing from Ireland because the expense of communication was too great and the connection "too unwieldy" to give general satisfaction. The cost of the Irish connection had been evident in 1835, when the union had to pay a week's lost wages and fares to the Londonderry delegate.[22]

There was something paradoxical in the formation of a printers' association covering the United Kingdom, for it occurred in the wake of financial troubles. In 1836 there were four regional unions: the Northern Union, the London Union of Compositors, the Scottish Association, and the Irish Typographical Union. They corresponded regularly and their officials met at Northern Union delegate meetings. A crisis brought about by shortcomings in the payment of "tramping" money prompted the creation in 1842 of a general fund, from which the Scottish and Irish unions were excluded on the grounds that they were already paying their fair shares. But the scheme was a failure in spite of a levy and a special loan made by the Dublin society. The Northern Union's remedy, adopted in 1844, was the formation of a National Typographical Association, to which Ireland contributed fifteen societies with nearly seven hundred members. The new association, aided by a trade boom, expanded rapidly and at the end of 1845 claimed a membership of some 5,500. It was a short-lived triumph, for a trade depression in the following year threw members out of work and

20. *Third Report on Condition of the Poorer Classes (Ireland)*, App. C, Pt. II, p. 8c.
21. Ibid., p. 23c.
22. S. Higenbotham, *Our Society's History*, pp. 13–15. The standard travel allowance was 3*d.* per mile from the delegate's home town.

encouraged master printers to run 'rat' shops employing nonunion labor and apprentices. A host of troubles—strikes, frequent levies, suspension of benefits, disaffiliation of some societies—fell upon the association, which finally went into dissolution early in 1848.[23]

In Ireland the onset of the great famine in the autumn of 1845 had been the first sign of trouble, shown in an excess of expenditure over receipts from Irish members at the end of the year. The collapse was swifter and recovery slower than in England. The Irish Typographical Association disintegrated, though in Dublin printers quickly reorganized themselves as the Dublin Typographical Provident Society and in the provinces a few societies led a precarious existence. Some applied to join the Provincial Typographical Association, the National Typographical Association's successor, in the late 1840s, but its Sheffield Executive soon decided that "no English Executive can successfully manage an association embracing branches so geographically distant, and so materially different in their regulations and their mode of remuneration, as those in the sister kingdom."[24] They recommended the formation of a separate Irish association and promised cooperation. After some abortive attempts the 1861 delegate meeting decided to send a mission to Ireland and prompted the Dublin society to make further efforts in 1863. Dublin tried, but had to admit defeat in 1867 in the face of great difficulties: low wages, an excessive number of apprentices, and a general apathy.[25]

Ireland's reentry into a United Kingdom association was ultimately made through the Relief Association, formed in 1863 for the sole purpose of rationalizing assistance to those "on the tramp." After covering England and Wales, the Relief Association took in nine Irish societies in the principal centers outside Dublin. When the Provincial Typographical Association dropped "Provincial" from its title in 1877, it absorbed the Relief Association, but it could not persuade London and Dublin to join.[26] The London Society of Compositors and the Dublin Typographical Provident Society have to this day retained their separate identities, though under altered names.

Unlike the cabinetmakers and printers, the tinplate workers did not wait until the combination laws were repealed before they launched a United Kingdom union. In April 1821, when the masters were using a trade depression as an excuse for lowering wages, the London Society of Tinplate Workers invited other societies to join them in the formation of a union covering both islands. To judge from the correspondence and reports extant, it appears to have been a federation that would supple-

23. A. E. Musson, *The Typographical Association*, pp. 52–69.
24. Ibid., p. 93.   25. Ibid., pp. 93–4.
26. Ibid., pp. 227–32.

ment the existing arrangements for "tramping" assistance and exchange of information with an organized scheme of financial help in lockouts and strikes. The risk of prosecution under the combination acts may have dictated methods of communication: the London committee dispatched a parcel to Liverpool via Belfast and Scotland, and when it wished to coordinate the activities of local societies it sent "a proper person" on a tour of the two islands, the mission, by extraordinary exertions, being accomplished in a month. The union's strength was soon put to the test, for in December the Wolverhampton masters, who had two years earlier reduced wages by 10 percent, attempted a further reduction; the ensuing dispute lasted for more than a year before the majority of the employers came to terms. London subscribed most of the 950 pounds raised to support the Wolverhampton men, but the contributors also included Dublin and Belfast. The annual report for 1823–24 noted successes in a number of other centers, one of which was Cork. In that fiscal year the union had a total of 945 members, 82 of them in the three Irish branches. The subsequent history of "The Union" (it seems to have had no formal name) is obscure, but it is probable that it dissolved into its constituent societies some years later.[27] Though London, in subsequent decades, continued to give generous aid to provincial societies in distress, it made no attempt to organize a successor. This task fell to Manchester, where the General Union of Tinplate Workers was formed in 1862. The new union was not, however, a duplicate of the earlier body, but rather a union of northern English societies except Belfast, listed as an affiliate in 1868. Repeated efforts over the next fifty years finally brought about the establishment in 1920 of the National Union of Sheet Metal Workers and Braziers, an organization that realized the dreams of those who had founded "The Union" a century earlier.[28]

In the trades already mentioned, relations between societies of the two islands were amicable, and instances of friction were rare. This was not the case among bricklayers and carpenters in Dublin, where the local societies were at loggerheads with branches of British unions. When Luke Seery, secretary of the British Friendly Society of Operative Bricklayers, appeared before O'Connell's 1838 committee he had a

27. A. T. Kidd, *History of the Tin-Plate Workers' and Sheet Metal Workers' and Braziers' Societies*, pp. 135–51. The records consist of correspondence and reports from London in the possession of the Liverpool and Glasgow societies. The files of local societies contain no references to "The Union" after 1825.

28. Ibid., pp. 152–3, 196, 236. The General Union had at one period branches in Cork and Limerick. Dublin was a member of the National Amalgamated Tin-plate Workers, which was formed in 1889 when a regional amalgamation secured the affiliation of London and Scottish societies. Dublin refused to join the National Union of Sheet Metal Workers and Braziers for political reasons.

cheerless tale to tell. His replies to questions revealed that his society could do little more than provide members with the usual friendly society benefits for sickness, accidents, and death: it did not insist on a fixed rate of wages; it was unable to prevent the practice of foremen paying wages in public houses, often at midnight; it expelled members aiding or assisting in any illegal strike; its members were considered "colts" by another society of bricklayers. He himself agreed that his combination had not been successful in any instance (it had not tended to raise wages) and that he had no reason to think that it did any good at present.

Seery believed that his difficulties were aggravated by the rivalry of a local Irish society, known as the Old Body of Bricklayers, favored by some Dublin employers because it had contributed to O'Connell's election fund; its members were employed in building an extension to Glasnevin Cemetery and received 4s. 8d. a day as against 4s., the rate asked by Seery's society. Even the 4s. rate could not always be maintained. Two firms, Messrs. Carolan and Messrs. Mullins, engaged in work on the Four Courts, the stately group of buildings housing the principal Irish law courts, found that they were paying different rates: Mullins, for whom Seery worked, 4s. and Carolan, 3s. 4d. Mullins then reduced his to 3s. 4d., Seery pathetically explaining that his society was in no position to object.[29] Not all Carolan's employees adopted the submissive attitude of the bricklayers, the carpenters especially being animated by a militant spirit; the resultant struggles figured prominently in the 1824 and 1838 reports on combinations. Allegations of intimidation, assault, and destruction of property were made against the carpenters and other trades, though no proof could be given that societies rather than individuals were responsible. Employers were not guiltless: Edward Carolan, Sr., head of the firm, had stabbed a workman in 1820 during a dispute over the employment of "colts," but when the carpenters prosecuted him and his two sons they were acquitted on the grounds that the act was justifiable homicide; this verdict led to further assaults on the Carolans.[30]

The Dublin carpenters who were members of a British union fared no better than Seery's bricklayers. Joseph O'Neil, giving evidence before the 1838 committee, stated that he belonged to the General Union of Carpenters and Joiners, which, he claimed, had nearly 400 members in Dublin. His society had two principal grievances against Dublin employers: that they tried to lower wages and that they took on

29. *Second Report on Combinations of Workmen,* pp. 145–8.
30. *Report Regarding Artizans and Machinery,* pp. 422–6, 292, 435–7; *Second Report on Combinations of Workmen,* pp. 172–3, 176–84, 195, 204–5, 207–8, 214–5, 232–3.

an excessive number of apprentices. When a member left an employer who attempted to lower his wages, the society paid him half his wages until he got another job, but it was powerless to limit the number of apprentices. O'Neil admitted that the "regular body" (the Irish carpenters' society) regarded his members as "colts" and refused to work with them. It would seem that O'Neil's society, if not as passive as Luke Seery's Friendly Society of Operative Bricklayers, was less militant than the Irish body, and made no attempt to prevent an employer from replacing a member discharged because he would not accept a wage reduction.[31] The Irish body claimed 500 members, refused to work with nonmembers, and attempted to limit the number of apprentices. Its secretary, James Kavanagh, stated that it had built an asylum for its aged and infirm members, intended to establish a practical school for its youth, and in addition carried out the usual benefit function of apprenticing orphans, assisting widows and distressed members, and burying the dead. Kavanagh admitted that the admission fee of £1 8s. 2d. before 1820 had been trebled by 1831, and subsequently raised until it reached £7 7s.; in 1838 "colts" could gain admission only by paying a prohibitive £10 10s. He had earlier pointed out that there had been a catastrophic decline in public and private employment since the Union and that 1838 was a particularly bad year, necessitating weekly levies to support unemployed members.[32]

The Dublin branch of the General Union of Carpenters and Joiners of Great Britain and Ireland cannot have been formed earlier than 1827, the year in which the British union came into existence. It is uncertain whether the Dublin branch had its origins in a breakaway from the Irish body, or consisted of carpenters who had worked in England or saw advantages in such a connection at a period when there was heavy unemployment in the Dublin trade; the evidence of building trade employers, some of whom were unaware of the existence of two societies, is vague and unhelpful. Two points seem indisputable: the General Union of Carpenters and Joiners with its relatively loose structure[33] was not likely to make detailed enquiries about the affairs of its Dublin branch, and the Irish society was a much more effective organization than its British rival.

The general pattern of British-Irish trade union relations before the mid-century is clear. Mutual recognition of one another's "tickets"

31. *Second Report on Combinations of Workmen,* pp. 143–5.
32. Ibid., pp. 202–6, 216.
33. See Higenbotham, *Our Society's History,* pp. 25, 34. Each society or lodge had practically complete local autonomy, fixing its own rate of contributions and framing its own rules. The union membership reached a maximum of 6,774 in 1834, but then declined steadily. When the union was reorganized in 1836, it had no Irish branches.

(membership cards), the provision of assistance to "tramps," exchange of information on wages, prices, and apprenticeships—these were common features in the period. Even loans in trade disputes were not unknown. Relations between English and Irish pipemakers were broken off, but this was exceptional and caused by the heavy influx into England of Irish tradesmen.[34] When a union covering both islands existed, it was a federation of local societies or regions, freely entered into. However, as the histories of the printers and cabinetmakers show, difficulties of organization and communication made its continuance on a United Kingdom basis impracticable. John Doherty's Grand General Union of Operative Spinners of Great Britain and Ireland included Belfast members from 1829 until its collapse in 1831[35]; the Journeymen Steam Engine and Machine Makers' Friendly Society (the "Old Mechanics"), founded in 1826, had some Irish branches that took part in the formation of the Amalgamated Society of Engineers in 1851,[36] but in neither case does it seem that there was any question of rivalry with existing Irish societies. The appearance of branches of British unions among Dublin bricklayers and carpenters was exceptional at this time, and even in these instances the consequent rivalries do not seem to have been caused by any political antagonism; resentment at English trade union "imperialism" was not to arise until the beginning of the twentieth century.

The Employers' Counterattack

The legislation of 1824 and 1825 on combinations removed some of the disabilities on trade unionists, who could now meet legally to discuss wages and hours of work and thus present agreed demands to their employers. They were not, however, allowed to enforce any limitation on the proportion of apprentices to journeymen, a matter of considerable importance when an employer tried to cut his wage bill by increasing the number of employees still apprentices or when the trade in question was stagnant or declining, as was frequently the case in Ireland. The provisions against violence or intimidation were stringent and the penalties severe, and efforts to obstruct those at work were forbidden, a clause that could be interpreted to make even peaceful picketing well-nigh impossible. Trade unionists were also vulnerable under the Master and Servant law, since an employee breaking a con-

34. *Third Report from the Commissioners for inquiring into the Condition of the Poorer Classes (Ireland)*, App. C, Pt. II, p. 32c, H.C. 1836.
35. *Second Report on Combinations of Workmen (1838)*, pp. 258–9.
36. Information supplied by the late James Morrow, Irish secretary of the Amalgamated Engineering Union.

tract by leaving his job was committing a criminal offense whereas an employer could merely be faced by a civil action.

It was not to be expected that the more militant trade unionists would refrain from action when an employer arbitrarily increased the number of his apprentices or engaged "colts," or proved obdurate in the matter of wages. Nor was it likely that the "turn-out" would suddenly be abandoned as a weapon in trade disputes even if it meant a breach of contract. Many employers on their part regarded combinations of workmen as prone to original sin, since even in the matter of wages workers were tempted to exchange a respectful manner for more forthright demands. In their turn the masters asserted their threatened authority. James Kavanagh produced, in evidence before the 1838 committee on combinations, a circular issued from the Dublin Chamber of Commerce in February 1838, signed by the secretary and sent to shopkeepers and businessmen generally:

I am directed by the committee for the suppression of illegal combination to transmit the following resolution, and to request the favour of a reply at your earliest convenience; the committee, which meets here every Wednesday at four o'clock, will thankfully receive and treat with strict confidence any information which you can give as to the injurious effects produced by illegal combination in your particular trade.[37]

Kavanagh's accompanying comment was that employers themselves entered into combination, as was shown by the circular, and that in reality they would only be satisfied if the trade societies abandoned their rules and left all contentious matters to the decision of the masters.

Prosecutions for offenses classified as combination cases were frequent. Apprentices who struck along with journeymen in a Carrickfergus, County Antrim, calico printing works in 1826 were immediately sent to prison.[38] Two convict hulks, the *Surprise* and the *Essex,* sailed regularly from Cobh (formerly Queenstown) and Dun Laoghaire (formerly Kingstown) to English penal colonies; during the years 1825–34 the *Essex* carried among its prisoners seven sentenced for combination offenses.[39] During the same ten-year period the *Surprise* carried 5,889 prisoners convicted of various offenses and ranging in age from ten to over seventy. Of these, 3,520 had received the minimum sentence of seven years, 121 fourteen years, and 2,248 life.[40] Given the

37. *Second Report on Combinations of Workmen,* p. 214.
38. R. B. McDowell, *Public Opinion and Government Policy in Ireland,* 1801–46, p. 62.
39. Swift, *Dublin Bakers,* p. 174.
40. Ibid., p. 174. Thirty-nine were between 10 and 12 years of age, 13 over 70.

nature of the penal code, with its emphasis on the sacred rights of property, it is reasonable to assume that among these thousands were some whose offenses were criminal only in a legal sense but who, whether peasants arrested for their part in the long drawn-out tithe war or urban workers driven to rioting in the course of industrial disputes or during spells of trade depression, were in effect the victims of a social and economic order that denied them in any real sense equality before the law.[41]

The year 1834 was the year in which the most ambitious effort was made by the English working class to transform their working conditions by the formation of the Grand National Consolidated Trades Union. It was also the year in which the employers fought back, ably aided by the Whig government, especially by Lord Melbourne as Home Secretary, who had six agricultural laborers of Tolpuddle, Dorsetshire, transported to Australia under a 1797 act that forbade the administering or taking of unlawful oaths for seditious purposes; the oath was part of a ritual enjoining secrecy, an understandable precaution in a period when mere membership of a trade union was sufficient to ensure victimization. These rituals and initiations were common in masonic and friendly society practice and in Ireland among such societies as the United Irishmen; they were sometimes accompanied by regalia, codes, and passwords, though in the case of trade unions there was no seditious intent.

In Ireland also 1834 was a year of intense trade union activity and of sustained counterattacks by employers.[42] Prosecutions for illegal combination involving attempts to limit apprentices, intimidation, conspiracy, strikes in violation of contracts, and even membership of a benefit society took place in Londonderry, Lisburn, County Antrim, Dublin, and Cork. Printers, sawyers, shoemakers, coachmakers, cabinetmakers, flaxdressers, and bakers were among those charged. Robert Watson, a baker, was given three months in jail for leaving his Belfast employer before his two-year contract was up; he had aggravated his offense by joining a trade union.[43] Flaxdressers employed in Mulholland's York Street flax-spinning mill, the first to employ steam power in Ireland, went on strike and three men were sent to prison for three months.[44] The egregious F. D. Finlay of the *Northern Whig,* engaged in

41. During the years 1843–9, 89 persons were tried in the Dublin metropolitan area for offenses connected with combinations or conspiracies to raise wages, 37 of whom were convicted (Swift, *Dublin Bakers,* p. 176).

42. During 1834 five prisoners in one Dublin prison (Newgate) were charged with combination offenses, three of them being sentenced to six months' imprisonment (Swift, *Dublin Bakers,* p. 176).

43. *Northern Whig,* 13 Feb. 1834.   44. *N.W.,* 5, 16 May 1834.

his prolonged struggle to eliminate society men from his printing establishment, succeeded in having one of the five men he charged convicted and sentenced to the usual three months.[45] Sawyers who met in a public house in Londonderry were arrested and sent to prison on the standard charge of combination.[46] Belfast coachmakers conducted a campaign in favor of the limitation of apprentices for three years and demanded that new employees possess a union card; some sixty men from various firms took part in stoppages and cases came before the courts in April.[47] Robert Murphy, an overzealous recruiter for the coachmakers' society, received two months' imprisonment with hard labor and a two-pound fine in July. He had threatened one Robert Gregory until Gregory attended a meeting in a public house and allowed his name to be entered in a members' book; later he resigned his membership and helped in Murphy's prosecution.[48] His employer, James Montgomery, found it impossible to persuade local coachmakers to give up the struggle and had to import scabs from London and elsewhere.[49] In Cork the police raided a mortality society, seized books, and arrested eight men, who were sent to prison for three months.[50]

The six men of Dorset, the "Tolpuddle Martyrs," had been sentenced to transportation in March. There followed demonstrations, the most notable being that in London marshaled by Robert Owen and attended by upwards of thirty thousand trade unionists complete with banners, petitions, and even an editorial in *The Times* pleading for clemency. In Belfast a meeting of the local branch of the Northern Trade Union was held during April in George's Market for the purpose of petitioning parliament on behalf of the Dorchester laborers. The chairman was a cabinetmaker, George Kerr, and other trades represented among the speakers included painters, coopers, sawyers, and carpenters.[51]

This meeting, like those in England, had no immediate effect on the fate of the Dorchester men, who were not pardoned until 1836, but it is an indication of the width of Irish workmen's sympathies in the convulsive year of 1834. A week later 200 Belfast trade unionists assembled to greet John Lawless, who had won their admiration by his radical record; he recalled the time that he had worn a 1782 Volunteer uniform.[52] Lawless, editor of various short-lived radical and liberal

45. *N.W.*, 5, 6 May, 5 June 1834.
46. *N.W.*, 10 Mar. 1834; W. P. Ryan, *The Irish Labour Movement*, pp. 79—80.
47. *Belfast News-Letter*, April 1834.   48. *N.W.*, 21 July 1834.
49. *N.W.*, 1 Sept. 1834.   50. *N.W.*, 18 Aug. 1834.
51. *N.W.*, 14 Apr. 1834. The Northern Trade Union may have been connected with the Grand National Consolidated Trade Union.
52. *N.W.*, 21 Apr. 1834.

papers and a one-time resident of Belfast, had campaigned for Catholic emancipation, freedom of conscience, repeal, and the abolition of tithes.[53] In February he had received a formal address of thanks for his labors, and in May he again appeared in Belfast to speak at a meeting for the purpose of arranging a petition against the compulsory tithes levied on all tenants, irrespective of religious affiliation, for the clergy of the established church.[54] Though on general grounds a supporter of O'Connell, he had taken a strong line against clerical influence in politics; in the same month of May he published an article in the London radical journal, the *True Sun,* condemning O'Connell's proposal to give glebe lands and houses to Irish Catholic clergy, a measure that would in effect have created a second established church in Ireland.[55] Nor would his radical sympathies, sympathies that earned him trade union admiration, allow him to give to the Whig administration the uncritical support that O'Connell required.[56]

In 1830 the southern English rural laborers had risen in revolt, smashing machines and burning ricks, especially those of tithe-receiving parsons. It was a short-lived and cruelly repressed revolt. By contrast the antitithe campaign which had started in Ireland in the same year spread over the countryside and did not end until 1838, when the system of collection was changed. It assumed in many cases the dimensions of guerrilla warfare, with assaults on tithe collectors; sporadic attacks by anonymous bands on landlords, land agents, and property; and, in retaliation, evictions of recalcitrant tenants by police and troops. Magistrates trying combination cases were mindful of this rural unrest. The long tradition of oath-bound agrarian secret societies in Ireland was an additional reason for the authorities to take alarm at any suggestion of oath-taking among urban workers, though there seems little evidence that trade unionists administered such oaths. The best documented instance of such an alarm concerns George Kerr, whose case in some respects resembles that of the Tolpuddle men, though with a less tragic ending.

Kerr, who published an account of his experiences in a twenty-two-page pamphlet, *Exposition of Legislative Tyranny and Defense of the Trade Union,*[57] was a Belfast cabinetmaker. Faced in 1834 with growing un-

53. Brian Inglis, *The Freedom of the Press in Ireland, 1784–1841,* pp. 143, 188, 195, 221–2.

54. *N.W.,* 21 Feb., 9, 12 May 1834.   55. *N.W.,* 26 May 1834.

56. *N.W.,* Lawless had earlier asserted the principle of an independent press against O'Connell's hostility in 1828. See Inglis, *Freedom of the Press in Ireland,* 221–22.

57. Copy in the Halliday tracts, V. 1811, Royal Irish Academy; text in A. Boyd, *The Rise of the Irish Trade Unions, 1729–1970,* pp. 113–31; summary in Ryan, *Irish Labour Movement,* pp. 78–82.

employment and heavy reductions in wages, the Belfast society decided to join the newly formed cabinetmakers' union started in Liverpool the previous year, and Kerr and two companions went to Derry to secure affiliations there. After the Belfast delegates had left, the mayor of Derry had two of the local men arrested, browbeat them into saying that the Belfast men had administered illegal oaths, and "swore by his immortal God" that he would have them transported if they did not confirm this testimony. Kerr was arrested in Belfast and sent off with a guard of four policemen armed with loaded muskets on an eighty-mile walk to Derry, being lodged in the local bridewell or station in each county town and taken on by a fresh guard. The mayor of Derry questioned him about his chairmanship of the Belfast meeting in support of the Dorchester laborers and about his membership of a trade union, and refused bail on the grounds that one surety was a union member and that others were not worth double the amount of bail. In Derry jail Kerr was stripped of all his possessions, put in prison clothes, and brutally treated by the prison barber. Finally released on bail he returned to Belfast where in May he was imprisoned to await trial at the next assizes.[58] Here his ordeal came to an end, for the grand jury threw out the bill of indictment against him and James Corbet, a fellow journeyman.[59] It is probable that his *Exposition,* published in Belfast at the request of his friends, had some part in his acquittal.[60] His work for the cabinetmakers was not in vain, for both Belfast and Londonderry remained in affiliation with the United Kingdom Union until its executive decided that it was impractical to retain Irish societies in it.

O'Connell, Trade Unions, and Chartism

After 1825 Irish workmen took a more active part in public life. In Belfast a number of "respectable workmen" joined the Belfast Reform Society during the agitation that preceded the 1832 Reform Bill.[61] In Dublin processions had long been dear to tradesmen, who assumed much of the pageantry of the guilds; a 1761 broadside ballad celebrates the order and procession of the journeymen woolcombers and weavers, who were accompanied by "the regular, registered, free and accepted masons belonging thereto."[62] Under the new legal dispensation they

---

58. *N.W.,* 5 May 1834.   59. *N.W.,* 7 Aug. 1834.

60. Kerr's *Exposition* was written between May 5 and July 27, since he mentions the latter date as that on which he was to appear before the assizes.

61. R. B. McDowell, "Consolidation of the Union," in T. W. Moody and J. C. Beckett, eds., *Ulster Since 1800, A Political and Economic Survey,* p. 21.

62. Gilbert, *Calendar,* xi, 496–9.

added to these demonstrations public meetings at which political resolutions were adopted. In 1830 the carpenters condemned the Act of
Union and called for its repeal, and other trades followed suit. A
subsequent combined procession to the house of Daniel O'Connell was
prohibited and the trades had to be content with representatives presenting an address to the "Liberator" and, at a later date, calling upon
"their brethren throughout Ireland" to seek parliamentary reform and
to oppose any candidate not pledged to support repeal. Cork and Tullamore also held vast open-air repeal meetings.[63]

O'Connell's unequaled mobilization of mass support in his successful
campaign for Catholic emancipation, which in 1829 swept away most
disabilities, opened to Catholics almost all offices of state, ensured
Catholic representation in parliament, and earned him his title of
"Liberator," though the relief measure had been bought at the expense
of disfranchising his most faithful followers in the countryside, the
forty-shilling freeholders, by a clause raising the property qualification
to ten pounds. But O'Connell's prestige remained immense, for in
Catholic eyes he was the leader who had restored to them their long-lost
dignity as human beings. If there was no immediate disillusionment,
such as that suffered by the English working class over the 1832 Reform
Act, it may be explained not only by continuing gratitude, but by the
hopes raised by O'Connell as he pursued his policy, however ambiguous
and hesitant, of repeal and reform, and alternately supported and
condemned the Whigs. Nor were his basic conservatism, his respect for
established property rights, or his horror of anything remotely subversive of the existing social and economic order (a dread strengthened by
his recollections of Jacobin France) immediately apparent as threats to
trade union claims. And for Dublin tradesmen repeal held out the
promise of renewed prosperity when Dublin again became the seat of an
Irish parliament.

As O'Connell's repeal campaign got under way Dublin trade unionists were drawn into it. In 1831 they formed the Dublin Trades Political Union (later known as the National Trades Political Union) as a
forum for the discussion of questions particularly affecting their welfare
as well as a sounding board for repeal and parliamentary reform. But
the "Liberator" captured it and deprived it of any independent function
by turning it into a registration machine. After condemning the strike
of Glasgow cotton spinners (five of whom were sentenced to transportation) in the summer of 1837 he then launched in November an attack
on combinations, choosing the Trades Political Union for his platform;

63. Rachel O'Higgins, "Irish Trade Unions and Politics, 1830–50," in *The Historical Journal*, iv, p. 212.

he secured the passage of a resolution denouncing their pernicious influence on trade and their addiction to intimidation and violence, and assured conbinators that "the vengeance of an outraged God, and the severe but just judgement of the laws will not fail to overtake their abominable crimes."[64] An aggregate meeting of the trades on December 26 repudiated O'Connell's charges and listed their benevolent work for their members, urging their critics to go and do likewise. Further meetings, at which O'Connell was present, were stormy, and neither his oratory nor the ecclesiastical strictures of Dr. Daniel Murray, the Catholic archbishop of Dublin, were sufficient to convince the Dublin combinators of their sins.[65] In February 1838 he denounced trade unionism in the House of Commons, singling out Irish combinations as being particularly baneful, as against the meritorious societies of Great Britain, and successfully urged the appointment of a select committee to investigate combinations in the whole of the United Kingdom.[66] Despite his presence on the committee, which he frequently chaired, its findings were obviously a deep disappointment to him, since the two reports contained no recommendations; the accompanying minutes of evidence, used earlier in this chapter, nonetheless are of value to the historian. As for the Trades Political Union, his attacks on trade unions drove all but his most unquestioning supporters out of that organization, which became completely subservient to him.[67]

During the revolutionary and Napoleonic period there had been mutual sympathy between Irish democratic nationalists and English reformers, a potential alliance that could have included more than the advanced radicals and Jacobins in both islands had objective conditions been more favorable. A second opportunity came in the 1830s. O'Connell was committed to a measure of parliamentary and agrarian reform and could have forged an alliance between Irish peasants and English industrial workers, as proposed by Fergus O'Connor, the Chartist leader, in his pamphlet, *A Series of Letters from Fergus O'Connor to Daniel O'Connell,* issued in 1837. But the personal antagonism between the

64. *F.J.,* 7 Nov. 1837, quoted in Clarkson, pp. 137–8.
65. Clarkson, pp. 138–41.
66. *Parliamentary Debates,* 3rd. ser., xi, 1084–97.
67. F. A. D'Arcy, in "The Artizans of Dublin and O'Connell, 1830–47," *I.H.S.,* xvii, no. 66 (Sept. 1970), pp. 221–43, points out (p. 238) that the artizans reserved their enthusiasm, not for Catholic emancipation, which they considered had brought them no economic benefits, but for repeal, which they expected would bring renewed prosperity to Dublin. He argues (p. 241) that O'Connell was responsible for the artizans' decision to rely in industrial disputes on "moral force and the irresistible impulse of public opinion" rather than on intimidation.

two men had already been evident as early as 1833, shortly after O'Connor was returned for a County Cork seat, which he lost in 1835. O'Connell had made his Lichfield House compact with the Whigs in 1835 and had supported their introduction in 1834 of the new English poor law, their opposition to trade unions, and their dislike of the trade union agitation for a ten-hour working day. O'Connor's wholehearted support of English working-class demands and his emergence as the leader of English Chartism were additional reasons for O'Connell's refusal to ally himself with the Chartists, whom he viewed as dangerous, violent, and subversive of social order. He denounced the People's Charter of 1838 and its demands for universal suffrage, abolition of property qualifications for parliamentary candidates, and implied power to shape social and economic policy. Following the failure of the Chartist rising in Monmouth in November 1839, the leaders of the revolt, John Frost, Zephaniah Williams, and William Jones, together with some of their followers were brought to trial, initially condemned to death, and later transported or imprisoned. The Trades Political Union, with a proper deference to O'Connell's views, to his personal antagonism to O'Connor, and even to his peculiarly baroque style of addressing royalty, sent an obsequious address to Queen Victoria: "May it please your Majesty, we your Majesty's most loyal and dutiful subjects express strongly decided disapprobation of the proceedings of the misguided persons in England who, under the name of Chartists, have committed themselves against the laws of the land, and have therefore justly incurred your Majesty's displeasure."[68] Some months earlier (August 1839) they had wrecked a meeting called by Dublin Chartists to hear Robert Lowery, an English Chartist leader. It is not surprising that Fergus O'Connor, the possessor of a power of invective scarcely inferior to that of O'Connell, should have described the Trades Political Union about this time as consisting of "briefless barristers, pettifogging attorneys, shopkeepers, clerks, and a set of fellows who haunt the public offices like locusts, their motto being Places or exposure."[69]

The leading part taken by such Irishmen as Fergus O'Connor and James Bronterre O'Brien in English Chartism is no guide to the success of the movement in Ireland, where O'Connell's dominance in Irish politics and the very different social and economic conditions presented formidable obstacles. At its peak the Irish movement seems to have had about one thousand members. Its initial support came from trade unionists in Dublin, Belfast, and Cork, and later it counted members

68. *F.J.*, 14 Jan. 1840, quoted in Swift, *Dublin Bakers*, p. 209.
69. O'Higgins, "Irish Trade Unions and Politics," p. 215.

in Newry, Drogheda, and Loughrea, County Galway, as well as radical small farmers in the neighborhood of these towns. A Chartist Association formed in Dublin during the summer of 1839 held weekly meetings and distributed O'Connor's *Northern Star* and other English Chartist publications. It was this body that invited the Chartist convention, sitting in Birmingham during July 1839, to send Robert Lowery to Dublin, only to have the meeting broken up by O'Connell's henchmen.

By 1841 the Dublin Chartists had recovered sufficiently to reorganize themselves and even to form groups in other towns, linking them in an Irish Universal Suffrage Association presided over by Patrick O'Higgins, a Dublin merchant. It was unable to imitate the militancy of the English movement but it issued pamphlets, *Chartism and Repeal* and *Civil and Religious Liberty,* which urged an alliance between Irish repealers and English Chartists and denounced the persecution its members suffered at the hands of O'Connell and Irish Catholic clergy. It organized several petitions to parliament in favor of the charter's six points and repeal of the Union, and even tried, unsuccessfully, to bring about a reconciliation between O'Connell and O'Connor in 1843. A turning point came in its fortunes in 1844. After the fiasco of the huge Clontarf repeal meeting of October 1843, dutifully cancelled by O'Connell when the authorities proclaimed it, the Liberator and his colleagues were tried on a conspiracy charge, sent to prison for some months, and then released in September when the House of Lords quashed the proceedings. With the onset of the trial the Dublin Chartists suspended their gatherings as a gesture to the "national feeling."[70] Membership fell off in the absence of meetings and made only a partial recovery in 1848. The anticlimax of the Kennington Common meeting on April 10 of that year marked the last high point in English Chartism; in Dublin the end as a coherent political group followed the arrest of O'Higgins in August on a charge of concealing arms and his subsequent release, after public protest, in March 1849.

If the general body of Dublin artisans kept aloof from the Chartists and lost faith in the National Trades Political Union, they continued to support the cause of Repeal. In July 1843 they held a large demonstration, drew up petitions to parliament, and, during the first nine months of 1844, contributed 600 pounds to Repeal Association funds.[71] But 1844 marked the end of their collective participation in Repeal politics, for an article in the constitution of the Regular Trades'

70. *United Irishman,* 4 March 1848, quoted in R. O'Higgins, "Irish Influence in the Chartist Movement," in *Past and Present,* no. 20, p. 89.

71. F. A. D'Arcy, Dublin Artizan Activity, Opinion and Organisation, 1820–50 (M. A. thesis, University College, Dublin, 1968), p. 71.

Association, founded in August, forbade the introduction at its meetings of any subject "of a sectarian, religious, political, or party" nature.[72] Individual workers did support the Young Ireland section of O'Connell's National Repeal Association on its expressing dissatisfaction with the Liberator's temporizing policy in December 1846, and when the Young Irelanders set up their own organization, the Irish Confederation, artisans joined the rank-and-file Confederate clubs and served on the Confederate Trades and Citizens Committee.[73] Confederate leaders who had hitherto dissociated themselves from the Chartists changed their attitude; Thomas Francis Meagher admitted at a meeting in March 1848 that "we have been guilty of sad injustice in our abuse of the English democracy" and spoke from the same platform as Fergus O'Connor in Manchester on St Patrick's Day.[74] John Mitchel had supported the Dublin Chartists when they formed the Irish Universal Suffrage Association; in London Irish Confederate Clubs were closely associated with the Chartist radical wing led by such men as Ernest Jones and William Coffey; at Oldham and Nottingham in May "Mitchel and Liberty!" and "Mitchel should be free!" appeared on Chartist banners.[75] James Fintan Lalor proposed in July 1848 that if he, as editor of the *Irish Felon,* should be arrested, one of its editors should be an English Chartist (he had been in correspondence with a well-known one, B. T. Treanor).[76] When Meagher and William Smith O'Brien, head of the Confederation, had gone to Paris to bear greetings from a Dublin demonstration, held in honor of the February revolution and attended by many artisans, the party received by Alphonse de Lamartine included Edward Hollywood, a silk weaver and trade unionist on the Council of the Confederation.[77] At the time of the Confederates' break with O'Connell Hollywood had suggested to Smith O'Brien that sympathetic repeal wardens in the North of Ireland should distribute free copies of the Young Ireland paper, the *Nation,* among the working class there, in view of the importance of winning over

72. *F.J.,* 24 Oct. 1844, quoted in D'Arcy, p. 71.

73. *Nation,* 5 Dec. 1846, quoted in K. B. Nowlan, *The Politics of Repeal,* pp. 112–13; O'Higgins, "Irish Influence in the Chartist Movement," p. 89.

74. *Nation,* 18, 25 Mar. 1848, *United Irishman,* 25 Mar. 1848, quoted in Nowlan, *Politics of Repeal,* p. 185.

75. See Nowlan, *Politics of Repeal,* for relevant newspaper references.

76. Thomas P. O'Neill, "James Fintan Lalor," in J. W. Boyle, ed., *Leaders and Workers,* p. 42.

77. Desmond Ryan, *The Fenian Chief,* p. 78; *Irishman,* 27 Sept. 1873. Other artisan council members were Michael Crean, a shoemaker, and Joseph Byrne, a hatter. Only Crean had been a member from the foundation (D'Arcy, Dublin Artisan Activity, p. 73).

the Protestant working class to Young Ireland ideals of democratic nationalism.[78]

The failure of the Confederate rising in August 1848 ended for the time being any possibility of large-scale participation in general political movements by Irish trade unionists. The country was already in the grip of the great famine that altered so profoundly the social and economic, and ultimately the political structure of Ireland, and in one sense the rising was a last despairing effort before apathy became total.

An Early Trades Council: The Regular Trades' Association[79]

Dublin trade societies had been forced to defend themselves publicly in the 1837–38 controversy with O'Connell over this allegations that they employed violence and intimidation in industrial disputes and that they had injured the prosperity of the city by their tactics. While they were not prepared to accept blame for the decline in trade, and continued to seek limitations on the number of apprentices, they did rely increasingly on appeals to public opinion rather than on direct action in their struggles with sweating employers. In the mid-1840s they took three unprecedented steps: they assisted workers outside the regular trades, did what they had been accused of doing at a much earlier date—forming an association of city trades—and, most surprising of all, attempted to revive the guilds.

During the summer of 1844 public interest was aroused by a prolonged strike of operative tanners for higher wages. The tanners were not regular tradesmen, since they had not served an apprenticeship, but could be counted as semiskilled. In August a letter from the Master Tanners' secretary denounced the strike as being directed by a central body, claimed that the wages paid in Dublin were higher than elsewhere—ranging from 8s. to 14s. per week—and emphasized that these tanners had served no apprenticeship.[80] The tanners' demand was for a standard wage of 14s. at a time when trade had recovered from an earlier depression.

The Master Tanners' secretary was correct in stating that the strike was centrally directed, for a strike committee of tradesmen—including a ladies' shoemaker, a broguemaker, a hatter, and a cartwright—had assumed charge. A reply to the Master Tanners was published, accompanied by a letter of support from some expatriates, the Irish

78. Text of Hollywood letter in Ryan, *Fenian Chief*, pp. 78–9.
79. Cork may have had a form of trades council in the 1830s (see app. 2).
80. *F.J.*, 9 Aug. 1844.

Operative Tanners of Litherland, near Liverpool; the Litherland tanners had also sent money.[81] The skilled men then held on 13 August a public meeting in support of the strikers in a theater in Fishamble Street, with a silk weaver as chairman and representatives present from twenty-one trades. The St. James's Temperance Society Band discoursed "fine and national airs" in the intervals. While the main business of the gathering was the plight of the tanners, one of the strike committee, the hatter J. H. Burke, announced that on the following Monday, 19 August, a meeting would be held to form a union of the trades of Dublin.[82] The Associated Trades of Dublin was formally inaugurated on 29 August. It changed its name to the Regular Trades' Association in October, when it adopted a constitution.[83]

A regular series of meetings in support of the tanners was held during August. At one it was announced that thirty trades had written letters of sympathy. Among the speakers was the English Chartist Henry Vincent, a compositor who had twice been imprisoned for his activities and had fought several parliamentary elections. While not surrendering his views on the necessity for parliamentary reform, Vincent, like his fellow Chartist Robert Lowery, had become a fervent propagandist for the temperance movement. He took the opportunity to refer to the "principle of universal suffrage" and the good work of Father Theobald Mathew, the well-known Irish temperance leader.[84] The following day he addressed a meeting of his own on working-class politics, stressing the importance of the temperance movement and condemning the imprisonment of repealers.[85] It is an index of the change of temper since Lowery's visit in 1839 that Vincent was well received and was given considerable publicity in the press. Another meeting in the Fishamble Street Theater, held on 27 August, was attended "by one of those numerous assemblages which of late have manifested such sympathy with the cause of the persecuted tanners of Dublin." The carpenter Richard McNamara presided and the secretary announced that the trades were coming forward generously in support of the tanners and, in a reference to the inaugural meeting of the Associated Trades of Dublin to be held two days later, "were fully alive to the necessity of forming themselves into a union by legal and constitutional means.[86] How successful the tanners were is not recorded, but

81. *F.J.*, 12 Aug. 1844.   82. *F.J.*, 14 Aug. 1844.
83. For the date of foundation see the annual report for 1846 in *F.J.*, 30 Dec. 1846; for the change of name and adoption of a constitution, *F.J.*, 24 Oct. 1844, and *The Guardian and Tradesmen's Advocate*, 2 Jan. 1847.
84. *F.J.*, 21 Aug. 1844.   85. *F.J.*, 22 Aug. 1844.
86. *F.J.*, 28 Aug. 1844.

as late as December a meeting was held to support their demand for
fourteen shillings a week. Organized by the bootmakers, it was the
occasion of a bitter speech by Thomas Clancy, the ladies' shoemaker
member of the strike committee: he declared that "labour has no
protection in this country; no voice. The tyrant can drag you before a
magistrate for something or for nothing. You have no voice in making
the laws that govern you, and therefore the law is against you.[87]

Though O'Connell and his colleagues had been imprisoned in 1844
for but a few months and were treated more as guests than felons, the
prison sentence was sufficient to arouse a new wave of sympathy and
admiration for the Liberator, mute the voices of his critics, and restore
some of the flagging enthusiasm for the repeal movement. The congregated trades of the city of Dublin, together with those of neighboring
Blackrock and Kingstown, took part in a large procession in May 1845
on the anniversary of O'Connell's imprisonment, and J. C. M. Brady,
secretary of the Regular Trades' Association, read an address to the
Liberator from his organization.[88] But it was the last occasion, if we
except their presence in the Liberator's funeral procession to Glasnevin
in 1847, on which the Dublin artisans took to the streets in support of
O'Connell. Disillusionment with politics had set in and subsequent
events merely deepened it. One of these was the curious episode of the
attempted revival of the guilds in an age of economic liberalism.[89]

In 1833 Benjamn Pemberton, chairman of the bricklayers and plasterers' union, but also a member of the bricklayers' guild,[90] proposed
that Dublin tradesmen should protect themselves against the sub-
contracting system that facilitated the employment of unapprenticed
labor by reviving the decaying guilds, which could then claim the right
to enforce the observation of guild regulations setting proper standards
of skill and working conditions. Some societies expressed interest, but
the passing of the Municipal Corporations (Ireland) Act of 1840 ending
guild representation on municipal corporations seemed to put an end to
the possibility. Pemberton, however, noted that the act ended guild

87. *F.J.*, 28 Dec. 1844. As a ladies' shoemaker Clancy belonged to the most skilled
and therefore highest paid division of his craft; the making of brogues, or men's heavy
working boots, required less skill.

88. *F.J.*, 31 May 1845.

89. This account of the attempted revival of the guilds is based on the article by
F. A. D'Arcy, "The Trade Unions of Dublin and the Attempted Revival of the Guilds,"
in *Journal of the Royal Society of Antiquaries of Ireland*, 101, pt. 2 (1971), pp. 113–27. I
am also indebted to Mr. D'Arcy for loaning me his valuable thesis on Dublin Artizan
Activity, Opinion and Organisation, 1820–50.

90. He twice held the office of Master of the Corporation of Bricklayers, in 1812
and 1836.

political but not trading privileges and succeeded after some delay in
having the validity of his guild's charter confirmed by the courts in
June 1845. As a result a number of the societies, notably the journeymen tailors who had suffered particularly from the depredations of
the sweating system, succeeded in persuading their respective guilds to
become active again, to proclaim their right to regulate trade, and to
threaten offending employers with legal action if they did not seek a
guild license to carry on their business. Among those served with a writ
during January 1846 was Thomas Arkins, prominent repealer and
master tailor to O'Connell. Though the Liberator did not at this stage
intervene on behalf of his henchman, he had earlier in the month
resumed, after an interval of some five years, his attack on trade unionism by expressing his anxiety at a repeal meeting about the dangers of
English trade unions enrolling Irish railway workers.

The war between the recalcitrant employers and the revived guilds
that had heeded the appeal of the societies lasted through the opening
months of 1846. The Dublin Chamber of Commerce organized a meeting that appointed a committee to defeat the attempt to establish "a
despotic authority over the employers and operatives," while the Regular Trades' Association sent speakers to a meeting of "merchants,
traders, manufacturers and operatives" under the chairmanship of the
lord mayor. The trades secretary, J. C. M. Brady, in moving a motion
calling on artisans and citizens to support the guilds, emphasized that
the guilds offered the great advantage of possessing arbitration machinery, something long desired by the artisans. In a supporting speech
John Harrison, the chandlers' secretary and delegate, admitted that
workmen's combinations had been guilty of violence in the past, but
pointed out that it was the result of "the working classes being chased
out of the pale of the charter granted for their protection," and claimed
that the general public, as well as the tradesmen, would benefit by the
revival of guilds that would ensure that good and fairly manufactured
goods were brought to market.

The meeting appointed a committee of artisans and masters to prepare an address to the lord lieutenant. But the Chamber of Commerce
had forestalled them, and its representative Jonathan Pim was able to
announce in April that the lord lieutenant and chief secretary had
agreed to have a bill drafted that would abolish the trading privileges of
the guilds. Both sides then drew up petitions to be submitted to
parliament. Those in favor of the bill included two to be presented by
O'Connell; those against it came from the Dublin guilds and trade
unions.

On 12 May the Regular Trades' Association held a meeting attended
by several thousand artisans. The first resolution, moved by the

sawyers' union secretary Bartholomew Redmond, reiterated the reliance of the societies on moral force, their determination to repudiate the baneful effects of turnouts or strikes, and their support for the guilds. The second, moved by the tailors' union secretary John Cosgrave, declared that guilds would help to prevent "imposition on the public, oppression on the part of the capitalist and aggression on the part of the operative." A third resolution asked the government to delay the bill until an enquiry into the nature and workings of guilds had been held. The request was ignored and on 22 August 1846 the bill to abolish the trading privileges of the guilds became law.

The Regular Trades' Association had been formed before the courts had confirmed Pemberton's belief that the guilds had a legal right to regulate trade, and its support for their revival can be seen as part of the craftsmen's campaign to protect themselves in an age of unbridled competition. When the brief alliance with the guildsmen was ended they were thrown back on their own resources. The normal activities of the association are described in the report for 1846 presented to the annual meeting in December.[91] They were those of trades councils, if somewhat more limited in scope, and as such may be said to make the Dublin body an early example of its kind in the British Isles.[92] The Regular Trades' Association had been formed with a two-fold object:

Firstly, to place before the working classes the rise, progress and objects of this association, and secondly, by doing so to create a feeling of interest and co-operation among their fellow-tradesmen, convinced as they are from past experience that nothing short of an entire human and peaceful union of working men can effect an amelioration of their condition, or tend to check the increase of oppression on the part of those so disposed.

John Harrison, the new secretary, read a list of deputations appointed during the year and emphasized "what successful and beneficial results united strength and concentrated action is capable of accomplishing," while the report retailed how "public meetings were attended, public contracts and works were watched, public boards were memorialled and waited upon with varying and alternate success." The Chartist movement was not forgotten, the report recalling that "during the period of the Charter agitation this association rendered material service in the general principle of the cause; but in common with their fellow-tradesmen they deeply regret the failure of their efforts." Perhaps the association's proudest achievement was the journal it

91. For the proceedings at the annual meeting and the text of the annual report see *F.J.*, 28, 30 Dec. 1846.

92. The first two bodies to be called trades councils were those of Glasgow (1858) and London (1860).

called into existence, having for its aim the elevation of the industrial and mechanical character of our country and her sons; the maintenance and inculcation of peace, law and order, the bringing out of trade reports, cheaply and correctly, before the public, and by these and by every other legal means in their power, to defend the character of our tradesmen from the many wanton and unfounded charges of combination, and to trace, as far as possible, the decrease of our trade and manufacturers to (at least) some of their causes.

This journal, *The Guardian and Tradesmen's Advocate,* was a penny weekly started on 31 October 1846; it bore the slogan "A fair day's wages for a fair day's work," and declared that its primary object was "to afford the operative classes of Ireland a channel by which their wants may become known, their rights asserted and their grievances redressed."[93] Devoted as it was "to the wants and wishes of the children of toil, to the noble task of elevating the social and moral conditions of our people," its "warning voice to those would-be tyrants of the fearful responsibility they incur who defraud the labourer of his hire"[94] was heard for nearly a year.

The brave words at the annual meeting in December were quickly belied. In January 1847 the new president, Frederick Ryan, a coachmaker, complained of the prevailing inactivity: "A most unaccountable apathy reigns and rules in the councils of all your societies. You seem to be passing through a state of collapse."[95] It was an accurate diagnosis. A depression in the printing trade brought about the collapse of Irish branches of the National Typographical Association during 1846, leaving only a reorganized Dublin Typographical Society to carry on at a later date.[96] The Dublin branch of the Bookbinders ceased to be the union's headquarters and the Dublin branch of the United Kingdom Society of Coachmakers was "blacked" by its union's executive committee. Nor can the discouraging effect of the failure to revive the guilds be omitted. And to these internal reasons for decline in the Regular Trades' Association must be added the impact of the Great Famine. During January 1847 starving city dwellers, together with an influx from the countryside, clamored for food, and bread carts were seized and the contents devoured. Some 36,000 men, women, and children were fed during the winter months by soup kitchens set up in

93. *The Guardian and Tradesmen's Advocate,* 31 Oct. 1846, quoted in O'Higgins, "Irish Trade Unions and Politics," pp. 215–6. It was owned and edited by Cornelius R. Mahoney and carried a statement that it was "especially patronised by the Associated Trades of Dublin."

94. *F.J.,* 30 Dec. 1846.

95. D'Arcy, Dublin Artizan Activity, p. 130. Unless otherwise stated, the sources for this account of the collapse of the Regular Trades' Association are to be found in D'Arcy's thesis, pp. 130–32.

96. See above, pp. 31–32.

the parishes. But as the famine continued, funds became exhausted and the city hospitals were crowded with those who suffered from typhus and other famine-induced diseases. At a public meeting of workers in March, organized to petition parliament for prompt measures of relief, John Harrison made a bitter comment:"No proposition had been brought forward to alleviate these conditions, and yet when the trades-men were wanted for any political array, they were quickly sought after."[97] In such circumstances the Regular Trades' Association per-ished. Aggregate meetings of the city trades might be held on special occasions, but a period of some fifteen years was to elapse before the individual societies had recovered sufficiently to create a successor in the United Trades' Association.

In a situation where *suave qui peut* was still the motto of hard-hit labor organizations, it is difficult to take seriously Bertram Fullam's Irish Democratic Association. The published objectives of the associa-tion are couched in rhetorical and repetitive language, but it is clear that it was to undertake the political education of the working classes so that, by realizing their power, they could secure "the recognition and just appreciation of the rights of labour and the overthrow of a heartless and useless oligarchy."[98] Founded in January 1850, it was supported by Fullam's paper, the *Irishman*. No prominent artisan ever had any con-nection with it, and when both journal and organization disappeared in May, nothing was left but a grandiose proposal quite unrelated to the harsh circumstances of the period.[99]

97. *F.J.*, 17 Mar. 1847, quoted in D'Arcy, Dublin Artizan Activity, p. 73.
98. *F.J.*, 6 Mar. 1850, quoted in D'Arcy, Dublin Artizan Activity, p. 78.
99. For the Irish Democratic Association see Rachel O'Higgins, "Ireland and Chartism" (Ph.D. thesis, Trinity College, Dublin, 1960), p. 160, quoted in D'Arcy, "Dublin Artizan Activity," pp. 77–8, and app. XII, pp. lix–lxi.

3

Recovery

The Dublin United Trades' Association

The early history of labor organization is characterized by the existence of short-lived bodies. Sometimes, however, they reappear, often with a new name but animated by much the same desires. The Regular Trades' Association, for instance, seemed to have lost the cohesion it possessed in the mid-1840s, but essentially the same personnel appeared for an aggregate meeting of the trades of Dublin. The meeting was held as before in Fishamble Street, to protest against the 1849 visit of Queen Victoria and the accompanying illumination of the city, as well as to demand repeal.[1] Working-class activity in the mid-century seems to have found expression in irregular meetings of the congregated trades, a pattern to be found in other Irish towns as well as in Dublin, when it was thought desirable that the views of trade unionists on some topic of public interest should be heard. But what organization existed was primarily of an *ad hoc* variety and tended to lapse when the immediate need was past. Though the congregated trades of a city might have a president and secretary, these officers did not of themselves guarantee the existence of an organization meeting regularly at this period; the Regular Trades' Association was thus an exception and, if it is correct to assume that its final collapse occurred in 1848, it is probable that the Dublin trades reverted to the looser and more infrequent type of assembly prevalent in such towns as Cork and Limerick.

The later 1850s were comparatively uneventful, the repeal movement was dead, and by 1852 the brief flurry of tenant-right agitation was over. Economically there was a gradual rise in living standards throughout most of the country. If we except the formation in 1851 of the first of the British "new model" unions, the Amalgamated Society of Engineers, which included Irish members from the beginning, little of importance occurred among the trade unions. Toward the end of the decade, however, there was renewed activity. The Dublin journeymen

1. *F.J.*, 27 July 1849.

bakers started a vigorous campaign in 1859 to abolish night work, Sunday work, and excessive overtime, publishing appeals to "clergymen, merchants and citizens" and holding public meetings, one of which, in May 1860, was attended by the lord mayor of Dublin, four Fellows of Trinity College, Dublin, and other prominent citizens. One of the speakers was a Belfast master baker, Bernard Hughes, who pointed out that day work had prevailed for many years in his city. The campaign continued, with meetings in many provincial towns. In Dublin only a limited success was obtained, when in 1863 an act made night work illegal for journeymen under eighteen years of age and required the inspection of bakeries.[2]

Disappointed in the results, the leading bakers' society of Dublin, the Bridge Street Society, welcomed a proposal for a new organization of the Dublin trades. Its projectors had originally come together to issue a journal but when they were unable to do so they decided in October 1862 to form a new body, the United Trades' Association. The bakers played a leading part in its formation and lent their committee rooms for preparatory meetings. Their secretary Patrick McNamee became the association's first president when it was formally constituted in January 1863.[3]

The new association's objective was, to quote from the speech of the secretary John Keegan at a dinner given in honor of the retiring president in April 1864, "the protection of the rights of labour."[4] It was not a militant body and its secretary was anxious to dispel any idea that it was bent on restraining trade. Good employers were cited as models and the public asked to patronize them. It was careful before committing itself to supporting wage claims to assure itself that the claim was justified and that the quality of the work done was adequate. But if it preferred a mediatory role it could point to some success early in its life; when in 1864 clay pipe makers struck against a 20 percent reduction in wages the association allowed the men 5s. per week strike pay and persuaded the employers to take them back and waive the reduction.[5] During its existence the organization continued to support members of affiliated trades involved in industrial disputes, as in the second quarter of 1870 when it paid strike allowances to men in four distinct trades.[6] It frequently aided societies by sending deputations to employers to

2. Swift, *Dublin Bakers*, pp. 236–9; Ryan, *Irish Labour Movement*, pp. 123–6.

3. Members of the Bridge Street Bakers' Society, 18, 22 Oct., 1, 29 Nov. 1862, quoted in Swift, *Dublin Bakers*, pp. 239–40. See also the first annual report of the United Trades' Association, *Irishman*, 6 Feb. 1864.

4. *Irish People*, 9 Apr. 1864, quoted in Clarkson, pp. 167–8; *Irishman*, 16 April 1864.

5. *Irishman*, 6 Feb. 1864.   6. Ibid., 17 Sept. 1870.

urge claims for improved wages and working conditions; it assisted in the formation of unskilled and semiskilled unions and, by setting up an arbitration committee in 1871, helped to reduce friction between rival trades.[7] If its policy seemed moderate, especially in the opening years when its officers were conscious of earlier failures in persuading Dublin societies to form a trades council, it gained confidence as its membership grew. When in 1871 one Moyers, a member of the Dublin Employers' Union, refused arbitration in a building trade dispute, John Keegan, still secretary of the United Trades' Association, said that up to the present the association had not intervened in the struggle, but Moyers's letter threw the onus on every Dublin workingman to come to the rescue—it was a question of capital versus labor, might versus right. Though the three societies affected (two local carpenters' unions and one plasterers') were not affiliated, Keegan promised the association's support and threatened to call an aggregate meeting of 30,000 Dublin tradesmen to raise a levy of 2*d.* per member, yielding £250 per week for strike pay.[8]

One of the permanent preoccupations of the United Trades Association was the steady decay in Irish craft and small-scale industries. The contrast between Dublin and Belfast could scarcely have been greater, for the northern city's expanding population and leading industries (shipbuilding, engineering, textiles) provided employment of a volume unmatched elsewhere in Ireland. Dublin, however, depended on a few large firms engaged in brewing, distilling, and food processing, and on its role as a transportation center for imports and cattle exports. For the skilled trades there was the building industry, which afforded but limited employment in a city that grew slowly, and handcrafts outmoded by changes in fashion or unable to meet British and foreign competition based on factory organization and power machinery. It is not surprising that the United Trades' Association should have spent much time and energy urging support for native industries. Its first annual report (for 1863) mentioned efforts to discourage the importation of such articles as clay pipes and clocks,[9] efforts repeated and indeed intensified in later years as trade after trade declined under the impact of competition and technological change. It was standard practice to lobby manufacturers, merchants, clergymen, local authorities, and committees engaged in erecting monuments to the patriot dead to use Irish-made goods and to employ Irish craftsmen; protests were frequent against the importation of such diverse articles as organs, corks, and clothing. Even the building trade was affected by the use of imported work, a plasterer announcing in 1871 that London cornices

7. Ibid., 15 May, 17 June 1871.   8. Ibid., 15 July 1871.
9. Ibid., 6 Feb. 1864.

were being installed by a firm that had been awarded a contract on the assumption that native work would be used.[10] The effects of competition were felt throughout Ireland; in provincial centers, with the exception of Belfast and other towns in the Lagan Valley, employment prospects grew darker as crafts decayed and more agricultural workers deserted the land. Artisans in such towns as Cork, Limerick, Waterford, and Sligo were at one with their Dublin fellows in denouncing the evils of importation, and, when the Irish Trades Union Congress was finally founded in 1894, resolutions on the subject appeared annually on conference agendas until the outbreak of World War I.

The United Trades' Association made plans early in its existence for a nationwide association. Aided by a guarantee of £20 from Sir John Gray of the *Freeman's Journal,* it entertained trade unionists from the provinces who were visiting the Dublin Exhibition during August 1864 and provided them with a *déjeuner* in the Mechanics' Institute.[11] The immediate result was to encourage a greater degree of organization in some provincial towns. The Cork trades followed the Dublin example and set up their own association.[12] In October a resolution from the committee of the Dublin association urged that in every town where three of more trade societies existed, a union should be formed "to be independent of, but in connection with, the United Trades' Association of the metropolis." Such an organization "knowing neither politics nor religion, but trade and protection of tradesmen's rights alone," would help to create a reciprocity of feeling between the various trades. It would also point out to the public the absolute necessity of encouraging native manufactures and discouraging importation, which had compelled "myriads of our most skilled fellow tradesmen to seek that employment abroad which they . . . were unable to procure in the land of their birth."[13]

The Dublin committee's suggestion was intended initially to increase the number of trades councils in Ireland and subsequently to link them in a federation in which Dublin would have a preponderant role. From such a federation might have arisen a national trade union center where individual societies or local branches would be represented indirectly through the trades councils with which they were affiliated. This development might well have led to a strong trades union congress capable of imposing a centralized structure upon the entire movement, of framing centrally directed policies, and of dominating, rather than being dominated by, a few of the bigger, nationally organized unions.

10. Ibid., 20 May 1871.
11. Clarkson, pp. 169–70; *Irishman,* 18 Feb. 1865.
12. *Irishman,* 5, 19 Nov. 1864.
13. *Irish People,* 29 Oct. 1864, quoted in Clarkson, pp. 170–71.

Support for the Dublin committee's plans came from Wexford, Enniskillen, Limerick, Waterford, Galway, and Ennis,[14] but the proposed federation does not seem to have had more than a theoretical existence.

In August 1865 the secretary of a cabinetmakers' society in Limerick asked for information about an amalgamation of trades extending throughout Great Britain and Ireland. The secretary of the Dublin association was instructed to acknowledge receipt of the letter but at the same time to correspond with the secretary of the Limerick congregated trades, an indication that Dublin preferred its own plan.[15] It was, however, in the same year that such a plan was suggested by Sam Nicholson, president of the Manchester and Salford Trades Council, to his friend Alexander Dronfield of the Sheffield Association of Organised Trades. Dronfield accepted the suggestion and in 1866 summoned a congress that set up the United Kingdom Alliance of Organised Trades. Its purpose was to raise a fund from trade unions to enable member unions to resist lockouts and reductions in wages, but it collapsed in 1867 when the affiliated bodies failed to pay levies regularly. Nicholson then summoned a congress at Manchester in 1868 with the less ambitious object of securing publicity for trade union opinions. Though it was not attended by delegates from the London Trades Council and though no formal decision was taken to hold annual congresses, the Manchester gathering turned out to be the first meeting of the United Trades Congress, as the British T.U.C. was called in its early years.[16] Dublin was represented at Manchester, however the relations between the British organization and Irish trade unionists are best dealt with separately.

The Dublin United Trades' Association was a less ephemeral body than its predecessor, the Regular Trades' Association. After two years it was firmly established with twenty-five affiliated societies of skilled artisans,[17] and receipts in 1864 of some £230;[18] the annual report for that year claimed that the association had united seven-eighths of the tradesmen in Dublin. It was still in existence in 1877,[19] with John Keegan as its secretary. It is not possible to fix the date of its disappearance, though it is clear that this must have taken place before 1880. In that year the British T.U.C. met in Dublin and the president of that congress, by custom a local man, lamented the absence of "some

14. Clarkson, p. 171; *Irishman*, 19 Nov., 24 Dec. 1864.
15. *Irishman*, 26 Aug. 1865.
16. Henry Pelling, *A History of British Trade Unionism*, pp. 70–73.
17. *Irish People*, 7 Jan. 1865, quoted in Clarkson, p. 169.
18. *Irishman*, 18 Feb. 1865.
19. Ibid., 26 Apr. 1877. The Regular Working Millers' Society of Ireland paid affiliation fees to it for the first quarter of 1877.

of the big, strong trades" of the city, trades whose presence would have enabled Dublin artisans to unite in "one solid compact body. . . . For it must be confessed that we have not in this city that trades council which is so essential to have in every large city, and as a consequence, we are much divided."[20] He expressed the hope that one result of the meeting would be the formation of a Dublin trades council, but this did not take place until six years later.

The United Trades' Association (U.T.A.) almost from the beginning had assisted by mediation and financial help affiliated bodies engaged in industrial disputes, maintaining a weekly levy of 1/2d. per head for the purpose. Such a fund was useful in small or short-term disputes but was unable to meet larger demands, so the association's meetings were used to announce the needs of striking or locked-out workers and to report subscriptions from sympathetic trades. We have already seen that the officials were prepared to recommend assistance to unaffiliated bodies in Dublin, but their concern on occasions could extend far outside the city. The most striking example was the reception given to delegates of the Lurgan (County Armagh) Damask Weavers in 1874. The depression that was to continue into the 1880s had begun and the weavers were trying to resist wage reductions that they claimed would lower their earnings some 25 percent below those prevailing twenty years earlier. The delegates reported that they had been warmly welcomed by the Dublin trades; the Letterpress Printers' Society voted twenty pounds, and the Boilermakers applied to their English executive committee for a special grant.[21]

As the title of their organization indicates, the founders of the United Trades' Association were concerned with securing the affiliation of unions of skilled workers. They were nontheless not unmindful of the plight of the unskilled and, when in 1864 a deputation of building laborers asked them for assistance in forming a union, they arranged for committee members to attend an organizing meeting.[22] The principal speaker at the meeting was John McCorry, a bricklayer, assisted by other U.T.A. members. McCorry drew attention to the exploitation of laborers at the Vartry (County Dublin) reservoir waterworks, where a "tommy" shop made inroads on their miserable wages, and at a later meeting cited cases of men working for as little as 2d. a day. McCorry claimed that with union organization they could raise their weekly pay to 15s. in summer and 12s. in winter (the rates in large English towns were £1 and 15s. respectively) and stressed the benefits that they could derive from cooperation as practiced by the Rochdale pioneers.[23] The

20. *F.J., B.N.-L.*, 15 Sept. 1880.   21. *Irishman,* 7 Mar. 1874.
22. Ibid., 2 June 1864.   23. Ibid., 11 June 1864, 11 Feb. 1865.

U.T.A., called upon in 1871 to assist striking ropemakers, secured a promise from Ringsend fishermen to use only twine and rope made in fair houses; in turn, the U.T.A. undertook to present a memorial to the lord lieutenant on the fishermen's grievances.[24] A year later the association intervened on behalf of scavengers employed by the Dublin corporation. Assuming that enlightened self-interest might prevail where other considerations would not, they called upon Dublin ratepayers to insist that the town council meet the modest demands of the scavengers, who were on strike for a pay rate of 14*s.* a week.[25]

If such actions on behalf of the unskilled or semiskilled seem less than militant, the context in which they took place should be remembered. Most of the skilled trades in Dublin were themselves in no strong position and the association shouldered a heavy burden in maintaining strike pay for its affiliated members.[26] To organize and take into membership large numbers of laborers, who would have found the utmost difficulty in paying dues, and support them during disputes, would scarcely have been possible in a city as permanently depressed as Dublin, so that appeals to public opinion on their behalf represented the utmost that the U.T.A. could do. In English towns where conditions were much more favorable for craftsmen and laborers, no effective organizing drive among general workers was undertaken until the late 1880s.[27]

A cherished ambition of the Dublin trades was to have their own headquarters. In September 1870 a member spoke of the need for a suitable trades' hall that would be a center for the association and also provide accommodation for individual trades; the association had been indebted to the Bakers' Society from the very beginning for providing a meeting place.[28] Though the scheme was welcomed by the trades, a levy of 1*d.* per member per week instituted, employers and citizens invited to contribute, and an impressive roll of trustees (Rt. Hon. Edward Purdon, lord mayor, Sir Arthur Guinness, bart., Jonathan Pim, M.P., Edward Dwyer Gray of the *Freeman's Journal,* and James Scott) drawn up,[29] the plan hung fire. A renewed effort was made in 1873 when it was decided to issue collection books to the various trades—it was estimated that "if only 10,000 of our members" con-

---

24. Ibid., 5 Aug. 1871.   25. Ibid., 6 Jan. 1872.

26. The United Trades' Association was still paying strike allowances to the employees of one rope-making firm three months after the strike began (*Irishman,* 6 Jan. 1872).

27. Clarkson's criticism (pp. 168, 170) of the attitude of the U.T.A. to laborers should be read in the light of the remarks above. Neither Clarkson nor Swift seems aware of the activities of the U.T.A. after 1865.

28. *Irishman,* 24 Sept. 1870.   29. Ibid., 31 Dec. 1870.

tributed 1*d.* a week for sixty weeks, £2,500 would be received and success assured.[30] Once again little progress was made and, when headquarters were at last secured in 1890, it was the U.T.A.'s successor, the Dublin Trades Council, that occupied them.[31]

Fenianism and Labor

In 1858 the Irish Republican Brotherhood (I.R.B.) was founded in Dublin by James Stephens, and its American wing, the Fenian Brotherhood, by John O'Mahoney in the same year. Both Stephens, the autocratic Head Centre or chief, and O'Mahoney had taken part in Smith O'Brien's Confederate rising in 1848 and had been fellow exiles in Paris, but had determined, when the time seemed ripe, to plan a revolutionary movement dedicated to establishing an Irish republic; the secret, oath-bound I.R.B. was the result. In "Fenianism, Past and Present," an unpublished article written possibly in the 1880s, Stephens described the growth of the I.R.B. in the face of clerical, aristocratic, and middle-class opposition and declared: "We had with us the farmers' sons, the mechanics, the artisans, the labourers and the small shopkeepers."[32] These represented the people of Ireland who, unlike their social superiors, had not lost faith in Irish nationality and needed only to be aroused; for these Stephens, as he explained in a parenthesis in his American diary late in 1858, wished to establish a democratic republic; "that is, a republic for the weal of the *toiler.*"[33] The republic once established, Stephens intended to retire from political life but was prepared to undertake the direction of a fraternal association, composed of volunteers, with the object of effecting a social revolution. At this point he lapsed into rhetoric. He hated landlordism and, though he did not quote Fintan Lalor, he shared broadly his aims to replace the landlord by the independent peasant proprietor. If he did not link the objective of the land of Ireland for the people of Ireland with the aim of an Irish republic, it was partly in deference to the views of his more conservative colleagues and partly because he was convinced at that time that the agrarian movement was dead. Nor was he persuaded that he could unite the rural and urban elements in his organization behind a movement for agrarian reform. To the urban worker, Stephens, rejecting socialism, communism, and

30. Ibid., 5 July 1873.
31. *Thom's Directory (1892)*, lists 114-16 Capel Street as occupied by the Dublin Trades Council in 1891. The council seems to have taken possession late in 1890 (*F.J.*, 22 Dec. 1890).
32. Desmond Ryan, *Fenian Chief*, p. 327.
33. Ibid., p. 133.

utopianism and showing no comprehension of what industrialization entailed other than regarding it as an English invention, appealed simply on grounds of nationality.

The Fenian chief did not appeal in vain. During the preliminary survey Stephens made after his return from Paris at the end of 1856, he met once again the silk weaver Edward Hollywood, then living in Manchester after an exile in Paris, and as a result of conversations with him and later with his brother William in Dublin, concluded that he would find support among Dublin trade unionists for the projected organization.[34] The I.R.B. or "The Organisation" as it was often referred to by members, was constituted on St. Patrick's Day of 1858 in the lumberyard of Peter Langan, a lath splitter.[35] Until Thomas Clarke Luby, a Protestant Fenian, successfully enrolled a substantial number of shop assistants in 1860, I.R.B. membership in Dublin and its neighborhood consisted largely of mechanics.[36]

If neither the Dublin United Trades' Association nor individual trade unions were officially associated with the Fenians, there is no doubt that Stephens was correct in describing the personnel of his organization as consisting, broadly speaking, of the urban and rural working class. After the abortive Fenian rising of March 1867, the list of those arrested in Dublin and other urban centers reads like a trades directory—almost every occupation, skilled, semiskilled, and unskilled, was represented among the prisoners.[37] Despite the denunciation of the Fenian leaders by Bishop David Moriarty of Kerry in February 1867 ("O, God's heaviest curse, his withering, blasting curse is on them. . . . It is a hard word and who can bear it? But when we look down into the fathomless depth of this infamy of the heads of the Fenian conspiracy we must acknowledge that eternity is not long enough, nor hell hot enough to punish such miscreants."[38]) and the hostility of many of the Catholic clergy led by the ultraconservative

34. Ibid., pp. 77–8, 81, 83.   35. Ibid., p. 91.
36. Ibid., p. 164.
37. 7 tailors, 1 gasfitter, 1 engine fitter, 5 boot and shoemakers, 1 plasterer, 1 car driver, 2 engine drivers, 1 coachmaker, 3 nailers, 6 laborers, 3 coopers, 3 iron workers, 1 tobacco spinner, 1 smith, 1 baker, 2 grocers, 1 ex-letter carrier, 2 messengers, 3 medical students, 1 shop assistant, 1 stationer, 1 brushmaker, 2 millers, 1 baker, 4 drapers, 1 draper's assistant, 1 rectifying distiller, 5 porters, 2 clerks, 1 cabinetmaker, 1 ropemaker, 1 mason, 1 bricklayer, 1 plumber, 3 carpenters, 2 slaters, 1 weaver, 1 dyer, 2 stonecutters and marble workers, 3 corkcutters, 1 printer, 1 painter (*Irishman*, 23 Mar. 1867). John O'Clohissey, first president of the Dublin Trades Council, had been a "centre," or head of a Fenian cell in Dublin and had acted as a marshal at the funeral of Terence Bellew MacManus in 1861; like many Fenians he had served in the British Army, where he was a soldier in the Bombay Horse Artillery (O'Brien Collection, MS. 13953, National Library of Ireland).
38. *F.J.*, 18 Feb. 1867, quoted in *Irishman*, 2 Mar. 1897.

primate Cardinal Paul Cullen, sympathy with the Fenians was widespread among many urban workers. The trials of leading Fenians, their speeches from the dock and the public hanging of the "Manchester Martyrs" (W. P. Allen, Michael Larkin, and Michael O'Brien) convicted on perjured evidence of the accidental shooting of a police sergeant during the rescue of Fenian prisoners, made 1867 a rival of 1798 in revolutionary nationalist annals.

A number of Fenian leaders had been arrested during 1865 and a campaign for their release, coupled with appeals for the financial support of the prisoners' families, began in 1866 and continued into the 1870s. It drew in those constitutional nationalists afraid lest their patriotism be impunged and evoked considerable popular support when Isaac Butt, later to lead a Home Rule party in the British parliament, organized an Amnesty Association in 1868.[39] The trades associations of several towns joined enthusiastically in the amnesty appeals; Cork, in September 1868, passed a resolution asking for the release of the prisoners wherever they were confined, and Dublin in the same month endorsed it.[40] The campaign continued in 1869, with resolutions carried and meetings held in various provincial towns by their congregated trades, culminating in a demonstration on the outskirts of Dublin attended, according to the organizers, by 300,000 on October 10. The forty-five trades parading included chimney sweepers and pawnbrokers' assistants in addition to the more conventional groups.[41] Though the campaign was suspended some weeks later in order to give the government time for reflection, the temper of some of the urban workers remained militant; the Cork Working Men's Association's *soirée* of December 27 was held in a room decorated with such slogans as "Our martyred dead—Allen, Larkin and O'Brien," and with portraits of patriot leaders.[42]

For some years a nominal distinction was preserved between the trades council (or congregated trades of a town) and the trades in general in the matter of political demonstrations, the more scrupulous

39. Butt began his career as a Unionist and Conservative and retained a conservative outlook on social issues; his experiences as defending counsel for Fenian prisoners persuaded him that some form of Irish autonomy was necessary if repeated disturbances and social revolution were to be averted. See L. J. McCaffrey, "Irish Federalism in the 1870s, A Study in Conservative Nationalism," in *Transactions of the American Philosophical Society,* new ser., lii, pt. 6 (1962); and D. A. Thornley, *Isaac Butt.*

One of the more unusual supporters of the amnesty campaign was the unorthodox Orange leader, William Johnston of Ballykilbeg, County Down; his letter of encouragement was read at a meeting of the committee of the Amnesty Association in December 1868 (*Irishman,* 5 Dec. 1868).

40. *Irishman,* 26 Sept. 1868.   41. Ibid., 16 Oct. 1869, suppl.
42. Ibid., 1 Jan. 1870.

trades councils barring the introduction of political or religious matters; in practice the distinction was not always self-evident when much the same personnel was involved. Certain anniversaries acquired over the years a national and therefore nonpolitical character in the eyes of some trades bodies, perhaps the most noteworthy being that of the Manchester Martyrs,[43] whose deaths were ultimately commemorated even by the most punctilious trades associations. The Limerick congregated trades never hesitated to take part in political demonstrations and paraded with bands and banners to greet Isaac Butt when, some months after his election as M.P. for the city, he came to speak at a banquet there.[44] The Cork trades meeting in the Mechanics' Hall were more prudent and in 1872 their officers disavowed a gathering held there to raise a monument to a deceased political prisoner, pointing out that the rules forbade the introduction of politics. Shortly afterwards they were again called upon to intervene when a meeting of the trades was called by printed placards to promote the parliamentary candidature of the lord mayor. Supporters of a rival candidate appeared, the officials barred all nonmembers, and fighting broke out, but disorder conveniently ended before the police arrived.[45]

It would not be correct to assert that it was the I.R.B. that had introduced trade unionists to national politics; O'Connell had exercised a very great influence on the Dublin trades who frequently demonstrated in his honor, even after his death, or for a cause he espoused. But O'Connell was a monarchist and demanded no more than repeal, whereas the Fenians were republicans; O'Connell was a thorough-going constitutionalist, but the Fenians were revolutionaries, political if not social; finally the Fenians had behind them the memory of the Great Famine and evictions, a powerful stimulus to hatred of British rule, however indirect; in the tradition of Wolfe Tone they were determined "to break the connection with England, the unfailing source of all our political evils."[46] If some of them were prepared to replace landlords by peasant proprietors, it was at least in part because landlords, as opposed to "the people," were not national-minded. The postrevolutionary Ireland of the Fenians' dreams was to be a democratic republic, with "the people" as master; further than that they did not go. And if their

43. The Limerick congregated trades took part in the organization of an anniversary funeral demonstration for the Manchester Martyrs in 1878 (ibid., 24 Nov. 1877).

44. Ibid., 30 Dec. 1871, 13 Jan. 1872.

45. Ibid., 16 Nov. 1872. The principal Cork trades, headed by their officers, took part in the funeral procession of John O'Mahoney, the Head Centre of the Fenian Brotherhood in America, when his body was brought back for burial in 1877 (ibid., 3 Mar. 1877).

46. *Life of Theobald Wolfe Tone*, ed. W. T. W. Tone (Washington, 1826), i., p. 51.

dreams lacked precision it was because for them the primary, indeed almost the only, goal was national independence, which would create a community where questions of class would be of minor importance.

Thus the Fenians reinforced in the minds of urban workers O'Connell's principle of the supremacy of nation over class. Their insistence on a nonsectarian nationalism (by no means uniformly present in O'Connell's speeches, which at times tended to identify Irish nationalism with Catholicism), combined with their revolutionary methods and oath-bound organization, brought them into conflict with the majority of the Catholic hierarchy and earned them a reputation for anticlericalism, not always undeserved. After 1861, when the I.R.B. leaders turned the funeral of Terence Bellew McManus, an 1848 exile, into a Fenian triumph, their influence increased rapidly and was further strengthened by a roll call of prisoners, exiles, and martyrs added after 1865. They could claim with justice that they had aroused a country sunk in political apathy; they could also assert that henceforward revolutionary methods would challenge constitutional ones in the Irish nationalist movement. When federalist, Home Rule, or other forms of parliamentarian activity failed to satisfy the hopes aroused, the advocates of stronger measures made themselves heard, invoking the long list of the patriot dead commemorated in story, song, and ballad.

Irish Relations with the British Trades Union Congress and Reform Organizations

Their preoccupation with domestic problems did not blind Dublin trade union leaders to developments in the British labor movement. Although the 1825 act had removed some disabilities, trade unionists were still in certain ways second-class citizens; under the Master and Servant law, for instance, employees could be sent to prison for any breach of contract whereas employers were subject only to civil, not criminal, proceedings.[47] Magistrates not infrequently acted as strikebreakers by threatening men with imprisonment if they did not resume work without delay.

Alexander Campbell and George Newton of the Glasgow Trades Council, assisted by the Scottish miners' leader, Alexander MacDonald, convened in 1864 a national conference of trade union delegates in London to further their campaign to amend the law. The conference made arrangements to have a bill introduced into parliament and to form local committees that would lobby for support. The United Trades' Association in June 1864 received a report of the conference

47. See Pelling, *History of British Trade Unionism,* pp. 63–4.

with great satisfaction and in September a letter, urging support, from John Smith, a Glasgow member of the executive committe in charge of the campaign.[48] The U.T.A.'s role seems to have been confined to approval and encouragement (it is probable that no Irish delegates were present at the London conference, described in the U.T.A. proceedings as a meeting of "the United Trades of England and Scotland"). A more active participation might not have been possible so early in the association's history, though the amending measure, enacted in 1867 and going some way toward meeting trade union desires (it still retained criminal proceedings in "aggravated cases") affected Irish and British workmen equally.[49]

Two of the thirty-three delegates to the Manchester United Trades Congress of 1868 were Irish, George Clare and John Keegan, president and secretary respectively of the United Trades' Association, which was listed among the supporting organizations. Clare spoke to a paper by George Potter of the *Beehive* on "Trade Unions: an Absolute Necessity" and remarked that some professional men, he singled out attorneys, adopted the principle of combination, which, strangely enough, they and "the kid-gloved class of society generally" deprecated among working men. Keegan contributed a paper supplementary to one by a Bolton mason on legalization of trade societies and Clare argued in the subsequent discussion that not only the funds, but the general objectives of trade unions should be legalized.[50]

Clare also attended the 1869 congress in Birmingham (he was the only Irish delegate) where he was nominated as president but declined on the grounds of ill health. He was nonetheless an active participant. When Potter read a paper ("The Disorganisation of Labour") denouncing the drink trade and referring critically to Tories and established churches, Clare disapproved of the introduction of "anything that would do violence even to the prejudices of persons anxious to assist the working classes"; it would "only distract their councils and give a triumph to employers who were hostile to their progress." He showed a similar moderation in a discussion on courts of arbitration and conciliation: when several speakers criticized the award of an arbitrator in a Manchester joiners dispute because he had dined with the secretary of the employers and then given an award displeasing to the men, Clare sided with those who said that this example did not invalidate the

48. *Manchester Guardian*, 3 June 1868; Edmund Frew and Michael Katanka, *1868, Year of the Unions*, p. 25.

49. *Manchester Guardian*, 6 June 1868; E. Frew and M. Katanka, *1868, The Year of the Unions*, p. 39.

50. *Report of the Second Annual Conference of Trade Unions*, p. 35. The name was later changed to Trades Union Congress.

principle of arbitration, adding that had Mr. Kettle (the arbitrator) found in favor of the men, he would have been a Daniel come to judgement. He argued that there might be many other remedies for trades disputes, but if they did not see their way to accomplish these remedies, let them continue to act upon the principle. At a public meeting Clare argued in favor of an international union of trade societies and earned applause when he asserted that such an extension of their bases would increase their power, influence, and ability to resist any attacks made on them. At the congress Clare also seconded a motion moved by George Odger to thank Sir Charles Dilke for introducing a bill to provide payment for M.P.s, but the motion was withdrawn since it would have led to a discussion. In a paper on the legal position of trade unions the Manchester tailor P. Shorrocks claimed, among other provisions, the same protection for trade union funds as for those of a trading company. Clare was disturbed because many of the subsequent speakers seemed indifferent to protection of funds and he warned them that such an attitude could lead government ministers to conclude that delegates were unstable in their opinions. Clare was included in a five-man committee to draw up a statement on the resolutions adopted to go out to the world, to trade unions, and to legislators as to the reasons why "we hold the opinions therein contained."[51]

Clare's prominence at the 1869 congress was a swan song rather than an augury of greater Irish participation in the affairs of the British body. No Irish delegate appeared at the third (1871) or fourth (1872) congresses. The U.T.A. passed a resolution adopting the preliminary agenda for the fifth (1873) meeting and urging the trades to have as large a representation as possible at Leeds, but no Irish delegate was present though the U.T.A. was represented formally by George Howell,[52] who had become secretary of congress in 1871. Howell corresponded with the Dublin body, and again acted as their representative at the sixth (1874) congress.[53] Even this tenuous connection was not maintained and there was no further Irish participation until 1880, when the T.U.C. met in Dublin.

The U.T.A. was also drawn into the campaign for a revision of the laws bearing directly on trade unions. Two events in 1866, the "Sheffield outrages" and the decision in the *Hornby v. Close* case, threatened to undermine the very existence of trade unionism. Violence in the cutlery trade in Sheffield, culminating in the blowing up of a nonunionist's

51. Op. cit., pp. 54–5, 169, 206, 94–5, 105–6.
52. *Irishman,* 5 Oct. 1872, 18 Jan. 1873: *Annual Report of Fifth Congress,* which listed the U.T.A. as having thirty-two affiliated societies.
53. *Irishman,* 5 July 1873; *Annual Report of Sixth Congress.*

house, led to a royal commission inquiry into trade unionism generally and to highly damaging disclosures of crimes committed in Sheffield and Manchester against nonunionists and hostile employers. In *Hornby v. Close* the Boilermakers' Society prosecuted the defaulting treasurer of their Bradford branch, only to find that the four judges (one of them the Lord Chief Justice) considered trade unions to be illegal (though not criminal) organizations as they acted in restraint of trade and were therefore not entitled to have their funds protected under the Friendly Societies Act of 1855. The five members (most of them officials of "new model" unions) of the London "Junta," to use the nickname bestowed on them by the Webbs, constituted themselves as the "Conference of Amalgamated Trades" and took charge of the marshaling of evidence to be given before the commission. The impressive nature of that evidence, showing the strength and respectability of some of the bigger unions, helped to offset the Sheffield and Manchester disclosures. The commission brought in majority and minority reports, the latter representing the views of Frederick Harrison and Thomas Hughes, middle-class friends of the unions. The Junta, together with the rival group led by George Potter of the *Beehive,* arranged for the introduction of a parliamentary bill based on the minority recommendations. It was to enlist their aid in support of the bill that Robert Applegarth, secretary of the Junta and of the "new model" Amalgamated Society of Carpenters and Joiners, wrote to the U.T.A.[54] Applegarth's letter was warmly received and the U.T.A. arranged to secure copies of the bill and lobby not only the M.P.s (two large employers, Sir Arthur Guinness and Jonathan Pim) representing Dublin constituencies, but parliamentary candidates for Trinity College, Dublin, and those Dublin residents whose seats were elsewhere.[55] The interest shown is the probable reason for the presence of Clare of the 1869 congress and his concern with the protection of trade union funds. No congress was held in 1870 and the 1871 meeting in London was designed to lobby M.P.s to amend the government's proposed bill. The result was only partially satisfactory; one bill, the Trade Union Act of 1871, protected union funds, but a second, the Criminal Law Amendment Act of the same year, prohibited peaceful picketing, thus taking away a right given by the Molestation of Workmen Act of 1859. At the 1871 congress, a parliamentary committee was appointed to maintain pressure on M.P.s and ministers; it was reappointed each year and became a permanent institution. It achieved notable success in 1875 when two measures, the

54. Applegarth also enclosed an address by Goldwin Smith, a friend of the Positivists Frederic Harrison and Professor E. S. Beesly, on the rights of electors.

55. *Irishman,* 7 Nov. 1868. Clare suggested the lobbying of Dublin residents whose parliamentary seats were elsewhere.

Conspiracy and Protection of Property Act and the Employers and Workmen Act (the latter replacing the Master and Servant law) legalized peaceful picketing and made workmen liable only to civil proceedings in cases involving breaches of contract. The absence of Irish attendance after 1869 can be plausibly explained by the U.T.A.'s confidence in the parliamentary committee as a pressure group and by a desire to avoid the expense of sending delegates to congresses or to meetings of the committee (if they were elected to it). It is also probable that the Dublin association members shared the views of its representative George Howell, who in 1875 felt that "legislation with respect to trade unions was then so perfect that the natural time had run for the existence of Trade Union Congresses so far as parliamentary action was concerned."[56]

The Reform League, formed in February 1865, had as its objective the enfranchisement of the working class; it demanded either universal manhood suffrage, or at least a householder and lodger vote, as well as a secret ballot. It was the creation of a group of London labor leaders and some advanced Liberals who undertook to raise money for agitation. It held an immense demonstration on 6 May 1867 in Hyde Park, though the government had proclaimed it, and if the meeting was perfectly orderly, the temper of the speeches and the determination displayed were notable factors (besides those of party advantage and realization that an extension of the franchise could no longer be put off) in bringing about the 1867 Reform Act.[57] The subsequent history of the League can only be described as disreputable from a labor point of view, for its secretary George Howell employed it as a tool of the Liberals in the general election of 1868, even to the extent of covertly hampering and discouraging trade union candidates and backing Whigs in certain constituencies.[58] It was dissolved in March 1869 amid recriminations from those who had hoped for the return of a solid group of labor representatives.

At its formation high expectations were roused, Marx being especially pleased; in a letter to Engels dated 25 February 1865 he declared: "The International Association has managed to constitute the majority in the committee, elected to found the new Reform League, in such a way that the *entire leadership* is in our hands."[59] The campaign for reform was fought mainly in England, and especially in London, but Ireland was not omitted. At the end of October 1866, Irish Liberals

56. Pelling, *History of British Trade Unionism*, p. 76.
57. See Roydon Harrison, *Before the Socialists*, chap. III, especially pp. 129–36.
58. Ibid., chap. IV.
59. International Working Men's Association (First International), *Documents of the First International: The General Council of the First International*, 1864–6, p. 386, n. 1.

entertained John Bright at a banquet where the radical M.P. expounded his policy of land reform and disestablishment of the Church of Ireland and called for Irish support for political reform. The O'Donoghue, M.P., a relative of Daniel O'Connell, presided; he expressed the hope that their guest's presence would "light up the flame of reform and rally them all for the great struggle to obtain such an extension of the franchise as would put an end to class supremacy—the curse and almost the ruin of Ireland." [60] Bright also spoke at a meeting organized by John McCorry in the Dublin Mechanics' Institute and devoted much of his speech to the unsatisfactory nature of Irish borough representation: twenty-seven M.P.s were returned by an average of 350 voters apiece. He reinforced an appeal for Irish support by reading a telegram of greetings from the Scottish Reform League. The working-class audience was in general sympathetic, though the chairman's introductory remarks were interrupted by Fenian supporters shouting "Fenianism forever" and "A cheer for Stephens." [61]

Two representatives of the Reform League, George Mantle and Thomas Connolly, attended the meeting on behalf of the executive of the League. Edmond Beales, the League's president, had persuaded its General Council to use the opportunity afforded by the meeting to introduce the League into Ireland. Connolly,[62] an Irish stonemason and one of the League's best orators, stayed for several weeks after the banquet to carry out an organizing campaign;[63] among the bodies he addressed was the Dublin United Trades' Association, to which he delivered "an able statement on the subject." [64] The U.T.A. seems to have taken no action, perhaps on the grounds that reform was a political matter and therefore beyond the scope of the association's activities, and the initiative passed to The O'Donoghue and his middle-class colleagues.

In November an Irish Reform League was founded with The O'Donoghue as president, Alderman P. P. McSwiney as vice-president, and

60. *The Times,* 29, 31 Oct. 1866.   61. *The Times,* 3 Nov. 1866.

62. Connolly was also active in the campaign to reform trade union law. He was admitted as the sole labor representative to the royal commission's sittings after trade union protests that the commission did not include a trade unionist. At a public meeting Connolly criticized the hostile attitude of one of the commissioners, J. A. Roebuck, M.P. for Sheffield, with the result that Roebuck successfully moved his expulsion from future sittings. George Potter's account of the incident, given at the first meeting of the T.U.C. (Manchester 1868), declared that the commissioners "had insulted working men in the person of Mr Connolly" (Frew and Katanka, *1868, Year of the Unions,* p. 36).

63. Reform League General Council minutes, 31 Oct., 7, 16 Nov. 1866; Executive Committee minutes, 9, 16, 23 Nov. 1866 (Howell Collection).

64. *Irishman,* 17 Nov. 1866.

P. J. Shanley, a compositor, as secretary. It issued an address to the Irish people, making the usual demands for a universal manhood franchise and the secret ballot. It also claimed that Irish trade and industry had declined because of "oligarchical rule." The modest yearly subscription of one shilling allowed for working-class membership, but the Irish organization seems to have remained small and its direction rested in the hands of its middle-class officers.[65] Several of these were made vice presidents of the English League and attended Council meetings and demonstrations in London.[66] But there seems to have been little activity of note in Ireland during the first half of 1867. The Reform Act passed in the summer applied only to England and Wales, so that a renewed effort resulted in meetings at the beginning of September in Dublin. Beales, Mantle, Ernest Jones (the former Chartist), and other English and Scottish reformers attended.[67] A deputation from Belfast was unable to attend the public meeting held in September as the northerners were busy with municipal reform.[68] Their absence was probably fortunate since, according to an acid report in *The Times* (5 September 1867), the audience seemed more interested in freeing Fenian prisoners than in extending the franchise. Beales reported to the General Council that he had been received most enthusiastically and that the foundation of an influential Reform League had been laid in Ireland. But *The Times,* which had pointed out the failure of Bright's earlier efforts and prophesied a repetition in the case of Beales's visit, was proved right in the event. In October The O'Donoghue protested to Howell against a meeting being held under League auspices "to support Garibaldi in his antipapal activities."[69] Though he affirmed his confidence in Edmond Beales he was evidently more concerned with preserving the temporal power of the pope than furthering the work of the League. The passing of an Irish Reform Act early in 1868 removed any remaining reason for the continuance of the League in Ireland. It is, therefore, not surprising that its successor, the Labour Representation League, evoked no support in Dublin.

The Junta formed the Labour Representation League at the end of 1869. It was so exceedingly moderate in its demands (Odger said he found it serving the Whigs) and infirm in its purpose (alternately sug-

65. Ibid., 1 Dec. 1866. Address in How. Coll.

66. Letters to Thomas Connolly (16, 17 Nov. 1866) and Edmund Keevil (21, 28 Nov. 1866) in Howell letterbooks; Council minutes, 12 Dec. 1866, 2, 9 Jan. 1867. The O'Donoghue and others attended the demonstrations on 3 Dec. 1866 and 6 May 1867.

67. *The Times,* 4 Sept. 1867.

68. Letter dated 31 Aug. 1867 to Howell (How. Coll.).

69. Letter dated 28 Oct. 1867 to Howell (How. Coll.).

gesting the creation of a Labour Party and inviting the railway tycoon
and Liberal M.P., Thomas Brassey, to be its president) that it made
little impression.[70] In 1874, its best year, it could return only two out
of twelve candidates, complaining that "the manager of the Liberal
party in nearly every constituency where they appeared regarded them
with suspicion and treated them in an unfriendly spirit,"[71] a pitiable
admission of its failure to persuade the Liberals to honor a Lib-Lab
policy. The Labour Representation League's only connection with
Ireland seems to be a letter received by its secretary Henry Broadhurst
(also secretary of the T.U.C.) in 1878, when the organization was
moribund; it was an enquiry from a member of the Amalgamated
Society of Engineers seeking information "as to the best means of
assisting to return a labour representative to parliament for Belfast."
The writer asked for pamphlets and added that "we made an effort here
at the last election, but the employers were too many for us."[72]

The Belfast engineer had no doubt a Lib-Lab candidate in mind. The
city was to have the distinction of putting forward Alexander Bowman,
the first Irish trade union candidate to stand without a party label, but
that was not until 1885. In the meantime there appeared a peculiarly
Belfast phenomenon—organized Protestant working-class support
for an independent conservative of evangelical sympathies. William
Johnston of Ballykilbeg, County Down, a barrister and landlord, was a
prominent Orange leader who had been sentenced to a month's imprisonment in 1868 for defying the Party Processions Act, a sentence
that did not prevent his election as M.P. for a Belfast constituency. He
was in some ways a decidedly unorthodox figure, his championship of
tenant right and his popular sympathies leading him to oppose official
conservatism. A body of Protestant artisans had met on 4 March 1868
to endorse his candidature and had the satisfaction of seeing him
returned as an independent conservative the following November.
When in 1871 conservative elements in the Grand Lodge of Belfast
opposed Johnston's reelection to the post of Grand Master, a meeting
was called in his support and a new body, the Belfast Orange and
Protestant Workingmen's Association, was formed "for the purpose of
protecting the political rights of the Protestant working men of
Belfast"; only Protestant artisans were to be admitted as members.

70. Harrison, *Before the Socialists*, pp. 234–301. See also G. D. H. Cole, *British Working-Class Politics, 1832–1914*, chaps. V and VI.

71. Circular issued after the general election, Minutes of the General Council of the Labour Representation League, 7 Mar. 1874 (British Library of Political and Economic Science).

72. Minutes of the General Council, Labour Representation League, letter from Stewart Gillespie dated 14 May 1878.

Speakers criticized official conservatism, one saying that there had been an earlier association but "the working men of Belfast had no voice in it. It was managed by aristocrats, who monopolized all the offices; therefore the working men did not consider themselves bound to assist in making a noise when called upon to do so." A barrister, John McKane, pointed out that when Johnston's election agent had moved a resolution in the Belfast town council to broaden the municipal franchise by assimilating it to the parliamentary one, "the old leaders" opposed it, saying that the working men of Belfast did not want it. He concluded by saying that when he saw an audience of upwards of 5,000 present without the face of a clergyman among them, he had no doubt of their success. The evangelical temper of the meeting was shown by Johnston's observation that if they had lost by the disestablishment of the Church of Ireland in 1869, they had gained by separation from the ritualistic Church of England; there were some God-fearing Protestants—descendants of the puritans of old—in the ranks of the Nonconformists of England and Scotland.[73] Though membership of the association was, by resolution, restricted to Protestant artisans, the social composition of the speakers was less homogenous; among them were small employers and professional men as well as craftsmen. These nonworking-class elements provided political leadership and indeed political representation, though the small employers, some of them former craftsmen who had set up in business for themselves, tended to seek office at the municipal rather than the parliamentary level.

The association remained in existence with the primary object of supporting Johnston of Ballykilbeg. It held an annual meeting in January 1872 in a hall decorated with banners and slogans in praise of Johnston. The meeting passed resolutions of confidence in their champion and when considering the parliamentary agenda gave approval to the forthcoming ballot act; the association would have preferred "the dignified and open system of voting" to the secret ballot had the older procedure not been accompanied by rioting and undue pressure.[74]

Johnston retained his parliamentary seat until 1878 when he resigned to become an inspector of fisheries. But before this date the association had lost its principal *raison d'être,* for Johnston had resolved his differences with the conservatives in 1873 and was an official candidate in the general election of 1874. The association, hopelessly split, was unable to contest the seat. It recovered again in 1876 when the Belfast corporation showed its hostility to the erection of a statue to Henry Cooke and in 1878 supported a barrister, Robert Seeds, as an

73. *N.W.,* 13 Jan. 1871.   74. *N.W.,* 26 Jan. 1872.

Orange candidate for a Belfast seat against the conservative William Ewart. This was its last action as an organization, though members supported Seeds again in 1880 and another Orange candidate, Edward S. W. De Cobain, with him in the 1885 election.[75]

If the Belfast Orange and Protestant Working Men's Association had but a brief existence, the desire for representation of the Protestant working class remained. De Cobain was a disappointment, for though he was successful in 1885, the Orange M.P. showed himself unfriendly to trade unions; his sudden disappearance from public life after being involved in a scandal concerning a male brothel was not regretted. Johnston returned to public life after he had been dismissed for violent speeches against the Land League and Home Rule (undesirable political activity on the part of a public official). He was elected to parliament in 1885 and held the South Belfast constituency until his death in 1902. His Unionist colleagues were less generous-minded than himself and, though he had made his peace with the conservatives, his Protestant working class voters saw in him a man who, while an Orangeman *pur sang* in his opposition to Home Rule and to any compromise with Rome or ritualism, did not regard them as voting fodder but as a Protestant democracy entitled to a voice in public affairs. These men, convinced of the necessity of preserving a common political front against Home Rule and Rome rule, yet conscious that their economic interests frequently conflicted with those of their employers, found an outlet for their pent-up irritation in revolting periodically against the domination of the Orange Order and conservative associations by landed aristocrats and large manufacturers. Their political role was for long confined to the supporting of dissident conservatives; not until the death of Johnston in 1902 did they have the satisfaction of returning a parliamentary candidate from their own ranks, the semiskilled shipyard worker Tom Sloan.[76]

75. I am much indebted to the late Mr. Aiken McClelland of the Ulster Folk Museum for this summary of the later activities of the Belfast Orange and Protestant Working Men's Association. Mr. McClelland was engaged in writing a biography of William Johnston when he supplied me with this information.

76. For the career of Tom Sloan see J. W. Boyle, "The Belfast Protestant Association and the Independent Orange Order, 1901 – 10," in *Irish Historical Studies,* xiii, no. 50, pp. 117 – 52.

4

Ireland and the First International

It was the Fenians who, by arousing a country sunk in political apathy, caused the First International (the International Working Men's Association—I.W.M.A.) to take up the Irish question. At its founding meeting in September 1864, Professor E. S. Beesly listed Ireland as one of the countries in which British policy was to be condemned, but the report of his address in George Potter's trade union paper, *The Beehive,* made no mention of it.[1] Fifteen months later the arrest and treatment of the Fenian leaders awakened the General Council's interest in Ireland. In January 1866 the council, on the initiative of Peter Fox, sent an appeal for funds for the relief of prisoners' families to the *Workman's Advocate,* which duly published it.[2] In February Fox drew the council's attention to a letter by John Pope-Hennessy in the *Pall Mall Gazette* describing the treatment of the Fenian prisoners in Pentonville jail, where solitary confinement drove a number of the inmates insane. The council asked the Home Secretary (Sir George Grey) to receive a deputation on the subject but was answered with a flat refusal. Neither the publication of the correspondence nor an earlier article by Fox, both published in the *Commonwealth,* had any effect.[3]

Two of the leading Fenians joined the I.W.M.A. in the United States. Shortly after his arrival in New York in 1866, James Stephens was enrolled by Cesare Orsini, the Italian political émigré and member of the General Council. Karl Marx, however, showed little enthusiasm

1. It was reported in *Le Phare de la Loire,* 2 Oct. 1964. See H. Collins and C. Abramsky, *Karl Marx and the British Labour Movement,* p. 35, n. 1.

2. International Working Men's Association (First International), *Documents of the First International, The General Council of the First International,* Minutes, I, 151–2 (2 Jan. 1866). The five volumes, published in Moscow and numbered only on the dust jackets, cover the following years: I, 1864–6; II, 1866–8; III, 1868–70; IV, 1870–71; V, 1871–2. Future references will be to *D.F.I.* The appeal for funds was issued by Mrs. O'Donovan Rossa and Mrs. Clarke Luby, wives of Fenian leaders.

3. *D.F.I.,* I, 159 (16 Jan. 1866), 166 (20 Feb. 1866), 168–69 (6 Mar. 1866), 327–34. Pope-Hennessy (1834–91) was an Irish conservative M.P. with reformist leanings. *The Workman's Advocate* was renamed *The Commonwealth* in February 1866.

for the new recruit and remarked in his letter of December 17 to Friedrich Engels that he was "one of our ambiguous acquisitions."[4] The comment was justified to a greater extent than Marx realized. Two days earlier, on December 15, the American Fenians had deposed Stephens as chief and the Irish members were not slow to follow, so that Stephens's slight connection with the First International lost what little importance it might have possessed. John Devoy, on his release from an English prison, went with other Fenian exiles to New York in January 1871 and within a month joined a newly formed Irish section of the I.W.M.A. He was appointed a delegate to the New York committee, but the energies he could spare from his work as a reporter for the *New York Herald* went into Fenian rather than I.W.M.A. activities.[5]

Marx and the General Council were not discouraged by the lack of interest on the part of James Stephens. In November 1867 at ordinary and special meetings they expressed their support for Fenian objectives and sent a resolution to the Home Secretary asking that the three Irish prisoners condemned to death at Manchester (the "Manchester Martyrs") be reprieved.[6] Marx made notes on Fenianism for a speech that he intended to deliver at one of the meetings, but decided that the excitement created by the executions was so great that it would be more suitable for an English council member (Peter Fox) to express sympathy with the Irish people and condemn the British government's act. These notes outline the principal changes in Ireland since the famine: the decline in population, the heavy emigration, the growth in the numbers of livestock, the increase in the number of evictions, an alteration in the character of English rule in Ireland—"government only instrument of landlords (and usurers)." Marx saw Fenianism as a socialist, lower-class movement, not a Catholic one, with no representative in parliament, its nationalism influenced by European movements and couched in English phraseology, and with three fields of action—America, Ireland, and England; it was republican because of American influence.[7]

Nearly two years passed before the General Council returned to the question of Ireland and once again the occasion was the position of

4. Ryan, *Fenian Chief,* p. 236; *D.F.I.,* II, 72 (4 Dec. 1866), 305.

5. Ryan, *Fenian Chief,* p. 236, n. 6; *D.F.I., IV,* 150.

6. *D.F.I.,* II, 174–83, 312–13. Marx framed the resolution, which referred to the evidence upon which the prisoners were convicted as "tainted" and declared that commutation of the death sentence would be "an act not only of justice, but of political wisdom."

7. *D.F.I.,* II, 253–58, 377 (n. 236), 400 (n. 349). See also letter from Marx to Engels, 30 Nov. 1867, in Karl Marx and Frederick Engels, *Selected Correspondence,* ed. S. Ryazanskaya (2nd ed., Moscow, 1965), pp. 195–97.

Fenian prisoners, some of whom had been in jail for several years. An amnesty movement had arisen in Ireland during 1868, and Gladstone was being urged to display the clemency for Irish prisoners that he had earlier called for in the case of the victims of Ferdinand II (King "Bomba") in Neapolitan jails. In October a large meeting in Hyde Park protesting against Gladstone's refusal of an amnesty prompted the council to draw up an address in favor of clemency,[8] but this was dropped when Marx, who was a member of the subcommittee charged with the task of framing the address, proposed instead a discussion of the British government's attitude toward the Irish question and of the English working-class's attitude toward the Irish.[9] Three lengthy debates ensued in November on a six-part resolution moved by Marx. It was severely critical of Gladstone's reply to amnesty appeals, accused him of "deliberately insulting the Irish nation," recalled his support for the American Confederate leader Jefferson Davis and expressed the council's admiration "of the spirited and high-souled manner in which the Irish people carry on their amnesty movement."[10] The council was divided on the issue. Robert Applegarth of the A.S.C.J., evidently under some pressure from Marx, supported the resolution, as did three other trade unionists, Benjamin Lucroft, George Milner and John Weston. But George Odger, secretary of the London Trades Council, temporized, pointing out that Gladstone had disestablished the Church of Ireland, and asked that the resolution be softened. Thomas Mottershead, a weaver, defended Gladstone at length, criticized Irish activities, and declared that Irish independence would threaten England's security. Vigorous replies by Milner, Marx, Johann Georg Eccarius (a German émigré and founding member of the I.W.M.A.), and Hermann Jung, a Swiss émigré, resulted in the resolution being adopted with the single omission of the word "deliberately" from the phrase accusing Gladstone of insulting the Irish nation.[11] The resolution was published in a number of English, German, Swiss, and Belgian newspapers.

The members of the General Council who supported the movement for Irish independence did so for the same reason that led them to support Polish independence—the right of a people to govern themselves. But for Marx there were other reasons, which he set forth in a

8. *D.F.I.*, III, 172–74.

9. *D.F.I.*, III, 176–77. It was felt that the government and the press would turn the council's views, if properly expressed, against the prisoners.

10. *D.F.I.*, III, 183.

11. *D.F.I.*, III, 178–90, 192–4. See also pp. 460–61, n. 258, for Marx's vivid description in a letter (dated 26 Nov. 1869) to Engels of the conduct of Applegarth, Odger, and Mottershead (referred to as "Muddlehead").

lengthy address from the General Council to the Conseil Fédéral de la Suisse Romande. *L'Égalité* and *Le Progrès,* two papers under the control of the Swiss Council, had attacked the General Council on a number of organizational matters and had criticized it for advocating an amnesty for Fenian prisoners. Marx vindicated the General Council and explained the political strategy that dictated its policy on Ireland. Starting with the proposition that England was the metropolis of capital, he declared that England could not be treated on the same basis as other countries. "Si l'Angleterre est le bulwark du landlordisme et du capitalisme européens, le seul point où on peut frapper le grand coup contre l'Angleterre officielle, *c'est l'Irlande.*" In turn, Ireland was the bulwark of English landlordism and if it fell there it would fall in England. If the forced union between the two countries were ended, a social revolution, though in outmoded forms, would break out in Ireland. English landlordism would not only lose its greatest source of wealth but also the moral strength it derived from English domination of Ireland.

Marx pointed out certain important consequences of continued English domination. The English proletariat, as long as it maintained the power of English landlords in Ireland, rendered them invulnerable in England also. The English bourgeoisie not only depressed the living standards of the English working class by the forced immigration of the Irish poor but divided the proletariat into two hostile camps. The English worker resented the Irish immigrant as a competitor who would accept lower wages and in additon felt for him national and religious antipathies. "He regards him almost as the poor whites in the southern United States regarded negro slaves." Moreover this hostility was reproduced in the United States; it fed English-American antagonisms and prevented the emancipation of the working classes on both sides of the Atlantic. The state of Ireland also provided the sole excuse for a large standing army that could be turned, if need be, against English workers.

Marx summed up the I.W.M.A.'s position on the Irish question as follows:

Its first need is to forward the social revolution in England. To this end the main blow must be struck in Ireland.

The resolutions of the General Council on the Irish amnesty serve only as an introduction to other resolutions which will declare, quite apart from any question of international justice, that a *preliminary* condition *of the emancipation of the English working class* is to transform the present *forced union* (that is to say, the enslavement of Ireland) into a *free and equal confederation* if possible, into a *complete separation* if need be.[12]

12. *D.F.I.,* III, 358–60. The original text is as follows: "Donc la position de l'Association Internationale vis-à-vis de la question irlandaise est très nette. Son pre-

During 1870 Marx and the General Council left Irish matters in abeyance,[13] but the proclamation of the French Republic early in 1871 raised the issue of possible English intervention and Ireland's attitude in such an event. A discussion on the Irish question suggested at a meeting on March 14 did not take place since the Paris Commune was established four days later and its fate dominated the council's proceedings for several months.[14] Marx, pessimistic about the chances of the Commune's survival, started to write his *Civil War in France* as early as April 18; he submitted the finished work for approval to the Council on May 30, and it was published over the signatures of the officers, corresponding secretaries, and Council members in June, in an edition of one thousand copies.[15] It was both an *apologia* and an elegy.

Among the signatories of the second and third editions was J. P. MacDonnell, corresponding secretary for Ireland.[16] MacDonnell was born in Dublin on 27 March 1847, and while a student at the Catholic University in that city joined the I.R.B. As his father intended him for the priesthood he should then have gone to the Maynooth seminary for clerical training, but the young Fenian refused because the Maynooth authorities insisted that their students take an oath to disclose knowledge of any secret society of a seditious nature.[17] MacDonnell became a

---

mier besoin est de pousser la révolution sociale en Angleterrre. A cet effet, il faut frapper le grand coup en Irlande. Les résolutions du Conseil Général sur l'amnistie irlandaise ne servent qu'à introduire d'autres résolutions qui affirmeront que, abstraction faite de toute justice internationale, c'est une condition *préliminaire de l'émancipation de la classe ouvrière anglaise,* de transformer la présente *union forcée* (c'est-a-dire l'esclavage de l'Irlande) en *confédération égale et libre,* s'il le peut, en *séparation complète,* s'il le faut." This was followed in the manuscript by a deleted portion explaining the difficulties faced by the General Council. The *Beehive* (George Potter's paper) had suppressed the amnesty resolutions and the council's discussion of the Irish question; as a result the council had been forced to print the resolutions and circulate them to the trade unions (*D.F.I.,* iii, 360, n. 2). The address was written about 1 January 1870 and published in part in the pamphlet *Les prétendues scissions dans l'Internationale,* Genève, 1872. Marx incorporated several of these passages verbatim in a letter (9 Apr. 1870) to S. Meyer and A. Vogt in New York (Marx and Engels, *Selected Correspondence,* pp. 235–8).

13. The Dublin United Trades' Association was sent a copy of the council's first address on the Franco-Prussian War (*D.F.I.,* IV, 37).

14. *D.F.I.,* IV, 125–26, 156–57, 162.

15. *D.F.I.,* IV, 204.

16. *D.F.I.,* IV, 411. MacDonnell was not a signatory of the first edition as he did not become a member of the General Council until July 4 (*D.F.I.,* IV, 220, 222, 226–27).

17. Unless otherwise indicated, details of MacDonnell's life are taken from the ten-page biography dictated by his widow to Miss Clara Commons in 1908. This and other MacDonnell papers are in the archives of the State Historical Society of Wisconsin. The Catholic hierarchy led by Cardinal Cullen denounced the Fenians. The Maynooth

member of the provisional council of the I.R.B., acted as an editor of the *Irishman,* and contributed to the Fenian *Irish People.* Some months after the suppression of the Fenian paper, he was arrested and detained in prison for nearly a year without trial, a detention made possible by the suspension of the Habeas Corpus Act. On his release in 1867 he started a provincial newspaper, but when it failed in the following year he moved to London. Here he earned a living in journalism, working for the *Universal News,* an Irish nationalist weekly, and the *Evening Standard,* and acting as London correspondent for the *Irishman.*

Early in 1869 MacDonnell with some fellow Irishmen organized for Irish immigrants a series of concerts consisting of patriotic readings, recitations, and songs.[18] He also formed an English Amnesty committee, with offices in Holborn, to carry on in Great Britain the movement started in Ireland the previous year.[19] He was responsible for a large number of public meetings in London and the provinces; one held in Hyde Park on October 24 was attended by a crowd variously estimated to be between 40 and 120 thousand strong.[20] It was Gladstone's refusal to grant this meeting's request for an amnesty that provoked the discussion on the Fenians and the Irish question in the General Council the following month.

During 1870 MacDonnell continued his amnesty campaign and won a following among the London Irish, who pressed him to stand as a parliamentary candidate for Southwark. He declined and urged the Irish there to support George Odger, then secretary of the London Trades Council. He was soon engaged in more strenuous activities. With the proclamation of the French Republic in September 1870, an ambulance corps was formed in Dublin to assist the new France and MacDonnell, at the request of the picturesque adventurer General Macadaras, undertook recruiting among the Irish in England. The ostensible ambulance corps was a cover for an Irish brigade that would gain military experience while fighting against the Prussians. The British government had its suspicions and MacDonnell was charged with infringing the Foreign Enlistment Act in October. After several months in prison and an inconclusive hearing he was released on bail,

---

College for Priests had been aided financially from its foundation in 1795 by British government grants.

18. Programs of concerts given in London and Cardiff during February 1869 are among the MacDonnell papers. MacDonnell also organized excursions and demonstrations on the anniversaries of the Treaty of Limerick and the American Declaration of Independence.

19. *Irishman,* 20 Feb., 6 Mar. 1869.

20. Collins and Abramsky, *Marx and the British Labour Movement,* p. 166.

but, though the charges were not pursued, the defense costs crippled him financially.[21]

MacDonnell's political activities brought him in touch with a number of members of the General Council of the I.W.M.A. Early in 1871 he was on visiting terms with Marx and Engels, who proposed him as a council member on June 20.[22] In letters[23] to Marx, he asserted that the prospects were good for enrolling the Irish in the I.W.M.A., since "Fenianism has, thank goodness, destroyed clerical power in Ireland"; that the I.R.B. had considerable influence among intelligent Irish immigrants in England; and that O'Donovan Rossa would do great things in America. He also defended himself against various charges—embezzlement of Amnesty Association funds, being in the pay of J. J. Merriman, selling the Irish vote in Southwark—and referred to his "never-failing devotion, imprisonment and toil" in Ireland. Marx used this material successfully when he and Engels had MacDonnell's election to the council carried unanimously in July.[24] In August he was elected on Marx's initiative as secretary for Ireland.[25] Again he had to defend himself against attacks, for Murphy, manager of the *Irishman*, alleged that MacDonnell had affiliations with the bourgeois class and not with the Irish revolutionary movement, which offered the only hope for the spread of the I.W.M.A. in Ireland. In addition, Murphy charged that MacDonnell's political views were "dwarfed" and that his general reputation was "that of an eccentric, agitating character, without steadiness or force."[26] MacDonnell maintained in a letter to Engels that his character would withstand any investigation, that the *Irishman* could bring no concrete charges against him and that Irish newspapers generally welcomed his appointment.[27] Murphy did not pursue his charges.

During his membership of the General Council, MacDonnell gave Marx and Engels consistent support against their opponents, whether Blanquists and Bakuninists at the London (September 1871) and

21. The hearing took place on 3 November 1870. A speech for the defense by Josiah J. Merriman, an English solicitor on MacDonnell's amnesty committee and a member of the General Council (1864–7) and the Reform League, was published as a pamphlet and is among the MacDonnell papers.

22. *D.F.I.*, IV, 220.

23. Marx–Engels Nachlass, D 3246, D 3247, International Instituut voor Sociale Geschiedenis, Amsterdam. D 3246, a covering letter to D 3247, is dated July 14.

24. *D.F.I.*, IV, 226–7. See also Collins and Abramsky, op. cit., p. 241.

25. *D.F.I.*, IV, 249, 285. 26. Jung papers, D 236, I.I.S.G.

27. M.-E.N., L 3661, I.I.S.G. Letter dated 30 Sept. 1871. See also Marx's letter to F. A. Sorge, 29 Nov. 1871, in Karl Marx and Frederick Engels, *Ireland and the Irish Question* (Moscow, 1971), pp. 298–9.

Hague (September 1872) conferences or in the council itself against John Hales, a persistent advocate of a separate British Federal Council, and Georg Eccarius.[28] He organized Irish immigrants and opened his first branch in Soho on 4 February 1872.[29] At the April 2 meeting, he reported that further branches had been formed in Bradford, Chelsea, and Marylelone, but his activities brought him into conflict with the General Council's secretary, John Hales. Hales had written him a letter refusing to give him copies of the rules and objecting to the formation of Irish branches in England on the grounds that it would perpetuate national prejudices and was opposed to the principles of the I.W.M.A.[30] The matter was a subject of a lengthy debate on May 14, when Engels defended the right of Irish sections in England to a separate existence and to make national independence their first objective; these sections were a base of operations for extending the First International to Ireland. Hales, who had finally succeeded in securing a separate British Federal Council for Great Britain instead of having the General Council acting in that capacity, wanted to bring these Irish sections under his council. Engels stated flatly that the Irish sections would not submit and if the General Council insisted it would be tantamount to turning the Irish out of the Association. If Hales's motion were adopted "the council would inform the Irish workingmen, in so many words, that, after the domination of the English aristocracy over Ireland, after the domination of the English middle class over Ireland, they must now look forth to the advent of the dominion of the English working class over Ireland."[31] Hales received only one vote for his motion.

MacDonnell, after his election as Irish secretary, set about extending the First International to Ireland. An *Irish Times* correspondent in October 1871 predicted that a strong effort would be made during the following months to set up Irish sections and that though so far the I.W.M.A. had found little favor, the General Council believed that the Association's principles would be "adopted by a large section of the Irish people."[32] Early in January 1872 MacDonnell announced to the General Council that considerable progress was being made, especially in the north, "branches of the association being in course of establish-

28. M.-E.N., L 3617 (letter to Engels postmarked 22 Sept. 1872); Collins and Abramsky, op. cit., pp. 251, 259–60, 263.

29. Collins and Abramsky, op. cit., p. 241.

30. *D.F.I.*, V, 141–2.

31. *D.F.I.*, V, 194–9, 297–300. Engels pointed out that French, German, and Italian sections in England were not under the jurisdiction of the British Federal Council.

32. *Irishman*, 28 Oct. 1871.

ment in numerous localities."[33] It was, however, in the south that the I.W.M.A. first attracted public attention. A branch was formed in Cork in late February and a resolution adopted designed to avoid wounding religious susceptibilities:

The Cork branch of the International Working Men's Association desires to make it known that the association does not in any way interfere with the religious convictions of the members, the bond of union being that the members acknowledge truth, justice and morality in their conduct towards each other and towards all men, without regard to creed, colour or nationality.[34]

An editorial in the *Cork Examiner* affected to believe that no branch existed, that the manifesto was the work of a few individuals, and that "the healthy moral conditions that prevail amongst our working men" would prevent the development of such institutions "hatched between English and Continental atheists."[35] Some working men were evidently less healthy than others, for on the very day that the editorial appeared the coachbuilders held a meeting to receive I.W.M.A. delegates who were engaged in an organizing tour. Of the five delegates one was described as a "very keen and clever man and a fluent persuasive speaker," while another was identified as a foreigner. The majority of those present joined the association by paying $1d$. subscription. This success is not to be explained by a sudden access of ideological fervor on the part of the coachbuilders but by the aid promised the men by the International's representatives. A campaign for the reduction of the working day to nine hours had gained successes in England and was now being carried on in Ireland. The coachmakers, heartened by what other Cork trades had won, had demanded the introduction of a nine-hour day and when the employers offered a reduction from a sixty to a fifty-seven-hour work week, the men rejected it. The I.W.M.A. delegates, according to one report, spoke of a levy of $1/2d$. on the International's worldwide membership, an amount sufficient to supply strike pay for two years.[36]

The counterattack against the I.W.M.A. came initially from the Catholic clergy. The Reverend Canon Maguire, a brother of John Francis Maguire, nationalist M.P. and publisher of the *Cork Examiner*, denounced the I.W.M.A. in sermons on successive days. Alarmed by the growth of the branch to not less than five hundred members,[37] he described the Internationalists as men who "put God, the priests, the

33. London correspondent (Belfast) *Morning News*, 10 Jan. 1872.
34. *Irishman*, 2 Mar. 1872.   35. *Cork Examiner*, 16 Mar. 1872.
36. Ibid., 18 Mar. 1872.   37. *N.W.*, 25 Mar. 1872.

altar and everything on one side to serve their objects. They were nothing more or less than murderers, they would bring out the priests and bishops, place them against the wall and shoot them."[38] He appealed to the women to destroy any of the association's documents they found and to hunt its agents out of the country. His brother abetted him in the *Cork Examiner* by editorials that dwelt on the horrors of the French Revolution and the Paris Commune: the International was saddled with responsibilities for the shooting of the archbishop of Paris.

The adherence of the coachbuilders and the rumored affiliation of the carpenters to the Cork branch called for immediate action if other trades were not to follow suit. The exhortations of clergy and press stirred a group of tradesmen to organize a counterdemonstration in the Athenaeum on Sunday, March 24. Notices calling upon the working men of Cork to attend were posted throughout the town. The twenty-one signatories included officials of the Working Men's Society, the Barrack Street Typographical Association Reading Room, and the Globe Lane Temperance Room. The posters carried what was regarded as the final proof of the iniquity of the I.W.M.A., the concluding paragraph of Marx's *Civil War in France:* "Working men's Paris, with its commune, will be forever celebrated as the glorious harbinger of a new society. Its martyrs are enshrined in the great heart of the working class. Its exterminators history has already nailed to that eternal pillory from which all the prayers of their priests will not avail to redeem them." The poster ended with the slogan, made famous by the Manchester martyrs, "God save Ireland." The Cork I.W.M.A. issued their own poster ending with the words, "Long live the People." It denounced the meeting as being organized by "capitalists, bondholders, brokers, employers of labour through their serfs," and called for an attendance of thousands whose cry would be "Nine hours and Liberty."[39]

The three-thousand-strong meeting began punctually but turned quickly into a Donnybrook fair. A group of Internationalists led by their secretary, John De Morgan, and wearing green ties like many of their opponents, occupied the orchestra behind the platform. The opening minutes were quiet, but when the chairman, Edward Murphy, an engraver, declared that the I.W.M.A. was connected with the communists of Paris and proceeded to read Marx's final paragraph, the group in the orchestra rushed the platform, bearing De Morgan with them. Pandemonium reigned: speakers tried to make themselves heard, the press tables were overturned, and the platform became a

38. *Cork Herald,* 18 Mar. 1872.   39. *Cork Examiner,* 25 Mar. 1872.

cockpit. Most of the audience were passive, but the contestants made free use of chairs and sticks to reinforce their arguments, while boys in the galleries ran along the cornices and hurled portions of plasterwork on the debaters. A cooper moved a motion that, while claiming the right of the working men to shorter hours and higher wages, called upon them "to avoid a society whose teachings are subversive of religion and morality, and which proposes to justify the atrocities committed by the Communists in Paris." His supporter, Daniel McCarthy of the Working Men's Society, could do little more than formally second the motion. Angered by imputations of atheism and by the refusal of the chairman to accept an amendment, the Internationalists made further speech impossible and the chairman declared the meeting dissolved. Fighting, which continued sporadically until 5:30 P.M., ended in the triumph of the I.W.M.A., and the hall was not completely cleared at 6:00 P.M. A ludicrous episode marked the end of the more formal portion of the proceedings. The chairman declared that as he was announcing the closure he heard a man exclaim three times in a loud voice, "No mass! No God!." After some initial confusion about the identity of the speaker, one Denis O'Leary gave his version: he had shouted at the chairman, "Murphy, you're a blasted sod!"; when he heard Murphy twisting his words, he was so shocked that he flung him off the platform.[40]

The Cork I.W.M.A. sent a triumphant telegram to MacDonnell who read it to a meeting called the same night in London to raise funds for the coachbuilders.[41] It was a short-lived victory. Canon Maguire preached a sermon the next night "appropriate to the Feast of the Annunciation." He waxed bitter over the failure of the working men of Cork, who had "allowed themselves to be triumphed over by a few men, the emissaries of the devil's legion." In Belfast and Dublin "those wretched people" had been expelled, but "the working men of Catholic Cork" had disgraced themselves "by tolerating for a single day the presence of such a body among them."[42] The sermon was effective. A group of angry parishoners surrounded a reporter taking notes for a local paper, cross-questioned him closely and only let him go after one

40. Ibid., 25, 27 Mar., 1 Apr. 1872; (London) *Daily Telegraph*, 25 Mar. 1872; (London) *Standard*, 26 Mar. 1872; *Irishman*, 30 Mar., 6 Apr. 1872. The account given in Collins and Abramsky, *Marx and the British Labour Movement*, p. 245, is misleading, since it gives the impression that the meeting was called by the Cork I.W.M.A. and that it ended in their rout.

41. *Irish Times, Cork Examiner*, 25 Mar. 1872; *Nation*, 30 Mar. 1872. See also leaflet dated March 26, appealing for aid to those on strike, issued by MacDonnell (MacDonnell papers).

42. *Cork Examiner*, 26 Mar. 1872.

of their number, a woman, had struck him. Other denunciations of the Cork Internationalists followed from J. F. X. O'Brien, later a nationalist M.P., and Father Patrick Lavelle, a politically prominent priest.[43]

Though a number of the Cork members suffered for their activities, the greatest animus was directed against John De Morgan, the founder and secretary. He had begun his career while still a boy by delivering orations on temperance; in the late 1860s he was traveling through Ireland and lecturing on current political and social topics, though occasionally he chose literary and historical subjects.[44] After some time in Belfast, where he spoke in favor of the disestablishment of the Church of Ireland, he moved to Cork to teach elocution in a number of academies. His youthful appearance—"he was the very model of a duck of a curate, and I am sure his eyes and voice would have been irresistible with the young ladies"[45]—half-theatrical, half-clerical dress, and eloquence brought him success. This he forfeited, initially by taking the side of some ironfounders on strike in 1870 and later by starting the Cork branch of the I.W.M.A. He was denounced by Protestant and Catholic clergy and the press and lost most of his pupils.[46] In vain he assured Canon Maguire that he believed in God, and would not be a member of a society of atheists intending to shoot bishops and priests. He offered to debate the whole matter in public but received no reply.[47] MacDonnell started a propaganda fund to aid him and others victimized in Cork and issued an appeal for subscriptions from Irish sections in late April.[48] But the I.W.M.A.'s days in Cork were already numbered. A meeting held on March 31 (Easter Sunday) had failed to attract an audience, possibly because armed police were present.[49] The coachbuilders inserted an advertisement in the press denying that they had any connection with the Internationalists or that they had received a penny from them; they had settled their differences with their employers, who had reduced the hours of labor by three and had promised them a nine-hour day by a further reduction in July.[50] MacDonnell, Marx, and Milner drafted a declaration[51] on police terrorism in Ireland, giving instances of harassment of I.W.M.A.

43. Ibid., 27, 30 Mar. 1872.

44. Material in this paragraph not otherwise footnoted is taken from Silvester St. Clair, *Sketch of the Life and Labours of Jno. De Morgan, Orator, Elecutionist and Tribune of the People* (Leeds, 1880). De Morgan published a list of 293 titles of lectures he had given.

45. Rev. Dr. Maurice Davis, *Unorthodox London,* quoted in S. St. Clair, *J. De Morgan,* p. 4.

46. *D.F.I.,* V, 141, 148.

47. *Irishman,* 13 Apr. 1872, *Irish Daily Telegraph,* 6 Apr. 1872.

48. Appeal dated 21 Apr. 1872 (copy in MacDonnell Collection).

49. *Cork Examiner,* 4 Apr. 1872.   50. *Cork Examiner, Irishman,* 6 Apr. 1872.

51. *D.F.I.,* V, 149–50.

members by the police; a thousand copies were distributed in Ireland and the contents published in the Cork papers. MacDonnell claimed that the I.W.M.A.'s intervention had produced positive results, for all the large firms in Cork and the south of Ireland had conceded a nine-hour day lest their employees join the International.[52] He also announced that he had made arrangements for De Morgan's support until the opposition to him had died down, but he underestimated the strength of anti-International feeling in Cork and De Morgan had to leave shortly afterwards and seek an living in England.[53] By early May the I.W.M.A. had ceased to exist in the southern capital.[54]

MacDonnell's reports to the General Council stated that branches had been established in Dublin, Belfast, and Cootehill (County Cavan) and that others were to be formed in Limerick, Ennis (County Clare), and Tipperary.[55] It is unlikely that the last three were ever more than plans in the minds of a few optimistic individuals;[56] the Cootehill branch's career was short and hidden in obscurity,[57] as might have been expected in so isolated and unpromising a center for revolutionary thought. Sections were undoubtedly formed in Dublin and Belfast but,

52. *D.F.I.*, V, 176.

53. *Eastern Post*, 14 April 1872, quoted in Collins and Abramsky, op. cit., p. 245. Shortly after De Morgan's arrival in England MacDonnell introduced him to Marx and Engels, whose side he took in the British Federal Council controversy. Though he was for several years in the utmost need his letters to them are filled with a pathetic optimism (M.-E.N., D 3469-72, L 5055-69, K 1315). He was prominent in the English republican movement and the Fenian amnesty agitation, was a member of the I.W.M.A. and the Reform League, and started a Working Men's Parliamentary Association. Despite frequent jail sentences he led demonstrations in the 1870s to preserve public access to common land and to secure a revision of the prison sentence on the Tichborne claimant. Further details of De Morgan's activites will be found in Seán Daly, *Ireland and the First International* (Cork, 1984), pp. 196–201 and passim.

54. A letter from Cork, signed by a pseudonym and dated May 9, alleged that "emissaries of the International" were at work in the villages and countryside during the lull in the storm of invectives from clergymen and some nationalists (*Irishman*, 11 May 1872). There was no sequel to this statement. The *Cork Examiner* of May 11 carried a report that the I.W.M.A. had "resolved to abandon for the present the Irish organisation, awaiting more favourable auspices for re-establishment."

55. *D.F.I.*, V, 140–41, 176. The Limerick and Cork branches were to be started by McCarthy of Ennis.

56. A report dated March 31 in the *Freeman's Journal* stated that the formation of a branch in Limerick had been postponed because of the troubles in Cork. Delegates were to appeal to those trades engaged in the nine-hour day agitation, but the correspondent thought that success was unlikely in view of the hostility of prominent nationalists (*Irishman*, 6 Apr. 1872).

57. The Cork branch's declaration of principle issued early in March congratulated the men of Dublin and Cootehill on the formation of sections (*Cork Herald*, 15 Mar. 1872). MacDonnell's report (May 4) that the Cootehill branch was progressing slowly is the last mention of this branch.

since the press was not welcomed at their meetings, there are conflicting versions of their proceedings. According to one account, the Dublin branch, known as the Hibernian Excelsior Labour League, was started in mid-February by a young Dane who had been introduced to Dublin by MacDonnell's father-in-law, Samuel McEvatt.[58] Several meetings were held in a loft in Chapel Lane. On March 10 a French delegate from London presided and he and others addressed a mainly working-class audience in uncompromising speeches justifying the shooting of the Versaillese generals Clément and Thomas and laying down the principle that only those who worked deserved to eat.[59] But the society was spied on by detectives and its more active members intimidated by police; a meeting on April 7 had to be abandoned when it was invaded by a drunken and hostile crowd.[60] The expected affiliation of the Dublin Painters' Society did not take place and the branch's secretary was persuaded by his family to leave Dublin. The interim secretary, McKeon, wrote to MacDonnell that the Dublin I.W.M.A. had decided "to work quietly and let the world believe that they were dead . . . until they were strong enough to defy the terrorism used against them."[61] Pretense and reality soon became indistinguishable.

The history of the I.W.M.A. in Belfast is more obscure than that of the Dublin section. Canon Maguire, agonizing in his sermon of March 25 over the failure of the Catholic workingmen of Cork to suppress the Internationalists, claimed that Cork stood disgraced before the Christian world, whereas Belfast (and Dublin) had driven out the devil's emissaries. This is contradicted by MacDonnell's April 2 report, which merely stated that efforts were being made to form a branch.[62] The earliest reference in the Belfast press to the local section was on May 28; a letter signed "Anti-Internationalist" announced that the International had gained a foothold in the city and that it had a president, a vice president, and nearly six hundred paying members.[63] The only description extant of a meeting is that of one held on June 30. A reporter managed to gain admittance after an initial refusal and found himself in a room dimly lit by candlelight. "A dark-dressed gentleman

58. McEvatt (1817–1901) took part in Irish revolutionary movements from the 1840s onwards. As a result he lost his shoe-manufacturing business and was imprisoned with MacDonnell in 1866. He lived at various times in Dublin and London and emigrated to the United States in August 1872 (Biographical sketch of MacDonnell, MacDonnell Collection; M.-E.N., L 3666; *Cork Examiner*, 1 Apr. 1872).

59. *Irishman*, 16 Mar. 1872.

60. *F.J., Saunders' News-Letter*, 8 Apr. 1872, reprinted in *Cork Examiner*, 9 Apr. 1872.

61. *D.F.I.*, V, 176 (May 4).   62. *D.F.I.*, V, 141.

63. *Northern Star and Ulster Observer*, 28 May 1872.

of foreign appearance" took the chair, claimed that the I.W.M.A. in
Belfast had 753 members, one-third of whom had joined within the
last month, and asserted that in Cork, Derry, Dublin, and Limerick the
International was in a thriving condition. He defined the object of
the I.W.M.A. as the protection of the workingman against the rapa-
ciousness of his master, but subsequent speakers soon turned to religion, a subject dear to the hearts of Belfast citizens. One man com-
mended Bismarck for his *Kulturkampf* and warned the audience against
Catholicism stealing a march on them. Though the chairman tried to
change the subject, the discussion continued with two speakers calling
for suppression of religion and a third asserting that it was the bible
that had made him an Internationalist. Harmony was restored by the
last speaker's peroration in which he predicted a new world in which a
genuine equality without distinction of creed, class, or party would
banish poverty, crime, and ill-will, a world to be attained only by the
work of the I.W.M.A.[64] A letter in the *Irishman* of July 20 from J. H.
O'Connor gave a somewhat different picture, for he stated that there
was no acknowledged branch in Belfast, though there were many
individual members. He was at pains to point out that the I.W.M.A.
did not interfere with religious convictions and that it was as much
opposed by the atheist Charles Bradlaugh as by Cardinal Cullen; membership was open to all—irrespective of creed, color, or nationality—
who accepted its objective, the abolition of class rule and the social and
political emancipation of the working classes.[65] The International's call
for working-class ecumenism fell on deaf ears; within a month the
antipopery tirades of the Reverend Hugh Hanna had provoked bloody
sectarian riots in which a number of Catholic and Protestant workers
were killed. A sardonic comment came from Paris to a reader of the
Belfast News-Letter: "Your religious troubles are now over; good! God
does not expect so much zeal from his servants."[66]

On Sunday, 17 November 1872, MacDonnell was entertained in
London at a banquet after the presentation of a green silk purse containing fifty-two guineas and the reading of an address in his honor before a
gathering of Irish, English, French, and German republicans and
members of the I.W.M.A.[67] Early in December he emigrated to the
United States, despairing of earning a living by journalism in England.

64. Ibid., 2 July 1872; *Irishman*, 6 July 1872.
65. *Irishman*, 20 July 1872.
66. Andrew Boyd, *Holy War in Belfast* (Tralee, Ireland, 1969). This is particularly
valuable for its detailed account of sectarian rioting in Belfast during the nineteenth
century.
67. *Irishman*, 23 Nov. 1872.

He never returned to the British Isles though he wrote some nostalgic letters to Marx and Engels recalling old times and enquiring about former acquaintances.[68]

Shortly before MacDonnell left for New York, a London journal commented that MacDonnell's departure would "probably give the *coup de grâce* to the attempt to introduce the International into Ireland."[69] The attempt had been made and had failed and the International itself had been written off by Marx; the decision taken at the September 1872 Hague conference to transfer the General Council to New York was followed by a rapid decline and the official ending of the organization in 1876.

The I.W.M.A. had a limited but definite appeal for British trade unionists; it offered "to augment their existing struggles, political and industrial, with the power of international combination."[70] The General Council in London acted as a clearinghouse for information about strikes and strikebreaking and was able to anticipate or prevent the use of blacklegs from abroad, especially in disputes affecting the building trade and the older crafts. It was unable to do as much for Irish trade unions; in fact the I.W.M.A. had passed its peak some years before MacDonnell started his work as Irish secretary. When Marx framed his thesis that English landlordism and capitalism must first be attacked in Ireland, he still had hopes for the International, but the fall of the Paris Commune and the ensuing reaction made it clear that social revolution was indefinitely postponed. It is difficult to imagine that he expected much from Irish branches formed after the Commune's collapse and the publication of his *Civil War in France,* or, indeed, that he was greatly concerned at such a time with the effect of these events in Ireland. Marx's elegy for the Commune, whatever its long-term justification might be, made it impossible for the International to secure a fair hearing in Ireland because, in the minds of Catholic workers, it identified the I.W.M.A. with irreligion and the execution of Catholic prelates; the International's sustained support for a Fenian amnesty had already antagonized Protestant workers. But any history limited to the

68. M.-E.N., D 3248-76. MacDonnell took a prominent part in socialist and labour activities in the United States. He acted as corresponding secretary for New York State in the I.W.M.A., edited several labor journals, and was imprisoned for publishing an exposure of working conditions in Paterson, New Jersey, brickyards. He organized several trade union locals, the Trades Assembly of Paterson and the New Jersey State Federation of Labor, of which he was chairman for fifteen years. The last time he left his house was to attend the Federation's congress, six months before his death in 1906. For further details of MacDonnell's career, especially in the United States, see S. Daly, *Ireland and the First International,* chap. 8.

69. (London) *Daily Chronicle,* 21 Oct. 1872.

70. Collins and Abramsky, op. cit., p. 288.

organizational failure of the First International in Ireland is incomplete; the I.W.M.A. continued and strengthened a tradition of social protest that had its origin in the United Irish period and was maintained in Chartist and Fenian times. When socialist bodies reappeared in Dublin in the 1880s, they counted among their members former Internationalists. Elements of Marxist thought, such as the reality of the class war and the necessity for working-class solidarity, can be discerned in the speeches of these socialists who first learned of them during the existence of the I.W.M.A. in Ireland.

5

The Growth of British Trade Unions
in Ireland

The brief attempt of the First International to extend its organization to Ireland was made at a time when the only body resembling a trades council then in being was the United Trades' Association in Dublin. It is therefore appropriate at this stage to attempt a survey of the trade unions existing in Ireland. Since, however, we are dealing with a movement and not a static framework, it will not be sufficient to make the survey at some arbitrary date; rather it will be necessary to extend it over the second half of the nineteenth century if it is to be of any value. Such an extension in time is all the more desirable since it was in this period that trade union membership increased substantially, amalgamated (i.e., British) unions expanded until they absorbed the majority of Irish trade unionists, and, toward the end of the century, general unions made serious efforts to organize large numbers of the semiskilled and laborers. It is convenient to group the unions under three heads: the societies catering for skilled tradesmen, the railway unions, and the unions of general workers—an arrangement that follows, incidentally, a chronological order. The survey concludes with some observations on the employers' strike-breaking organizations and on wages and working conditions.

The Skilled Trades

During the second half of the nineteenth century the most important development in the Irish labor movement was the success of British trade unions in enrolling Irish members of skilled trades. But the advance of the amalgamated unions was not uniform and varied considerably from industry to industry.

The Amalgamated Society of Engineers (A.S.E.) was formed in January 1851 and by the end of the year had nearly twelve thousand members. It earned the name of "new model" from Sidney and Beatrice

Webb in their *History of Trade Unionism* (1894) because of a combination of features that distinguished it from older craft unions. Though its district committees enjoyed a marked degree of autonomy it was above all a national union; most of its funds were centralized at its London headquarters, it had a full-time general secretary supervised by a resident executive committee drawn from the London branches, and it levied a high rate of contributions that enabled it to pay correspondingly generous sickness, retirement, and funeral benefits. Since the Dublin branch had taken part in its formation it would not be correct to say that the A.S.E. had invaded Ireland, as some unions did later. By the end of the year Irish membership amounted to almost four hundred, the strongest branches being in Dublin (104) and Belfast (230); the remaining members were in Cork, Drogheda, Londonderry, and Newry.[1] The continuing predominance of Belfast as an A.S.E. center was assured by the growth of the city's shipbuilding and engineering industries. By 1884, a speaker (S. Shearer) at an A.S.E. *soirée* could claim a membership of one thousand in Belfast and district.[2] In 1886 the A.S.E. had 14 branches in Ireland, 308 in England and Wales, and 42 in Scotland.[3] The Irish membership in 1891 was 2,228, Belfast branches accounting for 1,515 or nearly three-quarters of the total.[4] Dublin was second with 357, Cork third with 130; the remaining seven centers had less than 100 each.[5]

The absence of any rival Irish union points to the success of the A.S.E. in Ireland, and especially in Belfast, where turners, fitters, and smiths worked a 54- to 56½ hour week and received pay rates (37s. to 38s.) high in the British scale.[6] In Dublin the wage rates were slightly lower, 33s. to 34s. for a 54-hour week. The various trades in other branches of Belfast engineering and shipbuilding occupied the same

1. Monthly and annual reports in the archives of the Amalgamated Engineering Union. Branches of the "Old Mechanics" (Journeymen Steam Engine and Machine Makers' Friendly Society) were the nuclei of the A.S.E. in Ireland. I am grateful to Mr. Andrew Boyd of Belfast for his assistance in securing information about the A.S.E. The incomes of the Dublin (no. 23) and Belfast (no. 33) branches for 1851 were £138 15s. 11d. and £423 0s. 5d. respectively.

2. *N.W.*, 26 Apr. 1884.

3. *Statistical Tables and Reports on Trade Unions for 1886*, pp. 723–4, [C. 5104], 1887.

4. *Statistical Tables and Reports on Trade Unions for 1891*, p. 320 [C. 6990], 1893–4, cii.

5. Drogheda (28), Dundalk (62), Limerick (50), Lisburn (44), Londonderry (40), Newry (73), Waterford (19).

6. The highest rates in England and Wales were 38s. to 40s. for 53 to 54 hours; in Scotland 36s. was the top rate for 54 hours. Figures for engineering, shipbuilding, and building workers are taken from the appropriate tables in Abstract of Labour Statistics (Board of Trade) for the years 1899–1900, [Cd. 495], H.C. 1901, lxxxiii.

high position in wage scales: patternmakers, ironfounders, platers, riveters, and shipwrights all received wages at or near those paid in the leading English centers. These skilled workers were members of the appropriate British unions—the United Patternmakers, the Friendly Society of Ironfounders, the Boilermakers,[7] and the Associated Shipwrights Society.[8] The task of maintaining a high level of wages was made easier by the concentration of workers in a few large enterprises, by a high degree of militancy, and by the close connection between workers in Belfast and those in the major British shipbuilding centers. When each stage in the construction of a ship ended, it was usual for the workers engaged on it to move to another center if work was not available in the home port. Thus a well-known circuit was established; the main traffic was between Belfast, Clydeside, and Merseyside, but Tyneside and even London and Southampton attracted Belfast shipworkers. A further consequence is of sociological and indeed, in an Irish setting, of political interest; the high proportion of Protestants in the Belfast shipyards was reinforced by the immigration of Glasgow workers sharing the same fiercely partisan sectarian outlook and the same hostility toward Irish Catholics.[9]

In the building trade British trade union progress was slower. The Amalgamated Society of Carpenters and Joiners (A.S.C.J.), founded in 1860, did not have Irish participation from the beginning. In 1866 it formed eight Irish branches with 293 members;[10] twenty years later the number of branches had risen to twenty.[11] For more than a quarter of a century the A.S.C.J. made no headway in Dublin and Cork, where

7. The Boilermakers opened their first Irish branch, the Good Samaritan Lodge, in Belfast in 1841.

8. The Belfast Shipwrights (formed in 1855) in 1893 joined the Associated Shipwrights Society (itself founded in 1882) and had 526 members in 1892. Shipwrights in smaller centers (Passage West in County Cork, Queenstown, Wexford, Dublin, Carrickfergus, Newry, and Warrenpoint), with local societies formed between 1856 and 1889, joined the Associated Shipwrights between 1892 and 1894, but their total membership in 1892 amounted to only 371. See *Report on Trade Unions for 1897,* pp. 232 [C. 9013], H.C. 1898, ciii.

9. In 1901 Catholics formed 24.3 percent of the population of Belfast. They accounted for only 7.7 and 5.7 percent respectively of the two divisions of workers on ships' hulls. In the engineering trades the percentages were (1) engine and machine makers: 10, (2) fitters and turners: 11.1, (3) boilermakers: 9.9, (4) textile machine makers: 14. See *Census of Population (Ireland),* 1901, table xx, pp. 15–32 [Cd. 1123 (a)], H.C. 1902, cxxvi.

10. *Eleventh and Final Report of the Commissioners to Inquire into the Organisation and Rules of Trade Unions and Other Associations,* ii, app., p. 286 [C. 4124-1], H.C. 1868–9, xxxi.

11. *Statistical Tables and Reports on Trade Unions for 1886,* pp. 723–4 [C. 5104], H.C. 1887.

long-established local organizations (the Dublin Regular Society of Carpenters and the Ancient Corporations of Carpenters of the City of Cork) held virtual monopolies. The General Union of Carpenters and the Associated Carpenters and Joiners of Scotland (the latter, which opened a branch in Belfast in 1874, had two small branches there when it merged with the A.S.C.J. in 1911) were of negligible importance, especially after the A.S.C.J. finally succeeded in absorbing the Dublin and Cork carpenters' societies shortly after 1890.[12]

Irish cabinetmakers had formed part of a United Kingdom federation for a few years in the 1830s until it was decided that the cost of servicing Irish members was too great. In the second half of the century the Amalgamated Union of Cabinetmakers and the Alliance Cabinetmakers' Association formed Irish branches; the last important group of Irish woodworkers surrendered its separate identity in 1895 when the Dublin society joined the Alliance Cabinetmakers' Association.[13]

Local painters' societies were slow to respond to the advances of British amalgamated unions. The National Amalgamated Society of House and Ship Painters and Decorators, formed in 1886, opened Irish branches, but by 1896 had managed to absorb only a few minor societies (e.g., Sligo, Coleraine, County Dublin). The strongest resistance was put up by the painters of Cork, Belfast, and Dublin. The Cork House and Ship Painters (250 members) gave way in 1905.[14] The Belfast Operative House Painters lost members in 1905 and the following years, but not without a struggle; when the amalgamated branch applied for affiliation to the Belfast Trades Council in 1904 it was denounced by one delegate as the offshoot of a bankrupt society in Manchester and the council by an overwhelming majority endorsed its executive committee's decision not to grant affiliation.[15] The Dublin

12. S. Higenbotham, *Our Society's History,* pp. 37, 63, 135–8. The Regular Carpenters agreed to join the A.S.C.J. in 1891 when the Dublin Society and the small Dublin branches of the amalgamated union took part in a movement for a shorter working week. The Cork society, which claimed it had never lost a trade dispute in its whole history, resented the small amalgamated branch because it accepted the use of machinery. Unable to maintain the ban the society joined the A.S.C.J. in 1893.

13. *Ninth Report of the Chief Labour Correspondent of the Board of Trade on Trade Unions for 1896,* pp. 110–11 [C. 8644], H.C. 1897, xcix. The amalgamation of the A.S.C.J. and the cabinetmakers unions resulted in the formation of the Amalgamated Society of Woodworkers in 1918.

14. *Report of the Chief Labour Correspondent of the Board of Trade on Trade Unions for the years 1905, 1906 and 1907,* pp. 664–5, [Cd. 4651], H.C. 1909, lxxxix. The Belfast society had 550 members in 1905 and 50 in 1906 and 1907.

15. Belfast Trades Council (B.T.C.) minutes, 19 Mar., 5 May 1904. The quarrel was aggravated by the behavior of the amalgamated members in agreeing to work for 1 d. an hour less, according to evidence given before the executive committee of the B.T.C. The employers' representative claimed that the local men refused to work with

Metropolitan House Painters proved more obdurate and survived an attempt on the part of the Dublin amalgamated branch to take them over in 1909, when their resistance was given publicity in Arthur Griffith's paper *Sinn Féin* (20 February 1909).[16] The battle was still raging in 1911; in September of that year Treacy, a member of the amalgamated branch, attended the executive committee of the Dublin Trades Council to complain that his society did not get fair play as the local societies did not treat amalgamated societies fairly.[17]

Bricklayers, masons, stonecutters, plasterers, and slaters were organized in a multiplicity of local societies and generally showed little desire to join British unions. Belfast bricklayers led a more checkered existence. Founded in 1843, the United Operative Bricklayers' Trade, Sick, Accident, and Burial Society of Belfast and the North of Ireland joined in 1871 the British Operative Bricklayers' Society (formed in 1848), reverted to an independent status in 1896, and rejoined the British union in 1902.[18] The Regular Operative Slaters' Society of Dublin, claiming 1860 as its founding year, joined the Amalgamated Slaters and Tilers in 1896, but a dissatisfied remnant constituted themselves the following year as the National Operative Slaters and Tilers of Dublin.[19] Plumbers seem to have been members of the long-established (1832) United Operative Plumbers' Association of Great Britain and Ireland, if we except the brief appearance in 1896 of a local society in Limerick. Dublin brassfounders had their own society, dating from 1817, but their Belfast brethren, whose society dated from 1840, had become by the 1890s a constituent union of the British United Journeymen Brassfounders Association;[20] the Dublin society later followed the example of the Belfast men.

---

amalgamated members unless the latter joined the Belfast society and paid a £3 fine. The B.T.C. executive recommended the dismissal of *all* men who had remained at work during a dispute and their replacement by Belfast society men in good standing (B.T.C. executive committee minutes, 2 Apr. 1903). A similar quarrel had taken place some eight years earlier, when the Belfast society had secured the condemnation of the amalgamated union by the British T.U.C. at Edinburgh (1896) for undercutting and blacklegging (see Clarkson, pp. 189, 394).

16. Clarkson, p. 394, n. 1.

17. Dublin Trades Council (D.T.C.) executive committee minutes, 11 Sept. 1911. The committee had earlier (8 Sept. 1910) received complaints about bad relations between a local farriers' society and an amalgamated branch.

18. *Ninth Report by the Chief Labour Correspondent of the Board of Trade on Trade Unions for 1896,* p. 334 [C. 8644], H.C. 1897, xcix; *Report on Trade Unions for 1902–4,* pp. 82–3 [Cd. 2838], H.C. 1906, cxii.

19. *Ninth Report on Trade Unions for 1896,* p. 336 [C. 8644]; *Tenth Report on Trade Unions for 1897,* p. 204 [C. 9013], H.C. 1898, ciii.

20. *Ninth Report on Trade Unions for 1896,* p. 368, [C. 8644].

One of the most successful amalgamated unions was the Amalgamated Society of Tailors (A.S.T.). Dublin delegates took part in its inaugural meeting in 1866. Despite the difficulties of organizing what was in many areas a sweated trade, the A.S.T., whether by absorbing local societies or creating new ones, had branches in the principal Irish towns before 1890. The A.S.T., or the General Federation of Trade Unions on its behalf, spent large sums in fighting the battles of its Irish members and it is not surprising that this generosity, and the large number of Irish on its executive committee, evoked strong feelings of loyalty; two of its stoutest defenders against criticism from advocates of Irish unions were James McCarron of Derry and Patrick Lynch of Cork, despite their nationalist views.

Irish coachmakers had long been members of the United Kingdom Society of Coachmakers, which was founded in 1834. A number of crafts had, like the brassfounders, entered British federations while preserving their local autonomy; thus the coopers, with the exception of those in Dublin and Kilkenny, were constituent unions of the Mutual Association of Journeymen Coopers[21] by 1896, and the upholsterers in Dublin, Belfast, and Londonderry were in the same fashion members of the Amalgamated Society of Upholsterers.[22] Some minor or dying trades were also members of a British federation: Belfast shipriggers and sailmakers; Belfast and Dublin electrotypers and stereotypers; Dublin handsewn bootmakers, whose allegiance varied between the London and Provincial Hand-Sewn Boot and Shoe Makers and the Amalgamated Boot and Shoe Makers, to be owed finally, in 1897, to the amalgamated union.[23]

In the printing trade the Typographical Association (T.A.) absorbed Irish branches of the Relief Association in 1877. If it was the only printing union in Ireland, apart from the Dublin Typographical Provident Society,[24] it made slow progress in the face of competition from boy and nonunion labor in provincial towns until 1894 when Hugh McManus, a Liverpool-born Irishman, was appointed Irish organizer. Stationed in Belfast, he carried out a long-sustained campaign to over-

21. *Ninth Report on Trade Unions for 1896*, [C. 8644]. Some of these claimed foundation dates of considerable antiquity (Dublin, 1501; Cork, 1700), but most came into existence in the 1880s and 1890s. The Dublin coopers had been members of the federation in 1895.

22. The oldest society was that of Dublin (1872); the others were formed in 1893 and 1894.

23. *Tenth Report on Trade Unions for 1897*, pp. 264–5 [c. 9013].

24. It later changed its name to the Irish Graphical Society, having absorbed some minor allied societies, but refusing to join the T.A. The London Society of Compositors followed a similar course, changing its name to the Society of Graphical and Allied Trades (S.O.G.A.T.).

come "rat" shops and when he died he left the T.A. in Ireland with a substantial membership and a commanding position which it still retains.[25] The lithographic printers were connected with their British counterparts for many years. A Central Association of Lithographic and Copper Plate Printers—consisting of a number of local associations in towns in the north of England, Scotland, and Ireland—held its first recorded meeting in Dublin during August 1861; in 1862 Dublin and Belfast were represented at its Glasgow meeting. In 1880 the Amalgamated Society of Lithographic Printers was established and one of its first ten branches was in Dublin. Belfast joined the following year and a small branch was opened in Cork in January 1882.[26]

Two groups of skilled workers deserve separate mention, the bakers and the craftsmen engaged in the linen industry. Local bakers' societies had existed for many years, especially in Dublin where they underwent repeated reformations and amalgamations. Though communication between the various towns was frequent, no nationwide organization was attempted until the 1880s. In 1889 Murray Davis, the principal figure in the Belfast Baker's Society, and a leading member of the Belfast Trades Council, formed the Bakers' Federal Union of Ireland.[27] It was a loose federation and its principal value seems to have lain in the encouragement it gave to smaller societies in provincial towns—in Waterford, for instance, it helped to bring about a union of two rival groups.[28] While it is of interest as the only Irish federation in existence at this time, it did not lead to any stronger organization and it seems to have lost much of its cohesion in the first decade of this century.

With a few exceptions already noted, skilled workers in Belfast and the north of Ireland showed a marked readiness to join British amalgamated unions. No such possibility existed for the tradesmen in the linen industry, for during the second half of the nineteenth century it had become concentrated in Belfast and a few outlying centers; by comparison the numbers in the Scottish linen (and jute) trades were of minor importance. A series of local unions were formed from the 1870s onward, the most important being the Flaxdressers, started by Robert Gageby in 1872, and the Flaxroughers, dating from 1889; in the 1890s they mustered between them some 1700 members. With the exception of the Irish Linenlappers (founded in 1889) and the Yarn Bundlers and Drying Loftmen (1894), the other groups consisted of workers tending or making textile machinery: the Belfast and North of

25. Musson, *The Typographical Association* (London, 1954), pp. 112, 127.
26. I am indebted to Mr. Andrew Boyd for this information supplied to him (in a letter dated 14 Feb. 1956) from the files of the A.S.L.P.
27. Swift, *Dublin Bakers*, pp. 295–96.
28. *Ninth Report on Trade Unions*, pp. 450–51 [C. 8644].

Ireland Power Loom Tenters and the Belfast Power Loom Yarn Dressers (both started in 1877), the Belfast Hackle and Gill Makers (1880), and the Beetling Enginemen (1891). Though these latter societies had less than a thousand members between them, they, like the other linen unions, had considerable powers of survival and contributed a number of leaders to Belfast labor politics.[29]

A scattering of small local societies catered for workers in the provision trades. Limerick and Waterford, centers of the pork and bacon curing industry, produced in 1890 an Amalgamated Society of Pork Butchers in the two towns; it furnished a president (P. J. Leo) of the Irish T.U.C. in 1897 when the fourth congress met in Waterford. The quiet lives of the butchers' societies were disturbed in 1900 when the Belfast Journeymen Butchers and Assistants' Association, formed in 1891, became involved in the *Quinn v. Leathem* case, a pendant to the better known Taff Vale affair, but while the principle at stake was of general interest no marked change in organization among butchers followed.

The fate of certain societies was determined by changes in technology or in fashion, thus the unions of brushmakers, corkcutters, basketmakers, organmakers, ropemakers, lathmakers and packing-case makers either disintegrated or were reduced to a mere handful of members by the end of the nineteenth century. The Dublin silk and poplin weavers were an exception, a revival in the use of poplin for dresses bringing their numbers up to 198 in 1907; but another old craft, that of saddle and harness making, experienced no such renaissance. The once important Dublin society, which joined an amalgamated union in 1897 and left it in 1903, saw its numbers steadily shrink to sixty-seven in 1907.[30] On the other hand, workers in new industries tended to join amalgamated unions. Irish electricians, for instance, took part in the meeting that established the Electrical Trades Union in 1889; an Irish union (the Irish Electrical Workers), started in 1896 with twenty-five members, collapsed in 1897.[31]

Railway Unions

Railway workers constituted an important group in the poorly industrialized Irish economy. The Amalgamated Society of Railway Servants (A.S.R.S.), founded in 1872, opened its first Irish branch on 24 January 1885 through the efforts of Hugh Scammell, who had originally

---

29. Op. cit., pp. 408–10.

30. D.T.C. minutes, 30 Aug. 1897; *Report on Trade Unions for the Years* 1905–7, pp. 854–5 [Cd. 4651].

31. Gordon Shaffer, *Light and Liberty,* p. 6.

worked on the Brighton and London line before migrating to Ireland; he became the branch's first secretary and the first Irish representative on the A.S.R.S. executive committee.[32] In 1887 the Irish membership stood at 143 and in the following year, when it claimed representation at the Preston congress of the A.S.R.S., it had risen to 190, as against a Scottish membership of 237.[33]

Though the A.S.R.S. was not an industrial union (it did not, for instance, include railway clerks, and it had lost many engine drivers and firemen in 1880 to the Associated Locomotive Engineers and Firemen), its composition placed it somewhere between craft and general unions. It was profoundly affected by the great trade union agitation of 1889 and Irish railway workers were caught up in that year's movement. Goods porters and guards in the Glanmire (Cork) station of the Great Southern and Western Railway (G.S.W.R.) struck for increased wages early in December, and, though eighty blacklegs were imported from Dublin, the refusal of the freight train men to accept goods handled by the strikebreakers persuaded the railway directors to welcome intervention by officials of the Cork Trades Council (E. Crean and Michael Austin) and the Cork Chamber of Commerce; the porters and guards rceived most of their demands. Their example was followed by the passengermen in Cork and a similar movement took place at the Kingsbridge (Dublin) station of the railway company.[34]

Employees (other than engine drivers and firemen) of the second biggest Irish railway company, the Great Northern Railway (G.N.R.), expressed dissatisfaction with their working conditions during the same month and refused to accept the directors' contention that "on the whole, the employees were dealt with the most generously."[35] At a series of meetings in Belfast, Dublin and country stations strike action was threatened and was actually taken at Dublin. The agitation brought in many new members for the A.S.R.S., especially in country towns. A settlement was reached on January 14, but it left several grades and countrymen dissatisfied.[36]

In December 1889 the A.S.R.S. executive had sent William Fore-

32. G. W. Alcock, *Fifty Years of Railway Trade Unionism*, pp. 226, 256. Scammell, who served on the A.S.R.S. executive for 1891 and 1892, died in Nov. 1892 at age 43.

33. Amalgamated Society of Railway Servants, *Report and Financial Statement, 1887; Railway Review*, 5 Oct. 1888; Alcock, *Fifty Years*, p. 232. I am indebted to Dr. Philip S. Bagwell (author of the authoritative history, *The Railwaymen*) for details of Irish branch returns from A.S.R.S. records in the National Union of Railwaymen headquarters.

34. *F.J.*, 11–17 Dec. 1889.   35. *B.N.-L.*, 24 Dec. 1889.

36. *N.W.*, 2–4, 11–15 Jan. 1890. By 3 January, 33 men in Omagh (County Tyrone) and Clones (County Monaghan) had joined the A.S.R.S.

man to fill the new post of Irish organizer.[37] His arrival coincided with the wave of militancy and within a few months (February 1890) Edward Harford, the A.S.R.S. general secretary, claimed that four thousand had joined the union in Ireland in the previous twelve months. Branch returns for 1890 gave a total of 3,659. New branches in the twelve months from June 1889 to June 1890 included two in Belfast, six in Dublin, two in Cork, and single branches in over a score of country towns, mainly in Ulster and Leinster, but also in the other two provinces.[38]

The increase in A.S.R.S. membership took place against a background of continuing agitation. In February the discontented G.N.R. employees, especially the country men, renewed their demands, appealed to the A.S.R.S. executive for funds, and prepared to strike.[39] They were promised the support of the engine drivers and firemen,[40] but after negotiations a general settlement was reached in March and the strike averted.[41]

In the following month (April 1890) a serious dispute broke out on the G.S.W.R. when the company dismissed two men. Workers in Cork railway, shipping, and carrying companies struck on April 20. The strike spread to Dublin and intermediate stations and as the signalmen had also withdrawn their labor, rail traffic was at a standstill.[42] Michael Davitt, while condemning the signalmen for suddenly abandoning their posts, generally supported the men's claims. He was joined by the Catholic archbishop of Dublin (W. J. Walsh) who, however, withdrew proposals he had put forward to the directors on behalf of the men, declaring that the employees "had been dealt with by the directors in an altogether unjustifiable manner.[43] Feelings were further embittered when the directors prosecuted the signalmen for leaving their cabins. The Belfast A.S.R.S. branch passed resolutions of sympathy with the G.S.W.R. employees and expressed their resentment at the attacks made by the *Freeman's Journal* and the *Irish Times* on Foreman as an Englishman responsible for the strike.[44] The dispute was finally ended with little advantage to the men when on May 2 they voted overwhelm-

37. Foreman, who was born in Sunderland in 1855, worked on the North-Eastern railway (1870–86) before being appointed in 1886 assistant editor of the *Railway Review*. The *Trade Unionist* of 15 Aug. 1891 carried an account of his career to that date. See also Alcock, *Fifty Years,* and Bagwell, *The Railwaymen,* passim.

38. A.S.R.S. records. Again I am indebted to Dr. Bagwell.

39. *N.W.,* 19 Feb. 1890.   40. *N.W.,* 3 Mar. 1890.

41. *N.W.,* 4, 5 Mar. 1890.   42. *B.N.-L,,* 22–28 Apr. 1890.

43. *B.N.-L.,* 30 Apr. 1890.

44. *N.W.,* 30 Apr. 1890. Foreman and J. Havelock Wilson, founder of the Sailors' and Firemen's Union, were denounced as "foreign agitators" during strikes on the

ingly to leave arbitration to their representatives (Archbishop Walsh, Joseph A. Galbraith, Fellow of Trinity College, Dublin, and Edward Harford) and the railway directors.[45]

Irish membership figures fluctuated after the expansion of 1889–90. In 1893 the total stood at 3,313,[46] consisting principally of G.N.R. employees, for in the following year Harford claimed as members 2,154 of that company's labor force of 2,400; he also said that the increase in wages secured amounted to £16,000 per annum.[47] A drop to 2,893 in 1896 was followed by an extraordinarily successful recruiting drive in which the Irish membership rose to 7,500 by October 1897; the Irish organizer P. J. Tevenan estimated that this figure represented 53 percent of all Irish railwaymen eligible for admission to the A.S.R.S.[48] Since the British organizers were equally active, the grand total rose steeply, 47,381 new members being recruited by 26 November 1897.[49]

Within a year the union had lost almost all it had gained, the drop of 31,501 being described by Alcock, the union historian writing around 1920, as "the worst setback yet experienced."[50] Irish membership suffered even more severely. A fourteen-week strike on the Cork and Bandon railway in 1897–98 cost the union over £8,400; several men were imprisoned and fined, and fourteen were evicted from their houses. By the end of 1900 the union had only 1,093 members in Ireland; it did not recover its 1893 figure of over 3,000 until 1914.[51]

The Irish branches of the A.S.R.S. or of the National Union of Railwaymen (N.U.R.), as it was known from 1913 onward, were a financial liability to the union. The average annual loss for the fifteen-year period (1900–14) was over £1000,[52] and though Irish membership climbed temporarily to twenty thousand in 1920, the general secretary of the N.U.R., John Benstead, declared in July 1951 when his union withdrew from Ireland that "the loss to the union over the years was £250,000."[53]

Dublin, Wicklow, and Waterford line and on the British and Irish Company steamers in 1890 (*F.J.*, 18 Aug. 1890).

45. *N.W.*, 3, 5 May 1890. See also accounts of the strike in *F.J.* and *Irish Times* (*I.T.*) of relevant dates.

46. A.S.R.S. records.   47. Alcock, *Fifty Years,* p. 281.

48. Op. cit., 293–95.   49. Op. cit., p. 299.

50. Loc. cit.

51. Alcock, *Fifty Years,* pp. 298, 453. For a fuller acccount of the Cork and Bandon strike see Bagwell, *The Railwaymen,* pp. 189–91.

52. Alcock, *Fifty Years,* p. 453.

53. Statement to the annual general meeting of the National Union of Railwaymen

No Irish all-grades union for railwaymen seems to have existed. There was a Railway Porters' Association in Cork at the time of the December 1889 strike and this may have been the nucleus of an Irish A.S.R.S. that recruited some four hundred members in February and March. Delegates from the Irish branches of the A.S.R.S. at a conference held in Dublin during April rejected the idea of a separate union, a full-time organizer (W. Foreman), was appointed and the Cork society merged with the A.S.R.S.[54]

The Associated Society of Locomotive Engineers and Firemen (A.S.L.E.F.) was formed in February 1880 with headquarters at Leeds.[55] Its first Irish branch was not opened (in Dublin) until October 1910.[56] The thirty-year interval is partially explained by the existence of two Irish unions catering for locomotive men. The major union was the Belfast and Dublin Locomotive Engine Drivers' and Firemen's Union, which had been formed, like the A.S.R.S., in 1872, but was not registered until 1895.[57] In that year it had branches in Dublin and Belfast and a total membership of 355.[58] It seems to have lost some of its Dublin members to the A.S.L.E.F. when that body started a branch there in 1910; its main strength lay in Belfast. Its name was changed in 1917 to the Irish Locomotive Enginemen's Trade Union[59] and it continued its separate existence until it was absorbed by the British union. The second union, the Waterford, Limerick, and Western Railway Company's Engine Drivers and Firemen's Trade Union, was a tiny organization; formed in 1885, its membership, instead of growing, declined steadily from fifty-nine in 1890 to twenty in 1902. It was formally dissolved in 1903.[60]

(N.U.R.). In 1950, the last year in which the N.U.R. operated in Ireland, its Irish membership was 7,522.

54. Bagwell, *The Railwaymen*, p. 134. A meeting in Castleblaney (County Monaghan) addressed by the A.S.R.S. organizing secretary (Watson) resolved "to discountenance any connection with the Irish Association recently organised in Cork" (*N.W.*, 24 Jan. 1890).

55. Norman McKillop, *The Lighted Flame*, pp. 22–28.

56. Op. cit., p. 91.

57. *Report of the Chief Registrar of Friendly Societies for the Year 1895*, p. 90, 1896 (94), lxxviii.

58. *Eighth Annual Report on Trade Unions for 1895*, pp. 58–62 [C. 8232], H.C. 1896, xciii, 364–9.

59. *Rules and Regulations of the Irish Locomotive Enginemen's Trade Union*, 1917, p. 5. Its council consisted of 6 members from Belfast, 2 from Dublin, and 1 from Dundalk.

60. 59 (1890), 55 (1894), 42 (1895), 37 (1896). See *Ninth Annual Report on Trade Unions for 1896*, pp. 92–3 [C. 8644] and *Report on Trade Unions for 1902–4*, pp. 138–9 [Cd. 2838].

The Organization of General Unions

The unionization of unskilled and even semiskilled labor presented greater difficulties in Ireland than in Great Britain. With the exception of Belfast, where there were political and sectarian problems, Irish towns lacked the growing industries that could, as in England, absorb the numbers leaving rural areas. Many emigrated but there were still sufficient laborers and small farmers' sons to contribute to a pool of unemployed in the principal Irish towns or even to swell it in the winter months when farm work was slack. Though attempts had been made in the 1870s to form an Irish Agricultural Labourers' Union, this influx of rural labor had virtually no tradition of solidarity and it added to the difficulties of organizing the unskilled in stagnant or contracting urban centers.[61]

There were unions of semiskilled and unskilled workers in Ireland before the rise of general unionism in Great Britain in 1889. In the provincial towns ephemeral groups existed comprising laborers in different trades, occasionally including agricultural workers,[62] but unions in the bigger towns normally consisted only of those in specific trades and rarely had more than two hundred members before 1889. The Dublin paviors' union, founded in 1860, had declined in 1895 to fifty members and collapsed in 1897, and the Limerick dockers (organized

61. From 1870 onward agricultural laborers in several Munster counties held meetings at which they called for legislation to improve their working conditions, instancing what had been done for industrial labor in England and tenant farmers in Ireland. The executive of the English National Agricultural Labourers' Union helped in the organization of the Irish rural laborers, and Joseph Arch, its founder and president, spoke at the inaugural meeting of the Irish union at Kanturk, County Cork, in August 1873. But the union's success was limited for a number of reasons: a serious accident to P. F. Johnson, the secretary and moving spirit of the new union; the difficulty of organizing a labor force both scattered (few Irish farms employed more than two men) and declining; the agricultural depression that began in the mid-70s. [See *Irishman*, 22 Jan. 1870, 26 Apr., 10 May, 5 July, 23 Aug. 1873; J. W. Boyle, "The Rural Labourer," *Threshold*, iii, no. 1, Spring, 1959, and "A Marginal Figure: The Irish Rural Labourer," in S. Clark and J. S. Donnelly, Jr., eds., *Irish Peasants: Violence and Political Unrest, 1780–1914*, Madison, 1983; David Fitzpatrick, "The Disappearance of the Irish Agricultural Labourer, 1841–1912," in *Irish Economic and Social History*, vii (1980), pp. 66–92; P. L. R. Horn, "The National Agricultural Labourers' Union in Ireland, 1873–9," *I.H.S.*, xvii, no. 67, March 1971, pp. 340–52. The union, which seems to have changed its name to that of Labour League, existed until about 1879, when it was absorbed in the Irish Land League (*Royal Commission on Labour: The Agricultural Labourer in Ireland*, p. 34 [C. 6894] H.C. 1893–4, xxxvii). Labourers' unions reappeared in these Munster counties and reiterated the earlier demands for the provision of laborers' cottages and plots of land.

62. An account of a congress of laborers' unions held in Dublin in March 1891 includes a list of delegates from various towns and rural districts (*F.J.* 16 Mar. 1891).

in 1863) had over two hundred workers enrolled in 1896.[63] The Dublin Quay Labourers' Society assembled 1,500 dockers for a demonstration in 1875 to commemorate the centenary of O'Connell's birth,[64] but it began to disintegrate after 1880 and was replaced by a number of unions catering for laborers in particular commodities (coal porters, grain laborers, etc.). Building trade laborers, aided by the Dublin United Trades' Association, formed a union in 1864, but how long it endured is uncertain; in 1889 a new organization, the Dublin United Labourers' Society, appeared. The following year it had a membership of 2,300 and took a new name, the United Labourers of Ireland, but it soon lost ground in the reaction that affected general unions both in Great Britain and Ireland; its number fell to six hundred in 1897, a figure that it managed to maintain, despite some fluctuations, until 1907. Local laborers' unions in the building trade existed by about 1890 in Belfast, Cork, and Limerick, as well as unions of municipal workers.[65] If some laborers and semiskilled unions antedated 1889, there is little doubt that the stimulus of the agitation of that year helped to throw up a number of others between 1889 and 1891; the brewing industry, for instance, gave rise to several groups in Dublin and Cork, but they disappeared before the end of the century. Another laborers' union, the Irish National Labour Union, founded in 1892, was organized on a federal basis but its membership hardly justified its title; it rose to 1,200 in 1894, but sank to 600 in 1897 and disappeared in 1907.

It is probable that the total membership of Irish laborers' unions did not exceed four thousand at any one time during the years from 1889 to 1906, though the marked fluctuations in membership of even the larger bodies and the ephemeral nature of others make it difficult to arrive at more than a rough estimate. To this total may be added the Irish membership of British general unions. But before the impact of the "new unionism" is considered, the appearance in Ireland of a different form of unionism is worth noting, that of the Knights of Labour, an American organization.

The Knights of Labour, with a masonic ritual and a hierarchy of officials headed by the General Master Workman, Terence V. Powderly,

63. Unless otherwise indicated, the materials for this paragraph on unskilled and semiskilled unions are taken from the reports of the Chief Labour Correspondent of the Board of Trade during the years 1887–1909.

64. Swift, *Dublin Bakers,* p. 237.

65. In Belfast building trade laborers were organized in 1889 as the Bricklayers and Plasterers' Assistants Trade Union, which became a branch of the Gasworkers in 1890. With the collapse of the Gasworkers the old union was resurrected, its name being changed in 1896 to Belfast City Hodsmen; this union joined the English United Builders' Labourers in 1897.

was a body that included both skilled and unskilled in many centers of the United States and, by its primitive nature, recalled Owen's Grand General Consolidated Trade Union. It spread among workers in the English Black Country from 1886 to 1889, but after an embezzlement case it sank rapidly until by 1894 it consisted merely of a small benefit society.[66]

The first Irish local assembly of the Knights of Labour was formed in Belfast.[67] Some dozen workmen met in a public house on Donegall Quay in September 1888, and after the proprietor, a former Master Workman of an assembly in Columbus, Georgia, and another ex-Knight from the United States had explained the nature of the "Order," as it was commonly called, the men decided to organize an assembly. With the aid of the Birmingham organizer of the Knights and R. H. Feagan, the local official of the Bootmakers, L.A. 418 (Erin's First) was formally instituted in March 1889, with Feagan as its secretary for the first five months. Its membership consisted of shipyard workers and bootmakers and within a few months had reached three hundred. In June of the same year the Birmingham organizer opened a second assembly (L.A. 7566) consisting entirely of ropemakers and it, like Erin's First, built up membership and funds rapidly. But disaster fell upon both assemblies. Powderly, visiting England in the summer of 1889, sent a deputy to Belfast, but his substitute spent only a couple of hours with Feagan, did not address the assembly, and instead accompanied Henry George to meetings in the Temple of Liberty at Toombridge (County Antrim) and in Derry. Feagan, a pronounced Irish nationalist and secretary of the Belfast Fabian Society,[68] was accused by Unionist-minded members of political intrigue and he resigned. In December 1889, the second assembly became involved in a ropemakers' strike to raise wages from 18s. a week to 22s.,[69] the men being under the impression that the Knights paid a strike benefit of 20s. As the Belfast Ropework Company resisted the demand, L.A. 418 advanced money on the supposition that the American executive would refund it, but after a fourteen-week strike the men had to acknowledge defeat and only a few were being taken back. The assemblies received

66. For the history of the Knights of Labour in Great Britain see Henry Pelling, "The Knights of Labour in Britain, 1880–1901," in *Economic History Review*, 2nd ser., ix (1956, no. 2, pp. 313–31).

67. This account is, unless otherwise stated, based on the article "The Rise and Fall of the Knights of Labour in Belfast" in the *Belfast Weekly Star*, 17 Jan. 1891. For Irish membership in the United States see Carl Wittke, *The Irish in America* (New York, 1956), pp. 222–3.

68. *Belfast Weekly Star*, 10 Jan. 1891, contains a biography of Feagan.

69. The average wage of Scottish ropemakers was 28s.

no replies from Philadelphia (the Knight's headquarters), nor were they able to secure affiliation to the stronger Scottish district. Disheartened by their financial troubles and riven by the sectarian and political rivalries of their members, the assemblies fell apart; the officers of L.A. 418 sold its effects to members and the other branch ceased to meet.[70]

The Knights had one further Irish branch in the unlikely city of Londonderry. Alpha Assembly 1601 was founded shortly after the second Belfast assembly, in August 1889. By early 1891 the original fourteen members had grown to eight hundred and a contemporary account[71] gives a glowing picture of the "large and flourishing assembly" that formed such a contrast to "the humiliating failure in Belfast." Its premises contained an amusement room well stocked with nongambling games and papers and an entertainment room in which weekly concerts were given. The attendance at the weekly meetings averaged 250 and plans had been laid to form an Alpha band with performers from Catholic and Protestant musical groups. But by August the membership of eight hundred had shrunk to one hundred[72] and the formal end was not long delayed. The exact cause of the decline is uncertain but it is probable that on the religio-political battleground of Derry, a worthy rival of Belfast in this respect, the hopefully named Alpha became Omega under the combined assaults of employers and politicians exploiting sectarian passions.

The year 1889 is the great year of the "new unionism," when semiskilled workers and laborers were organized in general unions. These "new unions" asked only modest dues from their poorly paid members and initially made no attempt to pay benefits or build up a strike fund. Instead, they relied on aggressive strike tactics and demonstrations that would arouse public sympathy by exposing the sweated conditions under which they worked. Though the great London dock strike on August 1889 aroused unprecedented public interest, the union then formed—the Dock, Wharf, Riverside and General Labourers' Union—did not organize an Irish branch until some twenty years later.[73] The "new unionism" in Ireland was represented by the National Union of Dock Labourers (N.U.D.L.), the Gasworkers and General Labourers' Union, and the National Amalgamated Union of Labour (N.A.U.L.).

The N.U.D.L. was formed in February 1889 during a strike on the Clyde led by the Sailors and Firemen's Union, itself the creation of J. Havelock Wilson in 1887. At a strike meeting Wilson and other

70. Pelling, "Knights of Labour in Britain," gives the charter number as 1566, with thirty-five as the initial membership (early 1889).
71. *Belfast Weekly Star*, 7 Mar. 1891.
72. Pelling, "Knights of Labor," p. 331.
73. The annual report of the union (1912), p. 87, lists a branch in Cork.

speakers appealed to the dock laborers to stop work in order to bring pressure on the employers. At a further meeting dock laborers present agreed to support the sailors by withdrawing their labor and, in response to the suggestion of G. Galloway, the chairman, decided to form a union. Enrollment for the first branch of the N.U.D.L. started on February 5.[74] Simultaneously officials of Havelock Wilson's union proceeded to organize the Irish ports, beginning with Belfast, and with the Glasgow model in mind the N.U.D.L. followed suit. By May newspapers were carrying reports of successes in Belfast, some firms having conceded 6d. an hour, "the full round orb of the docker's tanner," to use John Burns's phrase in the later London dock strike, while the branch was "daily augmenting its strength." Further disputes broke out in the summer, the carters and dock laborers striking in support of the seamen and firemen in the autumn and in the opening months of 1890. In general the disputes ended with the men gaining advances in wages and feeling, in the words of a resolution of thanks to McGhee and McHugh in March 1890, that the two men "from the most unselfish motives and at great inconvenience to themselves [had] done . . . much to raise the dock labourers from the degraded position they once occupied." At this time the branch had four hundred members out of the two thousand men eligible in the port of Belfast.[75]

The Belfast branch was second only to Glasgow's in point of time (when it collapsed, the number was assigned to a second Glasgow branch) and had the honor of acting as host in 1891 for the union's third congress. By the middle of that year the N.U.D.L. had branches in fifteen Irish ports and a paid-up Irish membership of some two thousand. The executive committee's report was not, however, a tale of unbroken success; the Derry branch was unable to make a financial return but recovered the following year in the wake of renewed militancy on the part of the seamen, the Belfast secretary had defaulted with some funds (the same was to happen in Cork in 1894), and employers' counteroffensives had to be met in Cork, Waterford, and

74. At a meeting of the Belfast branch in March 1890, Richard H. McGhee stated that the union began on February 19 (1889) and that apart from himself and Edward McHugh there were only nine men present (*Brotherhood*, 15 Mar. 1890). Galloway replied (*Brotherhood*, Mar. 22), giving the correct sequence of events and underlining the part played by the Sailors' and Firemen's Union (later the National Union of Seamen). McGhee and McHugh, both of Irish origin, became president and secretary respectively of the N.U.D.L. shortly after its foundation. See also *N.W.*, 6 Feb. 1889, and N.U.D.L., *Executive Committee Report for Year Ending 30 June 1891*, p. 8.

75. This account is based on the reports in the *Northern Whig* for the months of February, May, June, September, November 1889 and January 1890; in the *Belfast News-Letter* for relevant dates in February, May, and June 1889; in *Justice*, 16 Feb., 2 Mar., 1 June 1889; in *Brotherhood*, 15, 22 Mar. 1890.

Drogheda. Yet the general picture was encouraging; wages in Irish ports which had been as low as ten shillings per week, with men working from 6 A.M. to 9 P.M. for two shillings, had advanced substantially by amounts ranging up to 30 percent.[76]

N.U.D.L. Irish membership remained substantial until 1893; though branches in the minor ports had earlier disintegrated, there had been an increased enrollment in some of the major ports. But in that year the Belfast branch succumbed. It had already weathered a succession of attacks from the Shipping Federation and its army of blacklegs, but it did not survive the political storms accompanying the second Irish Home Rule bill, because its secretary Michael McKeown, despite his devoted work for the dockers, participated in the Home Rule campaign and thereby lost the support of his Protestant Orange members.[77] The striking advance of the union in Dublin did not compensate for Belfast's defection. In 1895 there remained branches in only four Irish towns (Dublin, Derry, Drogheda, and Cork) and ten years later in only two (Derry and Drogheda).[78] In Belfast the dockers sank back into their degraded position in which two firms of stevedores (one Protestant, one Catholic) combined in a policy of *divide et impera* and reinforced, if they did not create, the situation whereby the cross-channel docks, providing better pay and more regular work, were manned by Protestants and the deep-sea docks by Catholics.[79] Not until 1907, with the coming of James Larkin, did the dockers of Ireland's most important port recover the gains they had lost in 1893.

In March 1889 Will Thorne, born in Birmingham of Irish parents

76. N.U.D.L., *Report for Year Ending 30 June 1891*, pp. 7, 9, 10, 28–39, and folded page.

77. Interview with Seán McKeown, son of Michael McKeown; N.U.D.L., *Reports 1892*, pp. 9, 28–39, *1893*, pp. 19–31. Numbers affiliated to Belfast Trades Council were 800 in 1891 and 367 in 1892; the entry for 1893 is "collapsed" [B.T.C. reports for 1891, 1892, (p. 10 and folded sheet)]. Other lapsed societies included the Sailors' and Firemen's branch.

78. N.U.D.L., *Reports 1894* (pp. 5, 30–35), *1895* (pp. 4, 5, 30–34), *1905* (pp. 6, 36–37). It seems that the N.U.D.L. in Dublin ceased to exist in 1900. There had been sporadic attendances of N.U.D.L. delegates at the Dublin Trades Council between 1894 and 1897; in 1899 six delegates attended, a number increased to seven, representing branches 18 and 19, after a visit by James Sexton, the Union's general secretary (D.T.C. minutes, 21 Jan. 1894, 10 May 1897, 10 April 1899, 1 January 1900). Affiliation lapsed shortly afterward.

79. Interview with Daniel J. McDevitt, active in Belfast labor circles from the 1890s until the early 1920s. This division was temporarily healed during James Larkin's organizing drive in 1907 and 1908, but reappeared when Larkin, expelled from the N.U.D.L. in late 1908, started the Irish Transport and General Workers' Union. Since then the Belfast dockers have belonged to separate British and Irish Unions.

and working in East Ham, a suburb of London, organized the Gas-workers and General Labourers' Union. Aided by Eleanor Marx (a daughter of Karl Marx) and other members of the Social-Democratic Federation, he enrolled twenty thousand members in four months and then successfully demanded an eight-hour day (i.e., three shifts of eight hours instead of two of twelve) from a number of gas companies.[80] In the closing months of the year branches were organized in Belfast and Dublin and demands for an eight-hour day soon followed. Gas in Belfast was a municipal enterprise and the corporation gas committee, though convinced that the wages of 5*s.* to 5*s.* 7*d.* a day were very liberal, offered in November an increase of 6*d.*, raised to 1*s.* a shift until the eight-hour shift could be introduced. The change was held up for some months until a new apparatus could be obtained.[81] A curious interlude occurred on January 1 when the monthly meeting of the city council heard a protest from a deputation, composed chiefly of "working men," against proposed increases in salaries to corporation officials; their speaker, one Craig, also said that his deputation was astonished by the large increase to the gasworks men as the expense involved could have been saved to the ratepayers if the corporation had acted properly.[82] This assertion evoked an immediate reply from W. N. Johnston, the Gasworkers' branch secretary, pointing out that the increase worked out at 1*d.* an hour, which was provisional until the men got what they wanted—shorter hours.[83]

Under the leadership of Johnston, the Gasworkers in Belfast carried on a vigorous organizing campaign among various classes of unskilled and semiskilled workers. In April 1890 Johnston intervened actively in a strike of the builders' laborers and brought their society (Bricklayers and Plasterers' Assistants) into the union and in the following June added the Belfast tramwaymen.[84] In 1891 the five branches had a total membership of 1,410 and covered, affiliated to the Belfast Trades Council, mineral water workers, coalmen, street cleaners, brickmakers, and provision workers.[85] For the year 1892, the district secretary, R. Greenlee, reported that the union was in such a flourishing condition that it had been necessary to appoint a full-time secretary and organizer and that the union now had branches in Lurgan, Newry,

80. Pelling, *History of British Trade Unionism,* pp. 97–100. See also François Béd-arida, *Will Thorne: La voie anglaise du socialisme,* Paris, 1987.

81. Belfast Corporation gas committee minutes, 7, 14, 15 Nov. 1889, 20 Feb. 1890.

82. *B.N.-L.,* 2 Jan. 1890.   83. *B.N.-L.,* 3 Jan. 1890.

84. *B.N.-L.,* 24 Apr., 23 June 1890.

85. *B. T. C. Report for 1891.* All branches of a union did not necessarily affiliate to a trades council, so that such numbers are normally below the full union strength.

Armagh, Londonderry, and Portadown in addition to those in Belfast. He made special acknowledgement of the valuable assistance he had received from Pete Curran, the union's Irish-born national organizer, and Adolphus Shields, the Dublin secretary. The yearly balance sheet gave a total of eighteen branches, eight in Belfast and four in Derry (where one consisted of female shirtmakers).[86] The union in Belfast seems to have reached its maximum strength in 1892, for though it took in the city carters, hitherto in a local union, several branches (brickmakers, provision workers) collapsed during 1893. Greenlee left the union and a series of disputes in the district cost it some £800 in strike pay.[87] Only six branches (four in Belfast, two in Newry) paid contributions to headquarters in 1894[88] and, though information is lacking, it appears that the Gasworkers then disintegrated. Some of the sections reverted to the status of local societies or were taken into the National Amalgamated Union of Labour.[89]

In Dublin the Gasworkers had a more spectacular rise and fall. The union in January 1890 demanded double overtime for Sunday work and a 7-shilling increase to 42 shillings in the weekly wages of its members employed by the Alliance Gas Company, a private concern. A weekend of reflection was sufficient to persuade the company's directors to reach agreement with the men's representatives and accept the three-shift system. It was introduced with no loss of pay and certain classes of workers received raises in basic pay and an overtime rate in addition.[90]

The euphoria that informed other trades as well as the Gasworkers during 1890 is indicated by the speakers at a May Day meeting in the Phoenix Park organized by the union to demand an eight-hour day by legislation. On the platform stood representatives of the skilled trades and of the new militant general unions engaged in what seemed an unbroken round of agitation, organization, strikes, lockouts, and negotiations; the Gasworkers' Dublin secretary, Adolphus Shields, introduced Michael McKeown, "one of the leaders of the great Liverpool dock strike," William Foreman of the A.S.R.S., the local secretary of the Seamen and Firemen's Union and P. A. Tyrrell, the A.S.E. Dublin branch secretary. Telegrams of support were read from Cunninghame-

86. National Union of Gasworkers and General Labourers of Great Britain and Ireland, *Report for Year Ending 31 Mar. 1892*, pp. 23, 24.

87. Gasworkers, *Report for Year Ending 31 Mar. 1893*, balance sheet; *B. T. C. Reports for 1892, 1893*, p. 10.

88. Gasworkers, *Report for Year Ending 31 Dec. 1894*, pp. 23, 46.

89. Examples are the building laborers (local society) and the mineral water operatives (N.A.U.L., date of accession uncertain, but this N.A.U.L. branch lapsed in 1898).

90. *F.J.*, 25, 28 Jan. 1890.

Graham, John Burns, Will Thorne, and several local leaders. Shields not only pointed out the gains won for gasworkers in Dublin and neighboring Kingstown, but claimed that the union had won substantial advantages for numerous classes of workers—within recent weeks they had "blacked" three ships belonging to the Great Southern and Western Railway Company. Solidarity was also the theme of a brickmaker (one Whelan), who spoke of a large body of men who refused to join any organization on the grounds that they had the best employers in the world, but stated that those men owed a duty to their fellow workers less fairly treated.[91] Whelan also asserted that Irish workers would no longer be content with M.P.s merely because they were nationalists, because they should have a workingmen's representative.[92]

The Gasworkers continued their hectic organizing drive throughout the summer, winning advances for men employed by coal merchants and the Grand Canal Company in the course of strikes and lockouts and despite the use of scab labor.[93] Membership was mushrooming and a wide variety of occupations were being unionized: an organizing meeting held in a Dublin suburb during August, attended by a crowd of three to four hundred and enlivened by a band, heard the secretary of the machinists, hammermen, steelworkers, and laborers section claim an enrollment of 1,019 in six weeks in his own branch; Michael Canty, an organizer, declared that the union had reduced the hours of operative pork butchers to fifty-seven a week, a concession the Dublin Trades Council had been unable to secure from the employers.[94] By early 1892 the union had twelve branches in Dublin that covered, in addition to gasworkers, coalmen and general laborers, glasshouse, biscuit, mineral water, and tobacco workers, bacon curers, machinists and hammermen, grain laborers, and Phoenix brewery employees.[95]

The brewery members did not include those at St. James's Gate (Guinness's brewery). Steady employment at wages somewhat higher than those prevailing generally in Dublin, and a range of fringe benefits that made the company a welfare state long before the term was in-

91. A fairly clear reference to the paternalistic brewing firm of Arthur Guinness and Son, Ltd.

92. The meeting is reported in *F.J.*, 5 May 1890. The Dublin branch was, like its union's executive committee, carrying out the directions of the Second International to hold international May Day meetings in support of the demand for an eight-hour day (*Gasworkers, Report for Year Ending 31 Mar. 1891*, p. 12). Whelan had been a brickmakers' delegate to the Dublin Trades Council (*F.J.*, 4 Feb. 1889).

93. *N.W.*, 1, 4, 5 July 1890; Gasworkers, *Report for Year Ending 31 Mar. 1891*, pp. 11, 18.

94. *F.J.*, 14 Aug. 1890.

95. *Gasworkers: Report for Year Ending 31 Mar. 1892*, p. 30.

vented, left the laborers with little incentive to join a union.[96] Nonetheless the activities of the Gasworkers were such as to prompt Sir Edward Guinness, who had recently retired from the chairmanship, to address a letter to the board of directors referring to the current debates on the relations between employer and employed and asserting his belief that the harmony that had existed between himself and his employees would not be disturbed:

I do not wish to express any hostility to trade unions, between which and myself most cordial relations have always been maintained in the past; but I cannot take leave of you without referring to the efforts which I have reason to believe are being made to induce the workingmen in your employment to become members of a union which has unfortunately been involved of late in disputes with employers. I would earnestly ask those who may have joined, or who intend to join that union, that they should very fully consider the possible consequences of their action. Hitherto the relations between employer and employed at St. James's Gate have been in no way complicated by questions outside the brewery, and I am convinced that it is for the advantage of all concerned that this should continue to be the case. I should be apprehensive of the employees being unwillingly drawn into disputes which might arise outside the brewery, with which they were not personally concerned.[97]

He added a *douceur,* as a personal gift from himself, of a month's salary to the two grades of clerks and a week's wages to the workmen. The laborers took his advice, at least to the extent of forming what seems to have amounted to a company union in 1891, but the life of the St. James's Gate Brewery Labourers' Trade Union was not prolonged beyond 1895.[98]

1890 was, however, not a year of unbroken success for the Gasworkers' Union. It had enrolled porters employed by coal merchants in the city, but McCormick, one of the largest, dismissed two men in July when he found them urging their workmates to join the union. He then brought in "free labourers" and persuaded other merchants to undertake deliveries to his customers. Shields and Canty, on discovering this, ordered their members to stop work. The strike became bitter, with attacks on scab laborers. Some of the smaller merchants, worried about

96. Some of these benefits were: pensions (including widows' pensions from about 1850), free medical and hospital services (dependents also qualified), and holiday travel allowances. Employees in the skilled trades were unionized.

97. *F.J.,* 23 Aug. 1890. Letter dated 21 Aug. 1890.

98. See appropriate reports by the Chief Labour Correspondent of the Board of Trade. James Larkin also tried unavailingly to organize Guinness's laborers before 1914 and it was left to his son, James Larkin, Jr., in the post-1945 years to succeed where so many had failed.

the loss of trade, then guaranteed that they would not supply coal to McCormick. A settlement was reached when it was agreed that all future disputes would be referred to an arbitration committee. But a dispute arose again because the men's grievances, low pay, for instance, had not been remedied. The union headquarters, hard pressed itself, sent some £200, but it was not sufficient to sustain the men, who had to agree to work with "free" labor.

Nor was a further attempt in late 1891 more successful. Thorne came to Dublin, but found the branch books in chaos. He paid strike money to some but not to those out of benefit or to those who had not been in the union for six months. A row erupted and Thorne and another English official took flight.[99]

Despite the troubles during the coal porters' strike in 1890, the Gasworkers dominated labor activity in the first half of 1891. In February they commemorated the first anniversary of their winning an eight-hour day, organized in March a conference of laborers' societies addressed by Parnell, and celebrated May Day in conjunction with the skilled trades. Later in May they held another demonstration with Edward and Eleanor Marx Aveling among the speakers.[100] Their success in recruiting members on an unprecedented scale has already been noted. But during 1892 there was a total change. The Gasworkers in Dublin fell apart. In addition to the losses that general unions suffered under employers' counterattacks, there seems to have been a deliberate and successful attempt to disrupt it. Bernard Doyle, editor and printer of the *Irish Worker,* denounced the Irish National Labour Union (I.N.L.U.), formed in 1892, when it applied for affiliation to the Dublin Trades Council. According to Doyle, the I.N.L.U. had been organized before the Gasworkers collapsed, and had poached members from it, from the National Union of Dock Labourers, and from a Dublin general union and offered a refuge to malcontents and black-legs.[101] Doyle's charges appear to have had some substance, for Michael Canty, after leaving the Gasworkers with printing and gas bills to pay, quickly became an organizer of the I.N.L.U. He soon shifted his allegiance, first to the Dublin Amalgamated Grain Labourers and then to the Dublin Corporation Labourers, soured by his experience with cross-channel unions.[102] Some of the local laborers' unions benefited temporarily from the breakup of the Gasworkers, but the net result was

---

99. See Dermot Keogh, "The 'New Unionism' and Ireland: Dublin Coal Porters' Strike, 1890," *Capuchin Annual,* 1975: 64–70.

100. *F.J.,* 18 May 1891.   101. *Irish Worker,* Mar. 1893.

102. *Gasworkers: Report for Year Ending 31 Mar. 1893; Report on Trade Unions for 1896,* pp. 430–31, [c. 8644]. Canty became a strong Sinn Féin supporter.

to leave a large mass of the Dublin unskilled unorganized and helpless.

The Gasworkers did not attempt to organize the Dublin Tramways Company employees, as this task was undertaken by William Foreman of the A.S.R.S. Foreman's efforts on behalf of railway workers from the time of his arrival in February 1890 prompted the tramwaymen to approach him with a request for help to improve their working conditions. They alleged that drivers and conductors worked from 7:00 or 8:00 A.M. to 12 midnight, a complaint that made a nationalist M.P., W. A. Macdonald, say that as a shareholder he would be willing to part with a portion of his dividend rather than allow such a state of affairs to continue.[103] Foreman held a midnight meeting and with the aid of the Dublin Trades Council formed a committee. He drafted rules for the new union, which enrolled 370 men at the first meeting, a figure raised to 700 by July of that year. Foreman, incidentally, disapproved of the Belfast Gasworkers enrolling tramwaymen, as he preferred a local union which could then federate with other tramway groups, instead of being absorbed in a general union.[104]

The Dublin and District Tramwaymen's Union faced considerable difficulties The company, headed by William Martin Murphy, a businessman with interests in two continents, could easily recruit nonunion labor from the pool of unemployed or young men from the country waiting to enter the Royal Irish Constabulary. In 1891 it refused to recognize the union when the men asked that the working day be limited to twelve hours.[105] In 1894 and in 1896 the T.U.C. heard renewed complaints that the company would not meet the men as a body or grant them a nine-hour working day, but congress seems to have taken no action.[106] In 1897 the union expired, its membership of 223 in 1896 being too discouraged to continue. It was refounded in 1901 and the men's case taken to the Dublin Trades Council and the Irish T.U.C. in 1902—they suffered from a split day, which ran from 7:00 or 7:30 A.M. to past midnight with a break of some three hours

103. *F.J.*, 10 Nov. 1890. Macdonald was replying to strong criticism of Irish M.P.s made at a previous meeting of the Dublin Trades Council.

104. *Belfast Weekly Star*, 26 July 1890. The entrance fee was 1*s.* and the weekly dues 3*d.* The union began enrolling members in August (*F.J.*, 11, 12 Aug. 1890). The rules (copy in the British Library of Political and Economic Science) provided for general meetings to be held at 12:30 A.M. (i.e., when the men ceased work). Foreman died in 1892.

105. *Belfast Weekly Star*, 6 June 1891.

106. *F.J.*, 30 Apr. 1894; I.T.U.C., *Report of Third Congress (1896)*, p. 43. It is possible that the I.T.U.C. leaders were reluctant to bring pressure to bear on Murphy, who had subscribed to the hospitality fund of the first congress (1894) and had given delegates free passes on the Dublin tramway system.

in the afternoon. Though Michael Davitt in a series of letters easily disproved Murphy's claim that his employees were better treated than Glasgow tramwaymen, he was unable to effect any marked improvement and the union collapsed in 1904.[107] The history of the Dublin tramwaymen shows how difficult it was to organize even transport workers in unfavorable economic conditions. It has the added interest that James Larkin's efforts to unionize the same men provoked the clash with Murphy that was the signal for the six-month dispute that paralyzed Dublin in 1913.

The most enduring of the British general unions in Ireland was the National Amalgamated Union of Labour. Unlike the N.U.D.L. and the Gasworkers, the N.A.U.L. began quietly, developed slowly but steadily in its initial phase, and, though it later lost members, it was not forced to dissolve. Formed in February 1889 as the Tyneside and National Labour Union, it began among semiskilled workers and laborers in the shipbuilding and engineering works of the northeast coast of England. It opened a branch in Belfast in 1890 and had 204 members by the beginning of 1891. The report for 1890 observed that "the London, Barrow and Belfast branches are doing as well as their somewhat isolated position would lead one to expect."[108] A quarterly report in 1893 noted that "with the exception of Sheffield and Belfast our members are practically centered on the North-East coast . . . and no effort is being made to extend the union in other directions"; this situation was regarded as a matter for regret.[109] In fact, the core of the union consisted of semiskilled shipyard workers and when the organization, in common with other general unions, lost members after initial gains, it owed its survival to these men.[110]

The fortunes of the N.A.U.L. in Belfast ran counter to those of the union as a whole. At the end of 1892, it had four branches with a total of some eight hundred members and had managed to raise wages by 3s. 6d. a week for some four hundred men.[111] During the second half of

107. Dublin Trades Council minutes, 24 Mar. 1902; I.T.U.C., *Report of Ninth Congress,* pp. 44–5. The union had 480 members in 1903. In addition to Dublin unemployed Murphy could draw upon country recruits for the Royal Irish Constabulary awaiting call-up.

108. National Amalgamated Union of Labour, Tyneside and National Labour Union, Report for Year Ending 14 Feb. 1891, pp. 6, 20. Subsequent annual reports ended December 31.

109. N.A.U.L., Tyneside and N.L.U., Report for Quarter Ending 1 July 1893, p. 11.

110. In 1891 nominal membership declined from 30,237 to 26,887, paid-up membership from 17,662 to 16,280 (N.A.U.L. Report for 1893, p. 6).

111. N.A.U.L. Report for 1892, p. 5.

that year and for most of 1893 the union was engaged in a series of disputes involving platers' helpers in the Belfast shipyards of Harland and Wolff and Workman, Clark. Negotiations were complicated because the helpers were paid not by the firms but by the platers, and, though they were nominally on weekly wage rates, they were in practice paid on piecework, so that actual earnings averaged 16s. a week instead of 28s. to 30s. Some progress was made when agreement was reached in Harland and Wolff, the platers undertaking to pay their helpers at the rates prevailing in the main British shipbuilding centers (Tyne, Wear, and Clyde) and the firm raising platers' rates accordingly. But in July 1893 when the Iron Shipbuilders and Boilermakers' Society (representing the platers) agreed to a 5 percent reduction in their members' wages, the unfortunate helpers in Workman, Clark had their wages cut disproportionately. The platers attempted to use blacklegs and the N.A.U.L., faced with similar tactics in two British centers, had to spend over £2,600 in strike pay before they managed to effect a settlement.[112]

Belfast's share of the strike pay was £312, covering 130 men for six weeks. It was money well spent, for at the end of 1893 the union had eight branches with 1,706 members.[113] The union continued to expand, increasing the number of its shipyard workers' branches and forming others to cater for general workers (e.g., builders' laborers, mineral water operatives) inherited from the defunct Gasworkers, a local society calling itself City Labourers. At the end of 1897 it had twelve branches with 2,856 members, including one in Dublin.[114] From this point it lost members for some years, mainly those outside shipbuilding and engineering, and had under 1,700 at the beginning of the new century.[115] But it managed to survive the difficult years and was able to benefit by the renewed upsurge in trade unionism toward the end of the first decade. It shared in the wartime boom (in the year ending June 1917, its Irish membership leaped from 5,408 to 8,876) recruiting members all over Ulster, including agricultural laborers in County Donegal.[116] In 1924, it was one of the unions that amalgamated to form the National Union of General and Municipal Workers.

112. N.A.U.L. Report for Quarter Ending 30 Sept. 1893. F. Wrightson, district delegate, reported that if 16s. was a good average wage, 11s. was the average in one large works. Wives had to hem handkerchiefs at 3/4 d. a dozen (supplying their own thread) or work in spinning mills (ibid., p. 8).

113. N.A.U.L. Report for 1893, p. 71.

114. N.A.U.L. Report for 1897, p. 10.

115. N.A.U.L. Reports for 1898, pp. 9, 10; 1900, p. 12; 1903, p. 11.

116. N.A.U.L. Report for 1917, pp. 17, 19, 41, 45.

The Shipping Federation and the National
Free Labour Association

The Shipping Federation was established by the shipping owners as a reply to the formation of the National Union of Sailors and Firemen in 1887 and the victory of the London dockers in 1889. It united seven-eighths of all British tonnage, established in all the main ports offices at which seamen were obliged to register before they could be employed, and in 1891 introduced its own ticket which pledged the holder to work with the union and nonunion men alike. It was in effect a strike-breaking organization directed against the new general unions in ports. It formed a special labor department which undertook to supply labor to employers involved in disputes. A common procedure was to quarter the men at the waterfront in boats, which served as floating hostels and were easily protected against picketing strikers.

The Shipping Federation's most spectacular victory was in Hull. By 1892 the dockers in that port were highly organized, but during a seven-week strike, in which military and police were employed to protect the Federation blacklegs, the union's power was broken. Hull became a stronghold of "free" labor in 1893. Disputes involving general unions were often marked by violence, and the Hull pattern of employing police and military to overawe strikers was frequently repeated. The "free" labor employed was often of poor quality, inefficient at work, drunken, and of the petty criminal class.

An early example of intervention by the Shipping Federation in Ireland occurred during a Dublin corn porters' strike in 1891. The masters of Federation corn vessels refused to employ a "tallyman" per vessel to check the discharge of cargoes by the grain laborers. The tallymen, weighmen, and corn laborers struck work on Friday, June 25.[117] Graeme Hunter, a Shipping Federation official, undertook to discharge the cargoes on the quayside, leaving the merchants to carry them away. The delegation of the societies (three local unions) representing the men had earlier reached an agreement on June 22 with the merchants whereby, in return for surrendering their right to have a tallyman on each vessel, the merchants would give them facilities for checking the grain laborers' work, not introduce steam winches, and withdraw the Federation men. But the men repudiated the agreement, and the merchants formed a Merchants' Protection Association and

117. *F.J.*, 26 June 1891. The tallymen had formed a union (the Port of Dublin Grain Weighers' Tally Clerks' Trade Union) in 1888. It had a membership of 40 in 1896 and 35 in 1900. It was in abeyance in 1901, was reorganized the following year, but broke up in 1903.

called in the Federation, which agreed to shift the cargoes from the quays to the warehouses.[118]

The strike spread, involving carters and other general laborers. Meetings of the men were held regularly during the strike and addressed by Dublin Trades Council spokesmen and leaders of several unions, including Adolphus Shields of the Gasworkers, E. Donnelly of the National Union of Sailors and Firemen, and R. Foreman of the A.S.R.S. Edward McHugh, general secretary of the N.U.D.L., arrived on July 8 and also addressed the men. But the speeches of the new union leaders did not please more conservative trade unionists. At a demonstration on behalf of the strikers, held in the Phoenix Park, John Martin, president of the Dublin Trades Council, said that the Dockers' Union had subscribed one thousand pounds to the Australian strikers but not one thousand pence to the Dublin men. He condemned as a firebrand a man who had addressed them and quoted Henry George.[119]

Adolphus Shields defended the new unions, but the controversy ended with the collapse of the strike. The men went back to work unconditionally on July 18. But the Federation men were slow and inefficient and were subjected to the ridicule of the old hands, who were not afraid of the sloping planks used as the vessels rose in the water and who could do three times as much work. As a result few of the "free" laborers were retained. Almost all the carters were taken back immediately and the nonunion carters, the sons of small farmers, left of their own accord. The store hands suffered, for the merchants took back only six of the fifty strikers, replacing the rest by the strikebreakers from the country.[120]

The Shipping Federation were prepared to bring blacklegs from long distances. While some of the "free" laborers in the corn porters' strike were recruited from the countryside, more came from Belfast, Scotland, and the north of England. The strikers did not take their arrival calmly, and when a number of them were escorted by police to lodgings in the town, a crowd followed and broke some windows. The landlady then refused to take in the Federation men, who had to seek shelter elsewhere. Though they were again escorted by police, the crowd attacked them and one man was slightly injured by a law clerk who sympathized with the corn porters.[121]

The "free" laborers also clashed with police. On July 13, seven—with addresses in Glasgow, Belfast, and transit sheds at the North Wall—were fined ten shillings or seven days' imprisonment for being

118. A summary of events up to July 5 is given in *F.J.*, 6 July 1891.
119. *F.J.*, 13 July 1891.   120. *F.J.*, 20 July 1891.
121. *F.J.*, 10 July 1891.

drunk and disorderly and for resisting arrest. The magistrate before whom they appeared then accepted the evidence of one of them and sentenced three men to three months' hard labor on a charge that they had assaulted the witness.[122]

The scabs in turn had grievances. Harry Stewart, a Federation official, imported a number from Belfast, telling them that there was not a strike in Dublin, just a dispute with tallymen. Three of the men engaged complained of misrepresentation by the official. The terms offered were: five pounds for a month's work and nine pence per hour overtime, three meals a day, and tobacco and porter *ad lib*. The diet was to have been breakfast—bread, butter, and two eggs; dinner—a pound of meat and bread and potatoes; supper—tea, bread, butter and cheese. The men complained that they got no such diet and scarcely any tobacco or porter, an experience that may have shaken their faith in the virtues of "free" labor.[123]

In 1893 the Shipping Federation passed over some of their problems to an organization which they subsidized, the National Free Labour Association. It established a free labor exchange and a district office in each main area. The officials, usually ex-policemen, maintained live registers of workmen who had signed the free labor pledge—to work in harmony with union and nonunion men alike. In the early years of the twentieth century the railway companies became the principal patrons of the association.[124]

Large-scale strikebreaking by the use of nonunion labor in the skilled trades had virtually ceased by the end of the nineteenth century. The A.S.E. lost its six-month struggle for the eight-hour day in 1897–98 because it could not afford the heavy expenditure on strike pay, not because a few employers used blacklegs, some of whom, incidentally, damaged machinery owing to their lack of skill.[125] Strikebreaking organizations were of use where little skill was required and they were frequently employed in disputes involving portworkers. Trade unions in Ireland had to contend with a steady influx of nonunion labor from the country, but they were also threatened by the importation of English and Scottish blacklegs. The Shipping Federation main-

122. *F.J.*, 14 July 1891.   123. *F.J.*, 20 July 1891.

124. Most of the material on the origin and development of the Shipping Federation and its subsidiary is to be found in John Saville, "Trade Unions and Free Labour: The Background to the Taff Vale Decision," in Asa Briggs and John Saville, eds., *Essays in Labour History*, pp. 323–39, and in the evidence of Cuthbert Law, general manager of the Shipping Federation, in *Report of the Industrial Council on the Enquiry into Industrial Agreements, Minutes of Evidence*, pp. 567ff., [Cd. 6953], H.C. 1913, xxviii.

125. J. B. Jeffreys, *The Story of the Engineers*, pp. 144–9; Pelling, *History of British Trade Unionism*, pp. 112–3.

tained officials in the principal Irish ports and intervened on a number of occasions in strikes and lockouts, the two most important being the Belfast (1907) and Dublin (1913) disputes in which the workers were led by James Larkin.

Wage Rates and Membership Figures

Wage rates for the different occupations are difficult to determine, especially where employers were numerous and employees largely unorganized, or where the nature of the work did not allow wages to be expressed in simple cash payments. With this proviso in mind, some useful comparisons may be made between wage levels prevailing in Great Britain and Ireland at the end of the nineteenth century.

The average weekly wages of agricultural laborers in 1898 (there were approximately 300,000 according to the 1901 census) varied from 8s. 7d. a week in County Mayo to 12s. 7d. in County Dublin.[126] The corresponding county figures for England were 14s. 8d. and 20s. 9d. On the evidence of these official returns the highest agricultural wage in Ireland was beneath that of the lowest in Great Britain. There were no doubt individual exceptions to this general pattern, but it is also certain that the Irish rates quoted were often more notional than real; a speaker at the Irish T.U.C. in 1901 found that some agricultural laborers in County Wexford were being paid only 4s. a week.[127] For the *buchaill aimsire* or servant "boy"—he was a boy as long as he remained unmarried—who was part of the farm household, 13 pounds a year in addition to bed and board was regarded in some districts as exceptionally high.[128] If emigration, whether permanent or seasonal, provided a way of escape for the discontented it also made the task of union organization more difficult and so perpetuated low wage levels.

Domestic service was the female equivalent of agricultural labor for men and 166,672 were so employed in Ireland in 1901. In the Belfast area, however, the linen industry did employ a considerable number of women workers.[129] A survey published in 1899 by the Labour Department of the Board of Trade showed that in Ireland over 20 percent of

126. *Report on Wages and Earnings of Agricultural Labourers in the United Kingdom, 1898,* [Cd. 346] H.C. 1900. The highest rates were paid in the vicinity of Dublin and Belfast.

127. I.T.U.C., Annual Report, Eighth Congress, p. 37. The speaker, James Chambers, was a poor law guardian. Meals were also supplied.

128. See Boyle, "A Marginal Figure: The Irish Rural Labourer" in S. Clark and J. S. Donnelly, Jr., *Irish Peasants: Violence and Political Unrest,* pp. 321–22.

129. There were 22,939 female linen workers in Belfast (48,886 in the entire linen industry—all processes) and 7,556 domestic servants.

domestic servants were over forty-five years of age, the corresponding percentage for Great Britain being under 10 percent.[130] The Irish version of Esther Waters was also worse paid than her British counterpart, the average yearly wage ranging from £15 1s. (Belfast) to £12 3s. (Cork and Limerick) as against a British scale of £17 8s. (London) to £16 (the rest of England and Wales).[131] The source and smallness of the Irish sample and the assumption that the proportion of one-servant households which paid the lowest wages was the same as that of London tended to inflate the Irish averages. The writer of the report was aware of the second deficiency and suggested that the Munster general average was probably not above £10 and that those of Ulster and Leinster fell between £12 and £14. Her wage rate for one-servant households in Dublin was £10 8s., but newspaper advertisements suggest that this is an inflated figure.[132] In 1899, £9 awaited a general servant whose character "must bear strictest investigation" and whose duties where to include plain cooking, early rising, and washing, while strength and humility were required of girls to be paid between £6 and £8.[133] There was, of course, no union for domestic servants, but the presence of such a large number of generally underpaid and overworked women should not be forgotten.

We have seen that the aristocrats of labor in Ireland were the skilled shipbuilding and engineering workers, especially those in Belfast, commanding wage rates high in the Belfast scale. Wages in the building trade throughout the United Kingdom varied according to area. The highest were paid in London, the next highest in large or strongly industrialized towns, and the lowest in the smaller country towns. The hourly rates in Belfast and Dublin for bricklayers, masons, carpenters, plumbers, plasterers, and painters at the beginning of 1901 were 8d.[134] In England and Wales the range was from 7½d. (Ipswich) to 10d. (London). The lowest Irish rates, those paid in the country towns, are not available, but even the highest Irish rates did not equal those paid in such comparable British centers as Sheffield. That the Dublin and

---

130. *Money Wages of Indoor Domestic Servants;* Report by Miss (Clara E.) Collet to the Labour Department of the Board of Trade, p. 11 [c. 9346] H.C. 1899, xcii. i. The report was compiled from forms sent to mistresses between 1894 and 1898. In a prefatory letter the Commissioner for Labour noted that one-third of the gainfully occupied female population of the United Kingdom in 1891 was engaged in domestic service. The 339 Irish returns came from Belfast, Dublin, Cork, and Limerick and their immediate neighborhood. They did not include domestic servants on farms or in small country towns. The large percentage of Irish servants over 45 is, despite Miss Collet, to be explained by the higher Irish emigration and lower marriage rates.

131. Ibid., p. 8.   132. Ibid., p. 10.

133. *F.J.,* 11 Jan. 1899.

134. The Belfast rate tended to be slightly higher.

Belfast rates were not below the British minimum is to be explained by the men's membership of long established craft unions and their ability to seek work in England.

Pay rates in one other skilled occupation—the tailoring trade—deserve attention. The Amalgamated Society of Tailors had strong Irish sections by the last decade of the nineteenth century and were prepared to spend generously in their interests. The hourly rates in 1888 were 4*d*. to 5½*d*. in Belfast, 3½*d*. to 5½*d*. in Dublin, and 4½*d*. in Cork. These figures were below those prevailing in London (5*d*. to 7*d*.), Birmingham, and Liverpool (6*d*.), but not out of line with the figure for Leeds (5*d*.), an important clothing center.[135] Enforcing reasonable wage rates in country towns was a very different matter, as the Typographical Association knew by bitter experience, but at least in the important centers Irish tailors were not seriously underpaid by British standards.

In general Irish skilled workers in the large towns were able to maintain wage rates and hours of labor that were not seriously out of line with those of British tradesmen; the position of the semiskilled and unskilled was decidedly inferior in so far as it is possible to judge by the evidence available. Despite the efforts of the A.S.R.S., the average weekly earnings of Irish railway workers in the coaching, goods, locomotive, and engineering departments were markedly lower, the figures for the first week of December 1899 for England, Scotland, and Ireland being 25*s*. 9¾*d*., 22*s*. 10¾*d*., and 19*s*. 4½*d*.; these differentials in wage levels had existed at least as early as 1896 and were not diminished by the notable but admittedly temporary increase in A.S.R.S. membership during 1896–97.[136] Belfast shipbuilding and engineering tradesmen were among the highest paid workers in the British Isles, but the semiskilled and laborers who assisted them were wretchedly paid, their weekly earnings of 16*s*. being some 6*s*. below those of platers' helpers in British centers in the early 1890s.[137] At a Gasworkers' organizing meeting for tobacco spinners in November 1890, W. J. McManus of the Belfast Trades Council stated that men had come to him in October to say that they worked seventeen hours a

135. *Statistical Tables and Reports on Trade Unions for 1888*, pp. 337–9, [C. 5808], H.C. 1889, lxxxiv, 156.

136. *Report on the Changes in Rates of Wages and Hours of Labour in the United Kingdom in 1902*, p. xliv, [Cd. 1562], H.C. 1903, lxvi, 839.

137. It seems that most of the Catholics in these Belfast industries were laborers. It should, however, be remembered that, quite apart from religious discrimination, there was a strong temptation for laborers' children to start unskilled work, which initially brought in more money than did the years of apprenticeship to a skilled trade. This was a factor that operated independently of religious or political allegiance and tended to check social mobility.

day for a weekly wage of 12s. to 18s.[138] It is not possible to cover in detail the wage rates or earnings of workers in the many semiskilled and unskilled occupations at the end of the nineteenth century, but it cannot be disputed that these Irish workers, though some qualification must be made in the case of Belfast, were at the bottom of the United Kingdom's social and economic pyramid.

Belfast offered better employment prospects and somewhat better housing than did Dublin, but it had its sweated occupations, notably those in the linen industry. The average weekly wages were 4s. and 12s. in 1886 and 1906 respectively. The labor force was very mixed, employing half-timers as well as juveniles and adults of both sexes. The flaxdressers and flax roughers, with unions of their own, earned wages which rose to over 1 pound a week in 1906 (roughers 12s. 8d., sorters 26s. 3d.). Much of the work was done by women and girls at wages averaging from 10s. 5d. for spinners to 11s. 6d. for weavers. The half-timers, aged between eleven and thirteen (the minimum age was raised to twelve in 1901) divided their week between school and work, earning approximately 3s. 6d. for a week of some twenty-eight hours. Linen workers, especially in the preparation and spinning processes, were liable to a series of occupational diseases of the respiratory system and the skin, or ran the hazards of accidents from poorly fenced machinery. The factory inspectors' reports even in the first decade of the twentieth century constitute a litany of complaints that singled out the Belfast district as the blackest spot in the industrial areas of the United Kingdom.[139] The Belfast Trades Council made several efforts in the last twenty years of the nineteenth century to unionize women linen workers, but the Textile Operatives' Society of Ireland, the union it formed in 1893, with great difficulty raised its enrollment from 1,050 in 1896 to 1,444 in 1903. The addition of over one thousand in 1907, bringing the membership to 3,023, reflected the general labor militancy in Belfast during that year.[140] The union did best in the more highly paid weaving end, though the greatest need for improved pay and working conditions was in the spinning mills.

The statistics furnished by British general unions are not sufficiently complete to allow an accurate determination of their Irish membership;

138. *Belfast Weekly Star*, 8 Nov. 1890.

139. D. L. Armstrong, "Social and Economic Conditions in the Belfast Linen Industry, 1850–1900," in *I.H.S.*, vii, 235–69; *Report of the Chief Inspector of Factories for 1906*, pp. 144–5, [Cd. 3586], H.C. 1907. Linen remained a low-wage, unhealthy industry until after 1945.

140. *Ninth Report on Trade Unions for 1896*, pp. 408–9, [C.8644]; *Report on Trade Unions for 1905–7*, pp. 826–7, [Cd. 4651].

nor have we satisfactory information on the strength of the smaller ephemeral Irish unions. It is nonetheless possible to reach some tentative conclusions. The year 1891 marks the maximum Irish membership of British unions catering for the unskilled and semiskilled, some five to six thousand. With the addition of four thousand members of Irish laborers' unions, the grand total in Ireland rises to about ten thousand. After 1891 there was a sharp decline, a veritable collapse in some cases, and though the N.A.U.L. continued to make progress it could not compensate for the disasters that befell the N.U.D.L. and the Gasworkers; after 1897 the N.A.U.L. itself lost 50 percent of its membership. General unions in Great Britain also lost heavily during the same period but the major bodies survived.[141] In Ireland the renaissance of general unionism had to await James Larkin in 1907.

When the Irish T.U.C. was founded in 1894, the Gasworkers had already vanished and the N.U.D.L., seriously weakened, had begun to decline. As a consequence of its ephemeral nature in Ireland, the "new unionism" could not have the impact on the Irish T.U.C. that it had on the British body. The A.S.R.S., though not a "new union," since its weekly subscription of 5 *d.* placed it above such a category, because of its size might have modified the influence of the older craft unions that dominated the Irish trade union center, but its own severe losses after 1897 put an end to such a possibility.

The progress of British skilled unions in Ireland resulted in a situation in which a large majority of Irish trade unionists belonged to British trade unions. We do not have the necessary details to determine the exact total of all union members in Ireland, or of those belonging to British unions, but the affiliations, mainly British, to the Irish T.U.C. give us some indication of the proportions in question. In 1895 affiliations amounted to 50,000 and the membership of Irish unions, as given by the Board of Trade, to 17,476; two years later the respective figures were 52,000 and 18,898.[142] This preponderance was even greater than the figures suggest since the statistics given by the Board of Trade for Irish unions were more complete than those furnished by Irish T.U.C. membership. It is clear that Irish members of British

141. See E. J. Hobsbawm, "General Labour Unions in Britain, 1889–1914" in *Economic History Review,* 2nd, ser., I, nos. 2 and 3 (1949).

142. *I. T. U. C. Report, Second Congress, 1895,* p. 17; *Eighth Report on Trade Unions for 1895,* p. 63, [C. 8232]; *I. T. U. C. Report, Fourth Congress,* p. 34; *Tenth Report on Trade Unions for 1897,* pp. 2–124, [C. 9013]. For 1895 the eighth report listed Irish unions separately and gave a grand total for their membership, but for 1897 the tenth report, which was much more elaborate, listed them under the various categories of trades, following the English and Scottish unions, and did not give a grand total for them, hence the reference to so many pages in the 1897 report.

unions must have accounted for at least three-quarters of the total trade union membership in Ireland at the end of the nineteenth century.

Trade unionists in Ireland were undoubtedly in a stronger position at the end of the nineteenth century than they had been fifty years earlier, for the great majority, those in amalgamated unions, could now count on the backing of their British headquarters in industrial disputes. But the reluctance of British unions to encourage the formation of autonomous Irish executives or to give the Irish T.U.C. adequate financial support left the Irish congress relatively powerless, and it remained for a number of years conservative in outlook, a preserve of craft unions, untouched by the surge of militant general unionism. It might have lost some of its conservatism had it or its constituent unions supported the formation of an Irish Labour Party, but such a decision would have forced it to take sides on the contentious questions in Irish politics, of which Home Rule was the most explosive. It clung to an uneasy neutrality that was preserved only by allowing individual delegates or groups to go their own political ways outside congress, but the indecisive debates that at times threatened the unity of the organization were evidence of the unresolved tensions that lay close to the surface of its deliberations.

6

The Origins of the Irish Trades
Union Congress

After an interval of eleven years Irish delegates resumed attendance at congresses of the British T.U.C. At its Edinburgh congress in 1879 the British organization, after considerable discussion, chose Dublin rather than Manchester as the seat of the 1880 conference. This first meeting on Irish soil drew twenty-four Irish delegates, all from Dublin. Nearly half represented British unions or Irish societies linked in a United Kingdom federation, the most notable being the Amalgamated Society of Engineers, the Amalgamated Society of Carpenters and Joiners, the Amalgamated Society of Tailors and the Ironfounders of England, Ireland, and Wales. In accordance with precedent, the president (John Murphy, an ironfounder) and secretary (John Ward of the Dublin Painters' Society) were local men.[1]

Irish contributions, whether by delegates at congress debates or by speakers at public meetings, were not of a temper to alarm upholders of private enterprise. The president assured the public that the congress did not come to Ireland to make an attack on capital—"for if I thought it did I should not be here."[2] William Abraham, a Dublin A.S.C.J. delegate and later an Irish nationalist M.P., objected to the encouragement given to the cooperative movement in the Parliamentary Committee's report and expressed his intention of moving that the coop-

---

1. This account of the 1880 congress is based of the report of the thirteenth annual congress of the British T.U.C. and on reports in the following newspapers: *F.J.*, 13–18 Sept. 1880; *B.N.-L.*, 14, 15, 20 Sept. 1880; *Irish Times*, 17 Sept. 1880. Clarkson, p. 178, n. 4, repeats the mistake of the British T.U.C. report in describing Ward as a baker. Ward himself said that, though a painter, he had to thank the bakers for electing him to represent them (*I.T.*, 17 Sept. 1889). Ward was one of the trades' representatives at various Dublin Home Rule and nationalist meetings in the 1870s (see *Irishman*, 12 June 1875, 1 Jan. 1876, 23 Feb. 1878), where he was described as president of the Painters' Society. Ward was also a delegate to the first congress of the Irish T.U.C. in 1894.

2. *B.N.-L.*, 15 Sept. 1880.

erative system would be unsuitable to Ireland and would destroy all private speculation.[3] J. K. Ingram,[4] a Positivist (Fellow of Trinity College, Dublin) read a paper to congress on "Work and Workmen." He asserted that the existence of a capitalist class and the maintenance of its independence were necessary to the public interest—"but *richesse oblige.*" He denounced attempts to depress wages in order to meet foreign competition and criticized those capitalist spokesmen whose aim, it would seem, was to have a working population content to live so miserably that they could drive others out of the markets of the world. But he dismissed producer cooperation as a solution and urged work-men to concentrate on securing decent wages, a well-regulated home, and adequate leisure and education. His conclusion was unexception-able: "What is really important for working men is not that a few should rise out of their class—this sometimes rather injures the class by depriving it of its more energetic members. The truly vital interest is that the whole class should rise in material comfort and security, and still more in intellectual and moral attainments."[5]

Ingram did not indicate how these objectives were to be attained. The attainment of one of them, adequate leisure through the limitation of working hours, provoked a debate that showed the ignorance of conditions in Irish industry prevalent among English delegates. The mover of a motion to protect the existing hours of labor had to recast it when he discovered that he was demanding the retention in some Irish trades of a working week of sixty-three hours. The Dublin joiner Abraham complained that the hours worked in the building trades of the city amounted to a day more in the week than in any other town or city in the United Kingdom, so that Irish tradesmen were encouraged to overstock the market in English towns and take the bread out of people's mouths there. John Ward replied that he was not in favor of a sixty-hour week but he did not see how they could get out of the difficulty without injuring the interests of employer and employed. Since payment was by the hour in Dublin any reduction in time would mean a reduction in pay. He denied that English workers resented Irish competition, just as the presence in his own trade of over one hundred English and Scottish workers did not provoke resentment among Dub-lin craftsmen.[6] Further information about working conditions in Dub-lin was supplied at a meeting organized to promote a women workers' union. One speaker, a London tailoress, said that the wages paid in the

3. *F.J.*, 15 Sept. 1880.

4. Ingram in his youth wrote a popular ballad, "Who fears to speak of '98?" In later years he was distressed by its vogue among militant Irish nationalists and claimed that its sentiments no longer applied in the happier conditions that then prevailed.

5. *F.J.*, 17 Sept. 1880.   6. *F.J., I.T.*, 17 Sept. 1880.

Irish capital in the best shops were scarcely paid in the lowest "slop shops" in London—such low wages were paid only in the East End among what they called the "German sweaters."[7]

The general tone of the Irish delegates' speeches was apologetic and in no sense critical of their English guests. Some references to the decay in Irish industries were made, but there was general agreement that a greater degree of trade union organization in Ireland and greater intercourse between English and Irish societies would solve many problems. A Manchester speaker considered it disgraceful that their Irish brethren had not helped English and Scottish trade unionists more, but blamed his fellow countrymen for not explaining the benefits of trade unionism to Irish workers.[8] An A.S.C.J. delegate, presiding at the annual dinner of his union, attributed his union's difficulties in Dublin to the short-sightedness of local societies and pointed out that in the last twelve months the A.S.C.J. had spent 200 pounds in unemployment benefit and 120 pounds in sick pay in the city.[9] Yet, apart from general exhortation, no steps were taken to ensure greater Irish participation in the work of the British congress, no Irish member being elected to its ruling body, the Parliamentary Committee.

Dublin trade unionists were not stimulated by the 1880 congress to resume attendance at subsequent meetings. With the exception of 1882, when John Murphy represented the Ironfounders, no Dublin delegates appeared until 1888, though an occasional modest subscription was sent. The burden of Irish participation was assumed by the Belfast Trades Council (formed in 1881) and its founder secretary, the energetic Alexander Bowman, a flaxdresser. Bowman attended in 1882 and 1883 and secured subscriptions to congress from a number of Belfast societies. Though he was unsuccessful in elections to the Parliamentary Committee he spoke frequently in discussions. When in 1882 Congress debated the desirability of making the Employers' Liability Act compulsory rather than permissive Bowman wanted it to be mandatory on the grounds that county court judges in Ireland were preeminently hostile to the working classes—a Belfast judge had described trades unionism as communism or nihilism.[10] In a later discussion of the powers vested in courts of summary jurisdiction Bowman repeated his criticism of Irish magistrates, busily engaged in trying defendants on charges of agrarian disturbances during the tumult of the land war (1879–82): "It was deplorable that outrages so often occurred, and that the law was so often violated, but there was a point beyond which

---

7. *F.J.*, 18 Sept. 1880.   8. *F.J.*, 16 Sept. 1880.
9. *F.J.*, 17 Sept. 1880.
10. British Trades Union Congress, *Report, Fifteenth Annual Congress*, p. 22.

submission ceased to be a virtue."[11] A Manchester A.S.E. delegate, who had lived in Ireland a decade earlier, claimed that Belfast magistrates were the most impartial in the Kingdom and could not believe that things had changed. The subsequent controversy over coercion ended only when the phrase implying that Ireland was "governed by coercion after coercion" had been withdrawn.

Bowman was a Liberal Home Ruler in politics and as a result of taking part in political controversy during the period of the first Home Rule Bill (1886) he was forced to resign as secretary of the Belfast Trades Council. No Belfast delegate attended the British T.U.C. in 1885 or the following year. In 1887 the Belfast representative was a compositor, Samuel Monro; unlike Bowman he was a Unionist in politics. When standing orders were suspended and a motion introduced condemning the suppression of a meeting in Ennis, County Clare, on the grounds that the right of free speech was being denied, Monro objected strongly. He considered it a political motion and insisted, despite laughter, on moving an amendment recognizing the necessity of law and order being established in Ireland and obedience to the law enforced before grievances were remedied. Renewed laughter greeted his defense of a coercion act, his amendment was overwhelmingly defeated, and the original resolution carried over his solitary opposing vote.[12]

For some years Irish political questions ceased to stir controversy at British congresses. In 1888 the Belfast and Dublin Trades Councils sent their secretaries as delegates, and in 1889 only Belfast was represented. A marked increase in attendance occurred in 1890, when five Irish delegates were present, two of them representing new general unions, the Gas workers and the National Union of Sailors and Firemen.

In 1891 six attended,[13] four from Belfast, including the Trades Council delegate, and two from Dublin, though the Dublin council would have been represented by its president had he not died shortly after his selection.[14] The following year the numbers rose to ten, largely owing to the increased representation of the Belfast Trades Council, which sent four delegates instead of one in a successful effort to have the 1893 congress held in Belfast. The invitation was issued by Samuel Monro and supported by H. Slatter of Manchester, a fellow compositor, who urged that trade unionism was the hope of Ireland and

11. Ibid., 26–7.
12. B.T.U.C., *Report, Twentieth Congress*, pp. 17–18.
13. B.T.U.C., *Report, Twenty-fourth Congress*, pp. 1, 5, 6, 12, 14.
14. *F.J.*, 27 July, 8 Aug. 1891.

added somewhat optimistically that the cause would be helped if the congress were held the following year in Belfast.[15] Influenced by such a plea, the delegates gave Belfast an absolute majority over Norwich, which had beaten it into third place the previous year.[16]

If the Irish attendance in the 1880s at the British T.U.C. was fitful, there was a pronounced development in the growth of local trade union centers. The Belfast United Trades' Council was formed in 1881,[17] and though its numbers were few at first, by 1892 it claimed twelve thousand affiliated members.[18] The corresponding Dublin body, a stronger organization than its predecessor the United Trades' Association, held its first formal meeting early in 1886,[19] and paid dues to the British T.U.C. on seven thousand members in 1892.[20] By this date trades councils also existed in a number of other towns, notably Cork, Newry, and Drogheda. Membership of such councils was drawn mainly from carpenters, joiners, bakers, painters, or tailors, but also included among affiliated bodies a number of general laborers' unions, at first organized on a purely local basis.

A fresh attempt to form an Irish federation was made in 1888, the Dublin Trades Council taking the initiative. Its treasurer, T. J. O'Reilly, a printer, impressed by the power of the Irish National League, the rank-and-file organization of Parnell's Irish parliamentary party, suggested organizing on the same plan "for an affiliation of the trades throughout not only Ireland but the United Kingdom." He was confident that the trades councils of Cork and Belfast would heartily cooperate. "By this means they could consult before elections, and they would in time be a power in the country. The Trades' Congress in England was a power which was not only respected but feared, and until they were feared they would never be respected. Why should they not have an Irish Congress meeting in Dublin?" His suggestion was supported by members of both Irish and amalgamated (British) unions, including two members of the A.S.E.[21]

Favorable replies were received from a number of trades councils (e.g., those of Cork, Clonmel, and Waterford),[22] but the Belfast Trades Council was more cautious. It set up a special committee to consider the matter[23] and received the following report: "Your committee are of

15. B.T.U.C., *Report, Twenty-fifth Congress*, p. 66.

16. B.T.U.C., *Report, Twenty-fourth Congress*, p. 76.

17. 29 Oct. 1881, according to a date stamp in old minute books. Those of 1881–5 are missing.

18. B.T.U.C., *Report, Twenty-fifth Congress*.

19. (Dublin) *Evening Mail*, 1 Mar. 1886; J. Swift, *Dublin Bakers*, p. 294.

20. B.T.U.C., *Report, Twenty-fifth Congress*.

21. *F.J.*, 12 May 1888.   22. *F.J.*, 3, 10 Dec. 1888.

23. Belfast Trades Council minutes, 24 Nov. 1888.

the opinion that a federation of the different trades throughout Ireland would be of great advantage to trade unionism. And would recommend the Belfast United Trades Council to assist the Dublin Trades Council in bringing the matter to a successful issue."[24] The report was accepted unanimously, but on the reception of a draft scheme it was decided that the affiliated societies should first be consulted before the council committed itself.[25] Though the coach-builders and patternmakers reported favorably, the painters' delegate said his society was opposed to a federation, and the whole matter was referred to an augmented committee of nine.[26] When it was finally decided to send delegates to Dublin, the original motion to send three was carried only after amendments to send one and two had been defeated. The council also recommended every society to send delegates.[27]

The Irish Federated Trade and Labour Union, the title finally adopted, held its first conference on 4 May 1889 in the Angel hotel, Dublin.[28] Thirty-three delegates were present from Belfast, Clonmel, Cork, Derry, Dublin, Limerick, and Waterford with Belfast (eight) and Dublin (ten) providing over half the number. Cork's six delegates included Eugene Crean, a town councillor, and Michael Austin, both of whom were later to be the two successful candidates among the seven labor-nationalists recommended by Michael Davitt for the general election of 1892.[29] The offices were filled with due regard to the importance of the various centers. Dublin provided the chairman (J. Ward, of the Dublin Regular Painters), Belfast the vice-chairman (W. J. McManus), and Cork (Michael Austin) and Dublin (T. J. O'Reilly) the joint secretaries. A central council of nine was elected, three from Dublin and one from each of the other centers. Derry's representative was James McCarron of the Amalgamated Society of Tailors, who was to preside at three conferences of the Irish Trades Union Congress in later years. A decision was taken to hold congresses annually and to meet the following year in Belfast.

The congress was gratified by British trade union blessings. Letters of goodwill were read from the temporary chairman (J. Drummond, secretary of the London Society of Compositors) and the secretary (George Shipton, London House Decorators and Painters) of the London Trades Council, and at a later stage in the proceedings J. Havelock Wilson, then secretary of the Glasgow Firemen and Seamen's Union

24. Ibid., 8 Dec. 1888.   25. Ibid., 12 Jan. 1889.
26. Ibid., 9 Feb. 1889.   27. Ibid., 23 Feb. 1889.
28. Report in *F.J.*, 6 May 1889, on which this account is based.
29. T. W. Moody, "Michael Davitt and the British Labour Movement, 1882–1906," in *Transactions of the Royal Historical Society*, 5th ser., vol. iii, 1953, p. 70.

and engaged in organizing a branch in Dublin,[30] entered amid applause and addressed the delegates. The chairman was highly sensible of the value of the British connection: "There is a great field for operation before us if we would only follow the grand example of our English and Scotch brothers, whom we this day salute, and to whose glorious union, I trust, we may be soon affiliated, and thus acknowledge in an unmistakable way our appreciation of the many Acts of Parliament passed through their organisation and which we enjoy today." Nor did he forget another aspect of British congresses when he hoped that at future Irish congresses "the wealthy members of the community would imitate the grand hospitality displayed by their English and Scotch peers."

The principal demands of the congress, whether by resolution or in the chairman's address, were the abolition of sweating and boy labor, a reduction in the hours of labor, more enterprise on the part of home manufacturers, additional factory inspectors, the provision of technical education and free libraries, and the formation of more trades councils and women's trade unions. The absence of workmen from local town councils and parliament was severely commented upon, and there was unanimous agreement that the municipal franchise should be assimilated to that of parliament, and that the expenses of elections and parliamentary representatives should be borne by the state. Unanimous too was the decision to postpone publication of a trade journal after W. J. Leahy (Dublin Regular Coopers) had pointed out that it would be unfair when the *Freeman's Journal* was giving them support. Harmony was the keynote of the dinner, also held in the Angel and attended by over 120, which concluded the congress. T. J. O'Reilly, echoing the chairman's tribute to "our Northern brethren who were, by their alacrity, the first to infuse fresh vigour into us," paid a compliment to Samuel Monro, the Belfast Trades Council president, who, amid applause, replied somewhat hyperbolically that there was "only an imaginary difference between the men of Belfast and those of the rest of Ireland."

Prospects for the growth of the Irish Federated Trade and Labour Union seemed bright, and it began to assume the appearance of a trades union congress. The Belfast Trades Council called its central council's attention to Fenwick's[31] bill for the payment of weekly wages,[32] and the Belfast delegates' report was considered very satisfactory in June

30. The branch became affiliated to the Dublin Trades Council shortly afterwards (*F.J.*, 10 June 1889).
31. Charles Fenwick, the "Lib-Lab" Northumbrian miners' M.P.
32. B.T.C. minutes, 8 June 1889.

1889.[33] But a storm suddenly blew up in August when the Dublin Trades Council asked for contributions towards a Sunday sports meeting to be run under the auspices of the federation. "A very warm discussion" followed the reading of the offending circular, and it was unanimously agreed that the secretary enter a "solemn protest" against associating Belfast with the Sunday meeting and request the removal of the name of the Belfast council's vice-president (W. J. McManus) from the circular.[34]

The incident was to have a damaging effect on the growth of the new body. O'Reilly followed up the unlucky circular with a letter asking what Belfast was likely to subscribe towards its funds, and it is not surprising that the Belfast council determined to defer the matter and at a later stage decided that its delegate W. J. McManus should not attend an executive meeting in Dublin.[35] A correspondence lasting some months ensued, Belfast expressing in a lengthy resolution its dissatisfaction with the federation's reply, which, while acknowledging that a mistake had been made in the past, gave no pledge against its recurrence. Such an action tended "to violate those principles of combination which are the basis of a true federation of labour."[36] The council turned its attention to less contentious matters and accepted the lord mayor's invitation to draw up a loyal address of welcome to be presented to the lord lieutenant on his visit to Belfast. But although the council increased its indebtedness (its expenditure for the previous year exceeded its income) the address, "beautifully engraved on vellum . . . and fastened with blue silk ribbon" was a source of irritation, for Richard Sheldon, the prime mover in the matter, complained that the council had been insulted; their representatives had neither been asked to present the address nor invited to represent the working classes at the civic banquet.[37]

The subsequent relationship of Belfast to the federation remained obscure, even to the Belfast delegates, for notice of a question on the matter was given twice during the opening months of 1890 without any answer forthcoming.[38] A letter from the federation president in May provoked a motion that the council sever its connection with the federation but pay its share of costs already incurred; this was amended to an instruction to the secretary to reopen correspondence and ascer-

33. Ibid., 22 June 1889.   34. Ibid., 10 Aug. 1889.

35. Ibid., 24 Aug., 28 Sept., 18, 26 Oct. 1889.

36. Ibid., 9 Nov. 1889.

37. Ibid., 21, 28 Dec. 1889, 1 Feb. 1890. The address was suitably loyal, but also included a moderately worded plea for improvements in working-class conditions (N.W., 18 Jan. 1890).

38. B.T.C. minutes, 22 Mar., 22 Apr. 1890.

tain how the council stood financially with the suspect body.[39] When the cabinetmakers later in the year asked that the ten shillings they had subscribed towards the formation of the federation should be forwarded to its executive, F. C. Johnston, a coachbuilder, carried an amendment that it be returned to the local branch as soon as funds permitted.[40] Johnston, who had been secretary of the council from January to October of that year, had distinguished his tenure of office by visiting England on a Unionist political mission;[41] he was to appear later as a Unionist candidate in municipal elections.[42]

The relationship between the trades councils of the two cities was for some time marked by considerable caution on the part of Belfast. When the Dublin body invited its cooperation in welcoming a visiting Australian trade unionist, John Fitzgerald, the secretary was instructed, "after considerable discussion," to seek further information and a guarantee that the "gentlemen named in the printed circular would not introduce political or religious questions during their visit to Belfast, but confine themselves to labour questions.[43] The word "federation" was out of favor, and even a circular from the Hull Trades Council on a proposed federation of all labor bodies was marked *read*.[44] The furious Parnell leadership controversy following the Parnell-O'Shea divorce case was an added reason for wary walking during 1891.

1891 was a year of much labor activity in Dublin. A meeting[45] was held on 28 February to celebrate the first anniversary of the Dublin gasworkers' success (they were members of Will Thorne's union) in winning an eight-hour day. The union's Irish organizer, Michael Canty, called for a federation of labor and its district secretary, Adolphus Shields, announced that they would have a conference with Parnell on the labor question. A fortnight later a conference, composed almost entirely of general laborers, both of town and country, gathered in the Antient Concert Rooms.[46] Canty successfully moved the adoption of a motion, to stand as the first clause in their program, for a universal legal eight-hour day. A motion for free and compulsory education was withdrawn, thus sidestepping an amendment to insert the word "secular," which, a speaker warned, would bring workingmen into conflict with a large section of the Irish clergy. They adopted all of the remaining clauses of the program: nationalization of land and transport; triennial parliaments; manhood suffrage; payment of M.P.s, local councillors, and election expenses; extension of the factory and employers' liability acts; taxation of land values; the employment of direct labor;

39. Ibid., 9 May 1890.
41. Ibid., 22 Mar. 1890.
43. B.T.C. minutes, 22 Nov. 1890.
45. F.J., 2 Mar. 1891.

40. Ibid., 10 Oct. 1890.
42. B.N.-L., 24 Nov. 1897.
44. Ibid., 24 Jan. 1891.
46. F.J., 16 Mar. 1891.

the removal of food taxes; evening sittings of local boards; greater liberty for labor combinations; the promotion of all Irish industries; increased building of laborers' dwellings and the lowering of their rents.

Having decided to call the new organization the Irish Labour League, the conference appointed an executive committee on which four places were to be reserved for delegates of the skilled trades and then adjourned until the afternoon, when they were to be addressed by Parnell. The nature of the afternoon session alarmed a Belfast delegate, who felt that Colonel Saunderson, the Ulster Unionist leader, might equally well have been invited, and that there was a danger of the meeting being given a political complexion. His fear had some substance, for Parnell's skillful speech, in which he contented himself with pleasing generalities, was greeted by applause and interjections directed against the anti-Parnellites. When he left the building he was preceded by the Gasworkers' band to a political demonstration.

The future of the Irish Labour League was not bright, for the skilled trades had taken no part in the meeting. The Cork Trades Council promised to "watch with interest the result of your proceedings," but the Dublin council had earlier voted overwhelmingly against sending any delegates on the grounds that "any such conference should be held aloof from all political parties."[47] The minutes of the Belfast Trades Council are significantly silent on the matter. While Parnell's early death removed a dubious labor champion, at this stage success could scarcely attend a body which the craft unions had not founded.

Despite the coldness they had shown, the skilled trades in Dublin joined with the laborers in a vast May Day demonstration,[48] in which over ten thousand trade unionists marched with banners and bands to the Phoenix Park. The call for an international Labour Day, first issued for May Day 1890 by the Second International, had been answered then in Dublin by only two of the newly established general laborers' unions, but in 1891 much stress was laid on the all-inclusive nature of that year's celebration. Three platforms were used so that the processionists and the thousands who accompanied them might have a chance of hearing the speeches. The president of the Dublin trades council, John Martin, was the chairman at the principal platform, and other officers of the council were among the speakers at the other two hustings. In spite of their presence there was a strong Parnellite tone in some of the speeches, particularly in that of Adolphus Shields, who claimed that Parnell had pledged himself to an eight-hour day, universal suffrage, and "almost . . . to land nationalisation and to many other

47. *F.J.*, 9 Mar. 1891.   48. *F.J.*, 4 May 1891.

reforms." The four resolutions, moved at each platform, called for an eight-hour day, "by legislation or otherwise," a greater degree of trade union organization, revision of laws affecting labor and capital, and the assimilation of the municipal and parliamentary franchise, with, as a corollary, representation of Irish labor in parliament. Visiting British speakers included one Davidson of the London Dockers and Pete Curran of the Gasworkers, and there was sympathetic reference to the imprisonment suffered by Curran and Havelock Wilson.[49] A car containing police notetakers, protected by a detachment of police, was stationed close to one of the platforms. There was, however, no sequel in the form of police action, and the *Freeman's Journal,* at that time still a Parnellite organ, commented favorably on the orderliness of the Dublin demonstration as against riotous behavior on the continent. Drogheda also had its May Day demonstration, at which the same resolutions were moved.

Labor activity continued unabated in Dublin. A fortnight after the May Day celebration, the Gasworkers held another demonstration. The speakers included Will Thorne, Pete Curran, and Edward and Eleanor Marx Aveling, all of whom were prominent in the organization of the unskilled in Great Britain.[50] Later in the same month the project of an Irish congress was revived by John Martin, president of the Dublin Trades Council, when he reported to that body that the executive had considered holding a trades conference in June to consider labor representation. He believed that there was every possiblity of carrying two seats in Dublin and two to four in the country by labor candidates selected by the conference and bound to no political party. Every trade body and society throughout Ireland should be represented at the conference, which would discuss the best means of supporting their representatives in parliament. In England, he pointed out, several districts were represented by workmen.[51]

This fresh start owed something to Michael Davitt who, in a conversation [52] with Martin and John Simmons (secretary of the Dublin Trades Council) late in 1890 had suggested that the labor leaders of the large towns be invited to confer with the Dublin officials upon the advisability of forming an Irish labor federation.[53] Davitt had earlier

49. Wilson was serving a sentence of six weeks' imprisonment on a charge of unlawful assembly and riot during a dock strike in Cardiff (*B.N.-L.* 8 Apr. 1891).

50. *F.J.,* 18 May 1891.   51. *F.J.,* 25 May 1891.

52. It was primarily concerned with arrangements for a Dublin meeting to be addressed by the Australian John Fitzgerald, John Burns, Tom Mann, and Cunninghame Graham.

53. *F.J.,* 10 Nov. 1890.

(21 January 1890) presided over the formation of an Irish Democratic Trade and Labour Federation at a convention in Cork;[54] it was mainly an organization of agricultural laborers and workers in country towns, and had Michael Austin as one of its joint secretaries.[55] Davitt's suggestion to Martin and Simmons was probably prompted by a desire to see the Irish trade unions exercising on the Irish party the influence that the British unions had on the Liberal Party in matters of social reform.

The conference was held in July in the new trade union headquarters (Capel Street), and was attended by delegates representing skilled and unskilled unions, mainly from Dublin, but including officers from the trades councils of Cork, Clonmel, Drogheda, Sligo, and Newry.[56] The Irish Democratic Labour Federation sent three delegates, one of whom was Michael Austin, and agricultural laborers were further represented by four delegates from midland branches of a local labor federation. Belfast and Derry were not represented, though it would appear that Belfast at least had been invited to attend.[57] John Martin and Michael Austin were elected president and vice president, and an executive committee "to form the nucleus of an annual trades congress for Ireland, towards the expenses of which each trades council and labour organisation be asked to subscribe," was appointed. It consisted of two members from each province, with John Simmons as secretary. Ulster had one representative only, from Newry, and it was agreed that Belfast and Derry be asked to select a second Ulster member.

The first resolution on the agenda was a strongly worded demand for direct labor representation in parliament. It declared that hitherto the interests of the "industrial classes" had been neglected by Irish parliamentary representatives, and the mover, John Simmons, in his speech complained specifically of the existing members of the Irish party. The resolution proposed that, in order to ensure the election of suitably representative workingmen, a candidate should receive the approval of the local trades council or other properly organized labor association of the division or district, who might then "more fully represent the views and wishes of his constituents." The second and third resolutions were the familiar demands for the payment of M.P.s, election expenses, and the assimilation of the municipal, poor-law, and parliamentary franchises. All these were adopted, though some remarks of Canty of

54. T. W. Moody, "Michael Davitt and the British Labour Movement," pp. 67–8.

55. D. D. Sheehan, *Ireland since Parnell*, pp. 172–4. Its nucleus was a local trade and labor association centred on Kanturk; events following the Parnell split disrupted the organization.

56. *F.J.*, 20 July 1891.

57. A circular from the Dublin Trades Council (contents unspecified) was marked read (B.T.C. minutes, 18 July 1891).

the Gasworkers on the third resolution (he thought that too much time was taken up at municipal meetings by discussion of political matters to the entire neglect of the interests of working men) provoked an exchange between him and Austin on the relative importance of labor and nationality. "One of the essential characteristics of every Irishman, he [Austin] thought, should be his nationality (hear, hear). While every man present was a working man, and was most desirous of forwarding the cause of the working classes, it was, beyond doubt, a fact that wherever a workman was to be found the country which gave him birth stood foremost (applause)." Canty replied that he was as good a nationalist as Austin, but persisted in maintaining that "the labour question came before so-called nationality."

It is a measure of the belated importance Irish labor had assumed in the eyes of the nationalist leaders that the *Freeman's Journal,* soon to opt definitely for the anti-Parnellite side,[58] carried an editorial in the same issue supporting the principles of the first three resolutions and declaring that it was high time there should be a real labor representation in the House of Commons. It pointed out that Parnell did introduce "one or two men who had a fair title to speak for labour," but that they were not elected as labor men. Payment of members was necessary if there were to be bona fide labor M.P.s and as this was now Liberal as well as Labour policy the outlook was promising. The following year did see the election of two labor-nationalists (Austin and Crean)—three if Davitt is included—and a scattering of similar representatives at the local government level, but such concessions by the nationalist leaders were insufficient to meet trade union wishes.

The remaining resolutions carried at the conference were in the main or orthodox trade union lines; only one, requiring a pledge from parliamentary candidates "to resist the establishment of a peasant proprietary" and declaring that the private ownership of land was the prime cause of low wages, overcrowding, and scarcity of employment, gave rise to a lengthy discussion, but in the end the resolution received only two votes.

A further attempt was made in September to secure the participation of the Belfast Trades Council, which was invited to fill the vacancy on the four provinces committee. The secretary was instructed to write for further particulars,[59] and, when the invitation was renewed in November, a motion that the letter be marked *read* was moved, followed by an amendment that a delegate be appointed. "After considerable discussion" the amendment was carried by 26 votes to 8.[60] But John Martin,

58. F. S. L. Lyons, *The Irish Parliamentary Party, 1890–1910,* p. 27.
59. B.T.C. minutes, 26 Sept. 1891.   60. Ibid., 13 Nov. 1891.

the moving spirit in the four provinces committee, had died in August[61] and the infant trade union congress did not survive beyond the end of 1891.[62]

The two most important Irish trades councils pursued their separate ways during the early months of 1892. In March the Belfast council held a labor demonstration[63] in aid of striking linenlappers; some thirty Protestant and Catholic bands took part in the procession, and lots were drawn to determine their positions. Samuel Monro, the president, addressing the British Trades Union Congress a year later, quoted with pride the comments of a local paper: "In the monster procession which passed through the principal thoroughfares of the city, orange and green rosettes decked the breast of the District Master of the Orange Lodge, in common with that of the vice-president of the Irish National Federation. A Nationalist band cut out a route for the Orange society, and many a stalwart body of Nationalist toilers beat tramp to the music of a Protestant fife and drum."[64] In spite of this amicable mingling of orange and green, or possibly because of it, the council refused an invitation in April to send three speakers to a May Day Demonstration in Drogheda on the grounds that they were considering one of their own. On May 13 a motion was moved that one be held in Belfast in May of each year, but it was amended to read that the discussion be postponed to February 1893. One of the three invited, Murray Davis (who was an official of the Irish Federal Union of Bakers founded in 1889 by delegates from Dundalk, Drogheda, Dublin, Newry, and Belfast)[65] did take part in the Drogheda meeting, where his speech was received with almost as much applause as that of the principal orator, Michael Davitt.[66]

Closer relations in 1892 were also brought about between the Dublin and Belfast councils by joint action on trade union issues. The Belfast council had appealed in April to the Dublin body,[67] among others, for aid in having objectionable passages referring to trade unionists deleted from the fifth standard reading book issued by the Commissioners of National Education, and the passages were omitted in a new edition distributed the following year.[68] In July, acting on behalf of the Belfast branch of the Typographical Association, they

61. F.J., 8 Aug. 1891.
62. Dublin Trades Council, appendix to Labour Day Agenda 1894.
63. B.T.C. minutes, 27 Feb., 4, 7 Mar. 1892.
64. B.T.U.C., Report, Twenty-sixth Congress, p. 25.
65. J. Swift, Dublin Bakers, p. 296.   66. F.J., 2 May 1892.
67. B.T.C. minutes, 2 Apr., 13 May 1892; F.J., 9 May 1892.
68. B.T.C. minutes, 7 Jan. 1893.

appealed to the Dublin council and the Dublin Typographical Society for help in dealing with the Belfast *Morning News,* which had its type set in Dublin by union labor but was printed in Belfast in a nonunion shop.[69] Help was prompt, and in less than two months the council delegates were informed that "as a natural result of blacklegging the rat newspaper office—the Belfast *Morning News*—had at last been compelled to close its doors.[70] A request from Dublin that Belfast's delegates to the British Trades Union Congress be instructed "to assist in promoting the candidature of an Irish representative" on the parliamentary committee was favorably received.[71] The Irish aspirant at the Glasgow conference of 1892 was Samuel Monro, but he came in last of the thirty-seven candidates for the ten seats, polling only 19 votes as against the 129 that secured the tenth place.[72]

The 1893 congress duly took place in Belfast. Of the 380 delegates 34 were Irish: 27 from Belfast, 1 from Newry, and 6 from Dublin.[73] The larger Irish attendance was understandable, given the place of meeting; the following year it returned to a more normal level, when eight delegates went to Norwich.[74] Samuel Monro presided, as president of the local trades council, and declared that "trade unionism is the 'ism' . . . whose mission it shall be to free our unhappy land from the incubus of religious bigotry and political intolerance," citing as evidence the successful demonstration of the previous year. He also made a strong plea for temperance, a cause which attracted much support among Belfast trade union leaders. He had little success, however, to report in the organization of women workers, for the three societies started by the Women's Trade Union Provident League's officers, the Misses Florence Routledge and M. E. Abraham, had all collapsed in spite of the efforts of the trades council.[75]

The number of Irish resolutions debated was greater than usual, but local susceptibilities were wounded by some incidents caused by tactlessness or indifference.[76] The parliamentary committee report regret-

---

69. Ibid., 10 June 1892.   70. Ibid., 25 July, 17 Sept. 1892.
71. Ibid., 26 Aug. 1892.
72. B.T.U.C., *Report, Twenty-fifth Congress,* p. 71.
73. B.T.U.C., *Report, Twenty-sixth Congress,* pp. 5–10.
74. B.T.U.C., *Report, Twenty-seventh Congress.*
75. B.T.U.C., *Report, Twenty-sixth Congress,* pp. 25, 31–32.
76. Clarkson (p. 185) is wrong in stating that congress "declined to heed the appeal of a Belfast baker [Murray Davis] that it lay special emphasis on the necessity of increasing the number of factory inspectors in Ireland"; Davis asked if the resolution could be made to apply to Ireland and the president (Monro) replied that there was nothing in it that would exclude Ireland (p. 49 of the report). Clarkson (pp. 184–5) also fails to point out that the "English" delegate who, when proposing a collection on

ted that no workingmen Justices of the Peace had been appointed in Scotland, while there were over seventy in England; Ireland, where none had been made either, was not included until a delegate drew attention to its omission.[77] Keir Hardie showed a wry tactfulness when, in moving a resolution declaring that independent labor representatives should always sit in opposition until they could form a cabinet, thought that "an independent labour party should follow the example of a certain other political party [i.e., the Irish Parliamentary Party], which it would not be in order for him to name in Belfast."[78] Tactfulness of any kind, however, was totally lacking in a discussion on the holding of labor demonstrations throughout the United Kingdom on the first Sunday in May of every year. The delegate of the Belfast Power Loom Tenters protested: "the people of Belfast were not in the habit of holding demonstrations on Sunday (hear, hear). . . . the trade I represent would not have sent me here if they had known that it was proposed to hold a labour demonstration on Sunday." A number of delegates sprang to their feet, delegates at John Burns's table described the protest as hypocritical, and Burns himself aggravated matters by repeating, after the resolution had been defeated by two votes, that bigotry had triumphed again, a sentiment which roused the gallery so much that the president had to ask them to control their feelings.[79]

A large labor demonstration, with Burns, Fenwick, Hardie, and Ben Tillett as the principal speakers, was held on the Saturday following the congress. The model was that of the 1892 demonstration in which Protestant and Catholic bands took part, but it was not marked by the same harmony. The second Home Rule bill, for which Burns and Hardie had voted during its earlier passage through the commons, had been rejected by the Lords the previous day, and there were appropriate Orange rejoicings. The Thomas Sexton flute band[80] was roughly handled (some of its members had to receive hospital treatment), speakers, especially Hardie and Burns, were severely heckled, and only the driver's rapid whipping-up of the horses saved Burns from a mauling when his brake was attacked by five to six hundred men armed with sticks.[81]

---

behalf of striking miners, maladroitly suggested that "Ulstermen should do more than entertain" (pp. 84–5 of the report) was E. McHugh, an Ulsterman himself. McHugh and Richard McGhee were officials of the National Union of Dock Labourers. Clarkson's main contention, however, is correct.

77. B.T.U.C., *Report, Twenty-sixth Congress*, p. 33.

78. Ibid., p. 49.   79. Ibid., pp. 77–78.

80. Thomas Sexton, nationalist M.P. for West Belfast (1886–92).

81. Recollections of the Labour Movement in Belfast, 1884–1920, by R. McClung, pp. 5, 6 (MS in the possession of the present writer); *B.N.-L.*, 11 Sept. 1893.

Some efforts were made at the Belfast congress to meet the difficulties of Irish participation. Monro received a greatly increased support, but missed election to the Parliamentary Committee by a handful of votes. Standing orders were also amended, on the motion of Hugh McManus, a Belfast printer, to allow the Parliamentary Committee to be increased by two, with the proviso that one seat should be reserved for "a duly qualified member of a trade union in Ireland."[82] Under the new standing orders in force at Norwich, Richard Sheldon, a cabinet-maker and secretary of the Belfast Trades Council, was elected as the first Irish member of the parliamentary committee.[83] But in spite of these changes, which seemed to foreshadow a greater involvement of Irish trade unions in the affairs of the British trade union center, the interval between the Belfast and Norwich congresses saw the birth of the Irish Trades Union Congress.

82. B.T.U.C., *Report, Twenty-sixth Congress,* p. 81.
83. Ibid., p. 74.

7

The Years of Conformity

The Trade Unionism of Moderation

The initiative in founding an Irish trade union center came once again from the Dublin United Trades and Labour League, or, to use its less formal title, the Dublin Trades Council. In March 1894 the secretary, John Simmons, moved a lengthy resolution proposing the holding of a convention in May 1894 to consolidate the interests of trades and labor organizations with the object of making "more effective the legislative means at present in existence, of protecting the lives and liberties of the workers generally, to consider how best reforms can be effected in the way of removing impediments to human progress at present existing within the constitutions under which we live, and to consider matters affecting trade and labour generally."[1] The resolution was passed and a committee appointed to make arrangements and issue invitations.

The Dublin Trades Council claimed, in 1894, some 15,000 affiliated members, ranging among the skilled trades from carpenters (1200) to members of such dying occupations as corkcutters (50) and silk weavers (20), and including a variety of laborers' unions, from the United Labourers of Ireland (2,000) and the Irish National Labour Union (1,200)—the latter a federal body—to the St. Andrew's and O'Connell's carmen with 100 each.[2] Its headquarters was the Trades' Hall, Capel Street: "a magnificent building containing a large theatre, billiard room, library, council chamber, and ample accommodation for the many trades who hold meetings within its walls—secured for the trade unionists of Dublin through the instrumentality of the council, assisted by the Rt. Hon. Ald. Meade, L.L.D., P.C., William Field, Esq., M.P. and Patrick Sheehan, Esq., as guarantors."[3] Influenced no doubt by civic precedent, it had instituted in 1887 an honorary roll which included such strangely diverse figures as Sir Charles Dawson

1. D.T.C. minutes, dated 18 (4?) Mar. 1894.
2. D.T.C., appendix, *Labour Day Agenda 1894*.
3. Ibid.; *F.J.*, 22 Dec. 1890.

(ex-lord mayor of Dublin), Mr. Michael Davitt, Archbishop Walsh, Arnold Graves, B. L., Alderman Sir Robert Sexton, and Lord Iveagh (then Mr. Edward Cecil Guinness).[4] It was in the building so patronized that the 119 delegates to the first Irish Trades Union Congress met on 27 and 28 April.[5]

Preparations for the hospitality to be extended to delegates troubled the minds of the reception committee. Its chairman, E. L. Richardson, acknowledging contributions to a hospitality fund, expressed his disappointment on 8 April: "Up to this time the traders and merchants of the city, notwithstanding some large individual subscriptions, had not given them the assistance that they had expected from them."[6] The fund reached a total of £67 11s., the main burden being borne by two breweries (Phoenix brewery £10, Guinness £10, and Lord Iveagh £10) and the Licensed Vintners' Association (£10),[7] as if to give substance to the allegation, made in 1891 by the vice-president of the Glasgow Trades Council, that the Dublin council had an unholy alliance with the publicans of the city.[8] Among the individual subscribers was William Martin Murphy, Esq., J. P., the foremost capitalist in Ireland, who sent £1.[9]

The Belfast Trades Council was represented at this first Irish congress by six delegates.[10] Like the Dublin body it claimed fifteen thousand affiliated members and the numbers at its meetings, usually under thirty at the beginning of the decade, had doubled by 1894.[11] When affiliation to the new congress was considered there was an exceptional attendance of eighty-five. There was some opposition to the sending of delegates to Dublin, but when a member moved the previous question, the amendment was defeated, the secretary noting that only twelve voted for it.[12] The Belfast council did not consider that this participation in the new congress ran counter to the British connection; indeed, the first of their resolutions for the Dublin agenda was the following: "That this congress is of the opinion that the time has arrived when, in the interests of trade unionists, there should be a general amalgamation or federation of the trades councils of the United Kingdom, for the more effective organisation of the workers in each country; a better method of enforcing the rights and privileges with regard to matters

4. D.T.C., appendix, *Labour Day Agenda 1894.*
5. *F.J.*, 28 Apr. 1894.   6. *F.J.*, 9 Apr. 1894.
7. *F.J.*, 2, 9 Apr. 1894; I.T.U.C., *Agenda*, 1894.
8. *F.J.*, 27 July 1891.
9. *F.J.*, 2, 9 Apr. 1894; I.T.U.C., *Agenda*, 1894. William Martin Murphy was to become James Larkin's antagonist in the Dublin industrial upheaval of 1913.
10. B.T.C. minutes, 4 Apr. 1894; *F.J.*, 27 Apr. 1894, I.T.U.C., *Agenda, 1894.*
11. B.T.C. minutes, passim.   12. Ibid., 16 Mar. 1894.

relating to labour, and whereby the combined organisation can be utilized for the betterment and strengthening of trade unionism." [13] The council forwarded the same resolution to the Norwich conference of the British Trades Union Congress some months later.

The agenda issued to the delegates was prefaced by an article reprinted from the *Irish Worker,* an independent labor and trade union journal edited by a Dublin printer Bernard Doyle; it clearly expressed the views of the Dublin labor leaders. After stating that the idea of holding an annual conference had been present in the minds of these leaders for some years past, it listed the reasons for starting an Irish congress. These were, in brief, the inability of Irish unions to bear delegates' expenses, [14] the meager results obtained when the Dublin and Belfast Trades Councils did send delegates, and the standing orders revised at the 1892 Glasgow conference that altered representation in an endeavor to check the growing numbers at conferences. [15] The principal source of dissatisfaction was not Ireland's repeated failure to obtain a seat on the Parliamentary Committee—though this was felt as a grievance—but the relegation to the last day of conference, known to delegates as "the sacrifice of the innocents," [16] of Irish resolutions, where they shared the fate of other embarrassing and unpopular motions. The *Irish Worker* article, moreover, pointed out that the trouble lay with "the overburdened congressional machine" and not with the few Irish representatives "who could not make any practical impression on an institution dominated by delegates of English and Scottish mining and manufacture." "We cannot . . . find fault with our English and Scotch friends in pressing forward their own claims first—that is quite natural, seeing that their interests are in the main identical and the facilities at their disposal favourable; they cannot be expected to understand the wants of a community largely agricultural, nor can we hope that they would, so to speak, cut their own throats by assisting in a revival of the languishing manufactures of Ireland." [17]

The introduction concluded by urging the delegates to institute their own annual congress and maintain their own parliamentary com-

13. Ibid., 13 Apr. 1894; I.T.U.C., *Agenda,* p. 31; *F.J.,* 30 Apr. 1894.

14. The expenses of the Belfast Trades Council's solitary delegate to the twenty-fourth annual conference of the British T.U.C. (Newcastle-on-Tyne, 1891) were £9 (wages, travel, hotel) plus 10*s.* to the Parliamentary Committee fund (B.T.C. minutes, 22 Aug. 1891); in 1892 (Glasgow conference) four delegates cost £28 plus £4 to the Parliamentary Committee fund (B.T.C. minutes, 17 Aug. 1892). The expenses of the Dublin Trades Council's two delegates in 1894 (Norwich conference) were £20 (D.T.C. minutes, 23 July 1894).

15. B.T.U.C., *Report, Twenty-fifth Congress,* p. 51.

16. Ibid., p. 51.

17. I.T.U.C., *Agenda, 1894,* introduction.

mittee, which, while securing attention for their own needs, would work in harmony with and assist the larger institution. The final words were a prophecy that the trades councils of Scotland would follow the Irish example, which they did three years later.[18]

The proceedings of the new congress[19] were eminently reasonable in tone. The chairman trusted that the demands and aspirations of the working men and women of Ireland would engage the serious attention not only of the parliamentary representatives of Ireland but also of the rulers of the United Kingdom. The lord mayor of Dublin, received with loud applause, said that they were powerful for much good and much evil, but assured his gratified listeners that having watched now for many years the proceedings of the Dublin Trades Council and the affiliated societies in Ireland, so far as he could see while they had an immense power in their hands he did not think that anybody could say that they had not exercised it with great discretion. Another visitor, W. J. Leahy, a cooper, recently elected to the corporation under the aegis of the local Parnellites,[20] while congratulating them on their large numbers, saw no imminent defection from the British Trades Union Congress. "He considered that at the annual congress of the United Kingdom, Ireland certainly had not got a fair share of attention," but suggested that "a special day ought to be devoted to Irish business." If further proof were needed of the subsidiary nature of the new congress, it was furnished by the adoption of the Belfast resolution calling for a United Kingdom federation of trades councils. This resolution's final clause asked that it be forwarded to the British Parliamentary Committee, the whole matter to be dealt with by them at the earliest opportunity, and—the wording is significant—"form part of the business of the next British Trades Union Congress."

The speech of the president of the new congress, Thomas O'Connell, a carpenter and president of the Dublin Trades Council, drew from Alexander Taylor, a Belfast linenlapper, the tribute that "their worthy president in his address had leaned to the side of moderation, and he thought it was a wise course." O'Connell reviewed the progress of trade unionism and its increasing acceptance by the public. Though rejoicing in the vindication of their right to strike, he warned the delegates

18. B. C. Roberts, *Trade Union Government and Administration in Great Britain*, p. 455.

19. See *F.J.*, 28, 30 Apr. 1894, for report of conference. No official report was issued.

20. Leahy made his first appearance on 1 Jan. 1893; *Dublin Corporation Minutes* of that date. He, along with T. J. O'Reilly of the D.T.C., J. Canty, and Adolphus Shields, had held a meeting in the Phoenix Park in support of Parnell. *F.J.*, 8 Dec. 1890.

that it would be criminal to resort to it if disputes could be settled amicably. On the eight-hour day question, he was in favor of trade option, for "with the hours at present worked in continental countries it would be suicidal to insist on its compulsory application to all industries," and he concluded amid loud applause with these words: "I trust, ladies and gentlemen, that your deliberations may be productive of general good, that they may tend to bring labour and capital in Ireland into close harmony, and hasten the time when each shall occupy its true place and recognize the fact that their interests are identical." Only once did he cease to be moderate; in a discussion on an employers' liability bill which contained an objectionable contracting-out clause not in the previous bill rejected by the House of Lords, he intervened to say that the sooner the house of nonentities ceased to exist the better. As for labor representation in parliament and local government, he declared it most unsatisfactory that in Ireland they had to rely on those gentlemen who had been returned from a political standpoint; not one of the 103 had been returned on purely labor lines. In England labor was represented at every level; in Ireland, where it was practically unrepresented, one of the essentials for reformation was the greater spread of trades councils.

The thirty-eight resolutions submitted were an Irish version of "Lib-Lab" reformism. Legislation, or its enforcement, accounted for twelve resolutions on industrial conditions. Hours, wages, and unfair domestic competition were the subjects of another five, while eight dealt with labor organization, housing, and technical education. All other political resolutions were strictly reformist, and called for a local government franchise on English lines, the payment of M.P.s, and the revision of jury laws; a slightly contentious resolution on the taxation of land values was condemned by an opponent of Henry George and was replaced by a vague declaration in favor of land nationalization. The remaining nine resolutions were along the familiar nineteenth-century lines of protection for decaying Irish industries, joined to demands for an Irish share of government and war department contracts. Similar resolutions were to be moved regularly at subsequent conferences: two concerned the use of Irish glass bottles and corks, a third, sponsored by the Dublin branch of the United Kingdom Society of Coachmakers, demanded that no lord mayor should hold his office for more than one year, as it deprived the coachmakers of employment.[21] This last resolution met with mounting opposition at each congress until finally Belfast delegates declared in 1901 that they would not accept dictation

21. It was the custom for the lord mayor to order a new coach on his election to office.

on the frequency with which their city might elect one person as first citizen.[22] Decaying crafts undermined by foreign competition were to occupy much of the time of later congresses. In 1896, for instance, a resolution[23] was adopted protesting against the importation of foreign brass work and calling upon clergymen, architects, and licensed vintners to use homemade work. Such pathetic appeals indicated the weakness of an economy that in some respects was still preindustrial in character.

The 119 delegates in the Trades' Hall, Capel Street, represented over 21,000 trade unionists directly and 39,000 indirectly, through the trades councils of Belfast, Dublin, Cork, Limerick, and Drogheda. Irish branches of amalgamated unions were strongly represented, for in the second half of the nineteenth century these British unions had absorbed many of the Irish craft unions.[24] Among those represented at the first congress were the A.S.C.J., the A.S.T., the Typographical Association, and the Amalgamated Society of Railway Servants; the A.S.E. sent no delegate. Four women delegates from Belfast and Dublin represented unions recently sponsored by the trades councils of the two cities, the Textile Operatives of Ireland in Belfast and the Bookfolders' section of the Irish National Labour Union in Dublin, but their membership totals did not exceed a few hundred. The few unskilled workers organized were in a number of local Irish unions or in new British general unions.

A parliamentary committee on the British model (one of its functions was "generally to support the parliamentary committee of the United Trades Congress upon all questions affecting the workers of the United Kingdom") was elected at the Dublin congress. It consisted of eight members and a secretary, all members of trades councils and belonging to skilled trades. Belfast and Limerick had two each, Cork and Drogheda one each, and Dublin three, including the secretary John Simmons, a member of the A.S.C.J. The Belfast members secured first and third places, Dublin second and fifth, the secretary being elected unanimously. This pattern in which the ruling body was dominated territorially by Dublin and Belfast and occupationally by the skilled trades, notably printers, carpenters, and tailors, persisted

22. I.T.U.C., *Report, Eighth Congress,* pp. 51–2. Though the resolution was carried by 33 votes to 12, it did not appear in subsequent years; the parliamentary committee report of 1902 quoted a letter from the Dublin town clerk, which stated that counsel had advised that the desired change in the standing orders of the Dublin corporation would be *ultra vires*. In Dublin the lord mayor received a salary; in Belfast the post was honorary.

23. I.T.U.C., *Report, Third Congress,* p. 36.

24. For the spread of British unions in Ireland, see Chapter 5.

during the early years of the congress. The unskilled workers were unrepresented except in 1895 and 1896,[25] when the United Labourers of Ireland won a seat. In reply to the complaint of a laborer at a later congress that his category of worker was unrepresented, the chairman of the parliamentary committee retorted that while he sympathized, the laborers had only themselves to blame because they split their vote by putting up more than one candidate.[26]

Delegates at the 1894 congress were suitably entertained. The Dublin United Tramways Company, of which William Martin Murphy was the principal shareholder, issued free passes—a gesture that was rendered ironic by a congress resolution complaining of the excessive hours worked by its employees and of the refusal of the company to meet the men as a body. The Gaiety Theatre admitted delegates to all parts of the house and the Phoenix brewery, already a subscriber, provided a carriage drive to Lucan and a free lunch. The meal was followed by the customary platitudinous speeches in an atmosphere of mutual good will, but when Richard McCoy, the high sheriff[27] of Dublin, referred to the late Mr. Parnell in his opening remarks some of his listeners considered that he had introduced "political and contentious matter." He attempted to explain, but his remarks were lost in the subsequent "interruption and uproar" and "the proceedings came to a somewhat abrupt conclusion." The banquet given in the evening by the Dublin Trades Council went more smoothly, attended by more tactful municipal officers, and the toasts honored included "Our native land," to which Mr. William Field, M.P., replied, and "The labour cause," supported by delegates from Dublin, Cork, and Belfast, the northern representative being William Walker, who was later to dominate the Belfast labor scene.

The second Irish congress met in Cork the following year, but in the meantime events in the British congress had occurred that made it certain that henceforth Irish trade unionists would be dependent on their own efforts. Richard Sheldon had been elected as the Irish representative at Norwich, but he held his seat only until the next congress (1895); the Parliamentary Committee of which he was a member drafted new standing orders that excluded trades councils from future meetings and also rescinded the provision for special representa-

---

25. E. Goulding (1895) and P. Golden (1896) were both Dublin laborers. Clarkson is in error (p. 195) when he states that 1895 was the only year in which laborers were represented. See I.T.U.C., *Report, Third Congress*, p. 45.

26. I.T.U.C., *Report, Seventh Congress*, p. 45. Only seven of the delegates represented laborers.

27. Richard McCoy, a strong Parnellite, chairman of the Parnell Leadership Committee. *F.J.*, 8 Dec. 1890.

tion for Ireland. The subsequent congress ratified these decisions.[28] The change was designed to bar the socialists, who had captured many of the trades councils and were undermining the "Lib-Lab" leaders of the Trades Union Congress,[29] but this was no consolation even to Belfast, where the names of Fenwick and his "Lib-Lab" colleagues were still powerful.[30]

The council made efforts to mobilize opposition to the ratification of the new standing orders and the resentment that followed the failure of these efforts resulted for some time in British Trades Union Congress correspondence being marked *read*. Henceforward Irish participation virtually ceased.[31]

The machinery of the Irish congress was consciously[32] modeled on the British T.U.C., a natural result of the fact that many of the leaders belonged to amalgamated unions and had attended British congresses. The rules governing election and procedure of the parliamentary committee were as far as possible identical with those of the British committee. Its finances were to be dependent on any surplus from delegates' fees and voluntary subscriptions from trades councils and trade unions. In 1895 income amounted to £111 15s., of which £54 5s. represented delegates' fees. Of the remaining £57 10s., trades councils supplied £26 (Belfast £10, Dublin and Limerick £7 each, and Drogheda £2), trade unions in Belfast £18, and small contributions, mainly

28. See B.T.U.C., *Report, Twenty-eighth Congress*, p. 32–9. The Norwich (1894) congress had entrusted to the Parliamentary Committee the drafting of new standing orders which came into force immediately. The Cardiff congress ratified them only in the sense that it defeated after a stormy and confused debate a motion of J. Havelock Wilson that they be submitted to congress before enforcement.

29. Roberts, *Trade Union Government*, p. 455.

30. When William Walker moved that the Belfast Trades Council delegates to the Norwich conference of the British T.U.C. be instructed to vote for the socialist Tom Mann as secretary of the Parliamentary Committee, an amendment, moved by R. Sheldon and T. Johnston, to postpone the question for six months was carried by fifteen votes to six. Johnston declared that "he knew no one fitter than Mr. Fenwick . . . . the only thing he knew about Mann was what he saw in the papers, that he had been an agitator" (B.T.C. minutes, 9 Aug. 1894).

31. A resolution submitted by the Irish Linenlappers' Association to the Cardiff Congress sought to have the Parliamentary Committee pronounced "guilty of a breach of faith, alike dishonest and dishonourable . . . in seeking to oust Ireland from representation on the Parliamentary Committee." It pointed out that the 1893 change in standing orders had been agreed to unanimously. On the few occasions that an Irish delegate was present at later British congresses he was a member or official of an Irish branch of a British union.

32. "We are not ashamed to admit that we took as our model the procedure and methods which resulted in bringing about material benefits for the workers of England during the past quarter of a century." (Address of G. Leahy, president, I.T.U.C., *Report, Seventh Congress*, p. 6).

from local unions, accounted for the rest.[33] Only two amalgamated unions, the Typographical Association and the General Union of Carpenters, sent subscriptions from their executives. The more powerful amalgamated bodies, such as the Amalgamated Society of Railway Servants, the National Union of Dock Labourers, the Amalgamated Society of Tailors, and the Amalgamated Society of Carpenters and Joiners, were represented by delegates but not by subscriptions. Richard Sheldon, who in 1895 was on the Parliamentary Committees of both congresses, moved the following motion, first in the Belfast Trades Council[34] and subsequently in the Cork congress:[35] "That it be an instruction from this congress to all delegates present, belonging to the various English and Scotch Trade and Labour organisations, to insist on their right to send a representative (who shall be a member of a branch in Ireland) to the Irish Trades Union Congress. The expenses of the said representatives to be paid out of the general fund." The last sentence was a strong hint to the union executives concerned, and the motion was adopted by congress. The Parliamentary Committee at the Limerick conference (1896) referred to it in their report, saying that most of the permanent officials of the amalgamated societies looked with disfavor on the Irish congress, but already in 1896 the resolution seems to have been effective, for in that year the A.S.R.S. and the A.S.T. subscribed £10 and £2 each from their Parliamentary Committee funds.[36] Though the executives of the amalgamated unions continued to be the largest contributors under the "voluntary" scheme until it was abolished in 1905, the Irish T.U.C. income remained small, and the Parliamentary Committee was handicapped in its work.

The anxiety shown by the founders of the Irish T.U.C. to rebut charges of disloyalty to the British congress prompted them to repeat their reasons for the new development at several successive conferences. The president of the 1895 congress, and the Parliamentary Committee chairman in 1896, repeated the arguments and assurances of the *Irish Worker* article of the previous year, and the 1897 president, emphasizing that their aim was "to supplement rather than clash with our brethren across the water," pointed to the institution of the Scottish Trades Union Congress as proving the wisdom of the course adopted. The first president of the Scottish body had in fact used much the same argument as the Irish leaders: "there were many questions which affect Scotland particularly to which our English fellow unionists cannot be expected to devote the necessary amount of time and attention which

33. I.T.U.C., *Report, Second Congress*, statement of accounts.
34. B.T.C. minutes, 9 May 1895.
35. I.T.U.C., *Report, Second Congress*, p. 15.
36. I.T.U.C., *Report, Third Congress*, statement of accounts.

they deserve." [37] The 1897 Irish congress was attended by Robert Smillie, Hardie's comrade, as a fraternal delegate, and relations between the two bodies were close and friendly for many years. If the action of the British T.U.C. had reduced the Irish body to an unwilling "external relations" position, it might nonetheless have its advantages, as H. McManus, chairman of the Parliamentary Committee, stated at Cork: "Sometimes heaven sends us a blessing in disguise; let us hope that this is one, and that the outcome may be the vitalising of the energy and self-reliance of the Irish workman." [38]

The Politics of Conformity

The political neutrality of the Irish Trades Union Congress was stated at the second congress by its president, J. H. Jolley of the Cork Trades Council, a compositor by trade: "I am not going to ascribe to this gathering any significance which it does not properly possess. The congress as such is of no party in politics. In regard to all those questions which divide Irishmen no less than others it holds itself absolutely neutral (hear, hear). Its members indeed do not abdicate nor suspend their rights for an instant to the fullest and freest expression of their own convictions, but the congress itself in its corporate capacity altogether refuses to throw its weight into one scale or the other." [39]

This perfectionist attitude, especially dear to the hearts of most of the Belfast delegates, was maintained with a remarkable degree of success for a number of years. There were minor disagreements when temperance advocates, from both Belfast and Dublin, considered time was wasted in protesting against the Guinness monopoly of bottled stout or the use of foreign-made bottles and corks. Alexander Taylor said that, provided goods were made under trade union conditions, they had not the right to protest: "It was too late in the day to try and build a Chinese wall of protection around Irish goods." [40] Another delegate argued that they should not acknowledge the principle that their neighbors in England had the right to starve them out: "Their first duty was to look after their own interests (hear, hear)." [41] The interpretation of the word "foreign" was vexing. At the Belfast con-

---

37. Roberts, *Trade Union Government*, p. 455. The Scottish unions were also influenced in their decision by Keir Hardie and other Socialists; they invited the Independent Labour Party founder to address their first meeting as a gesture of reproach to the British T.U.C., which had excluded Hardie by a change in the rules governing delegates' credentials.

38. I.T.U.C., *Report, Second Congress*, pp. 5–6.

39. Ibid., p. 11.

40. I.T.U.C., *Report, Third Congress*, p. 30.

41. I.T.U.C., *Report, Fourth Congress*, p. 30.

gress (1898), P. J. Tevenan, a Dublin railway worker who had spent some time in England, speaking on the King Charles's head resolution on homemade brass work, asked if it were possible to place goods from England (made under the fairest conditions) in the category of foreign products. Four Belfast delegates spoke against the resolution, which was carried by only four votes.[42]

But the subject provoking the greatest disturbance in the placid deliberations of congress was the report of the Childers Commission[43] on the financial relations between Great Britain and Ireland. As it concluded that Ireland had been overtaxed to the extent of nearly three million pounds annually for many years, it gave rise to an immediate agitation for a financial readjustment when it was published in 1896. An emergency debate at the Waterford (1897) conference revealed a division of opinion among the ranks of the northern delegates, Alexander Taylor (Belfast) and James McCarron (A.S.T. Derry) speaking in favor of the motion of protest against the overtaxation of Ireland. The opposition, led by Samuel Monro, claimed it had not been proved and that the whole matter needed further investigation, but McCarron denounced this claim as a tactical move that would suit Monro and those who were opposed to giving justice to Ireland. He waxed bitter over Mr. Arthur Balfour's statement that Ireland had received back every farthing given to England and his query as to Ireland's readiness to support the soldiers quartered there. McCarron said no: "They were peaceful in Ireland, and the country had no right to pay for them. This was a question on which all patriotic Irishmen should unite, and not allow themselves to be robbed by England any longer (hear, hear)."[44]

The motion was passed on a show of hands, but the subject came up for debate two years later at Derry, when McCarron presided. A similar motion was then passed by thirty-seven votes to three, after a heated discussion. Monro stated that every unwritten law as to politics had been broken, while Councillor W. J. Leahy (Dublin) declared that Ireland would never be fairly treated by England, and would never have justice done to her until she had the right to manage her own affairs. Charles Darcus, a Belfast printer who had supported Monro at Waterford, jumped to his feet on a point of order: "If this goes on I don't know where we are going to end." Murray Davis held that "Irishmen and Englishmen should be welded together as one man. . . . he was proud

---

42. I.T.U.C., *Report, Fifth Congress*, p. 52.

43. The chairman of this royal commission was H. C. E. Childers, who had numbered among his ministerial positions those of Financial Secretary to the Treasury (1865–6) and Chancellor of the Exchequer (1882–5).

44. I.T.U.C., *Report, Fifth Congress*, pp. 49–50.

to be part and parcel of the British Empire."[45] William Walker ended the debate by moving that the motion be put. Four years earlier in the Belfast Trades Council he had carried by a large majority an amendment that a circular on the Plunkett Recess Committee from the Dublin body be marked *read*,[46] and when he gave a report to the Belfast council after the Derry congress he complained strongly of the political complexion of the discussions: "unless the personnel of congress was changed he would recommend the council not to send delegates to it, as in his opinion the congress was not worth the money it cost."[47] He did not, however, press the point; five years later he was elected president of congress.

Direct labor representation, especially at the local government level, was considered to be primarily the responsibility of the trades councils. At the Cork congress, however, a resolution was passed that, had it been implemented, would have involved the T.U.C., at least financially. The Parliamentary Committee was to sponsor an election fund and appeals were to be made to friends of labor, trades councils, and organizations affiliated to congress; the fund itself was to be administered by the Parliamentary Committee. Parliamentary elections were not covered, since it was considered that payment of M.P.s would be necessary before workers could be fairly represented. The scheme did not envisage a distinct party as such, but "any labour representative chosen under this scheme must clearly understand that he should represent labour purely, and hold himself aloof from all political parties connected with such public bodies as he might be elected upon."[48] The motion was moved by Tevenan, the Irish secretary of the Amalgamated Society of Railway Servants, and T. Foy of the same union. The plan recalled the ideas of the English Labour Electoral Association modified by some of the proposals made by Tait and Hardie at the 1891 congress of the British T.U.C. Since, from lack of support, the scheme came to nothing, the responsibility for labor representation remained with the trades councils.

The Labour Electoral Association of Great Britain and Ireland had been supported by both the Dublin and Belfast Trades Councils. No Irish representative was present at the first congress (Sheffield) in 1888,

45. I.T.U.C., *Report, Sixth Congress*, pp. 48–50.

46. B.T.C. minutes, 16 Sept. 1895. The Recess Committee had been elected at a conference called by Sir Horace Plunkett, Unionist M.P. and cooperative enthusiast, during the parliamentary recess of 1895. It consisted of moderate Unionists and Nationalists and urged the adoption of a number of measures of social reform, especially in agriculture.

47. B.T.C. minutes, 17 June 1899.

48. I.T.U.C., *Report, Second Congress*, p. 36.

but John Simmons attended from the Dublin Trades Council in the following year and was elected to its committee. In moving the acceptance of its report, he said that it only required "some little stirring up" to make the Labour Electoral Association a success in Ireland as well as in Great Britain. Though he was himself an Irish nationalist, he regretted that "too much attention had been paid by the Irish members to a certain class of the Irish people and too little to the Irish workingman, who had been totally neglected."[49] Moving a motion later in the session urging the Irish people to return members pledged to support ameliorative legislation, he softened his charges by saying that he and those he represented had no serious fault to find with the Irish parliamentary representatives; he regretted "he should be compelled to say anything which might seem disrespectful to those gentlemen." But when a Bradford delegate protested and seconded a Liverpool delegate's amendment designed to take the sting out of the resolution, the congress insisted on adhering to the original motion.[50]

John Simmons was the only Irish representative among the thirty-seven delegates, but he must have been gratified by the attention paid to Ireland at the annual dinner. A fellow committeeman, W. Matkin, expressed deep sympathy with the people of the "Sister Isle," but thought that they were not trusting the democracy of Great Britain sufficiently: "if their Irish friends mixed with them a little more it would be better for all (applause)."[51] T. R. Threlfall, the Labour Electoral Association secretary, agreed with Matkin and thought such a course would solve the Home Rule difficulty; once the Irish question was out of the way "there were many questions affecting the welfare of the people to settle."[52] This indicated a feeling among the English labor leaders that social legislation was being held up by Irish demands for self-government. Two other speakers also made references to English sympathy with Ireland, and Simmons in reply could but hope that not only Dublin but all the other towns in Ireland would be represented at the next congress.[53]

Simmons's hopes were not realized. He was accompanied by a second Irish delegate in each of the two following years, in 1890 by Stephen Farrell of the Waterford Trades Council and in 1891 by T. McKevitt of the Dundalk branch of the Seamen's and Firemen's Union. Farrell denounced sweating nationalists,[54] while Simmons complained bitterly that absolutely nothing was done for labor by the Irish members.[55] In

49. Labour Electoral Congress, *Second Annual Report*, p. 11.
50. Ibid., pp. 28–29.   51. Ibid., p. 35.
52. Ibid., p. 36.
53. Ibid., p. 40. Simmons kept his committee seat in 1890 and 1891.
54. L.E.C., *Third Annual Report*, p. 27.   55. Ibid., pp. 19–20.

1892 Threlfall wrote to the Dublin council asking for assistance in getting the trades of Ireland to affiliate and send delegates, since his organization had taken up "strong, uncompromising and friendly co-operation on the Home Rule question,"[56] but no assistance was given and not even Simmons was present at the 1892 congress. He attended the congress for the last time in 1894.[57]

The Belfast council was hostile when first approached in 1887,[58] but from 1891 onward subscribed each year and expressed its sympathy with the Labour Electoral Association, though it was unable to send delegates.[59] An attempt on the part of Murray Davis to follow the example of some English boroughs and form a local branch, as distinct from mere affiliation, of the trades council was, however, opposed in an "acrimonious" speech by Hugh McManus and action was deferred.[60] There was irony in the discussion that took place in the Belfast council on the circular inviting delegates to the last conference of the dying organization. One member, a tailor, asked if the Labour Electoral Association was connected with any political party, whereupon the chairman answered "Not so far as I know," and the council then voted to send the usual delegate's fee of ten shillings, which was Belfast's last link with the "Lib-Lab" creation.[61]

Irish labor had no direct representation at Westminster. The obstacles which faced labor candidates in England were also present in Ireland, but an Irish labor candidate had in addition to surmount the barriers raised by Irish nationalism and unionism. Though labor was confronted by both barriers in Belfast, it was there that the first Irish labor candidate had appeared, in the general election of 1885, before the first Home Rule bill provoked the bitterest sectarian passions. He was Alexander Bowman, a flaxdresser, and secretary of the Belfast Trades Council.

The ground had been prepared for him by a small group of radicals, of whom the chief was a congregationalist minister, the Reverend

56. *F.J.*, 1 Feb. 1892. Point seven of the program of the L.E.A. in force from 1889 (L.E.C., *Second Annual Report,* p. 44) consisted of a demand for national parliaments for England, Ireland, Scotland, and Wales, with an imperial parliament for imperial affairs. One of the 1892 election leaflets (*Ireland and the Labour Question*) argued that British and Irish workers would benefit by the granting of self-government to Ireland. See L.E.C., *Fifth Annual Report,* p. 40.

57. D.T.C. minutes, 9 July 1894; see also I.T.U.C., *Report, Third Congress,* which includes short biographies of leading members.

58. A letter from Threlfall urging the formation of a branch was marked *read* (B.T.C. minutes, 21 May 1887).

59. Ibid., 25 Apr., 8 May 1891 and passim.

60. Ibid., 19 Dec. 1891.

61. Ibid., 25 May 1895.

Bruce Wallace, who late in 1884 had delivered a series of lectures to working-class audiences on subjects such as producers' cooperatives and land nationalization.[62] Bowman was associated with him and was secretary of a small organization, the Irish Land Restoration Society, which had the same ideals as its English and Scottish counterparts. It was this body that, in January 1885, brought Henry George to Belfast, where he addressed a packed meeting in the Ulster Hall, presided over by Wallace.[63] As Dr. Hugh Hanna, a prominent Presbyterian minister and Conservative champion known to his opponents as "Roaring Hanna," was denied the opportunity to deliver a speech at the meeting, Wallace arranged a debate with him in the same hall shortly afterward.[64] Encouraged by the growing public interest in radical politics, Bowman agreed to contest North Belfast at the general election of 1885. Though a member of the Belfast Liberal Association, he stood as a labor candidate.[65]

Bowman included in his election address the usual reforms demanded by trade unions (reduction in the hours of labor, additional factory inspectors, amendment of the Employers' Liability Act), a generous selection from Chamberlain's "unauthorised programme," and a demand for local option. On the Home Rule question he stood for the maintenance of the union between Great Britain and Ireland, but referred discreetly to his antipathy to any injustice in its operation. His own statements and those of his supporters make it clear that he stood as a trade union candidate. Though his campaign was hampered by intimidation and the wrecking tactics of his opponents, he polled about one-third of the votes secured by the Unionist, a linen manufacturer, William Ewart.[66]

The following year the debates on the first Home Rule bill took place and the Belfast Trades Council found itself involved unwillingly in the controversy. The introduction of the bill had split the Ulster Liberals.[67] A demonstration in the Ulster Hall on April 30 under Liberal (in reality, Liberal-Unionist) auspices passed resolutions against Home

62. *Northern Whig*, 11, 18 Mar. 1884. Wallace (1854–1939) published Christian Socialist periodicals, *Brotherhood* and the *Belfast Weekly Star*, in 1889–91. In 1891 he moved to England and took part in cooperative and community ventures. He contested the first Northern Ireland general election (1921) as an unofficial labor candidate. See W. H. G. Armytage, *Heavens Below*, p. 342.

63. *B.N.-L.*, 23 Jan. 1885.   64. *B.N.-L.*, 27 Feb. 1885.

65. He was present at the annual meeting of the Belfast Liberal Association (*B.N.-L.*, 30 Jan. 1885); see also *N.W.*, 20 May 1886.

66. For a fuller acount of this election and discussion of Bowman's candidature, see app. 3.

67. An account of the split is given in D. C. Savage, "The Origins of the Ulster Unionist Party, 1885–6" in *I.H.S.*, xii, pp. 185–208.

Rule; it was attended by a large number of workmen, including a hundred who marched from the Sirocco works, dramatically led by a man on a grey charger.[68] Bowman, though a member of the general council and the executive committee of the Belfast Liberal Association, was not allowed to move an amendment expressing confidence in Gladstone's leadership.[69] Instead, arrangements were made for a deputation of workmen to lobby, in particular, trade union and radical M.P.s. These working-class allies of the Ulster Unionists were in effect the first Labour-Unionists, and were given considerable support by the Belfast press. The deputation's secretary, William Currie, was extremely active and wrote to and interviewed a number of M.P.s including Joseph Arch (to whom he described himself as "Radical to the very heart") and Henry Broadhurst, secretary of the T.U.C.[70] Bowman, on the instruction of the Parliamentary Committee of the Belfast Trades Council, denied that the deputation had been appointed by the council or any trade union in Belfast.[71] His actions were upheld by a narrow majority (14 to 11) of the full council,[72] but some weeks later notice was given of a motion censuring him for violating "a fundamental principle of its government, that political questions of a party and contentious nature should be eliminated from its proceedings."[73] Joseph Mitchell, who was president of the Belfast Trades Council and who had signed Bowman's nomination paper in 1885, went so far as to say that if he had known of Bowman's views at the time he would not have proposed him: "Though differing politically from Mr. Ewart, I am glad to say that through him North Belfast will be found in opposition to a measure which, I am convinced, would be injurious not only to the best interests of Belfast, but to those of Ireland."[74] Bowman had allowed himself to be drawn, in letters to Henry Broadhurst, into a controversy with William Currie,[75] and had written as a Gladstonian liberal.[76] His attempt to persuade the council to distinguish between his public and private capacities failed, for though he succeeded in having the censure motion withdrawn, it was at the price of resignation

68. *B.N.-L., N.W.*, 1 May 1886.   69. *N.W.*, 20 May 1886.
70. *N.W.*, 13 May 1886, *B.N.-L.*, 15, 18 May 1886.
71. *B.N.-L.*, 10 May 1886, B.T.C. minutes, 15 May 1886.
72. Ibid., 15 May 1886.   73. Ibid., 5, 14 June 1886.
74. *B.N.-L.*, 18 May 1886. This Joseph Mitchell was an Ironfounders' delegate and should not be confused with the Bookbinders' delegate Joseph Mitchell who was assistant secretary in 1901 and subsequent years.
75. William Currie (not to be confused with W. A. Currie, secretary of the Belfast Harbour Board) was a linenlapper and later a clothpasser (*Belfast Directory* 1884, 1892) who, in addition to working in the same industry as Bowman, was a fellow member in the Belfast Debating Society and the Belfast Liberal Association.
76. *N.W.*, 20, 21 May 1886.

from his position as secretary of the body he had helped to create five years earlier.[77] The council's political chastity was ensured by the delegates voting 18 to 13 to have a report of the meeting published.[78]

The fierce rioting and loss of life that followed immediately on the defeat of the first Home Rule bill during its second reading in the House of Commons lasted throughout the summer months and involved shipyard workers. The Trades Council passed a resolution condemning "the cowardly ruffianism that has been and is disgracing our town" and calling upon all trade unionists to keep clear of disturbances.[79] Its desire to avoid political entanglements was strengthened by a not unexpected occurrence—decline in attendances and disaffiliation of a number of trade union branches. It was twenty years before another parliamentary labor candidate stood in Belfast.[80]

A restricted franchise had delayed the appearance of labor candidates in local government. Once again Belfast was first in the field, thanks chiefly to Thomas Sexton,[81] who had given it the widest franchise of any Irish town. In 1891 the trades council selected Samuel Monro, who accepted nomination for one of the five wards in the city with the knowledge that if elected he would be required by his employer to resign his job. He polled strongly and might have been successful if the polling booths had not been closed illegally between 7:00 and 8:00 P.M., so that many of his supporters were denied the opportunity of voting.[82] The Trades Council also supported in another ward Thomas Harrison, a barrister, who claimed on election to be the first labor candidate ever returned in Belfast.[83] As late as 1897 he continued to receive this support, as "the consistent advocate of the claims of the working classes in Belfast,"[84] though in that year he changed his affiliation from Independent to Liberal Unionist.[85] In 1893 the Trades

77. James Workman, a prominent member of the Belfast Trades Council, said in a speech at one of Bowman's election meetings that the candidate had conceived the idea of the trades council and with a few others had canvassed forty trades (N.W., 31 Oct. 1885).

78. B.T.C. minutes, 12 June 1886.   79. Ibid., 7 Aug. 1886.

80. Ibid., Dec. 1885 to July 1886, passim. Among the unions that withdrew were the Power Loom Tenters, the Associated Carpenters and Joiners of Scotland, two branches of the Amalgamated Society of Tailors, the Hackle and Gill Makers, and the Flaxroughers. The A.S.C.J. branch no. 2 announced that they would withdraw their delegates until Bowman was removed from office.

81. Thomas Sexton, during his period as M.P. (Nationalist) for West Belfast, introduced a section (5) into a local act, the Municipal Corporation of Belfast Act (50 & 51 Vict. c. cxviii), 1887, which abolished the ten-pound valuation for burgesses.

82. Cromac ward: Ritchie, 2,465, and Bell, 2,419, elected; Monro, 2,106 (B.N.-L., 27 November 1891).

83. B.N.-L., 27 Nov. 1891.   84. B.T.C. minutes, 23 Nov. 1894.
85. Ibid., 6 Nov. 1897; B.N.-L., 29 Oct. 1897.

Council tried again in another ward and, because Monro was unwilling to stand, nominated Murray Davis.[86] Davis was opposed in the council by delegates Unionist in outlook and was denounced by them at several election meetings held in support of McCammond and McCorry, his Conservative opponents in the ward.[87] He produced letters from two clergymen certifying that he was neither a socialist nor a nationalist, but it had no effect on the election result, for he was beaten two to one. In his speech made when the counting of the votes ended, he complained bitterly of the conduct of the opposition and recited an extended list of accusations made against him, all of which he denied— that he was a socialist, an atheist, an anarchist, a Home Ruler, and a nationalist.[88] Four days later the Trades Council passed a unanimous motion congratulating McCammond on his proposed election as lord mayor and calling him "the workers' best friend."[89]

In the absence of electoral successes, trades councils made a practice of lobbying candidates outside their ranks and endorsing them in cases where they had shown themselves in favor of such policies as the enforcement of a fair wage clause in local contracts and the employment of local labor.[90] The restricted local franchise in towns other than Belfast encouraged such a course, and one Dublin trade union leader (John Ward, who presided at the inaugural conference of the Irish Federated Trade and Labour Union) thought so highly of it that he preferred it for the time being to agitation for the extension of franchises.[91] A logical development of such a course was to request the dominant political party to include in its public representatives some labor men. The Belfast Trades Council never gave way to this temptation, for its leaders considered, with justification, that any political alliance would split the council. Owing to the threat of Home Rule, the Unionist party had a sufficient working-class following to make advances to labor interests unnecessary. Such advances, if made and

86. B.T.C. minutes, 27 Oct., 19 Nov. 1893.

87. *B.N.-L.,* 20–22 Nov. 1893. Two of his denouncers were Thomas Johnstone and F. C. Johnston; see app. 3, p. 423 and n. 2. Thomas Johnstone had appeared as a delegate of the Power Loom Yarddressers' Society at the Belfast (1893) conference of the British T.U.C.

88. *B.N.-L.,* 28 Nov. 1893. He was a member of the Masonic Order.

89. *B.N.-L.,* 2 Dec. 1893.

90. In 1897 Belfast Trades Council interviewed candidates and published their answers (B.T.C. minutes, 19 Nov. 1897). Dublin Trades Council lobbied candidates specifically on the extension of the municipal franchise and fair contracts (*F.J.,* 24 Nov. 1890).

91. "We do not follow Mr Dawson's advice to agitate for extension of the franchises . . . the best we can do now is to extract pledges from candidates." (*F.J.,* 6 May 1889).

accepted, would have weakened the ties between Belfast and British labor, for British trade unionists could not be expected to welcome the Irish allies of British conservatives. An alliance with Irish nationalists was repugnant to the majority of the council and would have been profitless, indeed damaging, in the Belfast area, whatever it might yield in an Ireland under Home Rule. Labor in Belfast was forced, willy-nilly, to find its political expression in independent labor representation.

Elsewhere in Ireland the temptation to ask for representation through the nationalist organization was strong. In 1890 William Martin Murphy, then a nationalist M.P., replied to a resolution of the Dublin Trades Council urging an extension of the municipal franchise by pointing out that the Irish parliamentary party had in vain introduced bills with that object, and another nationalist M.P. appeared before the council to deplore its harsh criticisms of his party. John Ward was not satisfied and retorted that Parnell should give labor at least one parliamentary representative.[92] The earliest nationalist concessions were made to the Cork Trades Council, the oldest in Ireland.[93] Its president, Eugene Crean, was elected to the corporation in 1886,[94] and in 1892 he and Michael Austin were elected as anti-Parnellite M.P.s. In the same year W. J. Leahy of the Dublin Regular Coopers was returned unopposed to the corporation; though he was described by the *Freeman's Journal* as "the workingman's candidate" and endorsed by the Dublin Trades Council, he owed his nomination and election to the Parnellite organization in the city.[95] The Dublin council supported him three years later[96] when there was a threat to oust him, but within a year they condemned him unanimously, declaring that he "should no longer be considered as voicing the opinions of labour in the municipal chamber" because he withdrew his support for the council's candidate for lord mayor.[97]

While the Dublin Trades Council as a body was pleased to have some of its members elected to councillorships under other auspices, there was an element in it that preferred "pure" labor representation. The first candidate of this description to have the council's full support (he was probably financed and initially selected by his union, the Amalgamated Society of Carpenters and Joiners) was John Simmons, its secretary and constant representative at Labour Electoral Association confer-

92. *F.J.*, 10 Nov. 1890.   93. See app. 2.
94. I.T.U.C., *Report, Second Congress*, p. 7.
95. *F.J.*, 11, 14, 18 Nov. 1892.
96. D.T.C. minutes, 11 Nov. 1895.   97. Ibid., 7 Dec. 1896.

ences. He stood for a councillorship in 1895.[98] His own statement makes his position clear: "When asked to come forward as a candidate for Fitzwilliam ward he refused to do so until he consulted the Executive of the Trades Council . . . and consenting to do so he had disclaimed any connection with any political body or organisation (cheers). He issued an address and he defied even the scrutinising eye of Her Majesty's sub-sheriff to find in it any political allusion."[99] If elected he would "devote himself to the interests of his class" and after that to the interests of the community generally.[100] Labor was unrepresented in the corporation, for of the two councillors who might be considered as labor-minded, one had rejected the description and the other (W. J. Leahy) had stated that he did not represent labor alone.

The election result was disheartening. Simmons came last in the three-cornered contest, beaten by a Conservative and an independent Nationalist, both of whom were engaged in the drink trade.[101] When he ran again in January 1899, his speeches, if not his election address, contained political allusions of at least historical interest. A resolution passed at one of his election meetings asked voters to show "our present representatives that we do not forget the manner in which they treated O'Donovan Rossa,"[102] an allusion to the efforts of J. P. Nannetti and John Simmons to secure a home for the old Irish-American Fenian leader. At a meeting in support of another candidate (John Gibbons, secretary of the Bakers' Society), Simmons said that "there were a good many parties nowadays, but he belonged to the old party called Fenian (cheers)."[103] The *Freeman's Journal* (9 January) described him as "an old '67 man." The Fenian card was no more successful than the nonparty one.[104]

In 1896 the Trades Council's preferred candidate was its president, E. L. Richardson,[105] who was also unsuccessful but[106] who was returned unopposed early in 1898, thanks to nationalist auspices.[107]

During the 1890s, a number of trade union candidates were elected to the corporation as the nominees of various nationalist organizations

98. Ibid., 4 Mar. 1895.   99. *F.J.*, 4 Mar. 1895.
100. *F.J.*, 5 Mar. 1895.
101. William Ireland (conservative) 223, Joseph Delahunt (independent nationalist) 176, John Simmons 141 (*Irish Daily Independent*, 7 Mar. 1895).
102. *F.J.*, 26 Nov. 1898.   103. *F.J.*, 12 Dec. 1898.
104. He was sixth in a ward of four seats (*F.J.*, 18 Jan. 1899).
105. D.T.C. minutes, 12 Oct. 1896.
106. Richardson polled 237 out of a total of 510 votes cast (*F.J.*, 26 Nov. 1896). One of his speakers was Thomas Harrison, who emphasized that Richardson was a labor (i.e., not a political party) candidate and could claim his support, though he (Harrison) was "a Unionist" (*F.J.*, 21 Oct. 1896).
107. D.T.C. minutes, 14 Feb. 1898.

and they normally received the Trades Council's blessing. Richardson, approving of one of these as "a practical workingman and a trade unionist," pointed out that another candidate who had submitted an election address for approval did not come within this description and added that the council recognized no politics in these cases. "He remembered Mr W. J. Leahy asking the assistance of the council and although he had strong political leanings the council willingly supported him on labour grounds."[108] So many of the Dublin trade union leaders were connected with outside political organizations that independent action was extremely difficult; Simmons complained that an ex-president of the council (Thomas O'Connell, who had presided at the first conference of the Irish Trades Union Congress) had lavished foul abuse on the council and on himself for intervening in one ward.[109] Even the council's president (John Fitzpatrick, a carpenter), when he contested a poor law guardian election in 1896, did so at the request of a ratepayers' association. The council, in endorsing him, expressed its gratitude to the local nationalist registration association for selecting him.[110]

The assimilation of the Irish parliamentary and local government franchises, object of so many and so oft-repeated resolutions, was effected in 1898, ten years after the similar British act.[111] There was an immediate increase in the number of candidates calling themselves labor, both in towns and in counties, and a number of trade unions and trade councils ran their own nominees.[112] The Dublin Corporation, "the stronghold of Parnellism," approved of a resolution calling for unity between the pro- and anti-Parnellite sections of the nationalist

108. Ibid., 26 Oct. 1896.   109. Ibid., 22 Nov. 1896.
110. Ibid., 28 Feb., 14 Mar. 1898.
111. Local Government (Ireland) Act, 1898 (61 & 62 Vict. c 37), s. 98. By ss. 2(5), 21(a) and 94(2), property qualifications were abolished for candidates who were required only to be registered local government electors.
112. E.g., Sligo Trades Council contested eight of the twenty-four seats and secured three; there were other "independent" labor candidates (*F.J.,* 10, 18 Jan. 1899). In small towns and rural areas some curious "labour" candidates appeared, as in Newcastle West Limerick), where a branch of the Trade and Labour Association selected a merchant, a J.P., and a house and land proprietor—though a voice from the crowd denounced the merchant as never having paid a pound in labor, to which his proposer replied: "That will do now. We don't want to insult anyone." (*F.J.,* 10 Jan. 1899). In Nenagh (Tipperary) another branch agreed on ten candidates for artisans and laborers and eleven for commercial, professional, and other interests, and appointed a committee to canvass on behalf of the twenty-one, who had been selected as nationalists (*F.J.,* 3 Jan. 1899). The Trade and Labour Association was a successor to Davitt's defunct Irish Democratic Labour Federation and like it had become a mere nationalist appendage.

movement.[113] But there was no corresponding development in the labor ranks. A Labour Electoral Association, formed in 1895,[114] but not connected with any English body, endeavored to distinguish between the motley crowd of candidates claiming to be labor. It produced a list of some eleven approved candidates but could not agree about others, because the chairman, Thomas Kearns, and George Leahy (both of the Trades Council) would not follow E. L. Richardson in regarding as bogus labor candidates those who opposed the Labour Electoral Association (L.E.A.) nominees.[115] One approved candidate said that he appeared before the L.E.A. "in the double capacity of a labour and a Nationalist candidate and would be faithful to his pledges to both,"[116] while Kearns attended a Parnellite ward meeting to ask that one place be reserved for a workingmen's nomination.[117] Even Richardson was proposed on nomination day by a parish priest who had done the same service for nationalist candidates.[118] Seven candidates endorsed by the Labour Electoral Association were returned, but apart from Richardson none was then prominent in the trades council.[119] The Irish Socialist Republican party put up its first candidate in this election. He was E. W. Stewart, manager of the party's paper, the *Workers' Republic,* and a member of the Shop Assistants (a British union); he finished at the bottom of the poll in his ward.[120]

The Belfast Trades Council had its first success a year earlier, in November 1897. The city boundary had been extended in 1896 and the electorate divided into fifteen wards (in every case returning an alderman and three councillors) instead of the previous five.[121] As the franchise had already been widened in 1887 and the sectarian passions attendant on the second Home Rule bill had subsided, the council was encouraged to put forward a candidate for councillor in each of seven wards. Six[122] were returned, five of them heading the poll in their respective divisions. They were Alexander Taylor, a linenlapper and

---

113. *F.J.,* 6 Dec. 1898.
114. D.T.C. minutes, 18 Mar., 27 May 1895.
115. *F.J.,* 13 Jan. 1899.   116. *F.J.,* 2 Dec. 1898.
117. *F.J.,* 10 Dec. 1898.   118. *F.J.,* 6 Dec. 1898.
119. *F.J.,* 18 Jan. 1899.
120. He polled 448 votes as against 613 for the last candidate elected (*F.J.,* 18 Jan. 1899).
121. Clarkson (*Labour and Nationalism in Ireland,* p. 350) overlooks the earlier extension of the Belfast franchise and assumes that the election took place after the passing of the Local Government (Ireland) Act, 1898.
122. William Liddell, a painter, stood in two wards: St. George's, in which he won the last seat, and Dock, in which he was at the bottom of the poll (*B.N.-L.,* 26, 27 Nov. 1897).

secretary of the Belfast Trades Council; Murray Davis, secretary of the Belfast Operative Bakers' Society; William Liddell, secretary of a Belfast painters' union; Robert Gageby, who had founded the Flax-dressers' Trade Union and been its secretary for the sixteen years of its existence; Edward McInnes, a district delegate of the National Amal-gamated Union of Labour; and Alexander Bowman. Bowman, who had spent some time in Great Britain, had returned two years earlier to organize and act as secretary of a branch of the Municipal Employees' Association in Belfast.[123]

The council's success in 1897, in contrast to its failures in earlier years, can be explained by factors other than the rearrangement of wards and the absence of an impending Home Rule bill. The most important were the prolonged dispute in the engineering industry,[124] which involved a number of Belfast as well as British firms, and the inquiry into the public health of the city. The engineering workers, despite the Orange and Unionist sympathies they shared with their employers, on this occasion raised a strike fund[125] and staged a large demonstration in October. The principal speakers included a number of the council's municipal candidates as well as John Burns, whose earlier associations with Home Rule were overlooked.[126] Some of the candidates were also witnesses in the public health inquiry, which produced damning evidence of the city's insanitary condition and of reckless jerrybuilding.[127] Public concern was increased still further by recurrent outbreaks of typhoid, which caused 354 deaths in 1897.[128] The council issued a manifesto to every municipal candidate; it de-manded proper measures to safeguard the health of the community,

123. *B.N.-L.*, 27 Nov. 1897, which gives short biographies of the successful candidates.

124. See Jeffreys, *Story of the Engineers*, p. 143–9, and A. Shadwell, *The Engineering Industry and the Crisis of 1922*, pp. 21–6.

125. The shipyard workers in Harland and Wolff, which had not locked out its men, levied themselves at the rate of 10s. a fortnight (contribution card of William Nesbitt, Oct.–Dec. 1897, shown to the present writer).

126. *B.N.-L.*, 11 Oct. 1897.

127. *Minutes of Evidence of the Special Committee Appointed 1 August 1896 to Consider and Report upon the Present High Death-Rate of Belfast and the Condition of the Public Health of the City*. The evidence included the following details: some 20,000 of the city's 50,000 houses had no back lanes (p. 9); the night soil from those with dry privies and the domestic refuse had to be brought to the front, in some cases through the living room, and dumped at the side of the houses, to be removed weekly or fortnightly (p. 41); some 11,000 pigs were kept within the city limits (p. 211); a proposed site for 102 houses was described by the committee chairman as an "enormous dunghill" (pp. 152–3). In 1897 there were over 26,600 dry privies in the city (H. W. Bailie, M.S.O.H., *Report on the Health of the County Borough of Belfast for the Year 1906*, p. 31).

128. Ibid., pp. 59, 113.

corporation dwellings for artisans, fair wages for municipal workers, and the enforcement of a fair wages clause in public contracts.[129] Faced with irrefutable evidence of their own gross corruption and negligence, the ruling municipal councillors fell back on "me-too-ism" as an election program, but this did not prevent the defeat of several prominent Unionist aldermen and councillors, including a former lord mayor and his son, and the election of labor candidates.

The labor councillors as a body gave no cause for alarm. The *Belfast News-Letter* described Taylor as of a peaceful turn of mind, holding sound views on most questions and not "of the forward school of labour candidates," and paid tribute to Murray Davis for the absence of strikes in the baking industry for many years.[130] A further reason for the success of Taylor and Gageby was their support for total abstinence. Gageby in particular excited approval as a respectable citizen; he was the superintendent of a Sunday school, and the Belfast Conservative Association put forward only two candidates in his ward, proclaiming that they were leaving the third seat for him. The two candidates, one of whom was F. C. Johnston, ex-secretary of the Belfast Trades Council, clung to his coattails, solicited votes for him, and, when they secured the two remaining seats, included his name in their thanks to the electorate.[131]

The trades council's victory was by no means complete. Taylor might state that "he did not claim their suffrages as the advocate of any political party," but the council did not venture into either of the two predominantly Catholic wards, Falls and Smithfield. These had been arranged during the negotiations for the extension of the city boundary as the compromise price that the corporation had to pay to overcome opposition from the Irish nationalist parliamentary party and English indifference.[132] These two wards immediately became the electoral battlefield on which a bitter and prolonged struggle, lasting until 1905, was carried on between the clerically dominated Catholic Association and the Belfast branch of the Irish National Federation led by Joseph Devlin.[133] One of the council's members (Francis Connolly) ran as a Devlinite, but when a speaker at an election meeting claimed that

129. *B.N.-L.*, 29 Oct. 1897. The adoption of the Notification of Infectious Diseases Act and the stricter enforcement of health by-laws had by 1906 reduced the number of dry privies and of pigs to under 3,000, while the death rate had fallen from 24.3 per 1,000 to 20.1 (Bailie, *Report on the Health of Belfast for 1906*), pp. 22–23.

130. *B.N.-L.*, 27 Nov. 1897.

131. *B.N.-L.*, 26 Nov. 1897. They were over five hundred votes behind Gageby.

132. See T. J. Campbell, *Fifty Years of Ulster*, pp. 45–7.

133. A full account is given in the chapter "Joseph Devlin and the Catholic Representation of Belfast 1895–1905," in F. J. Whitford, "Joseph Devlin," an unpublished thesis, approved November 1959 for the degree of M.A. in the University of

the candidate had the support of the council, that body denied it and disregarded Connolly's plea that, if elected, he would be a recruit to the labor party.[134] In Dock, where there was a substantial Catholic vote, Catholic Association candidates entered the field with the result that William Liddell, the council's candidate, was swept aside; he could only complain, when the count showed him at the bottom of the poll, that he was not surprised, as a political and religious element had been introduced at the last moment.[135] Because the prospects seemed bright the following year in the absence of a nominee of the Catholic Association, the Council contested the aldermanship with another candidate, Robert Fleming. The result was no different, for the Catholic Association gave him the kiss of death by supporting him publicly; he was described as being in alliance with Fenians and moonlighters, and two trade union secretaries worked for the return of his Unionist opponent.[136]

Until the close of the century the financing of labor candidates in Dublin and Belfast differed sharply. The Dublin Trades Council did not lack money, as was evident when it collected over £150 from its affiliated societies towards the Belfast Trades Council's appeal for the locked-out engineering workers in 1897.[137] But those of its delegates who were aldermen, councillors, or poor law guardians were almost all nominees of outside organizations and it did not seem to feel any special financial responsibility for them. The Belfast Trades Council logically enough considered that it should pay the piper in order to ensure the correct nonparty songs, and in 1892 set up a parliamentary and municipal elections fund.[138] The following year, fortified by a £100 surplus from the hospitality fund raised for the 1893 conference of the British T.U.C.,[139] it was prepared to subsidize its president (Monro), if elected a councillor, at the rate of £50 a year for his three years of office.[140] When Murray Davis stood instead, he was assured a maximum of £40 for his election expenses.[141]

The demand that local government bodies should hold evening meetings was the subject of frequent but unavailing resolutions by

---

London. Devlin persuaded some members of the Parnellite Irish National League to form a joint committee with his own organization.

134. B.T.C. minutes, 6 Nov. 1897.   135. *B.N.-L.*, 27 Nov. 1897.
136. B.T.C. minutes, 9, 16, 29 July 1898.
137. D.T.C. minutes, 1 Nov. 1897, 28 Feb. 1898. Simmons estimated that the total contribution from Dublin trade unionists amounted to about £800.
138. B.T.C. minutes, 2 Apr. 1892. A week later the fund stood at £69 7s. 7d.
139. Ibid., 31 Jan. 1895.   140. Ibid., 16 Oct. 1893.
141. Ibid., 22 Nov. 1893.

labor organizations; they had great difficulty compensating representatives for lost time, as was shown by the Belfast council's efforts to finance some of its councillors elected in 1897. A municipal labor representation fund started for the purpose was exhausted within six weeks of the election and the council was driven to issuing ballot tickets and circularizing the affiliated trade unions.[142] Ward committees failed to raise sufficient money and the burden remained with the council.[143] In 1899 it was estimated that £100 [144] a year was necessary to pay for the lost time of two councillors and one poor law guardian, a sum that would have amounted to almost two-thirds of the council's total income; with difficulty the three representatives were paid about half that sum.[145] In 1900 they received among them less than £17.[146] In November of that year the executive committee passed a resolution that the council should endorse those of its members seeking reelection, but should undertake no financial obligations on their behalf.[147] The new century opened inauspiciously with another financial liability. William Walker, already receiving lost-time money as a poor law guardian, was dismissed from his job for writing, as secretary of council, to the War Office about the violation of the fair wage clause in a castings contract,[148] and had to be paid 23s. 3d. a week until he found employment.[149] The council's liability ceased after some months, when Walker was appointed organizing delegate for the Amalgamated Society of Carpenters and Joiners, but the year ended with the council owing its two public representatives lost-time money.[150] Six years later the council still carried the same two names among its creditors.[151]

In January 1901 five of the six councillors had to seek reelection. The council nominated four others in the hope of striking a bargain with other parties, but they had to be withdrawn when no agreement could be reached.[152] Of the five retiring councillors, two (Bowman and Taylor) had to withdraw,[153] one (Gageby) was given an unopposed re-

142. Ibid., 11, 25 Feb. 1898.   143. Ibid., 13 Aug. 1898.
144. Ibid., 22 Apr. 1899.

145. B.T.C. account book, balance sheet for 1899. Total income amounted to £172 9s. 9d., including £30 12s. in the labor representation account: payment for lost time amounted to £51 2s. 6d.

146. Ibid., balance sheet for 1900. A further payment of £22 was made in January 1901.

147. B.T.C. executive committee minutes, 9 Nov. 1900.

148. Ibid., 3 Aug. 1900, 2, 18 Jan. 1901.

149. B.T.C. minutes, 7 Feb. 1901.

150. B.T.C. account book, balance sheet for quarter ending 2 Jan. 1902.

151. Ibid., assets and liabilities following statement of accounts for the quarter ending 7 Jan. 1907.

152. B.T.C. minutes, 12 Jan. 1901.   153. B.N.-L., 8 Jan. 1901.

turn,[154] and the remaining two retained their seats in low polls against a freak candidate who sought election in six wards simultaneously.[155] When Davis died early in 1902 the council's representation on the corporation was reduced to three.

Such a reduction did little to ease the financial burden of the council, and though it continued to fight elections, its candidates were seriously handicapped. Unless exceptional factors were present, as in 1897, the lack of a political machine such as that possessed by other parties prevented the council from returning a sizeable minority to the corporation. A proposal was made in 1900 to appoint a registrar to collect information and compile a list of labor voters, but even this modest attempt at electoral machinery failed.[156] The council itself possessed no full-time officials, and a resolution to secure a permanent secretary came to nothing when the executive committee advised that the first step should be the establishment of a £50 reserve.[157] Its income of about £100 per year came from dues of its affiliated bodies,[158] as the yield from special appeals for labor representation often had to be supplemented from it, the council on occasions found it difficult to meet normal expenditure and was forced to issue further appeals.[159]

154. *B.N.-L.*, 7 Jan. 1901.   155. *B.N.-L.*, 26 Jan. 1901.

156. B.T.C. minutes, 9 Feb. 1900.

157. Ibid., 7 Feb. 1901. The yearly salaries of the officials amounted to £27, of which the secretary received £20.

158. During the years 1899–1903 the total varied between £98 7d. 11d. and £106 9s. 8d. (B.T.C. account book, relevant years).

159. The council issued an appeal to meet the expenses of its three delegates to the Dublin (1900) conference of the I.T.U.C.; as sufficient funds were not forthcoming only one was sent (B.T.C. minutes, 19 May 1900).

8

The Voices of Dissent

The Social-Democratic Federation and the Socialist League

The steady flow of Irish labor to Great Britain in the nineteenth century is so marked that any movement in the opposite direction is apt to be disregarded. Most immigrants settled down permanently in the English midlands and in such ports as Liverpool and Glasgow, where many of them took an active part in trade union affairs; a glance at the lists of delegates to British T.U.C. meetings in the 1880s will reveal an astonishingly large number of Irish names. They might aid the Home Rule cause and follow the voting directives of Parnell and his successors, but they could exert little direct influence on labor politics in Ireland. A number did return, however, bringing with them the results of their experiences in the British labor movement; it is probable that they were of importance in assisting the growth of amalgamated unions in the country of their birth. Some of the leading figures[1] in the early years of the Irish T.U.C. had worked for a time in Great Britain, so it is not surprising that returned emigrants and those who had attended meetings of labor organizations should have been influenced by them. The work of the Parliamentary Committee of the British T.U.C. earned the whole-hearted admiration of Irish trade unionists, but the climate of Irish political opinion was decidedly less favorable to politics that were not of the "pure labour," that is, "Lib-Lab" reformist kind. Yet the principal varieties of advanced radical, socialist, or left-wing dissent in Great Britain were also to be found in Ireland, even if their adherents were few.

It is doubtful whether the statement of C. D. Greaves that there was continuity of socialist organization in Dublin from the 1840s is cor-

---

1. They include P. J. Tevenan (A.S.R.S.), R. P. O'Connor and Hugh McManus (T. A. McManus was born in Liverpool of Irish parentage), Michael Canty (Gasworkers and other unskilled unions), and Alexander Bowman (Flaxdressers). See short biographies of some of these in I.T.U.C., *Report, Third Congress.*

rect,[2] though Dublin was a Chartist center and did have a short-lived and somewhat shadowy branch of the First International. That indi-viduals provided continuity is less disputable: John A. Ryan, first treasurer of the Dublin branch of the Socialist League, had been a member of the First International's Dublin group, and when he died in January 1887 his funeral was attended by his comrades. Other "veteran Internationalists" were Adam O'Toole, J. Landye, George King, and John O'Gorman.[3] Socialist ideas were occasionally advanced in debates on topics of current interest, as in a discussion on the politics of social reform held in the Young Ireland Society rooms in June 1884. The principal speaker, H. Dixon, advocated votes for women on a property basis, whereupon a speaker from the floor urged him to put forward his proposal for socialist reasons. Dixon admitted the weaknesses of the wage system and the property basis of the qualifications, but regarded as inopportune any advance on socialist grounds.[4] Such discussion groups as the Saturday Club provided a forum for unattached socialists. Thus Alexander Stewart in a debate (June 1884) on compulsory educa-tion, which was generally approved, urged the provision of penny dinners for schoolchildren and found widespread support for his suggestion.[5]

Henry Hyndman's Democratic Federation, formed in London in March 1881, changed its title to Social-Democratic Federation (S.D.F.) at its fourth conference in August 1884. Its program included legis-lative independence for Ireland and land nationalization. The report of the executive committee to the fourth conference recalled the price paid by the Federation for championing Irish grievances: "There is no doubt indeed that the steady support given by the Federation from the first to the cause of the Irish people estranged English workingmen who, blind to their own interests, were for the most part bitterly opposed to real justice to their brethern in Ireland, and were unable to see that the Irish were fighting their battle in relation to the land."[6] There was no immediate response from the Irish people in the form of branches, but the S.D.F. paper *Justice,* stocked by news agents in Dublin and Derry, was circulating in Ireland six months after its founding in January 1884. A letter (*Justice,* 20 December 1884) signed by Alexander Stewart, a Glasgow patternmaker then resident in Dub-lin, Samuel Hayes, and Richard Grace Russell, invited those interested to assist in organizing a Dublin branch, which was formed in January

2. C. D. Greaves, *The Life and Times of James Connolly,* pp. 58–9.

3. *Commonweal,* 5 Feb. 1887, 2 Jan. 1888, 18 May 1889; O'Brien Collection, MS 13953.

4. *Justice,* 7 June 1884.   5. Ibid., 20 Dec. 1884.

6. Ibid., 9 Aug. 1884.

1885 under the name of the Dublin Democratic Association and held its first open meeting in February. It ran a series of public meetings once a fortnight on such general subjects as "The Social Question" and "Democracy—Competition versus Co-operation" as well as on working-class housing and town tenants' rights. It had some success in attracting a working-class audience and counted among its members several prominent trade unionists, notably P. A. Tyrrell, secretary of an A.S.E. branch, and Tom Fitzpatrick. It is not clear how seriously it was affected by the split in the S.D.F. between the followers of Henry Hyndman and those of William Morris or by the latter's formation of the Socialist League in December 1884, but as an organization the Dublin Democratic Association seems to have ceased functioning in the summer of 1885.[7] Not all links were broken, however, since *Justice* continued to be sold by former members.

Students who follow the history of socialism in Dublin for the rest of the nineteenth century may be forgiven for concluding that they are witnessing the maneuvers of a stage army, with familiar names appearing as members of successive socialist or radical societies. *Commonweal*, the organ of the Socialist League, announced in its December 1885 issue that a branch was being formed in Dublin: "several first-rate workers have foregathered, and look to place the red flag on Irish soil, so that it may soon gather a goodly army behind it." Two of the army were the former S.D.F. members Tom Fitzpatrick and Samuel Hayes, Hayes filling the position of branch literature secretary. The Socialist League (S.L.) engaged the old meeting place of the Democratic Association in the Oddfellows' Hall, Upper Abbey Street, for a quarter and held some successful meetings, but when the hall's board of management found out the nature of their new tenants they cancelled the verbal agreement abruptly. Members who turned up for a meeting found the building guarded by police and when they adjourned to a room in a tavern the owner was soon persuaded by the police to disallow further gatherings.[8] The branch found it impossible to hire permanent rooms at a reasonable rent and had to hold meetings in various halls during the remainder of its existence.

William Morris spent several days in Dublin in April 1886. After addressing a mainly middle-class audience on the aims of art and disappointing them by advocating socialism as a precondition for a new birth of art, he spoke to the Saturday Club on "Socialism—What It Is." There was a large audience of working men who listened atten-

7. *Justice* carried reports regularly until April, after which no further mention is made of the branch.
8. *Commonweal*, Feb. 1886.

tively despite their preoccupation with the first Irish Home Rule bill, which had just been introduced by Gladstone in the House of Commons. Morris was not impressed by the debate in the Saturday Club, for the first speaker to defend socialism described it as "the crystallisation of Christian ethics," a phrase which brought out "rampant theology and the bigotry which one certainly expects to find in an Irish audience." After a discussion with branch members in the rooms of F. Schumann, a Danish glassblower, Morris concluded that the immediate difficulty facing socialists was religious feeling, but that after the establishment of Home Rule the "Catholic clergy will begin to act after their kind and try after more and more power till the Irish gorge rises and rejects them." He was less sanguine about Protestants: "the Protestant religious feeling being dogmatic and not political is hopeless to deal with."[9] His Irish visit taught Morris one lesson that he reproduced in an editorial of 1 May: "the Irish (as I have reason to know) will not listen to anything except the hope of independence as long as they are governed by England." An article in a June issue of *Commonweal* noted the Irish obsession with Home Rule but asserted that some signs of progress could be seen, as the branch had not met with the hostility that had disrupted the First International in the 1870s. Open-air meetings were not possible but Socialist League members sold *Commonweal* and distributed leaflets.[10]

Dublin was not a congenial center for socialist bodies; the S.D.F. had disappeared after six months and the Socialist League as a branch of Morris's organization seems to have had a formal existence of about a year. It sent a delegate to the League's second annual conference held in London in June 1886, and paid affiliation fees up to the end of August of the same year.[11] The report of the third annual conference (May 1887) did not list any Irish branches,[12] and an attempt in April 1887 to refound the S.D.F. in Dublin suggests that the S.L. branch may have disintegrated.[13] Perhaps the most accurate way of describing the situation of Dublin socialists is to say that during these years their organizational links with such bodies as the S.D.F. and the Socialist League were, for the most part, informal rather than formal, that they received publicity in *Justice* and *Commonweal,* and that they were visited from time to time by British socialist speakers.[14] The most ambitious meeting they held in 1887 was on 17 March to celebrate the founding of the

9. Ibid., 8 May 1886.   10. Ibid., 5 June 1886.
11. Ibid., 26 June, 2 Oct. 1886.
12. Socialist League, *Report of Third (1887) Annual Conference.*
13. *Justice,* 2 Apr. 1887. Intending members were asked to communicate with J. E. McCarthy.
14. E.g., J. Sketchley, author of a series of articles in *Commonweal* and of a pamphlet

Paris Commune, when the attendance included French, Danish, Russian, and American socialists. After the Dane Schumann had read the manifesto of the Commune and a French member, A. Coulon, had led the singing of the "Marseillaise," came speeches, more songs, and a telegram of good wishes from London comrades.[15]

In these years the Dublin socialists were most active in "front" organizations that they created or penetrated. A committee was formed in September 1886 to start an International Club that would ensure the "promotion of solidarity among the various nationalities in Dublin and the establishment of socialism on a firmer basis."[16] Membership was open to persons of advanced opinions—"Radicals, Democrats, Secularists, etc." The Paris Commune meeting was probably held under its auspices.[17] At the same time Socialist League members were influential in the Saturday Club, which they were able to use as a forum, and in the City of Dublin Working Men's Club.[18] But the organization through which they reached the greatest audience in 1887 was the Irish (or National) Labour League. In February and March heavy unemployment led to several large spontaneous demonstrations. The Dublin socialists distributed local Socialist League pamphlets among the unemployed, and, at one meeting in a Dublin suburb, attended by several thousand workers, two members, J. B. Killan and A. Upward, both barristers, addressed them on the defects of capitalist society, declaring that the land and the instruments of production should belong to the whole community.[19] Other socialist speakers were favorably received at later demonstrations. Late in March the Labour League was started with the object of organizing workers, skilled and unskilled, and educating them so that they should understand their social rights.[20] The committee elected in May contained five socialists, and, with the appointment of J. E. McCarthy as secretary in June, the Irish Labour League passed

---

on the Irish question, visited the branch in August 1886 (*Commonweal*, 14 Aug. 1886). The hostility between the S.D.F. and S.L. leaders diminished in later years and did not prevent a degree of cooperation at lower levels.

15. *Commonweal*, 12, 26 Mar. 1887; *Justice*, 26 Mar. 1887.

16. *Commonweal*, 11 Sept. 1886.

17. The Commune celebration was held at the temporary address (50 Dawson Street) given at the formation of the club.

18. "Several of our members assisted in the formation of the Saturday Club for the coming session" (*Commonweal*, 11 Sept. 1886). During the 1886–7 and 1887–8 sessions Dublin socialists (they included T. Fitzpatrick, A. Coulon, J. O'Gorman, Adam O'Toole, P. Stephens, F. Schumann, J. B. Killen, J. Karpel, S. Hayes, G. King, and Richard Grace Russell) lectured or spoke in debates; meetings were listed in *Commonweal* and *Justice*. They also took a leading part in the Working Men's Club.

19. *Commonweal*, 5, 12 Mar. 1887; *Justice*, 19 Mar. 1887.

20. *Commonweal*, *Justice*, 2 Apr. 1887.

into the hands of S.L.–S.D.F. members.[21] Local branches were formed after large outdoor meetings had been held during May and June in Dublin and its neighborhood, but when the initial interest subsided the League became a discussion club concerned less with immediate economic issues and remedies than with socialist doctrine.[22] Difficulties in securing suitable premises for regular indoor meetings led to the suspension of activities in November and the organization lapsed.[23] Though its primary purpose was to carry out socialist propaganda, not to form trade unions, the League did help to create a climate of opinion that made possible the upsurge of general unionism during the following years.[24]

The Socialist League had played a part in the successful outcome of an industrial dispute involving glass bottlemakers. Early in 1886 the owner of a Dublin bottlemaking firm brought in Danes to break a strike but did not tell them that he was in dispute with his employees. Two S.L. members who were bottlemakers, F. Schumann and William Graham, aided by the newly founded Dublin Trades Council, informed the Danes of the true state of affairs and persuaded them to return to their native country. The Danes threatened to bring an action for false pretences against the employer, who ultimately had to pay their expenses; his essay in strike-breaking cost him over £3,000. As a result of the Dublin men's success, Schumann was asked to draw up rules for an international society of glass bottlemakers. He did so and, at a congress held during September 1886 in the London headquarters of the Socialist League in Farringdon Road, the international was duly formed. Graham attended on behalf of the Dublin group, which became a branch of the international society. The Dublin S.L. celebrated the success by holding a social evening at which Graham gave a spirited account of the strike.[25]

The international society proved its worth when a dispute arose at the end of the year in St. Helens, Lancashire. A deputation of workers went to Denmark, Sweden, and Germany and forestalled the firm's attempt to recruit blacklegs. The employers later managed to bring in thirty-nine Swedes, but some of them refused to scab and the rest had to work under police protection. A ten-thousand-strong demonstration was then held on a Saturday afternoon. Among the speakers were Schumann representing the Dublin Trades Council and Graham as

21. *Commonweal, Justice*, 4 June, 30 July 1887.
22. *Commonweal*, 6, 27 Aug. 1887.   23. Ibid., 5 Nov. 1887.
24. A number of local unions appeared in 1888, including the Labour Union of Ireland, a general organization (*Commonweal*, 28 July, 4 Aug. 1888).
25. Swift, *Dublin Bakers*, pp. 294–5; *Commonweal*, 5 June, 31 July, 23, 30 Oct. 1886.

president of the Dublin branch. The masters capitulated under such pressure, sent the Swedes back and came to an agreement with their employees.[26]

After the demise of the Irish Labour League, Dublin socialists could still make use of the Saturday Club, the Working Men's Club, or the Irish Industrial League. The Saturday Club was practically their preserve but it was at best a "front" organization suitable for reformist propaganda. What they hankered after was a society devoted to the discussion of socialist doctrine, and for this purpose John O'Gorman and George King formed the Dublin Socialist Club, "open to all schools of socialist thought,"[27] in December 1887. Its personnel was substantially that of its predecessors and the Paris Commune celebrations it held in 1888 and 1889 were identical with the one held in 1887.[28] It had links with the Socialist League and O'Gorman, its secretary, and other members corresponded with Morris. It seems to have held meetings less frequently than its forerunners, possibly because its small membership was already involved in the more "open" organizations. In August 1888 it lost two of its most active members, F. Schumann, who returned to his native Denmark, and Tom Fitzpatrick, who emigrated to London.[29] The Paris Commune meeting of March 1889 was its last undertaking; it is probable that its disappearance was hastened by the decline of its parent body, the Socialist League, which was captured by anarchists the following year.

Its successor had already been formed. In February 1889 the Progressive (or Progressist) Club was launched by A. Coulon at 16 Dawson Street, the premises used by the Dublin Socialist Club,[30] though later meetings were held at 87 Marlborough Street. While the nucleus consisted of familiar figures there were some new names, notably Adolphus Shields, a printer, who with William Graham of the International Glass Bottlemakers was to organize the Gasworkers in Dublin and secure an eight-hour day for them. "How to abolish human slavery," "Why I am a socialist," and "Prospects of the Irish workman," were some of the addresses given; J. Landye, a former I.W.M.A. member, spoke on the question "What do we mean by progress?," and "Comrade

26. *Commonweal*, 1 Jan., 5, 12, 19 Feb. 1887.

27. Ibid., 24 Dec. 1887.

28. Ibid., 10, 24 Mar. 1888, 9, 23 Mar. 1889. At the 1888 celebration a telegram of greetings was received from the Socialist League (London) and in 1889 the Dublin Socialist Club sent the following message to the London celebration, held in South Place Chapel: "Irish comrades join in honouring the memory of the martyred dead and in working for the realisation of the ideals of 1789 and 1871. Vive la Commune!"

29. *Commonweal*, 25 Aug. 1888. Fitzpatrick's emigration may have been temporary, as he attended a Dublin Socialist Union meeting in January 1891.

30. Ibid., 2 Feb. 1889.

Smith, late of Clerkenwell S.D.F.," lectured on "Poverty, its cause and cure."[31] The Progressive Club was less doctrinaire than the Dublin Socialist Club and its lecturers and audiences included nonsocialists, so that discussions were livelier; at one meeting addressed by George King on "The gospel of plenty," "two or three Gaels" created a slight disturbance, no doubt by asserting the importance of Irish nationality and the Irish language.[32] But normally meetings were concerned with general and theoretical subjects, for most members dismissed Irish political issues as bourgeois in character and considered that Home Rule and peasant proprietorship would not materially change the condition of the Irish worker. They were more interested by John O'Gorman's detailed account of the proceedings of the Possibilist congress he had attended in Paris during May 1889 as a delegate of the Dublin branch of the International Glass Bottlemakers.[33]

The Progressive Club met for the last time in late February 1890 when O'Gorman spoke on "The labour question from a socialist standpoint."[34] It was replaced by the Irish Socialist Union, which was a revival of the former Dublin Socialist Club and like it offered a common platform for "the various schools of socialist thought" in order to ensure "more effective propagation of the principles on which all are agreed."[35] It took over the meeting place of the Progressive Club and commemorated the anniversary of the Paris Commune in 1890, with O'Gorman as the principal speaker.[36] It observed another anniversary in November, this time in honor of the Chicago anarchists executed in 1886,[37] but the agenda for its regular meetings showed little that was new either in speakers or subjects. An article in a November 1890 issue of *Justice* claimed that "socialism is making great progress in Ireland, especially in Dublin and Belfast";[38] but it was not a claim that could be substantiated, for the Irish (or Dublin) Socialist Union[39] remained a small coterie, visited occasionally by S.D.F. speakers from Great Britain.[40] Its lofty attitude to the dominant question of Home Rule, dis-

31. Ibid., 27 Apr., 4, 11, 18 May, 1 June 1889.
32. Ibid., 6 July 1889.
33. Ibid., 17 Aug. 1889. The rival Possibilist (reformist) and Marxist congresses were held in Paris beginning 15 May, with the object of founding a new socialist international. Agreement between the two groups was reached some time later and it was a united Second International that met in Brussels in 1891. The S.D.F. attended the Possibilist congress, which explains why O'Gorman was a delegate to it; by this time the Dublin socialists had renewed links with the S.D.F.

34. *Justice*, 22 Feb. 1890.   35. Ibid., 8 Feb. 1890.
36. Ibid., 15 Mar. 1890.   37. *Commonweal*, 1 Nov. 1890.
38. *Justice*, 29 Nov. 1890.

39. It seems to have changed its name to Dublin Socialist Union in 1891 (*Commonweal*, Jan. –Apr. 1894).
40. *Justice*, 2 June, 28 July 1894.

cussed at a meeting in January 1891, is an indication of its refusal to recognize that it was an unavoidable issue. Most speakers declared that Home Rule would be detrimental to progress, or that it would be flying from known to unknown evils, or that it would mean the rule of "the farmer, the publican, the clergy-man and the party politician"; Fitzpatrick even asserted that until the power of the priest was broken it would be dangerous to introduce Home Rule. Only one speaker, A. Kavanagh, considered that the granting of Home Rule would open the way for "the intelligent electors" to demand reforms of greater social importance.[41] Some D.S.U. members were active in the Dublin branch of the Fabian Society in the nineties and most of them joined the Independent Labour Party branch started late in 1894, but it is difficult to avoid the conclusion that their eagerness to welcome successive British left-wing organizations sprang from a false conception of internationalism that enabled them to disregard central issues in Irish politics. When the I.L.P. branch disintegrated, the group reverted to the old name; in 1896 James Connolly used it to start his Irish Socialist Republican Party.

The Fabian Society

Some seven years after the founding of the Fabian Society in 1884 the first Irish branch was organized. A Belfast society was formed in February 1891, with Bruce Wallace as chairman, W. M. Knox as secretary, and a committee that included John Murphy of the Belfast Trades Council; for some months it carried on much useful work.[42] But the following year its membership had shrunk to six, and when two of its most active members left the city the secretary could only report that "its animation is suspended."[43] Knox was an indefatigable worker for good causes and he with some other ex-Fabians helped to found an I.L.P. branch in the autumn of 1892.

A Dublin branch formed in 1892[44] had a somewhat longer life. Its contingent and that of the Reform League marched together in the Dublin May Day procession of 1894, and it was represented by Adolphus Shields of the Gasworkers on the number one platform at the Phoenix Park demonstration that followed.[45] The society seems to have

41. *Belfast Weekly Star*, 24 Jan. 1891.

42. Knox and another member represented the society in a public discussion organised by the Belfast Trades Council on the eight-hour day in February (*Belfast Weekly Star*, 21, 28 Feb., 25 Apr. 1891).

43. Fabian Society, *Report of the Executive Committee for the Year Ending 31 Mar. 1892*, p. 18.

44. Ibid., p 23.   45. *D.T.C. Labour Day Agenda* 1894.

been most active in the middle years of the decade when it held weekly meetings advertised in *Justice*, but thereafter it gradually declined and by 1899 it was in abeyance.[46]

The success of a number of labour candidates in the elections following the 1898 Local Government Act had its effect on the Fabian Society executive. "Nearly a year before it occurred to the Queen to visit Ireland," they reported with unconscious humor, "the E.C. came to the conclusion that they too had hitherto neglected that country."[47] Considering that "the recent creation of District and County Councils must give rise to administration problems, towards the solutions of which Fabian experience might prove useful," they decided to extend the Hutchinson Trust[48] lectures to Ireland. As there were no trades councils, cooperative or socialist societies in many places, a preliminary tour had to be undertaken in order to set up local committees. Lectures were given by J. Bruce Glasier and S. D. Shallard, who undertook a series of month-long tours in various areas. In the first month the towns visited were Dublin, Dundalk, Drogheda, Maryborough, and Baltinglass; in the second, Limerick, Waterford, Wexford, Carrick-on-Suir, and New Ross. Encouraged by their success, the lecturers spent a further month in the work, Glasier visiting Munster (Cork, Tipperary, Thurles, and Cashel) and Shallard touring Ulster (Belfast, Londonderry, Enniskillen, and Lurgan). Shallard paid a return visit to Ulster in 1901.[49]

In Belfast, Dublin, and Cork, the trades councils made arrangements, but elsewhere the local organizers were mayors and councillors, assisted by the leading citizens, "lay and clerical." The Irish nationalist M.P.s William Field, J. J. Shee, and Kendal O'Brien, who were leading members of the Irish Land and Labour League and had attended early congresses of the Irish T.U.C., were especially helpful. The local organization made a selection from a list of subjects and arranged the place and time of the lectures. In the smaller towns, lectures were given in the court house; in Cork, in the municipal buildings lent by the corporation; and in Dublin, in the Trades Council's own hall. In Belfast the Trades Council, who had to hire a hall, charged 2*d.* for a single lecture and 3*d.* for the course of four (The Workers' Condition, Trade Unionists, Municipalities at Work, and Drink and Poverty).[50]

46. Fabian Society, *E.C. Report 1895* (p. 8), *1898* (p. 2), *1899* (p. 8).
47. Ibid., *1900* (p. 11).
48. In 1894 Henry Hutchinson left over £9,000 to be spent by five trustees for the educational purposes of the Fabian Society. His daughter died shortly afterwards and left £1000 for similar purposes (E. R. Pease, *A History of the Fabian Society*, p. 99).
49. Fabian Society, *E.C. Report, 1900* (pp. 11, 12), *1901* (p. 10).
50. B.T.C. minutes, 30 Dec. 1899.

The Fabian lecturer's tours had three results, none of them of any lasting significance. The Belfast Trades Council subscribed for a period to the Fabian book box service.[51] A local society formed in Cork in March 1901 included two town councillors, but its membership barely reached double figures; by 1903 six members had left the city and the four remaining ceased to constitute a society. Two pamphlets were prepared by Fabian headquarters on railway nationalization and local government, but sales were small, though both had a topical interest.[52]

More significant was an encounter Glasier had with James Connolly, an old fellow-agitator in Edinburgh in the days of the Socialist League. Connolly greeted Glasier at the end of a lecture: "And so, Glasier, you have become a Fabian!" Glasier, describing Connolly a few weeks later "stampeding with a mob through the streets [of Dublin, on the occasion of Chamberlain's visit], brandishing the Boer flag, and shouting for an Irish Republic and the defeat of Britain in the Transvaal," envied him his self-indulgence and irresponsibility. "How straight and broad, but ah! how exhilarating seemed the path along which he was careering with the policemen at his heels!"[53] Connolly's reply, in the S.D.F. paper *Justice*—"How I envied his self-restraint and sense of responsibility!"—was more than a retort; it was both a prophecy and an analysis of the different positions of the two men, and of the movements to which they belonged.

E. R. Pease, the historian of the Fabian Society, writing before 1916 and describing the work of the Fabian society as "the working out of the application of the broad principles of socialism to the industrial and political environment of England," remarked that "the application of the principles of socialism to Ireland has not yet been seriously attempted."[54] An Ireland obsessed with the question of national independence was not in a receptive mood for the Fabian gospel, and the attitude of leading Fabians like the Webbs was not calculated to change it. A letter written to Graham Wallas in July 1892, when they were on their honeymoon in Ireland, contains the following passage: "We will tell you about Ireland when we come back. The people are charming but we detest them, as we should the Hottentots, for their very virtues. Home Rule is an absolute necessity in order to depopulate the country of this detestable race."[55]

51. Ibid., 14 Nov. 1904.

52. Fabian Society, *E.C. Report, 1900* (p. 12), *1901* (p. 16), *1902* (p. 11), *1903* (p. 16).

53. *Clarion*, March 1900, quoted in Desmond Ryan, ed., *Socialism and Nationalism, A Selection from the Writings of James Connolly*, p. 8.

54. Pease, *History of the Fabian Society*, p. 240.

55. Janet Beveridge, *An Epic of Clare Market*, p. 9, quoted in A. M. McBriar,

The Independent Labour Party

Belfast, unlike Dublin, had no socialist tradition reaching back into the first half of the nineteenth century and the short-lived branch of the First International had no heirs in the 1880s. Samuel Hayes, the literature secretary of the Socialist League's Dublin branch, gave an address on socialism to a sympathetic Belfast audience in March 1887,[56] but his visit did not result in a S.L. branch. The S.D.F. struck no roots, and no local socialist societies or clubs similar to those in Dublin made their appearance in the northern city. The most radical groups were the Irish Land Restoration Society, the Ulster branch of the National Secular Society, and the Belfast Radical Association. The first group's purpose was to promote Henry George's social panacea of a single tax on land and it was responsible for his appearance in Belfast early in 1885. Alexander Bowman, its secretary, went in 1889 to Glasgow, where he became president of the Henry George Institute,[57] but his Belfast society had lapsed some time earlier. The National Secular Society did not confine its efforts to the abolition of religious tests in public life and held meetings of more general interest. In January 1890, J. Karpel, a member of the Dublin Socialist League and its successors but billed as a Russian nihilist, spoke under its auspices on "Russia and Nihilism."[58] W. M. Knox was the secretary of the Belfast Radical Association, which kept a reading room in the city center open each evening for its members and made the standard radical demands in its published program.[59]

No general support for more advanced political thought was to be found among Belfast trade unionists. Bowman's activities in the S.D.F. took place in England rather than Ireland. R. H. Feagan, an organizer

---

Fabian Socialism and English Politics, 1884–1918, p. 119, n. 1. With the exception of the last ten words ("in order to depopulate the country of this detestable race") and a postscript ("We are very very happy—far too happy to be reasonable"), the letter was written by Sidney Webb. The happy bride was the author of the additions (L. P. Curtis, Jr., *Anglo-Saxons and Celts,* p. 134, n. 47).

56. *Justice,* 19, 26 Mar. 1887.   57. *Belfast Weekly Star,* 11 Oct. 1890.
58. Ibid., 11 Jan. 1890.

59. Objects: promotion of radical principles in Belfast and district and their adoption in parliament; self-government for England, Ireland, Scotland, and Wales and an imperial parliament for imperial affairs; land nationalization; abolition of state pensions and sinecures; abolition of the principle of hereditary government; disestablishment and disendowment of the remaining state churches; payment of M.P.s and election expenses; removal of taxes impeding industry; adult suffrage; regulation of conditions and hours of labor; arbitration for international questions instead of war (Ibid., 7 June 1890).

of the bootmakers and secretary of a Knights of Labour Assembly, and John Murphy, later secretary of the Belfast Trades Council, were both committee members of the Fabian Society.[60] But the political leanings of the Trades Council were best represented by Samuel Monro, its first president, who "in his private capacity [had] been of considerable service to the conservative cause" and was opposed to socialism on the grounds of its impracticality.[61] Officially the Council was neutral in politics, but it would be more accurate to say that its neutrality implied an unquestioning acceptance, if not an active defense, of the Act of Union. While it forced Bowman's resignation as secretary on a charge of implicating the council on Gladstone's side in the Home Rule controversy of 1886, it was quick to exculpate a later secretary, F. C. Johnston, when he was accused of using his position on behalf of the Unionist cause during a lecture tour through England in March 1890.[62] A branch of the Fabian Society might escape because of its emphasis on reform, not revolution, and its avoidance of the Irish question, but the S.D.F. and the Socialist League were immediately suspect on the grounds of advanced socialist ideas and support for Home Rule. It was in this unpropitious climate that the Independent Labour Party's first Irish branch appeared.

The Belfast I.L.P. was established in September 1892.[63] Its chairman, reviewing its progress a year later, said that it had met with much opposition and that a number of the original members had left. Nonetheless he claimed that the branch had held a large number of open-air meetings and made progress. On the Sunday before the opening of the Belfast (1893) meeting of the British T.U.C., the branch held a conference for which invitations had been issued to all those in favor of independent political action, including members of the Independent Labour Party (I.L.P.), the Social-Democratic Federation, and the Fabian Society. The chairman was Alexander Stewart[64] and a four-part

60. Ibid., 10 Jan. 1891.   61. Ibid., 27 Dec. 1890.

62. *Brotherhood*, 22, 29 Mar. 1890. Johnston subsequently set up in business as a coachmaker and was elected as a conservative member of the Belfast Corporation.

63. *B.N.-L.*, 4 Sept. 1893. Alexander Stewart, the chairman, referred to the "Belfast Labour Party" as a young organization that had its first meeting 29 September 1892. Clarkson (*Labour and Nationalism in Ireland*, p. 349) assumes that it cannot have been formed before the Bradford national conference in January 1893, and places its inaugural meeting "a few months later." In fact a large number of I.L.P. branches were formed in the second half of 1892 as the result of a campaign in favor of independent labor representation by Joseph Burgess of the *Workman's Times*. See H. M. Pelling, *The Origins of the Labour Party*, p. 115.

64. Stewart had helped to found the Dublin Democratic Association in December 1884 and was now resident in Belfast.

resolution was proposed and seconded by two other local committee members, J. H. Gilliland and W. M. Knox. The visiting speakers included Edward Aveling, H. H. Champion, Pete Curran, Ben Tillett, Keir Hardie, and F. Brocklehurst, leading representatives of the three socialist groups. Little was accomplished at this conference. Part one of the resolution, which was substantially a demand for a legal limit on the hours of work, was passed, as was a motion by Aveling for the nationalization of the means of production and distribution. Part two dealt with organization and suggested that an annual meeting should be held during Congress week in the town selected by the British T.U.C., that a central executive should be chosen and paid agents appointed, and that members should contribute one penny per quarter to central funds. After Aveling had pointed out that those who were present belonged to various organizations and could not dictate a line of action to the I.L.P., part two was withdrawn except for the clause which laid down the time and place of the annual meeting. Part three, a rhetorical statement that now was the time to aim at a domination of the House of Commons, disappeared, and part four on electoral reform was debated. It demanded equal suffrage, labor representation on public boards and in parliament, a permanent ballot providing for second voting, payment of election expenses, and the use of the referendum (reference of all great cases to the people). Tillett urged the conference to adopt the policy of independent political action that was to be put forward by a group in the British T.U.C., and part four was replaced by a pious generalization declaring in favor of "any proposal for the democratisation of the system of government."[65]

In the afternoon of the same day, the I.L.P. held a meeting at the Custom House steps, Belfast's equivalent of Hyde Park. Here every Sunday socialist and labor speakers competed with a variety of orators, from the straightforwardly evangelical to the virulently sectarian, the greatest crowds being drawn by those speakers most intimately acquainted with infernal geography and papal duplicity. To the astonishment of the local branch—and of the *Belfast News-Letter*—the meeting was the most successful the I.L.P. had ever held. The crowd of over three thousand listened in "the utmost good order" to speeches by Aveling and Tillett, and a large number remained for a further meeting addressed by Pete Curran.[66]

Within a week the branch met with a different reception. A crowd, fired by rejoicings over the defeat of the second Home Rule bill, swept labor speakers from the steps and on the following Sunday organized a counter meeting. An attempt to distribute socialist leaflets resulted in

65. *B.N.-L.*, 4 Sept. 1893.   66. *B.N.-L.*, 4 Sept. 1893.

W. M. Knox being mauled and chased by a crowd of some thousands until the police made a baton charge.[67]

In the Belfast Trades Council there was opposition of a less violent kind. The Power Loom Tenters made a strong protest against the I.L.P. Sunday conference, and the Trades Council by a majority decision (27 to 19) hastened to disclaim "any connection with certain other so-called labour organisations"[68] and requested "the working men of the city to take no notice of irresponsible parties who are endeavouring to propound their ideas under the mantle of trade unionism and labour."[69] For these conservative members socialist doctrines were stumbling blocks in the way of trade union advancement.

The new year brought a fresh instance of hostility to the I.L.P. When the council was considering instructions for its delegates to the 1894 congress of the British T.U.C., Walker proposed that they move an emergency resolution sympathizing with the "friends and relatives of those who have suffered death by accident while following their usual avocation, and particularly the widows and relatives of those so suddenly bereaved by the late Albion colliery disaster . . . and that we regret that her Majesty's ministers in the House of Commons did not see fit to make their sense of regret at such a disaster known, by carrying a resolution of sympathy with the relatives, choosing rather to congratulate the Duke and Duchess of York on the birth of a son; and we think that the labour and Radical members failed in their duty by not supporting Mr J. Keir Hardie, who endeavoured to induce the House of Commons to sympathise with the sufferers of such disaster."[70]

Hardie's protest in the House of Commons on the same matter had provoked a wild scene. Walker's motion obviously terrified the council members, and Richard Sheldon, who was to run for office in the British T.U.C. under the new standing orders, hastened to move an amendment deleting all after the world "disaster." No one felt more sympathy with the victims than he, and he would support a resolution of sympathy if, as was more than likely, one was brought before the congress independently of the council. Sheldon's amendment was carried by 22 votes to 2. During the 1890s, Walker and his associates gradually acquired greater importance in the council until at the beginning of the twentieth century they were in a dominant position, but their rise was accompanied by a decline in their fervor. Walker clearly did not share the outlook of Hardie on Home Rule and disarmament. When a cir-

67. *B.N.-L.,* 18 Sept. 1893.
68. The conference called by the I.L.P. branch had been held in the Engineers' Hall, College St., where the Belfast Trades Council usually met.
69. B.T.C. minutes, 22 Sept. 1893.   70. Ibid., 9 Aug. 1894.

cular came before the executive committee from the labor subcommittee of the International Crusade for Peace, he moved that it be marked *read*, and an amendment by Bowman was necessary to secure its adoption.[71]

Belfast socialists continued their propaganda work outside the Trades Council, though there was no immediate improvement in the political atmosphere. H. Alexander, a visiting S.D.F. lecturer, spoke in Belfast on a Sunday in May 1894, but when he referred to Home Rule he had to close the meeting.[72] The opening months of 1895 were marked by severe unemployment and distress, soup kitchens were opened in February and March and the Belfast Trades Council collected £400 for relief. The I.L.P. decided that open-air meetings could be resumed on Sunday afternoons at the "Steps," and for some time all went well. In February William Rice and William Walker spoke to over two thousand who listened attentively for ninety minutes. The Sunday audiences continued to grow and, though Walker was interrupted at one meeting in late March by a local preacher in a tall hat,[73] he held his ground and a substantial crowd followed him and his supporters in a procession to the club rooms. Opposition increased in late April and, at stormy meetings on the first two Sundays in May, only a strong force of police saved Walker from severe treatment. Shouts of "Put him in the dock" (the Custom House backed on the river Lagan), "Three cheers for King William," and "To hell with the Pope," were the rallying cries of the mob.[74] On the second Sunday police had to charge the mob twice before Walker was rescued and later escorted him to his home from the club; he was subsequently given police protection for about a year.[75] At the end of May a Belfast correspondent for the *Clarion* sent the following report:

We think it advisable to discontinue the Custom House meetings until the spirit of the pious and immortal William cools down a bit. On Saturday evening, however, we went to the Queen's Bridge. As usual bigotry and brutality were well represented in the audience; but amidst cries of 'Throw him in the dock!' 'You're a home Ruler!' 'Drown him!' Walker held his ground, and said all that he went there to say. A large crowd followed us

71. B.T.C. executive committee minutes, 21 Jan. 1899. Alexander Stewart was successful (by 20 votes to 10) in securing the council's permission to have the officers sign the circular (B.T.C. minutes, 28 Jan. 1899).

72. *Justice*, 2 June 1894. Alexander held a successful meeting in Dublin some days later.

73. Probably Arthur Trew, the founder of the Belfast Protestant Association.

74. A summary of the I.L.P.'s activities during the first half of 1894 is given in *Justice*, 6 July 1895. See also *B.N.-L.*, 6 May 1895.

75. R. McClung, Reminiscences of the Belfast Labour Movement, a manuscript in my possession.

through the streets, but we divided, Walker jumping on a tram car, and they dispersed. We sold fifty 'Merrie Englands' at the meetings. We advertised it as an exposure of socialism; that sells it and minimises the risk of getting hit with something.[76]

Industrial conditions at the beginning of 1896, as in 1895, enabled the I.L.P. to make a fresh start. A shipbuilding strike on the Clyde and the Lagan made open-air meetings possible again and at one, addressed by Harry Orbell of the London Dockers' Union in January, a crowd of over four thousand attended and a collection was raised for the locked-out laborers. Two good meetings were also held in the new, centrally situated I.L.P. hall, and Walker announced that Pete Curran, Irish-born organizer of the Gasworkers and a well-known socialist, would contest North Belfast as an I.L.P. candidate against Sir James Haslett, who had declared in the Belfast Corporation that 12s. a week was quite a sufficient wage for a married laborer and his family.[77] But with the end of the strike the election plans faded. The I.L.P. continued to hold indoor meetings during the year and had a succession of cross-channel speakers, notably Bruce Glasier and his wife, Russell Smart, Pete Curran, Enid Stacey, and Ramsay MacDonald, as well as such local members as William Rice, W. N. Knox, J. H. Gilliland, Walker, and the recently returned Bowman.[78]

The year ended with a conference on organization and propaganda, to which all friends interested in socialist efforts were invited.[79] It marked the demise, not the rebirth, of the Belfast I.L.P. For the first few months of 1897 meetings were held, but the subjects were of a general nature and it was obvious that the branch had withdrawn from Belfast politics and was quietly fading away. Its place was taken by the Belfast Ethical Society, launched by the indefatigable W. M. Knox and his colleague J. H. Gilliland, who furnished audiences with lectures on literature, rationalism, spiritualism, evolution, and modern science—the staple intellectual fare of the ethical movement.[80] The society carried on into the twentieth century and continued to provide a forum for progressives of various hues. It occasionally offered a lecture on a

76. Millar, J., "Notes from the Front," "Belfast," *Clarion,* 1 June 1895, quoted in Emmet Larkin, *James Larkin, 1876–1947, Irish Labour Leader,* p. 316.

77. *Clarion,* 13 Jan. 1896. I am indebted to Dr. Larkin for his references also.

78. Ibid., 1896, passim.   79. Ibid., 19 Dec. 1896.

80. Ibid., 1897–1902, passim. The principal local speakers were Knox, Gilliland, Bowman, W. Rice, and John Murphy. Two visiting speakers were Margaret McMillan, best known for her work in nursery schools, and Hypatia Bradlaugh-Bonner, daughter of the well-known atheist Charles Bradlaugh. The Belfast Ethical Society was founded in 1897, joined the Ethical Union in 1898, and was dissolved in 1913 (G. Spiller, *The Ethical Movement in Great Britain,* p. 114).

political theme and in 1903 sent delegates to the inaugural conference of the Belfast Labour Representation Committee.

The attacks that ultimately drove the Belfast I.L.P. from the streets and caused its collapse were the work of Arthur Trew and his followers. Trew made his name as an open-air preacher at the Custom House steps from 1889 onward. He specialized in a particularly virulent form of politico-sectarian public speaking, attacking Home Rule, Romanism, ritualism, and tolerance shown in high places toward any manifestation of liberalism in politics or religion. Interlarding his diatribes with gross witticisms, he built up a regular Sunday afternoon audience that was willing to contribute to a collection to defray his expenses.[81] He led the initial attacks on Belfast I.L.P. speakers and subsequently formed the Belfast Protestant Association, a body that made him a force to be reckoned with and caused official Unionism and Orangeism much trouble. The subsequent history of the Belfast Protestant Association and its offspring, the Independent Orange Order, belongs to the first decade of the new century.

As in the case of Dublin, socialists in Belfast were not content with a "front" organization. In September 1898 a Belfast Socialist Society was formed and "Jewish, Christian, Protestant, Catholic and all other socialists" were invited to join.[82] Weekly meetings were held for a few months, after which the society ceased to advertise its existence and the handful of familiar figures confined their energies to the Belfast Ethical Society. A branch of the Clarion Fellowship, an organization recruiting members from readers of Robert Blatchford's paper, the *Clarion,* and leavening socialism with socials, appeared in Belfast in 1900.[83] The emphasis on entertainment and cycling excursions drew in a more youthful and less doctrinaire membership than the older societies; it acquired clubrooms, was encouraged by visits from Nunquam (Blatchford) and Dangle (A. M. Thompson), *Clarion* columnists,[84] and for some years stimulated the sales of the newspapers and of *Merrie England,* Blatchford's best-seller in warmhearted, undogmatic socialism. Clarionettes (Clarion Fellowship members) were to be found in Dublin and Cork as well as Belfast, a tribute to Blatchford's genius as a journalist. The Clarion Fellowship did not result in any sudden crop of socialist candidates in Belfast, but it did prepare the ground for renewed efforts to secure labor representation from 1905 onward.

At the I.L.P.'s organizing conference at Bradford in 1893, the com-

81. Trew originally was resident in Dublin and the collection was meant initially to cover his train fare (interview with William Boyd).

82. *Clarion,* 24 Sept., 8 Oct. 1898. This was really a branch of the Irish Socialist Republican Party; see the last section of this chapter.

83. Ibid., 24 Nov. 1900.   84. Ibid., 25 May 1901.

mittee said that their party had no existence in Ireland. "It was true that there was a very small branch somewhere about Belfast, but it had not put itself in evidence."[85] The branch directory made amends in 1894 and two years later added Waterford and Dublin to the list.[86] The Belfast branch had to contend with Orange hostility, but the Waterford I.L.P. fell a victim to nationalist dissensions when it became involved in the pro- and anti-Parnellite struggle that lasted for some years after the Parnell–O'Shea divorce case.

The I.L.P. in Dublin appears to have had a twofold origin. One of the Lyng brothers, members of the Dublin Socialist Union, met some of the personnel of the I.L.P. in Liverpool during a visit to that city and brought back some of its literature. As a result an invitation was sent to Hardie to address a meeting in Dublin.[87] James Connolly, then living in Edinburgh, made a similar suggestion to Hardie who was anxious to get support from the Irish in Great Britain for the I.L.P. Writing in July 1894, Connolly stated that he was well aware that both the Parnellite and anti-Parnellite groups were unfriendly to the labor movement and that their support for Irish tenant farmers arose from the necessity to back Home Rule "with some cause more clearly allied to their daily wants than a mere embodiment of the national sentiment of the people." Support from the nationalists would be forthcoming only if it could be shown that it was in their interest politically to do so. He then suggested a plan. There was the nucleus of a strong labor movement in Ireland, "which only needs judicious handling to flutter the doves in the Home Rule dovecote. Now if you were to visit Dublin and address a good meeting there, putting it in strong and sharp, without reference to either of the two main parties, but rebellious, anti-monarchical and outspoken on the feelings of both landlord and capitalist, and the hypocrisy of both political parties for a finale!" He urged Hardie to have a resolution passed at the meeting expressing the sympathy of the Irish people with the labor movement in Great Britain—it would force the hand of Redmond and his clique. The meeting should be arranged from the Dublin side and Field should take the chair: "The resolution, if rightly and judiciously used, would knock the bottom out of the Irish opposition to our movement."[88]

After a preliminary gathering in October,[89] the I.L.P. was launched

85. Shaw Maxwell, London, Executive Council, I.L.P. (*Report of I.L.P. Conference, Bradford, 1893*, p. 8).

86. *Labour Annual* (1896), pp. 103, 104, 115.

87. William O'Brien, *Forth the Banners Go*, p. 6.

88. Connolly to Hardie, 3 July 1894, O'Brien Collection, MS 13933, National Library of Ireland. This letter is a typed copy.

89. The meeting was to be held in York Street on Monday, October 29 (*Justice*, 27 Oct. 1894).

publicly at a meeting held in the Rotunda on 10 November. Hardie had evidently not followed all Connolly's suggestions, for though William Field, the cattle-dealer M.P., was on the platform, the chair was taken by Thomas O'Connell, president of the Dublin Trades Council, and E. L. Richardson, its vice-president, was selected to move the resolution. Hardie, the principal speaker, was neither antimonarchical nor as rebellious as Connolly would have wished. He claimed that he had been a member of the Home Rule League since 1879 and, in an assertion aimed at the Liberals, that the I.L.P. supported Home Rule as a matter of principle, not expediency. His policy was to unite the representatives of labor. "If independent labour men were returned from the north and south of Ireland it would do a great deal to break down the absurd prejudice which separates north and south." The motion, supported by Patrick Shelley and other Dublin Trades Council members, bears the marks of Hardie's drafting: "That in order to give effect to the resolution of the [British] Trades Union Congress [on independent labour representation] and to aid in the building up of an industrial commonwealth, this meeting of the workers of Dublin pledges itself to form and support an Irish section of the Independent Labour Party." [90] There were some *caveats* expressed when the possibility of putting up labor candidates in Dublin was mentioned. Field protested that he was there first as a Home Ruler and secondly as a labor man; he could not belong to the I.L.P. if its program interfered with the progress of the national movement. James Sexton, general secretary of the N.U.D.L., had come from Liverpool to aid Hardie, but he did little to soothe Field's fears; after asserting his *bona fides* as a Home Ruler and the son of an Irishman, he roundly asserted that the I.L.P. "were not going to consider the convenience of the Tory, Liberal, Welsh or Irish parties in opposition to the party drawn from the people." The resolution was passed, though with some dissent. An open-air meeting was held the following day (Sunday) in Beresford Place and Saturday's resolution adopted on the motion of Robert Dorman [91] and a N.U.D.L. member named Kennedy. Hardie was more outspoken at this meeting

90. *F.J.*, 12 Nov. 1894.
91. Dorman was appointed secretary of the branch. Born in 1859, Dorman joined the British Navy and was invalided out in 1880. A humanitarian socialist, he became a foundation member of Connolly's Irish Socialist Republican Party, but he had little success in his efforts to organize branches in provincial towns. In 1912 he returned to Belfast, where he joined the I.L.P. and helped to start a socialist Sunday school (R. McClung, "Bob Dorman" in *The Labour Opposition*, I, no. 6, Aug. 1925). In the 1920s he gained a seat in the Northern Ireland Senate, but lost it when the abolition of proportional representation in 1929 reduced the number of Labour M.P.s in the Northern Ireland House of Commons, which served as an electorate for the Senate.

and asserted that the Irish parliamentary party was playing into the hands of the enemies of both English and Irish workingmen by supporting official Liberal candidates against *bona fide* labor men. He warned that if this policy were continued "a very ugly feeling would grow up which would throw back the Home Rule movement and the labour movement for a considerable time."[92]

With the backing of leading members of the Dublin Trades Council the I.L.P. had good prospects of success. It absorbed the Dublin Socialist group, took premises in Bachelor's Walk in the center of the city and made an impressive appearance at the 1895 May Day demonstration in the Phoenix Park, accompanied by fourteen bands and a crowd of several thousand.[93] But unhappily it was more a mayfly than a May Day appearance and before the summer was over the Dublin I.L.P. vanished from the political arena. At the end of July the branch reported a change of strategy: "We are now entering a new era as far as socialism is concerned in Dublin. Our comrades have seen the wisdom of (for the present) dropping all attacks on other political parties, and setting themselves to work to educate the people in the principles of socialism."[94] At the beginning of 1896 the handful of remaining members reconstituted themselves as the Dublin Socialist Society. When they invited James Connolly to be their organizer they soon found themselves transformed into the Irish Socialist Republican Party.

The I.L.P. never took firm root in Ireland in the 1890s, despite its support for a measure of Home Rule and its championing of Irish grievances. In nationalist Ireland it faced a party even more entrenched than the Liberal Party in England. Persistent unemployment and a well-established patronage system discouraged opposition, which could also be denounced as imperiling national unity. The links with British industrial areas explain the early appearance of an I.L.P. branch in Belfast and its somewhat longer life, but the identification of Hardie and other I.L.P. leaders with Home Rule sentiments made it an easy target for Orange attacks. It is significant that when further attempts were made to introduce the I.L.P. into Ireland in the following decade, a temporary measure of success was achieved only in Belfast during a period of relative calm on the Home Rule front; here it survived in underground fashion through the second decade to reappear in the 1920s.

92. *F.J.*, 12 Nov. 1894.
93. Greaves, *James Connolly*, p. 59.
94. Buggins, "Notes from the Front," "Dublin," *Clarion*, 3 Aug. 1895, quoted in E. Larkin, *James Larkin*, p. 48.

The Irish Socialist Republican Party

The Dublin I.L.P. in its propaganda work had to face criticism because it was a branch of a British organization. Its decline during 1895 convinced its remaining members that the British connection was a real obstacle, especially since the literature issued was written with English conditions in mind. When a change of name to the Dublin Socialist Society brought no improvement, it was decided that an organizer was needed—somebody well versed in socialist literature who could devote most of his spare time to propaganda. Because no local candidate was available and there were obvious objections to an English organizer, the members sought for an Irishman with experience in the British socialist movement. James Connolly's name was suggested and Adolphus Shields, the Society's secretary, started negotiations with him.[95]

Connolly was born in Edinburgh on 5 June 1868.[96] The son of an immigrant Irish laborer, he joined the Queen's Liverpool Regiment at the age of fourteen after a succession of dead-end jobs had left him no choice but to follow the example of his brother John and of many other Irishmen.[97] The regiment was soon moved to Ireland, where Connolly

95. O'Brien, *Forth the Banners Go,* pp. 6–9.
96. Unless otherwise indicated this account of Connolly's life before his arrival in Dublin is based on Greaves, *Connolly,* chaps. 1–4.
97. There are conflicting versions of Connolly's early life. John J. (Jack) Lyng, the youngest of the three Lyng brothers, asserts that his brother Murtagh told him that Connolly was raised by foster parents [J. J. Lyng to William O'Brien, 29 April 1951, O'Brien Collection MS 13942 (1)]. In the same letter he states that Connolly served for some time in India and quotes him as saying in the Irish Socialist Federation Club (New York): "I was carried away by the John Boyle O'Reilly propaganda to infiltrate the British Army and find myself in India like most of the other Irishmen who enlisted for the same reason." Lyng adds: "You remember the series of articles in the *Workers' Republic* about the 'coming revolt in India.' Jim gathered the facts while serving in India, for that series." It should be noted that Lyng has confused "The Coming Revolt in India" (*Harp,* Jan., Feb. 1908) with the earlier articles "British Rule in India" (*W.R.,* Sept. 1898). In 1958 William O'Brien gave a copy of the *W.R.* articles to J. J. McElligott, Governor of the Central Bank of Ireland, for transmission to Prime Minister Nehru of India, telling McElligott that Connolly "when very young, joined the British Army and served some time in India." O'Brien noted that the final article contained the following statement: "The writer had for some time exceptional opportunities of learning the real position of affairs in that country." [O'Brien Collection MS 13942 (2)]. Greaves (*Connolly,* pp. 16–23) makes no mention of Connolly's possible service in India, but says that "very few details of Connolly's army life are known." Connolly's oldest brother, John, joined the Liverpool Regiment under a pseudonym and it is assumed that James Connolly did the same, since there is no record of his enlistment under his own name. After his army service, which included some time in India, John Connolly returned to Edinburgh and took part in the socialist movement in that city.

served nearly the whole of his seven years' engagement. He deserted early in 1889, some four months before he was due to be discharged, but owing to a confusion in the battalion records his offense was not discovered.[98] In April he married Lillie Reynolds in a Catholic church in Perth. The young couple settled down in Edinburgh where Connolly obtained work as a corporation carter.

Connolly spent the next seven years in the local socialist movement. He joined the Scottish Socialist Federation (S.S.F.), an amalgam of branches of the S.D.F., the Socialist League, and local socialist societies. The other socialist organization in the city was Keir Hardie's I.L.P., which grew rapidly in the early 1890s. The two bodies maintained friendly relations, with the S.S.F. engaging in propaganda and political education and the I.L.P. concentrating on building up an electoral organization. John Connolly, James's eldest brother, was secretary of the S.S.F. until in 1893 he lost his job as an Edinburgh Corporation carter because he had taken part in a May Day demonstration. When he resigned as secretary to seek work elsewhere, James took over, contributed branch reports to *Justice,* and carried propaganda into the nearby port of Leith. His work in that port enabled the I.L.P. to build up a large branch there.

The Edinburgh I.L.P. secretary was John Leslie, a socialist of part-Irish extraction, who had a profound influence on the political development of the young Connolly. Early in 1894 he contributed a series of articles to *Justice* and issued them later in pamphlet form under the title, *The Present State of the Irish Question.* Leslie contended that nationalism was not enough; Home Rule by itself would bring little benefit to the Irish people unless it was accompanied by a change in property relations that would substitute socialism for capitalism. The middle-class Irish nationalists were opposed to the labor movement and were at one with their English Liberal allies in wishing to continue the exploitation of the workers of both Great Britain and Ireland. Only an independent Irish working-class party, supported by the British labor movement, could abolish the age-old hostility between the two peoples, could end "the mastery of man over man, of class over class, of nation over nation . . . which has cursed both countries alike."[99] Two refugees, the Austrian Andreas Sheu and Leo Meillet, a major figure in Paris during the Commune, had a part in Connolly's political educa-

98. The reasons for the desertion may have been anxiety over a serious accident to his father in February 1889 at a time when his mother was chronically ill, together with the coming transference of his battalion from Dublin to Aldershot, where he would have been separated from his fiancée Lillie Reynolds.

99. Greaves, *James Connolly,* p. 41.

tion, but it was Leslie who insisted on the social content of the Irish question. A quarter of a century later, in an article published a few weeks before the Easter rising, Connolly wrote: "We are out for Ireland for the Irish. But who are the Irish? Not the rack-renting, slum-owning landlord; not the sweating, profit-grinding capitalist; not the sleek and oily lawyer; not the prostitute pressman—the hired liars of the enemy. Not these are the Irish upon whom the future depends. Not these, but the Irish working class, the only secure foundation upon which a free nation can be reared." [100] He summed up his belief in the opening sentences of the next paragraph: "The cause of labour is the cause of Ireland, the cause of Ireland is the cause of labour. They cannot be dissevered."

Connolly rapidly became a key figure in the Edinburgh socialist movement, organizing propaganda for the S.S.F. and I.L.P. and meeting national leaders: Keir Hardie, Bruce Glasier, Eleanor Marx and Edward Aveling, Hyndman, Pete Curran, George Lansbury, Tom Mann. When municipal elections were held in November 1894, he stood as a socialist candidate for the S.S.F. in St. Giles's ward and came third in a four-cornered contest against a Conservative and two Liberals, one of them unofficial. [101] In April 1895 he again fought the ward in a parish council election, but ran last of the three candidates. He continued his political activities even though his personal circumstances had become desperate. During the hard winter of 1895, the Edinburgh Corporation had laid off a number of the nonpermanent carters, of whom Connolly was one, and when he tried to earn a living by opening a cobbler's shop he failed dismally. He thought of becoming a full-time lecturer/organizer, and D. Currie, who was writing the S.S.F. reports in *Justice,* made a strong appeal in June to S.D.F. or I.L.P. branches to engage him, describing him as an excellent outdoor speaker and a martyr to the cause. [102] An advertisement in July in Keir Hardie's *Labour Leader* may have brought him some engagements but evidently nothing of a regular nature. He contemplated emigrating to Chile and Leslie asked him not to go on with his plans until he had made a special appeal in *Justice* on his behalf.

The appeal appeared in December. In it Leslie said that no man had done more for the movement in Edinburgh than Connolly; that he was the most able propagandist, in every sense of the word, that Scotland had turned out; and that, because of his ability and intrepidity, he was on the verge of destitution. He appealed to comrades in Glasgow,

100. *Workers' Republic,* 8 Apr. 1916.
101. Connolly received 263 votes out of a total poll of 1870.
102. *Justice,* 22 June 1895.

Dundee, or anywhere else to secure a situation for "one of the best and most self-sacrificing men in the movement. Connolly is, I have said, an unskilled labourer, a life-long total abstainer, sound in mind and limb (Christ in Heaven! how often have I nearly burst a blood vessel as these questions were asked of myself!). Married, with a young family, and as his necessities are therefore very great, so he may be had cheap."[103] The Dublin Socialist Society answered Leslie's appeal and invited Connolly to become its paid organizer. After some negotiations he accepted the offer, his traveling expenses being met from a fund raised by Leslie and others. Armed with books and pamphlets on socialism and Irish history, parliamentary papers, and press-cuttings on the London dock strike of 1889, and accompanied by Lillie and their young children, he arrived in Dublin in May 1896.

Within a few weeks Connolly had persuaded a number of the Dublin socialists to form a new party that had for its object "the establishment of an Irish socialist republic and the consequent restoration of social democracy in the island."[104] An informal meeting held on 29 May in the "snug"[105] of a Dublin public house was attended by eight people, six of them abstainers; they heard an address by Connolly and, after an exchange of views, resolved on the motion of Robert Dorman and Tom Lyng to constitute themselves the Irish Socialist Republican Party. The officers were Connolly, secretary; Dorman, treasurer; Tom Lyng, financial secretary; and Whelan, librarian. There was no president, a chairman being elected at each meeting.[106] Connolly as secretary/organizer was to be paid £1 a week as funds permitted, which frequently they did not. A clubroom was rented at 67 Middle Abbey Street, in the city center, and furnished with a few forms given by the Dublin Socialist Society, which then seems to have dissolved.[107] The Irish Socialist Republican Party (I.S.R.P.) book membership in Dublin was approximately fifty at any one time, about half of them active, and the weekly attendance rarely exceeded fifteen, eighteen being regarded as an exceptional turnout.[108] The burden of public speaking was borne initially by Dorman and Connolly and open-air meetings were held during the summer at various points, the principal forum being at the Dublin

103. Ibid., 14 Dec. 1895, quoted in Greaves, *James Connolly*, pp. 56–7.
104. I.S.R.P. minutes, 29 May 1896 (N.L.I.).
105. An enclosed compartment that gave some privacy.
106. I.S.R.P. minutes, 29 May 1896. Dorman later resigned in favor of Murtagh Lyng. There were frequent changes of officers; the secretaryship changed twenty-two times and was filled by fifteen different people during the period 1896–1904. [O'Brien Collection, MS 15674 (1)].
107. I.S.R.P. minutes, 17 June 1896.
108. O'Brien, *Forth the Banners Go*, p. 5.

Custom House, abandoned later for Foster Place outside the Bank of Ireland, formerly the seat of the eighteenth-century Houses of Parliament.

In a public statement issued on behalf of the new party, Connolly analyzed the Irish question as follows: "The struggle for Irish freedom has two aspects: it is national and it is social. Its national ideal can never be realised until Ireland stands forth before the world a nation free and independent. It is social and economic, because no matter what the form of government may be, as long as one class owns as their private property the land and instruments of labour, from which all mankind derive their substance, that class will always have it in their power to plunder and enslave the remainder of their fellow-creatures." [109] His conclusion was that "the party which would aspire to lead the Irish people from bondage to freedom must then recognise both aspects of the long-continued struggle of the Irish nation."

The principles and program of the I.S.R.P. were contained in a manifesto [110] written by Connolly and published in 1896. The manifesto bore as a motto a quotation from Camille Desmoulins, orator and journalist of the French Revolution: "The great appear great to us only because we are on our knees; LET US RISE." The object of the party was "the establishment of an Irish Socialist Republic based upon the public ownership by the Irish people of the land, and the instruments of production, distribution and exchange." A ten-point program, desirable in itself as helping to restrict emigration and palliate present social evils, was designed to organize "the forces of the Democracy in preparation for any struggle which may precede the realisation of our ideal." The program itself contained proposals for the nationalization of transport and finance and for the gradual extension of public ownership to other fields. Pensions for the aged, the infirm, widows, and orphans were to be financed by a graduated tax on all income over £400 a year, while a maximum working week of forty-eight hours and a minimum wage were to be fixed by law. There were to be free maintenance for all children, free education up to and including the university, and public control and management of national schools by elected boards—the last was a direct blow at the clerical managerial system then in force in almost all Irish primary schools. Connolly was not to live to see the working week reduced to forty-eight hours, or universal suffrage introduced; another proposal, the establishment of rural depots of agricultural machinery to be lent out at a rent covering cost and management, was a partial anticipation of the Soviet tractor stations of a later date.

109. Ryan, ed., *Socialism and Nationalism*, pp. 11–12.
110. For the full text of the manifesto see *Socialism and Nationalism*, pp. 184–6.

The manifesto ended with a statement of principles clearly Marxist in inspiration. Private ownership by a class of the means of production, distribution, and exchange was "the fundamental basis of all oppression, national, political and social," its abolition was necessary to establish the democratic principle as the foundation of the economic as well as the political system of a free people. The subjection of one nation by another could "only serve the interests of the exploiting classes of both nations."

The nucleus of the I.S.R.P. consisted of the three Lyng brothers (Murtagh, Tom, and Jack), Thomas and Daniel O'Brien (William, the youngest O'Brien, joined in 1898), W. J. Bradshaw, E. W. Stewart, and W. McLoughlin, all clerks or tradesmen. When Dorman left Dublin, Connolly set about training the others as propagandists. Under his forceful direction the tiny party engaged in so many activities that an outsider, decrying the suggestion that the socialists took up a lot of room, asserted that in the whole of Dublin there were only five hundred of them altogether, when the actual membership amounted to about one-tenth of that number.[111] Thanks to Connolly's determination,[112] the party organized a series of meetings and counterdemonstrations during the celebration of the diamond jubilee of Queen Victoria in 1897. Maud Gonne, daughter of an Irish father and an English mother, brought up in aristocratic circles and presented at court but by this time a fervent republican, was an enthusiastic ally. She helped in the preparation of the most spectacular of the I.R.S.P. demonstrations held on Jubilee Day (22 June). A procession, carrying banners designed by her and recounting famines and evictions during the sixty years' reign, paraded through the center of Dublin. It was headed by an imitation hearse containing a black coffin labeled "The British Empire" and accompanied by a band playing the Dead March. W. B. Yeats, Maud Gonne, and others distributed black flags to those taking part in the parade. When the procession was halted at O'Connell Bridge, by police, Connolly ordered the coffin to be thrown into the Liffey to a chorus of "Here goes the coffin of the British Empire! To hell with the British Empire!"[113] In Cork the I.S.R.P. branch, led by Con O'Lyhane, tore down the Union Jack from the fire station and replaced it by a black flag. By these activities Connolly voiced a radical, republican protest

111. O'Brien, *Forth the Banners Go,* p. 5.

112. "Bravo! All my congratulations to you! You were right and I was wrong all the evening. You may have the satisfaction of knowing that you saved Dublin from the humiliation of an English jubilee without a public meeting of protestation. You were the only man who had the courage to organise a public meeting and to carry through in spite of all discouragement—even from friends!" [Maude Gonne to James Connolly, n.d. (1897?), typewritten copy, O'Brien MS 13939 (2)].

113. Greaves, *Connolly,* p. 72; O'Brien, *Forth the Banners Go,* p. 9.

against British attempts to demonstrate how loyal Ireland was to the empire and against the accommodating attitude of Irish Home Rule M.P.s and their alliance with the Liberal Party.

Connolly was less successful in his struggle with Irish Home Rulers over the centenary celebrations of the United Irish rising of 1798. A movement to secure an amnesty for Fenian prisoners still in jail had given rise during 1897 to a number of clubs formed to commemorate the rising. The membership of these clubs was mixed, but if only a minority were avowed republicans or advanced nationalists, they were not under the control of the Irish parliamentary party and its subordinate organizations. When it was evident that political capital could be made out of the occasion and that their own influence might be lessened if the celebrations took place without them, the Home Rule politicians took command in the name of national unity by creating a Centennial Association; its platform included such unlikely rebels as William Martin Murphy, Dublin's leading capitalist and a supporter of the monarchy, and Tim Harrington, an M.P. who had antagonized the normally friendly Dublin Trades Council by his denunciation of a building trade strike. Connolly consoled himself with reprinting writings of the United Irishmen, open-air propaganda, and articles that emphasized the radical and separatist aims of Wolfe Tone and his companions, their relevance to his own day, and the fundamental difference between them and those of Home Rulers pledged to the English Liberal alliance. The success of the antirepublican, antilabor politicians convinced Connolly that the I.S.R.P. must have a paper of its own. The first issue of the *Workers' Republic* appeared in August 1898, to be sold at Centennial Association meetings and to disabuse its readers of illusions about the sincerity of Centennial speakers who rattled the bones of the patriot dead.

The eight-page weekly printed by a Dublin jobbing firm was made possible by Connolly's energetic fundraising. He obtained £50 from Keir Hardie, but as the paper ran at a loss, only £10 was ever repaid.[114] Publication was maintained until October, when funds were exhausted. Connolly then decided that commercial printing was impossible and, when it reappeared in May 1899, it was the product of a hand press operated by Connolly, who was also editor, contributor, and publisher. Even these economies were insufficient to ensure regular publication, which was often interrupted for weeks or months when the I.S.R.P. ran out of money. On one occasion during the height of agitation against the Boer War, the police smashed the printing press. The paper's life was almost that of a clandestine journal, yet Connolly

114. O'Brien, p. 10.

and his few helpers managed to bring out issues every year until shortly before his final departure for the United States in 1903.[115]

The articles which Connolly wrote in the *Workers' Republic* provided a commentary on day-to-day politics, municipal and national, or on events such as the Jubilee celebrations of 1897, the '98 Commemoration, the Boer War, and the coronation of Edward VII. Subjects of less immediate interest—the Irish language, physical force in politics, modern war—were discussed, always with reference to their social significance. The doctrinaire attitude might at times have discouraged readers, but the vigor and directness of the writings, and the analytical power of the writer, made other labor journalism appear vague, sentimental, and verbose. History, and especially the neglected history of the Irish working-class and radical movements, was Connolly's peculiar interest, and it was in the pages of the *Workers' Republic* that there appeared the opening chapters of his pioneer work, *Labour in Irish History*, later to be published in book form. He also wrote and printed manifestoes, pamphlets, and handbills for emergent occasions and contributed articles to other papers, notably Alice Milligan's *Shan Van Vocht*, Maude Gonne's *L'Irlande Libre*, Hardie's *Labour Leader*, *Justice*, and the Scottish *Socialist*.[116]

The outbreak of the South African war in 1899 gave Connolly and the I.S.R.P. another opportunity to mount a campaign against imperialism. Even before it began Connolly denounced it as springing from the desire of "an unscrupulous gang of capitalists to get into their hands the immense riches of the diamond fields."[117] The Party was the first to hold a public protest meeting in Ireland (27 August 1899); at it, an uncompromising resolution was passed denouncing British rule in Ireland, India, Egypt, and other colonial countries, characterizing as an act of aggression "the interference of the British Capitalist government in the internal affairs of the Transvaal Republic," and calling upon Irish residents there to assist in the Transvaal's defense.[118] In Great Britain the war evoked opposition from some Liberals, the S.D.F., the I.L.P., and, in the early stages, the British T.U.C., but it was a decorous opposition compared with its Irish counterpart.[119] In Ireland,

115. Eighty-five numbers were issued between August 1899 and May 1903, when it ceased publication (Clarkson, p. 210, n. 1).

116. The *Shan Van Vocht* was published in Belfast and *L'Irlande Libre* in Paris; both were republican in tone. The *Socialist*, which appeared in August 1902, was published by the Scottish Council of the S.D.F. and was initially printed on the I.S.R.P. press.

117. *Workers' Republic*, 19 Aug. 1899, in Ryan, ed., *Labour and Easter Week*, p. 27.

118. Ibid., p. 30.

119. F. Bealey, "Les travaillistes et la guerre des Boers," in *Le Mouvement Social*, no. 45 (Oct.–Dec. 1963), pp. 39–70.

outside Unionist east Ulster, sentiment was generally against the war, and the initiative of the I.S.R.P. was followed by the appearance of a somewhat informal Irish Transvaal Committee that included the Home Rule M.P., William Redmond (brother of John Redmond, later leader of the Irish parliamentary party when the Parnellite and anti-Parnellite sections came together in 1900) advanced natonalists and republicans. Maud Gonne and her women's organization *Inghinidhe na h-Eireann* (Daughters of Erin) actively opposed Irish enlistment in the British forces, as did Arthur Griffith, editor of the *United Irishman*. It was a temporary alliance of very disparate elements. Griffith, for example, was actuated by an unqualified anglophobia and by a racist chauvinism best expressed in the following sentence from his preface to an edition of John Mitchel's *Jail Journal:* "The right of the Irish to political independence never was, is not, and never can be dependent upon the admission of equal right in all other peoples."[120]

Initially, protest meetings were held without much harassment from the authorities. One, arranged to denounce Joseph Chamberlain as an arch-apostle of imperialism on his visit to Dublin in December 1899, was proclaimed, but the organizers, mounted in a brake, amused the crowds by keeping ahead of the slow-moving foot police and giving a series of whistle-stop speeches. Mounted police finally halted Connolly, who had earlier taken the reins when the driver had been pulled off the box, but the only charge they could bring against him was that of driving in a public place without a licence.[121] This comparative freedom did not last long. Antiwar agitation was continued through the visit of Queen Victoria to Dublin in March 1900, but demonstrations were broken up by savage baton charges. In April Maud Gonne's article entitled "The Famine Queen" in the *United Irishman* led to its seizure and a general attack on civil liberties followed. The I.S.R.P. managed by a vigorous open-air campaign to lessen its impact, but when the Conservative government was reelected in the jingoistic "khaki" election later in the year all public meetings in Dublin were proclaimed.

Connolly was well aware of the limitations of a purely political republicanism. In the January 1897 issue of the *Shan Van Vocht* he addressed himself forcefully to its advocates: "If you remove the English army tomorrow and hoist the green flag over Dublin Castle, unless you set about the organization of the socialist republic your efforts would be in vain. England would still rule you. She would rule you through her capitalists, through her landlords, through her financiers. . . . Nationalism without socialism . . . is only national recre-

120. John Mitchel, *Jail Journal* [Dublin, n.d. (1913?)], p. XIV.
121. Seán O Lúing, *Art Ó Griofa*, pp. 58–61.

ancy." [122] He was equally insistent on the use of the ballot box and parliamentary processes, for only if the party of progress had shown that it possessed the suffrage of the majority of the people and had exhausted all peaceful means was it justified in taking arms to assume the powers of government. Those who made a fetish of physical force were utterly regardless of principle and attached importance only to methods—"an instance of putting the cart before the horse, absolutely unique in its imbecility and unparalleled in the history of the world." [123]

When the extension of the local government franchise in 1898 abolished property qualifications, the I.S.R.P. contested the annual Dublin municipal elections from 1899 to 1903. Its candidates were E. W. Stewart, Murtagh Lyng, William McLoughlin, Tom Lyng, and Connolly, but none was successful. [124] The party's opponents were in the main nominees of the rank-and-file Home Rule organizations (after 1900 the United Irish League) supported by clergy and M.P.s. In his 1903 election address to the voters of the Wood Quay ward, Connolly described the tactics of his opponents of the previous year: "Let us remember how the paid canvassers of the capitalist candidate—hired slanderers—gave a different account of Mr. Connolly to every section of the electors. How they said to the Catholics that he was an Orangeman, to the Protestants that he was a Fenian, to the Jews that he was an anti-Semite, to others that he was a Jew, to the labourers that he was a journalist on the make, and to the tradesmen and professional classes that he was an ignorant labourer, that he was born in Belfast, Derry, England, Scotland and Italy, according to the person the canvasser was talking to." [125] Referring to the wholesale corruption of voters who were issued with free drinks by publican members of the corporation, he declared that "there can never be either clean, healthy, or honest politics in the City of Dublin until the power of the drink-sellers is absolutely broken—they are positively the meanest and most degraded section that ever attempted to rule a city." Connolly, however, was not content only to denounce, or to present an immediate program; he also insisted on including a lesson

122. Ryan, ed., *Socialism and Nationalism*, p. 25.

123. *Workers' Republic*, 22 July 1899, quoted in Ryan, ed., *Socialism and Nationalism*, p. 55. Connolly was referring to physical force nationalists on the '98 Executive who proclaimed the principle of national independence "as understood by Wolfe Tone and the United Irishmen" but within a year rejected a similar resolution and elected monarchists to the governing body.

124. For the election campaigns and results see the January file of the *Freeman's Journal* in 1899 and subsequent years.

125. D. Ryan, ed., *The Workers' Republic*, pp. 46–7.

in first principles. Arguing the necessity for the working class to establish a political party of its own, he stated that every political party was the party of a class. "The Unionists represent the interests of the landlords and the big capitalists generally; the United Irish League is the party of the middle class, the agriculturalists, the house jobbers, slum landlords and drink sellers."

The small attention paid in the *Workers' Republic* to trade union and labor matters at this time is an index of Connolly's absorption in socialist politics. But if his energies were mainly employed in political affairs, he belonged to a trade union, the United Labourers of Ireland, and represented them on the Dublin Trades Council for some months.[126] The solitary motion moved by him during this period was practical and constructive; criticizing the enmity shown by corporation contractors to organized laborers, he proposed that corporation work in the future should be carried out by direct labor.[127] Despite the conservative nature of the Trades Council, the I.S.R.P. municipal candidates were usually endorsed by that body, Connolly himself being proposed and seconded by two craftsmen.[128] He received the warm approval of Arthur Griffith, who described him as the foremost among the few able and honest candidates in the municipal election of January 1903 and urged every nationalist voter to support him, opposed as he was "by the shoneens, the tenement house rack-renters of the poor, the publicans, and we regret to say, the priests."[129]

In September 1900 the I.S.R.P. sent three delegates (Daniel O'Brien, Mark Deering, and E. W. Stewart) to the fifth (Paris) congress of the Second International and claimed that it was "the first time in the history of socialism that Ireland was represented by delegates from a properly constituted and organised socialist party."[130] John O'Gorman, the First International veteran and member of the Dublin Socialist Club, had attended the Possibilist congress in 1889, but as a trade union delegate from the Dublin branch of the International

---

126. He first appeared as a delegate in 1901 and was replaced in 1902 (D.T.C. minutes, 4 Nov. 1901, 7 Apr. 1902).

127. Ibid., 10 Mar. 1902.

128. Ibid., 2 Dec. 1901. The proposer was a tailor and the seconder (C. Comiskey) a member of the local painters' society. Comiskey was a Gaelic League supporter and signed his name in Irish (D.T.C. minutes, 7 Apr. 1902).

129. *United Irishman*, 10 Jan. 1903, quoted in Clarkson, p. 259.

130. I.S.R.P. minute book, 18 Sept., 9, 16 Oct. 1900; O'Brien, *Forth the Banners Go*, p. 27. O'Brien and Deering represented the I.S.R.P. proper and E. W. Stewart, by arrangement, the Cork Fintan Lalor Club. Walter Kendall is incorrect in stating that Connolly was present (*The Revolutionary Movement in Britain*, p. 14). It is highly probable, as Greaves suggests (p. 103), that Connolly was unable to afford the cost of attendance.

Glassbottlemakers. At the 1896 (London) congress George Bernard Shaw, though resident in London, represented the Dublin Fabian Society, and when the French delegation split over an issue, he requested in typical Shavian fashion to be allowed to constitute himself as the Irish national section.[131] There was no such levity in the I.S.R.P.'s attitude. Through an oversight, admission cards had not reached the Irish delegates before they set out, and until the error was rectified it seemed as if they would have to withdraw unless they attended as part of the British contingent, "a course of action which could not have been entertained."[132] The appearance of a separate Irish delegation and the report it gave impressed the editors of the official and unofficial reports of the congress, both expressing surprise at the progress made in so impoverished a country.[133]

The most contentious issue at the congress was the question of socialist participation in a capitalist government. It had arisen in 1899 when the French socialist Alexandre Millerand had joined a cabinet that was all the more repugnant to the left because it included as war minister General Gallifet, who had earned the title "butcher of the Commune" for his part in its suppression. Millerand's supporters, among whom was Jean Jaurès, defended him on the grounds that the republic was in danger as right-wing, clerical attacks mounted during the Dreyfus affair. When the congress opened Jules Guesde (France) and Ferri (Italy) moved a resolution forbidding socialists to join any bourgeois government. The prolonged and bitter debate might have disrupted the International, but a compromise resolution framed by its leading theoretician, Karl Kautsky of the powerful German Social-Democrat Party, carried the day. The compromise allowed participation in exceptional circumstances, provided party authorization had first been secured. Twelve of the twenty-one national delegations voted *en bloc* for the Kautsky compromise (each delegation was allowed two votes), five split their votes, Norway abstained, and only two (Ireland and Bulgaria) voted solidly for the Guesde—Ferri resolution.[134] But the

131. *Cinquième congrès socialiste international: Compte-rendu sténographique (non-officiel)* (*Cahiers de la Quinzaine*, seizième cahier de la deuxième série, 1901), p. 51, n.

132. I.S.R.P. minute book, 16 Oct. 1900; *Workers' Republic*, 6 Oct. 1900.

133. "Les progrès de l'idée socialiste y sont considérables, si l'on tient compte surtout de l'extrême misère du pays" (*Cinquième congrès socialiste international: Compte-rendu officiel*, p. 33). "C'est l'indication d'un grand progrès de voir que dans un pays aussi malheureux, aussi retardataire, un pays d'agriculture, dépourvu de ressources comme l'Irlande, aient pu se développer et se former des associations socialistes" (*Compte-rendu non-officiel*, pp. 51–52).

134. *La Revue Socialiste*, xxxii (Jul.–Sept. 1900), p. 487; Cinquième congrès, *Compte-rendu officiel*, p. 89; *Compte-rendu non-officiel*, p. 110. Germany, England, Austria, Bohemia, Denmark, Spain, Sweden, Belgium, Holland, Argentina, Portugal,

left was itself divided. The Polish socialist Rosa Luxemburg, one of the most forceful of the anti-Kautskyite speakers, had objected to the seating of the Poles as a separate national section and had denounced as dangerously utopian any plan to recreate Poland, then partitioned between Germany, Austria, and Russia. It is not difficult to imagine what Connolly, had he been present, would have said in reply to her plea that the proletariat should accept capitalist political geography and organize itself on existing political foundations.[135]

History has vindicated Connolly as against Rosa Luxemburg in his insistence on the necessity for combining national with social liberation. On another issue, that of a legal minimum wage, congress reached a decision with which Connolly also disagreed. Though supporting the long-standing demand for a legal maximum working day of eight hours, a majority of the delegates declared that a minimum wage fixed by legislation was impracticable and could only be achieved where strong trade union organization existed. When the I.S.R.P. discussed the report of its delegates, Connolly strongly dissented from the congress decision;[136] some nine years later the British Trade Boards Act of 1909 allowed legal minimum wages to be fixed in poorly organized, sweated industries.

Though the *Workers' Republic* and pamphlets carried the name of the I.S.R.P. beyond Dublin, the party had few members outside the capital. There was a small group in Belfast, a branch in Cork, and individual sympathizers and supporters in other provincial towns. The group in Belfast was formed by Ernest Milligan, brother of Alice Milligan of the *Shan Van Vocht*. At his sister's prompting Milligan sought out Connolly and other members during a visit to Dublin, where he was given a number of the socialist classics then popular (Henry George, Robert Blatchford, John Ruskin, Ernest Bellamy). He joined the party and on his return to Belfast started the Belfast Socialist Society in September 1898 after advertising in the *Clarion*. But the group owed only its origin to the I.S.R.P.; its name avoided any suggestion of republicanism or nationalism. Milligan, a law student, enrolled three other students, Robert Lynd, Samuel Porter, and James Winder Good, as well as William Rice, W. M. Knox, and J. H. Gilliland, veterans of Belfast left-wing radicalism. The *Workers' Republic,* sold at the meetings held in the Typographical Hall, College Street, seems to have been the only link with the I.S.R.P. Robert Lynd, in his October 1916 preface to Connolly's *Labour in Irish History,* describes the outlook of

---

and Switzerland supported Kautsky; France, Poland, the United States, Russia, and Italy split their votes.

135. See Greaves, pp. 102–3.   136. I.S.R.P. minutes, 16 Oct. 1900.

the members of the short-lived coterie. "We were doctrinaire inter-nationalists in those days, and scarcely realised, as many of us do now, that imperialism equally with capitalism means the exploitation of the weak by the strong. Socialism seemed to us like a creed for the world, while we regarded nationalism as a mere noisy indulgence in flags and bands not different in kind from the patriotism of London stockbrokers."[137]

The Cork branch was openly anti-imperialist. In 1897 Con O'Ly-hane,[138] a young butter merchants' clerk, had led some friends in antijubilee demonstrations. During the following year he turned the group into the Wolfe Tone Literary Society, a '98 club that shared Connolly's hostility to the Home Rule politicians who took over the 1798 centenary commemoration.[139] In January 1899 the society adopted the I.S.R.P. program and became the Cork branch of the party under the name of the Fintan Labor Club.[140] O'Lyhane brought Con-nolly to Cork in February to address a meeting under the club's auspices on Labour and Irish Revolution. But the fortunes of the club then declined and O'Lyhane's reports to Connolly and E. W. Stewart were depressing. A meeting in August to revive it was unsuccessful, and sales of the *Workers' Republic* fell off so badly that O'Lyhane was reduced to distributing copies free.[141] In February 1900 he declared the branch defunct; he had come to the conclusion that he and his associates had

137. *Labour in Irish History* (Dublin, 1922), p. XX. Ernest Milligan, in a letter to William O'Brien [27 Jul. 192?, O'Brien Collection MS 13961 (2)], thought that the *Workers' Republic* would have been a success in Belfast had the Catholic Bishop Henry of Down and Connor not proscribed it. Milligan also related his difficulties in persuading "the Protestant section . . . to any connection with the national movement," mention-ing his failure with the Christian Social Brotherhood that had as its leaders William Walker, Alexander Brown, and Alexander Taylor. The Belfast Socialist Society agreed to an open-air propaganda drive but left Milligan to carry it on. The society's early demise was probably caused by his having to withdraw from political activities when serious and prolonged illness befell him in 1899. See also Greaves, *James Connolly*, pp. 69–70.

Lynd later became a well-known essayist, Porter stood as an I.L.P. candidate in the 1920s and was appointed a justice of the Northern Ireland Supreme Court by the British Labour government in the late 1940s, and Good made a reputation as a journalist and author of several books on Ulster Unionism.

138. O'Lyhane, born 21 November 1877, began life as Cornelius Lyhane, adopted Carroll O'Lyhane as a *nom de guerre* and called himself Con Lehane when he went to London in December 1901.

139. O'Lyhane supported Connolly in the *Shan Van Vocht* of 12 March 1898; the two met during the August commemoration later in the year (Greaves, pp. 70, 87).

140. *Clarion*, 4 Feb. 1899.

141. O'Lyhane to Connolly, 15 Aug. 1899; O'Lyhane to E. W. Stewart, 18 Nov. 1899. Unless otherwise indicated, these and subsequent letters are in the O'Brien Collection, MS 15700 (1).

done the movement in Cork more harm than good and that members of a different caliber were required if the club were to be resuscitated.[142] The membership consisted substantially of clerks and students having little contact with Cork trade unionists and, though on Connolly's prompting O'Lyhane approached a number of them, he met with a lukewarm response. One of them, Cody, the secretary of the local Labour Electoral Association, agreed to give assistance, but unfortunately he seemed to be more attracted by Bruce Glasier's Fabian lectures than by the stronger meat of revolutionary socialism. O'Lyhane himself was elected a vice-president of the local branch of the National Amalgamated Union of Shop Assistants, Warehousemen and Clerks, but decided that he must be tactful in his new position.[143] For the remainder of 1900 he had nothing to report from the dormant branch. A few debates in the Catholic Young Men's Society could neither counter sermons against socialism preached in Catholic churches nor compensate for the lack of organized propaganda. His discouragement is evident in a letter to Connolly dated 12 November. He had been appointed as a delegate from his union to the Cork Trades Council but preferred to attend evening classes in chemistry and physics—"I have determined not to be a clerk much longer if I can help it."[144]

The new year brought an unexpected revival. O'Lyhane was able to announce in March 1901 that they had "again floated the Cork branch, this time, I hope never to fall again."[145] They drew up a municipal program and planned to fight a corporation seat the following January. There were, however, some adverse signs later in the year. Two prominent members, W. J. Gallagher and W. D. Horgan, embarked on full-time studies that left them little time for political activities.[146] Thinking better of his earlier decision, O'Lyhane made up his mind to attend the Cork Trades Council, only to find that that body would not accept him as his attitude had "been too uncompromising to suit the books of the fakirs in office."[147] In addition, O'Lyhane and the club were denounced from the pulpits of several Catholic churches. Yet, though forced out of their club room, they held successful open-air meetings and sold dozens of the *Workers' Republic*.[148] When gasworkers went on strike O'Lyhane assisted them and the club benefited by the resultant

142. O'Lyhane to Connolly, 3 Feb. 1900.
143. Ibid., 6 Mar. 1900.   144. Ibid., 13 Mar., 12 Nov. 1900.
145. Ibid., 27 Mar. 1901.
146. Gallagher entered medical school and Horgan resumed courses for a Bachelor of Arts degree.
147. O'Lyhane to Connolly, 2 Aug. 1901.
148. O'Lyhane to M. J. Lyng, 10 Sept. 1901.

militancy. But the Cork Trades Council intervened to produce a settlement of the dispute that victimized the president, vice-president, and
secretary of the gasworkers' local branch and barred them from employment in the Cork Gas Company.[149] Dr. O'Callaghan, the Catholic
bishop of Cork, issued a pastoral letter condemning the club. It fought
back by holding a meeting in his own neighborhood, but members
dropped away and subscriptions declined, the result of priests bringing
pressure to bear on individual members.[150] Even the infant Fabian
Society collapsed before the bishop's onslaught. In a letter to Connolly
dated 4 November 1901 O'Lyhane comforted himself by observing
that at least clerical opposition had made the club's position clear and
that any future additions to membership could be relied upon. His next
letter to Connolly was written from London in February 1902—he had
given up the struggle in Cork, which he had left at the beginning of
December.

Connolly's reaction to the club's demise was one of intense bitterness.
Patrick J. Tobin, one of the few left in Cork, informed him of the
situation. Several members had been sacked by clerical influence. As
for himself, he had decided to join Gallagher and Horgan in a course of
studies so that within three or four years they hoped to be "at least on
terms of intellectual equality" with their opponents.[151] Connolly's
reply was to pour scorn on the students' long-term plan to reequip
themselves for the fight and to call Gallagher, Horgan and O'Lyhane
deserters. Tobin replied temperately that the students wished to establish themselves on a secure financial basis in Cork, that Gallagher
and Horgan were completely dependent on their families, and that
O'Lyhane, sacked from his job, was blacklisted with every Cork employer. Within a few years they hoped to bring O'Lyhane back to Cork
and keep him there.[152]

Connolly was not to be placated by any apologia on behalf of the lost
leader. O'Lyhane acknowledged that he understood Connolly's motive
(that propaganda would cease in Cork), but claimed that he was "free to
work for the cause in any place I choose." He continued on a more
cheerful note to tell of his joining the S.D.F. in London and to ask
Connolly's advice on moving a motion calling for complete independence for Ireland that could go before the next annual conference of the
S.D.F. He signed his letter "yours fraternally."[153] Connolly's reply was

149. Ibid., 26 Sept. 1901.   150. Ibid., 2, 9, 29 Oct. 1901.
151. Tobin to Connolly, 2 Dec. 1901, O'Brien MS 15701 (1).
152. Ibid., 4 Dec. 1901.
153. O'Lyhane to Connolly, 14 Feb. 1902.

devastating, to judge from the summary he gave John Cairstairs Matheson, his Scottish correspondent:

In a letter I wrote to Cork about the matter I said that in my opinion O'Lyhane was a deserter, and that the Cork men as a whole were behaving in a cowardly fashion. Also that for a man to say he was boycotted because when sacked out of one job he did not find a capitalist at the corner of the street waiting to give him another job was absurd. And that Fenians, Land Leaguers and Parnellites had been attacked by the clergy and they did not run away. O'Lyhane wrote to me saying that he had a perfect right to change his residence. I answered that he had, but when a man at the head of a regiment made up his mind to 'change his residence' at the moment the enemy attacked he was usually called a very ugly name. So you need not wonder at that man's enmity.[154]

O'Lyhane's answer, addressed, "Dear Sir," and signed, "yours fraternally," thanked Connolly formally for his prompt reply.[155]

In a survey of the debacle, Tobin concluded that the Cork branch might have fared better had they circulated their propaganda from the start among trade unionists, given the support they had obtained at public meetings. But they fought shy of "boring from within" lest, it would appear, their revolutionary doctrine become contaminated. And the clerical onslaught drove away the majority of members who had joined in the first rush; their excuse was that "the bishop being the temporal no less than the spiritual director of his flock, that consequently the flock were bound to obey him in matters economical too. The more advanced among us don't acknowledge his authority either way—but the majority preferred not to come under his anathema."[156]

Though it would appear from some of Tobin's remarks that Connolly, or at least the Dublin I.S.R.P., was prepared to modify the strictures on Gallagher and Horgan, the "sentence" on O'Lyhane stood. It left a legacy of bitterness. O'Lyhane wrote to Horgan in February 1904, some eight months after Connolly had presided in Edinburgh at an inaugural conference of the Socialist Labour Party, composed of dissident Scottish members of the S.D.F. He complained of misrepresentation by M. J. Lyng, but held Connolly, who claimed to be "genuinely revolutionary and tactically scientific," responsible:

Quelch and the S.D.F. are strong supporters of 'secular education,' but Catholic Connolly, the founder of the great I.S.R.P., had not the pluck to put it on the I.S.R.P. programme. Now the I.S.R.P. is dead, and Connolly is a discredited man who (after telling his friends in Scotland that he could not find

154. Connolly to Matheson, n.d. (March 1903?), O'Brien Collection, MS 13906 (2).
155. O'Lyhane to Connolly, 20 Feb. 1902.
156. Tobin to Connolly, 6 Jan. 1902, O'Brien MS 15701 (1).

employment in any of the *three countries*) has gone to America to see if he can't carry on the game there where he is not known. . . . Again, when 'Dr.' O'Callaghan tried to rouse the city of Cork against our little band, what did Catholic Connolly do? He said 'Oh! I'm a Catholic too! Socialism has nothing to do with religion—and we are very sorry your lordship is against us.' What would Quelch have said? Why even Blatchford hit out in the *Clarion,* but Connolly could not see his way to defend the Party against clericalism in the *Workers' Republic.*[157]

Clerical opposition to socialism of any kind was slow to disappear, as the following letter from Cork, dated 8 February 1908, shows:

DEAR SIR,

I beg to resign membership of the Socialist Party of Ireland, by advice of Catholic clergymen.

C. O'Leary.[158]

If Connolly regarded some of the Cork members as deserters, they in turn felt that it was they who had been unfairly misjudged in difficult circumstances. They assumed, not incorrectly, that Connolly, like themselves, did not acknowledge Dr. O'Callaghan's spiritual or temporal authority.[159] But they seem to have been unaware of Connolly's

157. O'Lyhane to W. D. Horgan, 5, 6 Feb. 1904, O'Brien MS 13919 (2). O'Lyhane obtained employment as a clerk in the London Road Car Company and later became a successful journalist, taking over the *Evening News* edited by Frank Harris. In politics he stood aside from the S.D.F.–S.L.P. controversy, but in June 1904 joined dissident members of the London S.D.F. in forming the Socialist Party of Great Britain, of which he became the first secretary. At the Albert Hall meeting (2 Nov. 1913), held in support of the men involved in the Dublin dispute of 1913 and addressed by Connolly, Ben Tillett, and such notables as George Bernard Shaw and Æ (George William Russell), he led a group of stewards that ejected the students trying to wreck the demonstration. In 1914 he emigrated to the United States, where he died in December 1918. See obituaries by Frank Harris, *Pearson's Magazine,* Feb. 1919, and P. S. O'Hegarty, *Irish World,* 15 Mar. 1919 [O'Brien notebook, MS 15674 (1)].

158. O'Brien Collection, MS 15700 (1).

159. In the postscript to a letter dated 22 Dec. 1907 [O'Brien Collection, MS 13906 (1)] Matheson asked Connolly: "What is the position of socialists who are Catholics (are you still in the bosom of the Church?) in view of the encyclical of the Pope on modernism? So far as I can see the Pope has asked you what the hell you are doing in the Church and has intimated that, in his pontifical opinion, your room is a damsite [*sic*] better than your company (I use the swear words to give the proper ecclesiastical and excommunicatory colouring)." Connolly replied in a letter dated 30 Jan. 1908 [O'Brien Collection, MS 13906 (2)]: "Theoretically it was not *ex cathedra,* therefore it was not binding. For myself, tho' I have usually posed as a Catholic I have not gone to my duty for fifteen years, and have not the slightest tincture of faith left. I only assume the Catholic pose in order to quiz the raw free-thinkers whose ridiculous dogmatism did and does annoy me as much as the dogmatism of the orthodox. In fact I respect the good Catholic more than the average freethinker."

determination to avoid being entangled in what he regarded as ultimately destructive controversies over questions of religious belief. None of them became what he was and remained: a full-time professional revolutionary, who occasionally displayed the contempt he had for those he regarded as dilettantes or as men whose revolutionary enthusiasm withered at the first adverse blast. O'Lyhane realized that the Dublin I.S.R.P. was having its own difficulties, but it is unlikely that he knew of their exact nature or of the endless and well-nigh hopeless struggle that Connolly had to make ends meet. The not infrequent bitterness shown by Connolly is to be explained by the double task of making political headway with the aid of colleagues who had not the same singlemindedness as himself and of trying to provide some food and shelter for his growing family.

When Connolly was appointed as organizer in 1896, he was to be paid £1 a week, but in fact it was rarely paid. In March 1899 he asked Daniel O'Brien for a loan of £2 in order to set up as a peddler as a last resort. It would tear out his heartstrings to leave Ireland after so much toil and privation, but unless his peddling succeeded the necessity of feeding his family would leave him no alternative. He had got a corporation job doing unskilled labor but had to stop after a few days because he had been ill-fed for so long that he was unable to do such work. The organizing business was a failure—7s. a week—and he did not wish to draw money from a few comrades.[160] Four years later Connolly's position was unchanged; he still lived in a one-room tenement and had no promise of steady employment. In March 1903, when his disagreement with the I.S.R.P. was at its height, he wrote to Matheson that he intended to leave Dublin at the first opportunity. "As to work I would 'prefer', well, Chancellor of the Exchequer would do. But I have been a proof-reader, a tilelayer (ten years ago); a while-you-wait shoemaker, a mason's labourer and a carter. It is so long since I did hard manual labour that I feel queer at the thought of it."[161]

Wretched as Connolly's financial situation was, it would have been even worse had it not been for frequent visits to Great Britain. Initially, as in 1897, 1898, and 1900, he wished to see relations (his father died in 1900) or to raise funds for the *Workers' Republic;* thereafter, like the Irish migratory harvester, he spent the summer months in Scotland and England, but sowing and reaping political crops. He undertook engagements, principally for the S.D.F., lecturing and organizing.

160. Connolly to Daniel O'Brien, 11 Mar. 1899, O'Brien Collection, MSS 13940 (1) and 13932 (typewritten copy). Connolly mentioned that an earlier effort at peddling had failed because the stock he could afford was exhausted within a few days. His I.S.R.P. wages for Christmas 1900 amounted to 2s. (Greaves, p. 104).
161. Connolly to Matheson, 9 Mar. 1903, O'Brien MS 13906 (2).

Within the S.D.F. the tightly knit leadership of Hyndman, Harry
Lee, party secretary, and Harry Quelch, editor of *Justice,* roused opposi-
tion from younger members, especially from a Scottish group led by
J. C. Matheson, a Falkirk school teacher, and G. S. Yates, an engineer.
The influence of Daniel De Leon, the leader of the American Socialist
Labour Party (S.L.P.), made itself felt in the Scottish S.D.F. through
pamphlets and De Leon's *Weekly People,* which began to circulate in
Glasgow and Edinburgh from 1898 onward.[162] The S.L.P.'s insistence
on revolutionary doctrinal purity appealed to the Scots who could
express in the *Weekly People* the "clear-cut," "impossibilist,"[163] anti-
reformist views that were excluded from *Justice.* The S.D.F. delegation
(with the exception of Yates) had voted for the Kautsky resolution in
1900, whereas the S.L.P. delegates had supported the Guesde-Ferri
motion. In the ensuing controversy in S.D.F. branches, De Leonite
sympathizers were prominent. The dissidents were defeated when they
attempted to have the Kautsky compromise repudiated at the S.D.F.
annual conference at Birmingham in August 1901, but they continued
to agitate against the leadership's policy of collaboration with reformers
and nonsocialists. Connolly, who had pointed out in a letter[164] to *Justice*
(25 May 1901) the illogicality of denouncing Millerand while defending the Kautsky resolution, was, not surprisingly, engaged as orga-
nizer/lecturer in 1901 by those branches that shared his views. In 1902
he covered much the same ground as in 1901 and arranged with the
S.D.F. Scottish Council, now strongly De Leonite, to print its new
paper, the *Socialist,* edited by Matheson, on the I.S.R.P. press in
Dublin. The first issue appeared in August and set a course that was
sharply critical of the Hyndman leadership. When Connolly set out on
his 1903 tour,[165] confined this time to Scotland, it was to make preparations for the launching of a new party that was the inevitable outcome
of the defeat of the De Leonites and the expulsion of a number of their
leaders at the April 1903 conference of the S.D.F. He presided over its
inaugural conference in June. Despite some misgivings, its founders
called it, on Connolly's suggestion, the Socialist Labour Party.[166]

Before Connolly went to Scotland in April 1903 he had already met
De Leon and the leaders of the American S.L.P. On that party's invita-

162. Kendall, *Revolutionary Movement in Britain,* pp. 13–14.
163. A synonym for "revolutionary" as opposed to "reformist." See Kendall,
p. 324, n. 83.
164. Greaves, p. 106, prints a summary and extracts from the letter.
165. The most detailed and accurate account of Connolly's tours in Great Britain,
his relations with Scottish and English socialists, and his 1902 tour in North America
is given by Greaves, pp. 85–134.
166. The British S.L.P. survived until 1925. See Kendall, *Revolutionary Movement
in Britain,* pp. 314, 414, n. 122.

tion and with some assistance from his own union, the United Labourers of Ireland, he had spent the last four months of 1902 addressing meetings all over the United States (as well as a few in Canada) on
behalf of the S.L.P. and gathering funds and subscriptions for the
Workers' Republic. It was a highly successful tour in terms of the reception he was given in many centers and of the amount of money he sent
back to the I.S.R.P.[167] Nonetheless, his relations with his own party
were strained at times. He had a not unfounded suspicion that during
his absences party activities fell off, and he was not slow to voice it in a
manner that produced some resentment. In August 1901, M. J. Lyng,
replying to some of his complaints, acknowledged that the members
should show appreciation of Connolly's work by their own efforts, but
felt that he underestimated the difficulties they faced, adding, "As a
matter of tactics I think the tone of some of your remarks has been much
too *vitriolic*—tending to produce the opposite effect on some of us to
what you desired."[168] During his American tour he grew increasingly
irritated by the way in which the *Workers' Republic* was being run;
despite his repeated complaints, it was reaching American subscribers
late or not at all. Exhausted by incessant traveling and speaking, and
exasperated by the failure of those at home to honor his promises to
subscribers of regular publication, he wrote to Lyng in November:
"You may think it all a joke, but I think you all ought to be damned
well ashamed of yourselves."[169]

Recriminations ceased when, on his return in mid-January 1903, he
plunged into a municipal election, but they broke out again in February. The party's finances were chaotic. Connolly had assumed that his
remittances had freed the party of debt; instead he discovered that they
had been dissipated by an ill-advised attempt to run a bar and hopelessly muddled accounts. The party was in debt to the landlord (sixteen
weeks' rent was owed), to the paper manufacturer, and to the Labor
News Company of New York; the production of the *Socialist,* for which
the party had been paid in advance, was suspended. Differences—to
some extent political, but personal for the most part—among members, many of whom were unemployed, came to a head on 17 February.
Connolly proposed that a week's rent be paid, but his proposal was
turned down and he offered his resignation. To his bitter astonishment
it was accepted. The weeks that followed were filled with a welter of
accusations and counteraccusations, quarrels over financial priorities
and the ownership of the printing press, readmissions, resignations,

167. His letters written during these months frequently mention enclosures of
money, usually about $20.
168. Lyng to Connolly, 3 Aug. 1901, O'Brien MS 13912 (1).
169. Ibid., 3 Aug. 1901.

and simple loss of members. Some improvement was made in the party's finances, but the party as a whole had suffered severely. Connolly was readmitted after some delay. E. W. Stewart, whom he regarded as his principal opponent, then resigned because of Connolly's refusal to withdraw allegations of "besting," [170] but so did others, among them William O'Brien, whose departure he regretted. [171] What recovery had taken place was only temporary. In May, during his Scottish tour, Connolly expressed himself as stupefied—"it is as if I had lost a child"—at news from John J. Lyng that chaos had come again. [172] In July the dissidents set up a Socialist Labour Party, but though the rest retained the original name, the Irish Socialist Republican Party was dead. [173] When, after prolonged negotiations, the two factions came together on 4 March 1904, they called themselves the Socialist Party of Ireland. [174]

170. Connolly to Stewart, n.d. [Feb. 1903], O'Brien Collection, MS 13908 (1). Connolly alleged that the party seemed to have adopted a policy of "besting," i.e., defrauding creditors.

171. He offered to resign if O'Brien would come back, on the grounds that he felt that O'Brien was a younger man with fewer ties than himself, and one who could be depended upon to run the movement upon the correct lines [Connolly to O'Brien, 27 Mar. 1903, O'Brien Collection, MS 13908 (1)].

172. Connolly to John J. Lyng, 15 May 1903, O'Brien MS 13912 (1).

173. This summary of dissensions in the I.S.R.P. is based on letters written by Connolly, E. W. Stewart, M. J. Lyng, J. J. Lyng, W. O'Brien, and J. C. Matheson in the following files of the O'Brien Collection: 13906 (2), 13908 (1), 13908 (3), 13912 (1), 13914, 13915 (1). See also Greaves, pp. 126–7. Greaves is in error (p. 133) in stating that the I.S.R.P. proclaimed itself the Irish section of the Socialist Labour Party, though Connolly had at one time made such a suggestion to J. J. Lyng [Connolly to Lyng, 25 May 1903, O'Brien Collection, MS 13912 (1)].

In the surviving sheet (pp. 7–8?) of a letter [O'Brien Collection, MS 13942 (1)], correspondent and date unknown, W. O'Brien stated that he enclosed some of Connolly's letters to Matheson "from which you will see that you and I were 'moderates' and 'kangaroos' à la the S.L.P. of U.S.A. The references in his letters to Matheson (8 Apr. 1908) and to me (5 July 1909), taken in conjunction with what he said to Jack Lyng and yourself in New York, convinces me he realised he was responsible for the split in 1903. I propose to write a full account of what happened on 17 February 1903. The reason why I propose to write fully about Connolly's resignation is that some misleading reference may be made to it. This I admit is not very likely, but in view of Connolly's importance now it could happen. I was told some years ago about who said 'William O'Brien is the man who drove James Connolly out of Ireland.' I did not get his name." O'Brien does not seem to have written this account. The term "kangaroos" was S.L.P. jargon applied to unstable reformists as against doctrinaire revolutionaries.

174. D. O'Brien to secretary, I.S.L.P., 4, 9 Feb. 1904; John Brannigan (to D. O'Brien?), 20 Feb. 1904; draft minutes (in pencil) of I.S.R.P.–S.L.P reunion meeting of 4 Mar. 1904 [O'Brien Collection, MS 13915 (2)]. The name Socialist Party of Ireland was adopted on W. O'Brien's motion after the rejection of National Socialist Party and Socialist Revolutionary Party.

W. O'Brien [O'Brien Collection, MS 15674 (6)] gives the following chronology for the I.S.R.P. and its successors: I.S.R.P., 29 May 1896–4 Mar. 1904; S.L.P., July

In early March, while he was still outside the party, Connolly had made up his mind that he would leave Dublin at the first opportunity, irrespective of the outcome of the controversy. He kept to his decision when he rejoined the party later in the month, but he was unable to make precipitate plans, given "the trifling circumstance of having a family to lug around." Yet he could not "wait with equanimity, for I have not been so poverty-stricken for six years. I have only drawn 20 *s.* wages since I returned from America." Finally, in early April, he told Matheson in confidence that he had decided to go to America in the autumn, after his Scottish tour, and bring his family out after him. He regretted that he had not known the state of affairs when he was in the United States, as he had received tempting offers to stay, and it was unlikely that, having turned them down, they would be made again.[175] On 18 September 1903 he left Dublin for New York.

The depth of Connolly's disillusionment and bitterness is best conveyed by a letter he wrote in August replying to William O'Brien, who had expressed his surprise and sorrow on learning of his decision to leave.[176] Admitting that conditions for his family and himself in Ireland had been very hard, he still denied that they were sufficient to drive him from the country—"the glory and pride of that feat were reserved for my quondam comrades, whose willingness to believe ill of me, and to wreck my work, seems to have grown in proportion to the extent I was successful in serving them." After rehearsing his grievances against party members and declaring that "no amount of belated praise" from those responsible could "gild the pill or sweeten the bitterness of exile," he asserted that "men have been driven out of Ireland by the British Government, and by the landlords, but I am the first driven forth by the 'Socialists.'"[177]

If Connolly's seven years in Dublin are to be judged by his failure to make the I.S.R.P. a mass party, then they were seven lean years. The party had not acquired any appreciable support from the urban working class or organized labor. Conditions generally were notably unfavor-

---

1903–4 Mar. 1904; S.P.I., 4 Mar. 1904–11 June 1908; Irish Socialist Society, 20 Aug. 1908–14 Sept. 1909; S.P.I., 13 June 1909–June 1912; Independent Labour Party (Ireland), June 1912–July 1914; S.P. I., July 1914–Easter Week 1916; S.P.I., restarted 1917.

175. Connolly to Matheson, 9, 24 Mar., 8 Apr. 1903, O'Brien Collection, MS 13906 (2).

176. O'Brien to Connolly, August 1903 (typewritten copy), O'Brien Collection, MS 13908 (3).

177. Connolly to O'Brien, n.d., from a Glasgow address (c/o Clark, 10 Risk St.), O'Brien Collection, MS 13908 (1).

able—a trade union movement composed of conservatively minded skilled workers obsessed with the protection of decaying industries, an unorganized mass of unskilled workers in a city marked by persistent structural unemployment, a reunited nationalist party that had recovered much of the ground lost before 1900 and still retained support by holding out alluring promises of the golden age that would follow the granting of a measure of self-government, a religious climate of opinion more rural than urban in character and immediately hostile to any suggestion of social change. Connolly's major contribution, as evidenced by his writings, was, as Greaves has said (*Connolly,* p. 134), his persistent battle against the opportunism that marked the politics of the period. And if his propaganda was at times overtly doctrinaire for its recipients, if his temperament, understandable in view of his own circumstances, frequently made heavy demands upon his associates, both were to be sensibly modified by his experiences during his seven years' exile in the United States.[178]

178. For Connolly's years in the United States see Greaves, chaps. 10–13.

9

Ferment

The Struggles in the Irish Trades Union Congress, 1900 to 1906

The end of the nineteenth century brought little apparent change in the ruling body of the Irish labor movement. The Dublin congress of 1900 was a very splendid affair. The lord mayor the Right Honourable Sir Thomas Pile, Bart., in robes and chain of office and attended by mace and sword-bearers, received the congress in the council chamber of the city hall where he addressed "the parliament of labour" in well-rounded clichés, expressing his confidence that their decisions would be of lasting benefit to the workers and the country itself. Two nationalist M.P.s, William Field and Michael Austin, and large numbers of aldermen and councillors were also present. Field, stressing the importance of home manufacturers, declared that "capital and labour should work harmoniously together to keep the work at home instead of sending it abroad." [1] The president of congress, George Leahy, a Dublin plasterer, stated that the Irish Trades Union Congress (I.T.U.C.) was founded "to do for ourselves what had hitherto been attempted for us in a somewhat perfunctory manner by our brethren across the channel" and urged an alliance between the forces of labor and temperance "both movements having much in common . . . [being] non-political and non-sectarian." [2] At a later stage congress adopted a resolution asking that no intoxicating liquor be served to a child under sixteen (an amendment to fix the age at twelve was decisively defeated), but there was no interference with the arrangements of the Dublin Trades Council's reception committee. The lord mayor gave a reception, followed by a picnic at the Scalp, a well-known beauty spot, and the Dublin Press Club (representing printing and kindred trades) provided a dinner for some sixty delegates. Hospitality reached its peak at the Trades Coun-

1. I.T.U.C., *Report, Seventh Congress*, p. 3.
2. Ibid., pp. 18–19.

cil's banquet for delegates, friends and guests (130 in all), who sat down to five courses with appropriate wines, followed by toasts and songs.[3]

The composition and organization of the Irish T.U.C. underwent little change. The numbers represented by delegates at conference had climbed slowly from 50,000 (Cork congress, 1895) to 67,000 (Sligo, 1901), but for the rest of the decade it fluctuated around 70,000. The finances of the organization were meager, and the parliamentary committee depended for its income on any balance remaining from delegates' fees and the response to its annual appeal, which rarely yielded more than £50. The main contributors were a few of the amalgamated unions, notably the A.S.R.S., and the Belfast and Dublin Trades Councils. It was not until 1905 that the decision was taken to replace subscriptions by affiliation fees based on Irish membership.[4] The change produced a steadier, if not much greater, income.

Dublin and Belfast continued to dominate the Parliamentary Committee, though an attempt to limit their representation to a maximum of two (and representation of any other town to one) was defeated only by the casting vote of the chairman (Alexander Bowman of Belfast) at the Sligo congress of 1901.[5] Laborers' unions were unrepresented until 1906, and on that occasion George Greig (N.A.U.L., Belfast) owed his election to a standing order disqualifying a candidate with a higher vote.[6] In the same year a new standing order was adopted declaring the secretary a member *ex officio* of congress and parliamentary committee, and as such, permanent as long as he gave satisfaction.[7] John Simmons had been secretary for the first five years and was succeeded in 1899 by Hugh McManus. The following year there were four candidates for the secretaryship and E. L. Richardson topped the poll, beating Simmons, McManus, and Daly. Richardson remained secretary until 1910, when

3. The menu and entertainment are of interest as showing the social inclinations of the "old unionism." Ibid., pp. 13–15. Menu: Soups—Oxtail, Julienne (Sherry); Fish—Fillets of sole, turbot and lobster sauce (Amontillado); Entrees—Lobster cutlets, Jardinière, savoy pie (Hock); Rôti—Roast beef, Horse-radish (St. Julien); Vegetables—French beans, peas, cauliflower, new and mashed potatoes; Sweets—Rhubarb tart, apple tart, Chancellor pudding, compôte of pears, peaches, apricots (Port). Toasts: "Our Native Land," "The Irish Trades Union Congress," "Our Guests." *Songs:* "Il Bacio," "The Meeting of the Waters," "The Green Isle of Erin," "The Sailor's Grave," "Maying" (a duet), "Alice, Where Art Thou?," "The Snowy-Breasted Pearl."
4. I.T.U.C., *Report, Twelfth Congress*, p. 50. See Appendix 6 for lists of officers and committee members.
5. I.T.U.C., *Report, Eighth Congress*, p. 57.
6. I.T.U.C., *Report, Thirteenth Congress*, p. 76. Not more than one representative of the same trades council could be elected; of the two D.T.C. delegates (James Chambers and George Leahy), Chambers (36 votes) was elected. Leahy had 23 votes, Grieg (Belfast) had 15.
7. Ibid., p. 79.

he resigned to become manager of the Board of Trade labor exchange in Dublin.[8] A printer by trade (member of the D.T.P.S.), he was a conservative craft unionist, but his administrative ability pleased William Walker, who complained that his successor P. T. Daly was much less efficient.[9] There were no full-time officials.

William Walker approved of the 1900 congress in his report to the Belfast Trades Council. Confessing that "he had not been at all favourable to the Irish Congress from the beginning," he said that the Dublin conference was most successful; "there was evidently a desire on the part of all to redeem the past."[10] This redemption consisted of the absence of Home Rule sentiments. Resolutions on the need for technical education (and labor representation on its national board), for temperance, and for free books and meals for poor children were approved, as were the stock resolutions on matters of Irish trade union interest. These demands had been and continued to be the staple of congresses: the protection of home manufacturers, the appointment of additional factory inspectors, the enforcement of safety regulations and of the fair wage clause in government and municipal contracts, a greater Irish share in supplying British military requirements, the payment of returning officers' charges out of the public purse.

Yet if the personnel, income, and majority of resolutions were scarcely different from those of the founding congress, a new tone and new resolutions revealed the changes that were taking place. They were evident in the activities of the Dublin and Belfast Trades Councils,[11] but the ferments working in the lower levels of labor organizations ultimately affected the national body, so that the years from 1900 to 1906 constituted a transitional period in the history of Irish labor. The resolutions in question were concerned with socialism, or more accurately nationalization, versus reformism, and with issues that involved, directly or indirectly, Irish nationalism—the political representation of labor, whether through existing Irish political parties or through an independent labor party, and the rival merits of Irish and British trade unions.

Nationalization and Reform

At the 1893 congress of the British Trades Union Congress held in Belfast, James Macdonald was at last successful in carrying his resolution confining support to candidates prepared to endorse the nationalization of the means of production, distribution, and exchange.

8. I.T.U.C., *Report, Seventh Congress*, p. 43.
9. B.T.C. minutes, 7 Sept. 1911.
10. Ibid., 29 June 1900.   11. See chapters 10, 11, 12.

In 1895 William Walker moved in the Belfast Trades Council a resolution to be submitted to the Irish congress of that year declaring that "the ultimate solution of the labour problem is to be found in the nationalisation of land, also the means of production, distribution and exchange," and adding a demand for the immediate state purchase and working of the Irish railways.[12] Though the Trades Council struck out "the ultimate solution," Walker was not defeated, for he had the deleted paragraph moved at the Cork congress (1895) by James McCarron of Derry. McCarron, described in the annual report (p. 10) of the fourth congress (Waterford, 1897) as having, in labor questions, "a leaning to what is considered by some the extreme side," was an official of the Amalgamated Society of Tailors. He was an energetic and forceful trade unionist: in a big strike in Derry he had been imprisoned for vigorous picketing. A full-faced, expansive man, he was extremely popular with delegates, who elected him regularly to the parliamentary committee, usually at the top of the poll.[13] He was president of congress three times and in his own city successively councillor and alderman. In spite of his "extreme" reputation, he was essentially an "old unionist"; he combined membership of an amalgamated union with support for the Irish parliamentary party. In proposing "the ultimate solution," he shocked the more conservative delegates by asserting that the land laws forced agricultural laborers into the towns and brought down wages. If land could be nationalized, so could every source of production, distribution, and exchange. "Labour created capital, which was the fruit of the tree of labour."

Alexander Taylor, president of the Belfast Trades Council, moved an amendment declaring that the quickest way to attain the ultimate solution was to have carried into effect reforms with which the vast majority of workers agreed: "The resolution meant that private property was a thing that could not exist."[14] The amendment's seconder (E. L. Richardson, Dublin, later secretary of the I.T.U.C.) declared that the resolution practically said that trade unionism was played out, and William Field[15] warned the delegates that the resolution would do them infinite harm, for "the theory of socialism was all right if they had

12. B.T.C. minutes, 27 Apr. 1895.   13. See Appendix 6.

14. Taylor opened a small shop after he ceased to work as a linen lapper (interview with D. McDevitt). He is described as a stationer and newsagent in his nomination paper for the aldermanship of Court ward in 1901 (*B.N.-L.*, 7 Jan. 1901).

15. Field was a cattle-dealer and attended the Cork congress as a delegate of the Land and Labour Association. Ostensibly an organization of rural workers it was in effect an appendage of the nationalist party. At the following congress (Limerick 1896), Field and two others (J. J. Shee, M.P., and Kendal E. O'Brien, later an M.P.) were not accepted as delegates on the grounds that they did not satisfy standing order 2, which required delegates to have worked or be working at the trade they represented.

to deal with angels and not with human nature." In spite of a Dublin delegate's remark that "socialism might be bad, but it could not be worse than the present condition of things" and McCarron's conclusion that the cooperative commonwealth was not an impossibility but the only way to prevent social injustice, the delegates decided that they were not angels and carried the amendment by 57 votes to 25.[16] Walker raised the issue in the Belfast Trades Council when the congress delegates gave their report, saying that congresses should exercise an educational social influence in the state rather than merely record agreed decisions, and calling Taylor's attitude reactionary. Taylor held that the passing of the resolution would have damaged congress and described nationalization as a will-o'-the-wisp; he was supported by 27 votes to 3.[17]

At the Limerick congress (1896) of the following year, McCarron moved the same resolution, but again Taylor's amendment was carried by a comfortable majority.[18] At Waterford (1897) McCarron changed his tactics, and acknowledging that previous congresses had rejected nationalization of all industries, asked that it be applied to land, mines, and railways. Congress accepted this installment unanimously.[19] How small the installment was can be realized on examination. A demand for the nationalization, or at least the state purchase of Irish railways, had been made as early as the 1860s, and the second congress (1895) had endorsed it. Mining was negligible as an industry in Ireland and had none of the importance it had in Great Britain. Land nationalization was unlikely to arouse opposition in a congress attended almost exclusively by urban delegates who felt that the woes of the tenant farmers had hitherto engrossed political energies to the exclusion of their own. McCarron contented himself with moving the same resolution regularly at subsequent congresses up to 1906, changing his seconders annually.

The tone of presidential addresses was almost invariably reformist. Ruskin and Carlyle were frequently quoted when speakers exalted the dignity and rights of labor, but no new view of society was given until 1904 when Walker presided at the Kilkenny congress. In a highly rhetorical speech he looked forward to a time "when all men shall feel they are brethren . . . when we shall enforce the dictum of St Paul that he that shall not work neither shall he eat, and when we shall be able to declare that our laws give equal opportunities to all the sons and daughters of men."[20] The vice-chairman of the parliamentary commit-

16. I.T.U.C., *Report, Second Congress*, pp. 25–26.
17. B.T.C. minutes, 22 June 1895.
18. I.T.U.C., *Report, Third Congress*, pp. 40–41.
19. I.T.U.C., *Report, Fourth Congress*, pp. 34–35.
20. Urging a platform common to all creeds and parties in Ireland, he said it "will

tee (James Chambers, a Dublin saddler), impressed by Walker's oratory, hoped that his ringing voice would be heard ere long in the House
of Commons, demanding equality and justice for the workers of his
native land;[21] but when Chambers himself presided at the Wexford
congress (1905) he issued a warning against "irresponsible people pre-
suming to act in the name of trade unionism. . . . we recognise only
those demands that tend to secure to the worker at least a living wage, a
just percentage of the profits of his toil—in short, a fair day's pay for a
fair day's work, whether that work be for the state, the local authority or
the private employer."[22] But the 1906 congress (Athlone) heard the
first unequivocally socialist presidential address which, while quoting
from Carlyle and Ruskin, also drew upon William Morris. Stephen
Dineen, a Limerick baker, inviting the delegates to "come join in the
only battle," turned his back on reformism: "In spite of the palliatives
mentioned the unemployed problem will still be with us until the
workers' party becomes the dominant force in the state, and the evil of
the capitalist system . . . is finally got rid of by the substitution of
public for private control of industry."[23]

Irish Trade Unionists and Irish Members of Parliament

The principal business of the I.T.U.C. parliamentary committee was to
lobby members of parliament and ministers in support of congress
resolutions. They made two unsuccessful attempts to see the chief
secretary for Ireland (John Morley) after the first congress, but finally
secured an interview with him through the intervention of William
Field.[24] The support of Irish nationalist M.P.s was sought on Irish
affairs, but this did not indicate any political preference on the part of
Irish trade unionists. In the early years the committee sent congress
resolutions to labor M.P.s in general, but on specific matters (e.g., the
fair wage clause) they wrote to Sir Charles Dilke, Sidney Buxton,
Michael Davitt, T. W. Russell, and John Burns. Anxious to have a fair

---

enable us to cast around the poor and the weak of our brethren the protecting mantle of
a united people's love and care (loud applause). In the alembic of a Divine mysteria, it is
hard to reason the whys and wherefores of our conflicting opinions" (I.T.U.C., *Report,
Eleventh Congress,* Walker's address, pp. 7–17). Clarkson (*Labour and Nationalism in
Ireland,* p. 213) is wrong in stating that Walker was the only resident of the Irish
T.U.C. from 1894 to 1907 to declare for political action of the workers through a party
of their own; Stephen Dineen also did so, in less rhetorical language.
  21. Walker was a prospective labour candidate for North Belfast.
  22. I.T.U.C., *Report, Twelfth Congress,* p. 6.
  23. I.T.U.C., *Report, Thirteenth Congress,* p. 36.
  24. I.T.U.C., *Report, Second Congress,* p. 6; Report, I.T.U.C., *Third Congress,* p. 2.

wage clause inserted in the Local Government (Ireland) Act, 1898, the committee wrote to fifteen of the principal M.P.s of all parties. They received a number of favorable replies, "perhaps the most important from John Dillon" (chairman of the Irish parliamentary party), who promised his best support.[25] Though an appeal to trades councils to provide expenses for a deputation drew a response only from Cork,[26] McCarron, Simmons, and Taylor went to London and interviewed Irish and other members of parliament.

In their 1901 report the committee thanked Keir Hardie and Sir Charles Dilke for assisting the Irish trade unionists. More significant, however, was the announcement that they had sought the help of the Irish party and had received a reply that the party was in entire sympathy with their resolutions on the Factories and Workshops bill and would support them. The committee also reported the election to parliament of J. P. Nannetti,[27] who would fill the gap left by the recent defeat of Michael Austin. Occasionally during the rest of the decade the help of British Labour M.P.s was sought, but most of the parliamentary work on behalf of the Irish T.U.C. was done by nationalist M.P.s.

The new century brought with it a change of the Irish party's attitude to organized trade unionists. When the divided nationalists were brought together in the United Irish League, its National Directory adopted new rules governing the conventions for the selection of parliamentary candidates.[28] Each convention was to be composed of delegates representing almost every organization that could conceivably be considered nationalist (e.g., the National Literary Society, the Gaelic Athletic Association) as well as all nationalist public representatives in the constituency. Each branch of the Land and Labour Association was entitled to six delegates, each trades council could send six, and the local United Irish League executive could also invite additional representation of trade and labor bodies. The Local Government (Ireland) Act, 1898, had resulted in a large number of working-class representatives being elected to local councils. This development, and the apparently greater control exercised by the rank-and-file organization over the Irish Parliamentary Party, made the nationalist M.P.s much more sympathetic to trade union requests.

Nannetti rapidly became a liaison officer between Irish trade union-

25. I.T.U.C., *Report, Fifth Congress*, p. 38.

26. It was a constant complaint of the Parliamentary Committee that they were seriously handicapped by want of money, so that deputations to London could be sent only on rare occasions.

27. Nannetti had been secretary and later president of the Dublin Trades Council; he was elected as a nationalist.

28. *F.J.*, 20 Sept. 1900, quoted in Lyons, *The Irish Parliamentary Party, 1890–1910*, p. 151.

ists and his party. Even the Belfast Trades Council, normally cautious in its approval of politicians, endorsed a circular from the Dublin council appealing for subscriptions to Nannetti's testimonial and emphasized to its affiliated trade bodies that Nannetti's position was unique in Irish trade union annals, "he being the only trade union M.P. Ireland sends to Parliament."[29] When a resolution was passed at the Sligo conference (1901) on the motion of two Belfast delegates, both members of the Belfast branch of the Typographical Association— Hugh McManus (chairman of the Parliamentary Committee) and John Murphy (president of the Belfast Trades Council)—that returning officers' expenses should be paid out of the rates, the resulting petition to parliament was presented on behalf of congress by Nannetti.[30] Two years later another petition, signed by the officers, on working-class housing in Ireland was also presented by Nannetti to the chief secretary.[31] But the strongest indication of the dependence of congress on the Irish party was the interview Nannetti arranged with the party's chairman (John Redmond) and some of his colleagues in 1902; the meeting took place in Dublin's Mansion House, lent by the lord mayor. Redmond promised assistance on most of the matters mentioned by the deputation and hoped that there would be more frequent meetings between the two organizations than in the past.[32] The same procedure was followed in 1904 and was repeated on a number of occasions after 1906. Nannetti received constant tributes to his work,[33] and the Irish party was frequently praised in annual reports of congress, and at times by presidents, for its activities on behalf of Irish trade unionists.

In spite of the satisfactory performances of Irish nationalist members, there was a feeling among some northern delegates that assistance should also be requested from Irish Unionist members. Edward McInnes (National Amalgamated Union of Labour, Belfast) urged such a course while at the same time paying the nationalists "the tribute of being sound labour men," though he was opposed to them in politics.[34] The Parliamentary Committee thereupon invoked the help of the Irish Unionist leader but had to report to the following congress (Newry, 1903) that not even an acknowledgement of their request was received

29. B.T.C. minutes 5 (?) Sept. 1901.

30. I.T.U.C., *Report, Ninth Congress*, p. 20.

31. I.T.U.C., *Report, Eleventh Congress*, p. 30.

32. I.T.U.C., *Report, Ninth Congress*, pp. 24–5.

33. "Your committee trust this feeble expression of appreciation of valuable services rendered will be endorsed by Congress in a more emphatic manner." Parliamentary Committe's report of a letter of thanks to Nannetti (Ibid., p. 33).

34. Ibid., pp. 34–5. McInnes was moving a resolution requesting noncontributory old age pensions.

from Colonel Saunderson.[35] The Parliamentary Committee took care in succeeding reports to list the names of members who voted against desirable measures.[36]

At the second congress (Cork, 1895) Samuel Monro, who had presided at the Belfast congress of the British T.U.C. (1893), replying to a toast (The Labour Cause) said that they were assembled in Cork for one purpose—"to improve their condition and that of those dependent on them, and with that view they gladly accepted the help of influential men like the mayor and the M.P.s."[37] Mayors and nationalist M.P.s continued to attend congresses, and even on occasion expressed the hope of seeing more labor representation in public life. Tevenan's scheme for labor representation on local government bodies was put forward at the Cork congress (1895), which was attended by Alderman E. Crean, then one of the two labor-nationalist M.P.s. Crean, who joined in the mayor's welcome to the delegates, anticipated the debate on Tevenan's resolution by claiming that nearly nine years earlier, while president of the Cork Trades Council, he had been elected to the corporation "purely and simply as a labour representative. He was a working joiner then, and he was a no better man now."[38] Though Tevenan's scheme came to nothing for lack of finance and though the nationalist party grew more benevolent in its attitude to trade unionists, the desire for more direct labor representation persisted.

Direct Labor Representation

In Belfast William Walker was the strongest advocate of labor representation free of party political taint. Seconded by a Dublin fellow A.S.C.J. delegate he moved a resolution at the Dublin (1900) congress instructing elected representatives of labor to abstain from publicly supporting the nominees of any political party unless such a nominee was endorsed by the local trades council (or trade union where no trades council existed). P. T. Daly,[39] making his first appearance at the Irish

35. I.T.U.C., *Report, Tenth Congress*, p. 31.

36. The Parliamentary Committee received a reply from the secretary of the Irish Unionist members promising to consider "with an open mind" a Trades Disputes bill. All the official Unionists who voted opposed the bill (I.T.U.C., *Report, Twelfth Congress*, p. 32).

37. I.T.U.C., *Report, Second Congress*, p. 38.

38. I.T.U.C., *Report, Second Congress*, p. 7.

39. Daly was already deeply involved in the political schemes of his D.T.P.S. fellow-member, Arthur Griffith; in Nov. 1900 he was present at the first annual convention of Cumman na nGaedhael, one of the forerunners of Sinn Féin (R. P. Davis, the Rise of Sinn Féin, 1891–1910, p. 17; unpublished thesis approved for the degree of M. Litt., 1958, T.C.D.).

Trades Union Congress as a Dublin Typographical Provident Society delegate, proposed an amendment that branches of the Labour Electoral Association be established in every town in Ireland and that a pledge-bound labor party be created, pledged to vote as the majority should decide. Daly's amendment, with its echoes of Parnellite pledges,[40] was ruled out of order, and the original resolution narrowly defeated (24 to 21).[41] A year later the resolution (moved by John Murphy of the Belfast Trades Council and seconded by Walker) was passed.[42]

From 1893 onward the legal rights trade unions enjoyed under the Trade Union Act of 1871 and the Conspiracy and Protection of Property Act of 1875 were assailed by a series of adverse judgements.[43] The climax came in two cases: the Taff Vale case, in which it was decided that a trade union could be sued in its corporate capacity for tortious acts committed on its behalf, and the *Quinn v. Leathem* case, where the judge's decision made a strike or boycott, or a threat of strike or boycott, in certain circumstances a conspiracy to injure. As a result of the Taff Vale case, the union funds were liable for damages in such an event.[44] The right to picket had already been severely circumscribed by decisions in earlier cases, with the end result that unions were seriously concerned about their position. The employers' counteroffensive—hostile newspaper articles, the organization of strike-breaking forces by such bodies as the Shipping Federation and the National Free Labour association—had been provoked by the initial success of the new general unions in 1889, but the legal decisions in the main concerned members of craft unions, who had previously been able to manage

40. An earlier attempt at a pledge-bound party was made in 1850, when a tenant league conference recommended that the new league (the "League of North and South") should support only "representatives who will give a written pledge that they will support in and out of Parliament a tenant law, based upon, and carrying into effect, the principles adopted by the Irish Tenant League; and that they will withhold all support from any cabinet that will not endorse these principles" (*F.J.*, 10 Aug. 1850, quoted in J. H. Whyte, *The Independent Irish Party*, p. 13). The Parnellite pledge was as follows: "I . . . pledge myself that in the event of my election to parliament I will sit, act and vote with the Irish parliamentary party and if at a meeting of the party convened upon due notice specially to consider the question, it be decided by a resolution supported by a majority of the entire parliamentary party that I have not fulfilled the above pledge I hereby undertake forthwith to resign my seat." (C. C. O'Brien, *Parnell and his Party*, p. 143).

41. I.T.U.C., *Report, Seventh Congress*, p. 29.

42. I.T.U.C., *Report, Eighth Congress*, p. 56.

43. See John Saville, "Trade Unions and Free Labour: the Background to the Taff Vale Decision," in Asa Briggs and John Saville, eds., *Essays in Labour History*.

44. See F. Bealey and H. M. Pelling, *Labour and Politics, 1900–1906*, chaps. 3 and 4.

disputes in a quiet fashion, even to the extent of paying subsistence and traveling allowances to persuade nonunionists to leave factories where they had been introduced.[45] The resultant state of alarm was a powerful influence in increasing trade union affiliation to the Labour Representation Committee and in preparing the way for the election of a greatly increased number of labor members of parliament. The unions received their reward in 1906, when the Trades Disputes Act of that year protected their funds against legal actions and restored the right of picketing.

The legal decisions in the Taff Vale and *Quinn v. Leathem* cases had aroused the fears of Irish as well as British trade unionists, since all were affected by them. Indeed, the *Quinn v. Leathem* case was of direct Irish interest, for it arose out of the efforts of the Belfast Journeymen Butchers' Association (Quinn was its treasurer) to persuade Leathem, an employer, to dismiss his nonunion assistants. Both the Belfast Trades Council and the Irish Trades Union Congress were concerned in raising funds.[46] The Irish T.U.C. printed the legal opinion obtained by the Scottish T.U.C. on the new status of trade unions and a second opinion by the barrister Clem Edwards.[47] The result was that labor representation ceased to be an academic question and A. Taylor (Belfast Linen Lappers) and Robert Gageby (Belfast Flaxdressers' secretary) had no difficulty getting a motion passed declaring that, in view of the Taff Vale judgement, money would be more usefully spent on advocating direct labor representation in parliament than on legal expenses.[48]

At the same conference (Cork, 1902), Taylor (seconded by W. Hayes of the Belfast Bakers' Society) moved the usual motion forbidding labor representatives to support the nominees of any political party "unless such nominee is approved of by the local trades council or other recognised labour organisation." Daly proposed an amendment that the recognition be by congress and that the parliamentary committee be

45. In the case of a Dublin bottlemakers' strike in 1866, the Dublin Trades Council persuaded the employers to pay the expenses of the seventy Swedish workers who had been brought to Dublin under false pretenses (Swift, *Dublin Bakers*, pp. 294–5).

46. The council advised the butchers to affiliate to the B.T.U.C. and attend the Huddersfield congress; Walker and Bowman accompanied them and were successful (B.T.C. executive committee minutes, 30 July, 20 Aug. 1900; B.T.C. minutes, 21 Sept. 1900). The Dublin butchers contributed £20 and the Dublin Trades Council circularized its affiliated societies.

47. I.T.U.C., *Report, Ninth Congress*, pp. 26–29. Clem Edwards (1869–1938) started as a farm laborer, studied law, and was called to the bar in 1889. He played an important part in the '90s as trade union organizer, publicist, and labour journalist. He became a liberal M.P. in 1906 (Briggs and Saville, *Essays in Labour History*, p. 324, n. 4).

48. I.T.U.C., *Report, Ninth Congress*, p. 48.

instructed to draw up a scheme for the creation of a pledge-bound labor
party, "controlled by and answerable to the Irish Trades Union Congress." He complained that Taylor's resolution had no binding force
and that in Dublin candidates not endorsed or even condemned by the
Trades Council had received the public support of labor men. John
Murphy (Belfast) announced he would vote against the amendment,
because it was based on insincerity—no doubt a reference to Daly's own
political commitments[49]—but after the lengthy debate was closured,
Daly's amendment and the substantive motion were carried by 45 votes
to 12. Among his varied supporters were William Walker and E. W.
Stewart (of Connolly's Irish Socialist Republican Party).[50]

One of the grievances of Irish trade unionists against the British
Trades Union Congress (and one that helped to maintain the Irish
congress in existence during its initial years) was the exclusion of trades
councils from representation. John Simmons, opening the proceedings
as vice-chairman of the parliamentary committee at the Sligo congress
(1900), referred to this exclusion and declared, in the presence of two
fraternal delegates from the Scottish congress, that "if the gentlemen
who had forced Irish and Scotch trade unionists to establish their own
congresses were aware of the success which had since followed these
undertakings, they would have been very slow to drive Irish and Scotch
workers from the fold."[51] In spite of the repeated declarations at Irish
congresses, and in a circular to amalgamated unions, that the Irish
body had not been founded in any spirit of rivalry—its work was
"analogous and auxiliary to the British United Trades congress"[52] relations between the organizations had grown cool. A formal acknowledgement by the secretary of the British T.U.C. of a number of resolutions forwarded to him by the Irish Parliamentary Committee
produced an irritated report to the 1899 congress that nothing further
had been done.[53] Two years later the British secretary expressed sympathy with the Irish resolutions, but only widened the breach by adding
his Parliamentary Committee's views on the "unfortunate existence of
these sectional congresses." His committee, he wrote, was convinced
"beyond the shadow of a doubt" that the time had come for both the
Irish and Scottish congresses to return and again be "part and parcel of

49. Daly, who retained his connection with the bodies that later produced Sinn
Féin, was endorsed by the Dublin Trades Council (minutes, 10 Aug. 1903) for a
councillorship in the Rotunda ward, and congratulated by them on his election at the
head of the poll (minutes, 9 Sept. 1903).
50. I.T.U.C., Report, Ninth Congress, pp. 42–43.
51. I.T.U.C., Report, Eighth Congress, pp. 3–4.
52. I.T.U.C., Report, Seventh Congress, pp. 15–16.
53. I.T.U.C., Report, Sixth Congress, pp. 34–35.

the British Trades Union Congress as in days of yore." In an obviously restrained reply, the Irish committee unanimously defended their organization, which "has greatly benefited trades organisation in this country and has fully justified the necessity for its existence."[54] The days of yore did not return.[55]

The Belfast Trades Council had greatly regretted the broken connection with the England of the United Trades Congress, but an opportunity to renew it in a somewhat altered form came with the formation in February 1900 of the Labour Representation Committee (L.R.C.). Its growing trade union membership made it a much more respectable body than the Independent Labour Party, which in any case no longer had a Belfast branch, and the legal battering that trade unions had received counseled political remedies. In addition the "old unionists" had lost influence in the council and William Walker, who had been secretary for a year and a half until his appointment as an official of the A.S.C.J., was the dominant figure (he became president in 1902).[56] The initial conference of the L.R.C. fixed the affiliation fee for trades councils at £5, a figure most councils regarded as beyond their means, but the conference of the following year made the minimum £1. The Belfast council, on Walker's motion, decided unanimously in 1902 to affiliate and send two delegates to the next conference.[57] They were instructed to invite speakers to visit Belfast and address the council on the possibility of fighting "one or more" of the city's parliamentary divisions at the next general election.[58]

The delegates duly attended the important L.R.C. conference at Newcastle-on-Tyne (February 1903). The efforts of the trade unions to reverse by legislation the situation created by "judge-made law" were obvious in the Newcastle resolutions that there was need of an organization with a tighter political constitution and an adequate fund for maintaining M.P.s. James Sexton[59] moved a motion requiring candidates seeking ratification by the executive committee of the L.R.C. to be promoted by affiliated societies (or a conference of affiliated societies in the district to be fought); they were also to accept the L.R.C.

54. I.T.U.C., *Report, Eighth Congress*, pp. 3–4.

55. A further effort was made in 1910, when two delegates of the Postmen's Federation (from Cork and Glasgow) moved an instruction to the Parliamentary Committee to confer with the B.T.U.C. committee for an amalgamation of the two congresses. The previous question was moved by James Larkin and a delegate of the Irish Glass Bottlemakers and carried by 23 votes to 15 (I.T.U.C., *Report, Seventeenth Congress*, p. 48). Some amalgamated executives sent representatives to Irish congresses, hence the Glasgow delegate's presence.

56. B.T.C. minutes, 19 Jan. 1902.   57. Ibid., 18 Oct. 1902.

58. Ibid., 5 Feb. 1903.

59. James Sexton, secretary of the National Union of Dock Labourers.

program and, if approved, to appear in constituencies under the title of labor candidates only. Hugh McManus, a Belfast delegate, proposed a Parnellite pledge for such M.P.s: "How had Mr. Parnell's programme been made effective? Every man was bound by a pledge similar to that which he asked the conference to accept. They would also be asked to sit and vote on questions that have been settled by a majority vote in the House of Commons."[60] The addendum was carried on a card vote of 501,000 to 194,000.[61] The Belfast delegates also carried out their instructions to invite speakers to visit Belfast. Keir Hardie and J. Ramsay MacDonald accepted the invitation and, when they had fulfilled their engagement, accompanied the Belfast contingent to the Newry congress of the Irish T.U.C.

Delegates at Newry were frequently reminded of the importance of labor representation. Their fraternal delegates to the Scottish congress reported that it was the main subject discussed at Ayr, and the Scottish fraternal delegates in their turn emphasized that, if trade unionists wished to protect themselves, they must have political power. Hardie summarized the unions' basic demands (right to peaceful picketing, protection of union funds against compensation claims by employers, right of a union to bring out men in support of another union) and also stressed the absolute necessity for political action by labor if the growing power of employers were to be checked. He looked forward to the return to parliament of Irish labor members who would work together realizing they had one common interest "which was greater than national feeling, greater than religious differences, the principle of seeking to uplift the people to whom they belonged."[62] MacDonald repeated Hardie's message and, as secretary of the new organization, pointed with pride to its phenomenal growth, for it now represented about 900,000 trade unionists.

It was somewhat anticlimactic that when the Parliamentary Committee's report was presented it contained no mention of political representation. Daly was quick to point out that the committee had failed to carry out the previous year's instruction to draw up a scheme for a pledge-bound labor party; he warmly praised MacDonald's speech of the day before. The president (Walter Hudson, Irish secretary of the A.S.R.S.) could only explain that his committee was daunted by the task of reconciling the conflicting political opinions of Irish industrial workers, but invited delegates to see the standing orders committee if they had a suitable resolution. Murphy and Walker did so and were

60. L.R.C., *Third Annual Conference Report*, 1903, pp. 32–33.

61. It was repealed at the 1904 (Bradford) conference and the exact procedure left to the executive committee to decide (Cole, *British Working-Class Politics*, p. 175).

62. I.T.U.C., *Report, Tenth Congress*, pp. 18–19.

gratified to have their motion passed: "That this Congress of Irish trade unionists heartily recommends to the trade unionists of this country an immediate affiliation with the Labour Representation Committee to promote the formation of independent labor representation in Ireland." [63]

The resolution was ineffective [64] and was moved regularly at later congresses by Belfast delegates (with occasional support from Dublin members of amalgamated unions) who found it provoked opposition. The debates, however, showed that politically the congress consisted of three groups: the majority content with the Irish parliamentary party, a smaller group favoring affiliation to the Labour Representation Committee (after 1906 to the British Labour Party), and a handful, led by P. T. Daly, who demanded the formation of a distinctively Irish labor party. The two minority groups might unite temporarily, but their aims were too dissimilar for the alliance to be lasting.

The debate on labor representation at the Kilkenny congress (1904) was spirited. The Parliamentary Committee's report that preceded the debate gave a lengthy account of the committee's interview with John Redmond, in which Walker thanked the leader of the Irish parliamentary party for the way "he guided the destinies of the Party for the amelioration of the welfare of all Irishmen" and sought support for a trades disputes bill. [65] It also listed the numbers of Irish M.P.s. who voted for and against the bill and pointed out that over fifty nationalist M.P.s made the London-Dublin crossing on two successive nights in order to support labor. [66] Finally, standing orders were suspended in order that McCarron might move and W. Hudson (A.S.R.S., Dublin) second a motion of thanks to Redmond and his colleagues. McCarron pointed out that the bill would not have passed its second reading if fifty-five Irish nationalist M.P.s had not voted for it—the Parliamentary Committee and its energetic and able secretary (E. L. Richardson)

63. Ibid., p. 54.
64. Belfast was the only Irish Trades Council that affiliated to the L.R.C. and sent delegates, but occasionally an amalgamated union might include an Irish delegate from another town; e.g., H. O'Rourke (A.S.R.S., Dublin) attended the Liverpool conference. Belfast had four present at this conference, W. Walker (A.S.C.J.) and E. McInnes (N.A.U.L.) in addition to the Trades Council representatives, John Murphy and Alexander Boyd (L.R.C., *Fifth Annual Conference Report*, 1905, pp. 4–21).
65. I.T.U.C., *Report, Eleventh Congress*, pp. 31–5.
66. Ibid., pp. 35–6. There was a nationalist convention in Dublin on 21 April and a division on the bill the following day. The bill passed its second reading but no more was heard of it. The prime minister, A. J. Balfour, was not prepared to support it because a commission, to which the trade unions refused to give evidence, was sitting on the matter.

had taught the Irish members "what the labour question was." Hudson, with a certain realism, said that the Irish party, in acting as they did, also took action with regard to their own immediate interests, because the subject struck at the bedrock of all organizations, political and otherwise. His remark, that it was the duty of the Irish party to go with the workers, provoked two Dublin delegates to praise the altruism of the nationalist members and rebuke the ingratitude of prominent labor men who were an obstacle to the very party from which they never sought assistance in vain.[67]

It is not surprising, therefore, that when the Belfast delegates moved their usual motion on labor representation, the debate[68] that followed should be concerned with the merits of the Irish parliamentary party. Its defenders claimed that there was no need for a labor party. W. J. Leahy (Dublin Regular Coopers) maintained that they had a labor party in the House of Commons in the nationalist party: "No man outside Belfast was prepared to go forward as a candidate without declaring his political opinions, whether Conservative or Nationalist. As an Irish Nationalist he could not see his way to sink his Nationalist opinions by voting for such a resolution as this, which would pledge him to vote for a labour candidate." His assertion that no candidate would have a chance in Dublin unless selected by a nationalist convention drew a retort from George Leahy (Dublin, plasterer) on the number of bogus labor men there, and an assertion that he "yielded to no one as an Irish Nationalist, but believed in the principle that labour should go first and nationality afterwards. Until they had independent labour representation in Ireland they would never get their grievances remedied." To a delegate who cited George Leahy's defeat in a municipal election, E. W. Stewart pointed out that the other Leahy (W. J.) had himself been defeated though he "was always assuring them that his politics were his first concern." Walker, in putting the resolution to the vote, declared that if "they were to secure economic emancipation they should find a neutral platform on which men holding different political opinions could meet"; the resolution was then carried by 41 votes to 14. The same resolution was carried in 1905 (Wexford) after the withdrawal of an amendment, moved by McManus and a Cork delegate (Councillor Michael Egan), agreeing with the principle of the motion but affirming that the main duty of Irish trade unionists was the financial support of the work of congress and its Parliamentary Committee—that is, propaganda for trade unionism, the material welfare

67. The two Irish unorthodox Unionist members, T. W. Russell and E. Mitchell, together with the independent Unionist Tom Sloan, also voted for the second reading.

68. I.T.U.C., *Report, Eleventh Congress,* p. 55 et seq.

of the workers, and the development of Irish industries.[69] That McManus should move such an amendment after his speech in an earlier L.E.A. conference is less surprising when the weak financial position of congress (a position to which he referred) is remembered— in itself a reflection of the large number of Irish workers, especially the unskilled, still unorganized—but it is also an indication of his nationalist views.

Irish Versus British Trade Unions

The net effect of the Athlone congress (1906) was to relegate to the debatable land the organization of trade unions as well as labor-representation. A resolution urging the formation of an Irish federation of trade unions and asking for the assistance of amalgamated executives in carrying out the scheme, provoked a sharp debate on the rival merits of Irish and amalgamated unions. Though the resolution was moved by the delegates of two amalgamated unions (Councillor M. Leahy, Limerick, Typographical Association, and J. Treacy, Dublin, Amalgamated Painters), it had its origin in the Dublin Trades Council. The executive committee of that body had brought in a report that the existing federation (The General Federation of Trade Unions)[70] was the best that could be obtained at that time. E. L. Richardson and W. P. Partridge (an A.S.E. delegate who spoke warmly of the aid given by the existing federation to Dublin members on strike) moved its adoption, but an amendment referring back the report in order to ascertain the possibility of forming an Irish federation of trade unions was carried on the casting vote of the president, P. T. Daly.[71]

George Greig (N.A.U.L., Belfast) proposed an amendment drawing the attention of Irish trade unionists to the desirability of affiliating to the General Federation of Trade Unions. In the debate that followed,

69. I.T.U.C., *Report, Twelfth Congress*, pp. 48–9.

70. After many attempts from 1874 onward, the B.T.U.C. founded the General Federation of Trade Unions at a special conference in 1899 with Pete Curran as president and Isaac Mitchell (A.S.E.) as secretary. Its advocates intended it to be a powerful organization capable of carrying out the industrial functions shirked by the Parliamentary Committee. It was to secure unity of action among its federated societies, to promote industrial peace by methods (arbitration, mediation) that would avoid strikes, lockouts, and interunion disputes, and to establish a fund for mutual assistance. At the outset 44 societies with 343,000 members (about one-quarter of the T.U.C. unions) joined. A collection of loosely bound autonomous unions, it possessed limited powers. Most of the larger unions stayed outside it, not wishing to have their own authority diminished and seeing no financial advantages in it. See B. C. Roberts, *The Trades Union Congress*, p. 162.

71. D.T.C. minutes, 10 July 1905.

P. T. Daly produced what in effect were Sinn Féin arguments for Irish-based unions and an Irish federation—that while broadly speaking the interests of Irish and British workers were the same, their practical interests did not coincide, and that the money taken out of the country by amalgamated unions left that country so much poorer. He also criticized the limited autonomy allowed Irish members of such unions and rebutted Greig's assumption that "Britain" included Ireland as well as Scotland. Rather surprisingly a Belfast printer, Charles Darcus, sympathized with both Greig and Daly. He admitted that English executives were loath to allow their Irish members to spend money except as a last resort, but he used this as a reason for supporting the amendment. Michael Canty (Dublin, Corporation Labourers) argued that the reasons for the formation of the I.T.U.C., inadequate representation and neglect of Irish interests by the British T.U.C., applied equally to the federation question. An Irish federation ought to be able to maintain itself; he believed in the policy of Sinn Féin. But the Belfast delegates took their stand on the international character of trade unionism; one (E. Deane of the Belfast Operative Bakers) declared that there were ten thousand members of amalgamated unions in his city and ironically informed Daly that he would have to consult an encyclopedia to see whether Ireland was British or not.

But the chief defenders of the amalgamated unions were their nationalist members, and especially Alderman McCarron of Derry and Patrick Lynch of Cork, both of the Amalgamated Society of Tailors. Lynch said he happened to be a member of an amalgamated union himself and "he and the association to which he belonged thanked God that they were amalgamated (hear, hear), because by being so they had obtained benefits they never could have received otherwise. He could say with authority that Ireland was receiving ten times more money than ever she sent across the water."[72] McCarron reiterated Greig's statement that the great bulk of amalgamated unions in Ireland were affiliated to the General Federation of Trade Unions, which had spent five thousand pounds on behalf of the A.S.T. in the very city from which Daly came. Three thousand pounds had been spent fighting the master tailors of Limerick. He said that at a recent congress of his society in England six of the eleven delegates were Irish, and as the Irish were the pioneers of the labor movement in England they were being asked to fight with their brothers who were prepared to help them in any struggle. He reminded delegates of the trouble the congress had in getting contributions from societies and in keeping up their membership—what would happen if societies had to contribute an additional

72. I.T.U.C., *Report, Thirteenth Congress*, p. 64.

8*d*. per member? His financial argument was reinforced by a Dublin brassfounder, who said that they had received from the federation of their own trade fifteen times the amount they paid into it, 2*d*. per week per man. His society would not give up that benefit. E. W. Stewart, now an official of his own amalgamated union, attacked Daly and the other Sinn Féin delegates who had "skedaddled from their own amendment because it was not possible to produce that scheme."[73] When the lengthy debate was closured the amendment was passed and the substantive motion carried by 36 votes to 14. The 14 votes for the motion asking for an Irish federation represented Sinn Féin strength at the congress; the 36 votes were the combined efforts of the Belfast and nationalist members of amalgamated unions. The alliance of the last two groups was, however, limited in scope and time.

Stalemate

The striking success of labor candidates in Great Britain at the general election of 1906 had excited renewed interest in Ireland in political representation. The Parliamentary Committee rejoiced "at the awakening of the British democracy and the consequent founding of an Independent Labour Party in the new parliament," and their pleasure was tempered only by their regret at losing Walter Hudson, who had been elected one of the new M.P.s.[74]

When John Murphy moved the usual Belfast motion[75] recommending affiliation to the Labour Representation Committee, he was careful to moderate his criticism of the nationalist party. "He had no fault to find with the Irish party, but as such they did not represent entirely the views of the voters of Ireland. There were Unionists in Ireland as well as Nationalists, and he contended that they should have a distinct Labour party." But the movers of the amendment, that there was no need for a new party as "the Irish party is everything that labour requires," were not content to be moderate. P. Hayes (Limerick, Mechanics' Institute)

73. The amendment Daly carried by his casting vote in the Dublin Trades Council. E. W. Stewart had been appointed an official of the National Union of Shop Assistants (D.T.C. minutes, 19 Sept. 1904) and was having interunion trouble with the Irish Drapers' Assistants led by M. J. O'Lehane, a Sinn Féin member.

74. I.T.U.C., *Report, Thirteenth Congress*, p. 3. Hudson had been elected as senior member for the two-member borough of Newcastle-on-Tyne by a comfortable majority. He had served as a guard on the North Eastern railway (England) for twenty-six years until his appointment as Irish secretary of the A.S.R.S. (1898). It was not uncommon for amalgamated unions to send English officials to Ireland. Clarkson's comment (page 400, n. 3) that Hudson had to go to England to find a constituency is therefore scarcely relevant. Hudson was a member of the outgoing Parliamentary Committee.

75. The debate is given in I.T.U.C., *Report, Thirteenth Congress*, pp. 70–73.

argued that national unity was the primary consideration ("a country fighting for its independence from an alien Government could not be too united") and recommended Murphy to confine his scheme to the north of Ireland—its representatives had in all cases voted against the interests of labor. His seconder, Councillor M. Leahy (Limerick), thought it might be a good plan for north of the Boyne, "but any man from the South who would try to put in a man purely on the labour ticket . . . should be inside a lunatic asylum." Daly opposed both the motion and the amendment, referred to his own scheme for an Irish labor party that he had proposed at Cork, and attacked Murphy for opposing it. He regretted Walker's absence,[76] as he had a word to say to him which he would not say behind his back. An Athlone councillor (David Barry) was less concerned with niceties and denounced him for "a pledge he signed against his co-workers on sectarianism, also on the Home Rule principle"[77] and said that he was not surprised at Walker's election defeat. Thomas McConnell (Belfast Operative Bakers) endeavored to explain Walker's defeat—he had a difficult job to handle, for the workers of Belfast were divided in many ways—and excepted Thomas Sloan and Joseph Devlin[78] from the charge that Belfast M.P.s never voted in the cause of labor. Sixteen speakers took part in the debate, including Walter Hudson (now an M.P.). Michael Canty (Dublin Corporation Labourers) was the last speaker and, like his leader P. T. Daly, condemned both the motion and the amendment. As if in anticipation of the 1907 Belfast strike, he complained, amid cries of dissent, that the skilled men ignored the claims of the unskilled.

The debate, like that on an Irish federation, ended only when the closure was applied. The amendment was put to the vote and defeated by 31 votes to 17; the motion itself was rejected by 33 to 18, thus leaving the congress with no fixed policy on labor representation. The amendment had been defeated by a combination of Belfast and Sinn Féin delegates against the nationalists, while in the vote on the motion itself the nationalists joined with Sinn Féin delegates to defeat Belfast.

Nannetti, newly elected lord mayor of Dublin, had made a special journey to speak to the congress and to receive an address from the Athlone Trades Council. In his speech,[79] delivered after the debate, he pleaded with the delegates to regard the Irish parliamentary party as a labor party.

76. Walker was detained in Belfast by a strike (ibid., p. 48).
77. The reference is to Walker's fight in North Belfast and his answers to questions put to him by the Belfast Protestant Association. Appendix 7.
78. For the parts played by Sloan and Devlin in Belfast politics, see chap. 12, first and third sections.
79. I.T.U.C., *Report, Thirteenth Congress,* pp. 74–5.

Where was the necessity of setting up new parties? The platform on which he was proud to stand was broad enough for any workingman. They could make the Parliamentary Party do everything they wished. . . . They were purely labour as well as Nationalist and he as a worker could not be with them on the platform that day were it not that he was a Nationalist as well (hear, hear). He could not be a Member of Parliament were he a purely labour candidate, and he challenged contradiction when he said that not a single constituency in Ireland would return a man on the labour question purely.

Hurt by Canty's reference to the neglect of laborers' claims, he explained that he and his colleagues, who had founded the Dublin Trades Council, had made it their principal charge to protect the unskilled. But the Irish party's liaison officer had done no more than carry out a holding operation in both matters, for labor representation continued to provoke disagreement, and the claims of the laborers were to be vindicated, in a fashion thoroughly uncomfortable for many old-style unionists, by the arrival of James Larkin the following year.

The Control of Education

One further contentious subject was raised at the Athlone congress, though it was not debated. The president, Stephen Dineen, had in his address put forward two schemes for education: (1) that the state should confine itself to secular education, giving equal facilities to all denominations to provide the religious education desired by parents for their children; and (2) that the state should provide religious education for all, according to the wishes expressed by parents. He himself favored the first course.[80] E. W. Stewart, moving a vote of thanks to Dineen, seized the opportunity to attack denominational control, saying that Irish education was unsatisfactory because "the education question was used as a football by contending religious bodies striving for supremacy."[81] He was cut short by the chairman (McCarron), who asked him to confine himself to the vote of thanks.

The control of education had already been discussed with acrimony at an earlier congress. In 1901 Walker moved a motion in the Belfast Trades Council (after circulars from the National Labour Education League had been read) asking for the establishment of elective school boards in Ireland and declaring that popular education should be "free from the great obstacles to all educational reform, a) sectarianism, b) political wire pullers and vested interests."[82] Keown (Plasterers)

80. Ibid., p. 32.　　　　　　　　　81. Ibid., p. 37.

82. B.T.C. minutes, 16 Nov. 1901. Walker was elected to the committee of the National Labour Education League (B.T.C. E.C. minutes, 12 Dec. 1907).

opposed it, saying that the scheme would not remove sectarianism but would only make matters worse. McManus pointed out that English education was financed out of local rates, while in Ireland the money came from the consolidated fund; the two systems therefore were different. An attempt was made to adjourn the discussion, but Walker carried his motion by 22 votes to 2. In 1903 Walker again successfully moved a somewhat similar motion to be submitted to congress: "That in the opinion of this council and congress the time has arrived when an educational system should be established in Ireland, placing elementary, secondary and technical education under the control of an administrative body elected for that purpose only; as we believe that the present system of education in Ireland does not tend to foster that true educational spirit which should prevail in a community such as ours."[83]

The motion was rephrased by standing orders committee and combined with another protesting against the Irish equivalent grant being applied to anything other than primary education.[84] Walker, in proposing it, severely criticized the arrangements for education in Belfast and said that all schools should be conducted upon the system of the Belfast model school,[85] absolutely free from all denominational control." E. L. Richardson moved an amendment that would reduce the motion to a simple affirmation of the need for improvement in primary education, and deplored Walker's suggestion, coming as it did at a time when there was a cessation of strife. McManus, seconding, declared that education was one of the most difficult questions of the day. McCarron went further and moved the rejection of the motion, expressing surprise that such a controversial subject should have been introduced at all. "If they passed the resolution they would be approving of what was opposed to the Catholic church and to Catholics. Catholics refused to send their children to any school where the children would not get religious training."

The opposition to Walker's motion was not confined to Catholics.

83. B.T.C. minutes, 18 Apr. 1903.

84. I.T.U.C., *Report, Tenth Congress*, p. 47. The equivalent grant was a sum of £183,000 from the British treasury given for Irish expenditure; the motion condemned a proposal to use it for increasing the compensation given to landlords willing to sell out to tenants.

85. The model schools were controlled and financed by the commissioners of the Board of National Education. Twenty-eight schools were opened between 1848 and 1867. They were to promote the united education of Protestants and Catholics in common schools giving combined secular and separate religious instruction, to exhibit the best examples of national (i.e., primary) schools and to give a preparatory training to young teachers. The hostility of the Church of Ireland and the Roman Catholic Church to nondenominational education was the major cause of the decline of the model schools.

Charles Darcus (Typographical Association, Belfast branch) declared that any attempt "to divide the schools from a certain amount of clerical control in Ireland would be simply beating the air. . . . He was of the opinion that the fundamental truths of Christianity ought to be taught to the children to make them fit for life. Any other step would be backward. He would oppose separating the youth of the country from religious instruction." He was supported by speakers from Kilkenny and Limerick who gave additional proofs of his contention that the model schools were steadily losing numbers. Despite denials by other Belfast delegates, and by E. W. Stewart of Dublin, of any desire to interfere with religious training or "ostracise Catholics from their religion," the amendment was carried by 47 votes to 14, and the resolution defeated by 38 to 16.[86]

Denominational control of education in Ireland had been firmly established by the second half of the nineteenth century and was supported by the vast majority of Catholics and many Protestants. Connolly had included its abolition in the program of the Irish Socialist Republican Party, but the group he led was numerically unimportant. Walker's proposal was that of the Belfast Trades Council, which he dominated, and, more important, was a part of British labor's program.[87] It was an additional reason in the opinion of most delegates for opposing affiliation to the Labour Representation Committee.

The End of a Period

The Athlone congress marked the end of a period in the history of the national trades union center. The heat and bitterness of the prolonged debates on such subjects as labor representation and Irish versus British trade unions had been entirely absent from the harmonious discussions of the Dublin congress of 1900. By 1906 the failure of the attempt to exclude politics was plain. It was no longer possible to confine discussion to trade union affairs and the desire to obtain representation raised immediately the question of political organization. The fate of the resolution on labor representation at the Athlone congress meant that henceforth a three-cornered struggle would be carried on among supporters of the nationalist party, those affiliated to the Labour Representation Committee, and the group desiring an independent Irish labor

86. I.T.U.C., *Report, Tenth Congress*, pp. 47–49.

87. A resolution, proposed by the Gasworkers and agreed to, included a clause "that all schools, whether elementary, secondary or technological, shall be under popular control—that is, under the control of the directly elected representatives of the people" (L.R.C., *Third Annual Conference Report, 1905*, p. 55). At the Swansea congress (1901) of the British T.U.C., a similar resolution had been passed.

party. The resolution, which was virtually a demand for Irish-based trade unions, was defeated comfortably, but it was significant of the growing support for Sinn Féin ideas among a section of Dublin workers. Canty's complaint of the neglect of the unskilled by the craft unions, though it was brushed aside, emphasized the weakness of trade union organization among Irish laborers and the unrepresentative nature of the congress itself. Even the reference to secular education was a reminder of another element—denominational differences—in Irish political life. When the congress concluded, it had asked, with varying emphasis, the questions that the Irish labor movement had to answer in the succeeding years.

Clarkson, in describing the state of the Irish labor movement at the end of this period, wrote that it was about a generation behind the British labor movement; "the old unionism still held sway; the political weapon was almost neglected."[88] The reasons for the weakness of general unions in Ireland have already been considered, though it should be remembered that even in Great Britain the new unions had lost ground by the middle of the 1890s and did not make a permanent recovery until 1910.[89] The political backwardness of the Irish labor movement is not surprising in view of the very different conditions obtaining in Ireland. The British movement was not hampered by the claims of nationalism, yet it was slow to break its dependence on the Liberal Party. Irish trade unionists in the 1890s were prepared to make use of the parliamentary services of both Unionists and nationalists and ceased to apply to the former only because of their general indifference to labor's claims. The members of the Irish parliamentary party were socially much closer to trade unionists than were the M.P.s of the two main British political parties, and dependent to a greater extent on popular support.[90] The small number of labor members in the House of Commons before 1906, and the growing attention paid by the Irish party to trade union demands, helped to extend the period of dependence of Irish trade unionists on nationalist members.

Irish Nationalists and British Labor

The chief advocates of independent labor representation were Belfast delegates, who wished to rid themselves of the necessity of relying on

88. Clarkson, p. 214.

89. E. J. Hobsbawm, "General labour unions in Britain, 1889–1914," *Econ. Hist. Rev.*, 2nd ser., I, nos. 2 and 3 (1949), p. 214.

90. Over one-third of the Irish nationalist (anti-Parnellite) M.P.s during the years 1892–1900 consistetd of local shopkeepers, farmers (including tenant farmers), labor leaders, and salaried workers; a similar proportion were paid what amounted to a

Irish nationalist M.P.s. Affiliation to the Labour Representation Committee was an umbilical cord connecting them with a British political party, so that, though they opposed Unionist candidates, they maintained the connection with England and satisfied both their Unionist and labor ambitions. Yet the political sustenance transmitted was at times hardly to be stomached. William Walker was the strongest supporter of the British connection, and it was he who was responsible for the visit of Keir Hardie and Ramsay MacDonald to Belfast and Newry in 1903, but it was in spite, not because, of their views on the Irish question that he brought them.

British labor leaders, from Walker's point of view, had an unfortunate tendency to favor Irish Home Rule.[91] Hardie and MacDonald were discreet during their visit, and their addresses to the Irish Trades Union Congress were chiefly concerned with cooperation between British and Irish labor in the pursuit of their common interests. Nevertheless Hardie had long favored Irish independence and, in 1898, had helped Connolly to start the *Workers' Republic*.[92] His attitude toward the Irish parliamentary party was warmly approving. On his return to the House of Commons in December 1900, he had taken his seat on the top bench below the gangway among the members of the Irish party. The first survey of his parliamentary work that he gave to the Independent Labour Party conference of 1901 contained a remarkable passage dealing with the Irish nationalists:

The outstanding feature in this parliament was the way in which it was dominated by the Irish party. A considerable number of the representatives from Ireland were men who, by training and instinct,[93] were in the closest sympathy with the claims and aspirations of the workers, and they had given many proofs of the fact that their sympathies in this direction were not bounded by the Irish sea. The truest representatives of Democratic feeling in the house *of commons* were the Irish Parliamentary Party, a fact which the workers of Britain would do well to recognise.[94]

---

parliamentary salary when party funds were available. See Lyons, *The Irish Parliamentary Party, 1890–1910*, chapt. 6.

91. See chap. 6 for the hostility shown by a portion of the crowd at a Belfast labour demonstration in 1893 towards John Burns and Keir Hardie, who had voted for the second Home Rule bill.

92. He lent Connolly £50, but only £10 of the loan was repaid (O'Brien, *Forth the Banners Go*, p. 10).

93. He might have added that their financial position resembled his own. At this conference it was agreed that Hardie be paid £150 a year towards his expenses as M.P., the money to be raised by subscriptions from trade unions and individuals [I.L.P., *Report of Ninth Conference (1901)*, p. 11].

94. Ibid., p. 40.

J. Bruce Glasier at the same conference referred, amid applause, to the presence in the House of Commons of eighty Irish representatives, "who were proud to call themselves rebels" and said that they were a reminder that they had "a little India and another Transvaal at their own doors. . . . It [Ireland] was still disloyal, still like the Transvaal—unsubdued."[95]

Whatever might be the shortcomings of the Irish nationalists in Irish labor eyes, at Westminster they were regarded as the natural allies of the trade union members. In August 1901 they supported the United Textile Factory Workers Association in securing the amendment of a clause in a Factory and Workshop bill relating to a general stoppage of work at noon on Saturdays.[96] Their abstention on a motion (14 May 1902) calling for legislation to remedy the situation following the Taff Vale decision, resulted in its defeat (by 203 votes to 174),[97] but they enthusiastically supported bills with the same object in every one of the following years.[98] Hardie habitually voted with the Irish members, and they responded by supporting measures of trade union interest.

This cooperation was not confined to parliament. William Redmond (brother of the reunited Irish party's leader) supported Robert Smillie in a by-election in Northeast Lanark (September 1901), though his help was not an unqualified asset as there were Ulster Unionists among the Lanarkshire miners. Michael Davitt, in the last years of his life when the antagonism between himself and Hardie had disappeared, did his utmost to rouse Irish support for labor. In a speech at Glasgow he declared that the "party which should hold the balance of power in the next House of Commons should be the British Labour Party" and urged Irish voters to refuse assistance to a Tory or Liberal in any constituency where their votes might help to elect a labor candidate.[99] His last campaign was in the general election of 1906, when he spoke for a large number of labor candidates in London, the midlands, South Wales, Lancashire, and Yorkshire; it was fitting that he was able to take part before his death (30 May 1906) in the labor victory demonstration in the Queen's Hall on 16 February 1906.[100]

Proposals for what might be called in modern terms a popular front

95. Ibid., p. 29.

96. Bealey and Pelling, *Labour and Politics,* p. 100.

97. Ibid., p. 93.

98. Ibid., p. 204. The bill in 1903 was introduced by David Shackleton (Labour M.P., Clitheroe), that in 1904 by J. H. Paulton (Liberal M.P., Bishop Auckland), and the 1905 bill by T. P. Whitaker (Liberal M.P., Spen Valley).

99. Bealey and Pelling, *Labour and Politics,* pp. 243—4.

100. For a fuller account of Davitt's relation with the British labor movement, see

were made on a number of occasions. W. M. Thompson, the editor of *Reynold's Newspaper,* after the extinction of his National Democratic League (founded October 1900), called for a new version, a Radical Democratic Party, to be led by Sir Charles Dilke and allied to the Irish party, which he considered "intensely sympathetic with labour."[101] Hardie himself, in a speech during the North-East Lanark by-election, calculated that a combination of the Irish, the radicals, and the labor forces "would dominate politics inside the next dozen years."[102] He made his most detailed suggestions in March 1903, a few months before he visited Belfast, in an open letter to Lloyd George. He proposed that, after the next general election, Lloyd George should found a new party, the Party of the People, consisting of an alliance between 85 Irish, 50 labor, and 25 independent radical M.P.s.[103] Hardie's suggestion was not taken up; instead there followed negotiations between Ramsey MacDonald and Herbert Gladstone, the Liberal chief whip, resulting in an agreement to share constituencies and so contributing to the Liberal and Labour victories of 1906.[104] In November 1905 the Irish nationalists made their alliance with the Liberals and secured Campbell-Bannerman's commitment to Home Rule.[105] It did not prevent them from giving support to any L.R.C. candidate who was sound on Home Rule, except in cases where he was standing against "an old and tried friend of the Irish cause."[106]

Moody, "Michael Davitt and the British Labour Movement, 1882–1906," in *Transactions of the Royal Historical Society,* 5th ser., vol. iii, 1953, pp. 53–76.

101. Bealey and Pelling, *Labour and Politics,* p. 135.

102. *Labour Leader,* 28 Sept. 1901, quoted in Bealey and Pelling, p. 135.

103. Bealey and Pelling, *Labour and Politics,* p. 145.

104. For the MacDonald-Gladstone *entente* and its results see Bealey and Pelling, pp. 125–59, 288; and Philip E. Poirier, *The Advent of the Labour Party,* pp. 175–93, 263.

105. See Lyons, *The Irish Parliamentary Party,* pp. 112–3.

106. *Northern Star,* 6 Jan. 1906. The manifesto was adopted at a meeting of the executive committee of the United Irish League in Great Britain with T. P. O'Connor, M.P., in the chair and John Redmond in attendance. The full text of the manifesto is as follows:

The working people of Great Britain have never up to this been fairly represented in the House of Commons. The Irish National Party have always been steady and consistent supporters of the claims of labour, while the Labour members who have succeeded in getting into the House have always been courageous and steady supporters of the Irish National demand. A great opportunity now seems to offer itself to increase the representation of British labour in the House. For these reasons we recommend our people in all cases where a Labour candidate, who is sound on the question of Home Rule, is in the field to give their votes to that candidate, except in cases where he is standing against an old and tried friend of the Irish cause, or where the support of the Labour candidate would ensure the return of the Unionist candidate.

In rank-and-file organizations the alliance with the L.R.C. went further than mere cooperation. At the constituency level at least one L.R.C. branch (Leeds) made provision for the affiliation of local groups of the United Irish League.[107] The Independent Labour Party in Great Britain was even more accommodating and as late as 1918 Irish nationalists could join local branches. The chairman, Philip Snowden, dealing with the possible Labour candidature of the chameleon-like Colonel Arthur Lynch, said that "the I.L.P. had always admitted members of the Irish Nationalist Party without requiring that they should sever their connection with it. Members of the Liberal and Conservative parties were not eligible for membership of the I.L.P., but that rule had never been applied to the Irish Nationalist Party."[108]

In spite of occasional clashes that occurred when their candidates suffered by the Irish vote in Great Britain going to Home Rule Liberal rivals, British Labour Party leaders accorded the Irish parliamentary party *de facto* recognition as a labor party, and thereby hampered the growth of an Irish political labor organization.[109]

107. Bealey and Pelling, p. 237.

108. I.L.P., *Report of Twenty-Sixth Annual Conference* (1918), pp. 53–4. Lynch was born in Ballarat, Australia, in 1861, and educated in Melbourne, Paris, and Berlin. In 1899 he organized the second Irish brigade of the Boer army and led it in the South African war. He was later charged by the British authorities with treason and sentenced to death but reprieved (1903). In the British House of Commons he represented Galway City (1901–9) and West Clare (1909–18). In 1918 he was given the rank of colonel in the British army and conducted recruiting campaigns in Ireland. He was also a physician (M.R.C.S. and L.R.C.P., 1908) and a voluminous author (over thirty works in prose and verse, science and fiction, in English and French). He died in 1934. See J. S. Crone, *Concise Dictionary of Irish Biography*, p. 282, and Lynch's own autobiography, *My Life Story* (1934).

109. For the subsequent fortunes of the Irish T.U.C. see Charles McCarthy, *Trade Unions in Ireland, 1894–1960*.

10

The Divided Aims of Dublin Labor

The respective decisions of Irish and Scottish trade unionists to form their own national centers meant that there were three trades union congresses in the British Isles at the beginning of the twentieth century. The British T.U.C., which in 1902 had 1,500,000 members drawn from an industrial labour force of nearly 6,000,000 in England and Wales, was a giant compared with the other two organizations.[1] The Scottish T.U.C. grew more rapidly than the Irish congress formed three years earlier, and in 1902 had an affiliated membership of 128,000 against the Irish figure of 70,000.[2] The explanation for the more rapid Scottish growth is to be found in the different economic structures of the two countries. Each had a population of approximately 4,500,000, but Scottish industry in 1907 employed almost 900,000 workers, some three times the size of the corresponding Irish labor force.[3] Irish agriculture was a poor source of trade union recruitment. Much of the land was farmed by tenants or peasant proprietors requiring only seasonal assistance, and persistent underemployment drove large numbers of rural laborers from the land, or even from the country. The great majority of unskilled or semiskilled workers in industry and transportation remained unorganized, and until these general workers were unionized no marked increase in the membership of the Irish congress could be expected.

A trades union congress was not initially a body with a permanent membership. Some continuity was ensured by the election of a parliamentary committee that functioned as a pressure group between congresses and presented an annual report, but a trade union or trades council was formally a member only during the annual meeting to which it sent delegates and paid their fees. Not until 1905 did the Irish

1. H. M. Pelling, *A History of British Trade Unionism*, p. 261; *Final Report on the Census of Production of the United Kingdom (1907)*. [Cd 6320], H.C. 1912, cix. 1.
2. I.T.U.C., *Report, Ninth Congress*, p. 36.
3. *Final Report on the Census of Production of the United Kingdom, 1907*, p. iii.

T.U.C. replace dependence on voluntary subscriptions and any surplus from delegates' fees with affiliation fees based on Irish membership. This change brought no dramatic increase in finances but did diminish the *ad hoc* element hitherto present in the organization.[4] It is therefore understandable that the proceedings of the annual body give but an incomplete account of developments in the Irish labor movement. For a fuller version we must turn to the trades councils—bodies that met at regular intervals throughout the year, transacted the bread-and-butter business of the movement at the local level, and debated issues that ultimately were of national concern.

At the end of the nineteenth century the number of trades councils in Ireland had not reached double figures. Belfast and Dublin were the only urban areas of importance and the Irish T.U.C. was dominated by delegates from their trades councils (each claiming around sixteen thousand members in 1898) and trade union branches. Cork ran a poor third in size and its council's membership was normally under, rather than over, two thousand. Limerick's numbers fluctuated around one thousand, while most of the smaller towns had difficulty in maintaining councils, which lapsed from time to time to be revived under the stimulus of some external event.[5]

With the possible exception of Derry, which occasionally was divided in its allegiance, the minor towns followed the lead of the capital, so that Irish labor history is substantially the history of organized labor in Dublin and Belfast. The minutes of the two cities' trades councils, while not complete, are sufficient when supplemented by other records to show us how they functioned and what their attitudes were toward the leading issues of the day. The two cities had approximately the same population, about 350,000, but had little else in common.[6] Belfast, strongly Protestant in religion and Unionist in politics was (with shipbuilding, engineering, and textiles) economically a creation of the industrial revolution. Dublin, overwhelmingly Catholic in religion and nationalist in politics, depended on food, drink, and building industries, a large distributive trade, and a conglomeration of minor

4. I.T.U.C., *Report, Twelfth Congress*, p. 50.

5. *Report by the Chief Labour Correspondent of the Board of Trade on Trade Unions in 1898*, pp. 204–5. [C 9443], xcii, 493.

6. The Belfast city boundary was extended in 1896, raising the population to 348,180 in 1901. A similar extension of the Dublin city boundary, to include the suburbs of Pembroke, Rathmines, and Rathgar, would have raised the capital's population to 349,039. Cork had a population of 76,122 and the other towns less than 40,000 [W. E. Vaughan and A. J. Fitzpatrick (eds.), *Irish Historical Statistics: Population, 1821–1971*, pp. 29, 33, 37]. For the growth of the Dublin suburbs see Mary E. Daly, *Dublin, The Deposed Capital*, chap. VI.

crafts and manufactures. The extent to which the two councils could agree on common objectives and methods was of importance in determining the fortunes of urban labor in Ireland.

Irish Industries and "Fair" Houses

One of the less rewarding legacies inherited by the Dublin Trades Council from its predecessor, the United Trades' Association, was an obsession with the protection of moribund trades. Much energy was spent in denouncing the importation of goods of non-Irish origin as the cause of unemployment among craftsmen. Church authorities were persistent offenders; between 1895 and 1897, for instance, the council censured Catholic and Protestant clergy for importing a wide range of ecclesiastical goods, including Belgian first communion cards, German stained glass, Italian church furniture, and—a severe blow—a complete chapel-of-ease made in England.[7] The organ builders, who had affiliated on a membership of twenty in 1894, condemned the purchase of foreign church organs, but were particularly incensed when the Royal Dublin Society, founded in 1731 "for the improvement of husbandry, manufactures and other useful arts,"[8] disregarded the praise bestowed on Dublin organs by "Herr Lizst" (sic) and ordered an instrument from Leeds.[9] The council had appealed for support in their campaign to the Catholic archbishop of Dublin (W. J. Walsh), but the nationalist prelate, while offering his sympathy, replied that he was tired of urging people to buy Irish goods, since it was no use unless these were as cheap and as good as the imported articles.[10]

Foreign competition affected more than the small number of workers engaged in such specialized crafts. Retail traders in large numbers modernized their premises by importing entire shop fronts. The Dublin corporation ignored pleas to patronize local manufacturers when decorating the city for King Edward VII's visit in 1903.[11] Even the Irish literary movement had an Abbey Theatre series of plays printed in London.[12] New developments in transport brought fresh grievances, for coachmakers and cabinetmakers, previously concerned with competition in horse-drawn carriages, were alarmed at the importation of motor cars in 1906 and appealed in vain for the bodies to be made in Ireland.[13] They renewed the appeal in 1908, protesting at the purchase of 1,250 railway carriages and lorries outside Ireland.[14] The council,

---

7. D.T.C. minutes, 30 Mar. 1896.
8. Maxwell, *Dublin under the Georges*, pp. 172–3.
9. D.T.C. minutes, 1 Feb. 1897.   10. Ibid., 30 Mar. 1896.
11. Ibid., 15 June 1903.   12. Ibid., 20 Feb. 1905.
13. Ibid., 9 July 1906.   14. Ibid., 20 Jan. 1908.

in the hope of stimulating local industries, subscribed regularly to the Dublin Industrial Development Association, but had on several occasions to express dissatisfaction at the wages paid by industrial revivalists.[15]

Allied to the problem of importation was that of goods made in nonunion houses. The promoters of memorials to the patriot dead were at times negligent of the claims of the living, and protests were useless when contracts for the railings around Parnell's grave and the Fontenoy memorial were entrusted to unfair houses.[16] In spite of years of energetic lobbying, the council too often received dusty answers from the sinners, who included ecclesiastical dignitaries. When in 1908 plasterwork in two Dublin convents was done under unfair conditions, unsatisfactory replies from the superioresses and the archbishop, who refused to receive a deputation, provoked the delegates' wrath. A coachmaker, T. Milner, asserted that clergy of all denominations were to blame because they were inclined to beat down the wages of the workers. He was supported by a brassfounders' delegate and the condemnatory resolution was passed unanimously.[17]

It is a measure of the council's single-mindedness in pursuit of fair wages that even the vice-regal menu did not escape notice; they backed the successful appeal of a poulterers' delegate to Earl Dudley that only fair houses should tender for the supply of poultry and game to his excellency's table at Dublin Castle and the vice-regal lodge.[18] A more astonishing demand for vice-regal patronage was made twelve years later. In April 1915, in a period of acute political feeling, and less than a year before the Easter 1916 rising, the council unanimously passed a motion protesting against the action of the newly appointed lord lieutenant in ordering his state uniform from a London firm and directed that copies of the resolution be sent to the vice-regal delinquent, the press, and the Dublin Industrial Development Association. The motion was moved by William O'Brien, a tailors' delegate and a close associate of James Connolly, who was himself present at the meeting.[19] The tradition of protection was evidently too strong to be lightly disregarded even in time of war and incipient rebellion. The provincial

15. Ibid., 9 Feb. 1903.
16. Ibid., 30 Mar. 1896, 10 Dec. 1906. Exiles in the Irish Brigade played a prominent part in the French victory at Fontenoy (1748) over English and Dutch forces led by the Duke of Cumberland.
17. Ibid., 17 Mar. 1908 (clipping from *F.J.*).
18. Ibid., 29 June, 27 July 1903.
19. Ibid., 19 Apr. 1915. Connolly may not have been present during the discussion, which was the last item reported in the minutes, but his announcement of the forthcoming publication of the *Workers' Republic* is recorded immediately before O'Brien's motion.

towns were at one with Dublin in such demands. They left their mark on congress agendas, which became so crowded with resolutions against importation in the years before 1914 that it became the custom to group them together and pass them *en bloc*.

"Social" Politics

The Dublin Trades Council in its corporate capacity prided itself on keeping clear of politics. What constituted politics was not always plain to delegates. When a lathmaker wished to ban the introduction of any question having a political tendency, E. L. Richardson pointed out that the matter under discussion, an employers' liability bill, was a social question—"there were social politics as well as politics pure and simple."[20] That definition was given in 1894. Five years later the lathmaker seconded a motion to send a deputation to a meeting dealing with the erection of a statue to Parnell. It was opposed by delegates on the grounds that the motion was political; Alderman William Doyle regretted that, though a Parnellite himself, he could not vote for it. A supporter of the motion argued not unreasonably that the project was no more political than that of the Wolfe Tone and United Irishmen Memorial Committee, to which the council had sent its officers and Alderman Doyle. The power of logic, or more probably the strength of the Parnellites, carried the motion by 34 votes to 8.[21]

The council's aversion to politics was in practice an aversion to being embroiled in the faction fighting that followed Parnell's fall and did not rule out support for nationalist activities. Delegates who adjourned a meeting in November 1888 to attend a Manchester Martyrs' commemoration ceremony in Glasnevin Cemetery were following a long-established custom.[22] Some months later the council, with J. P. Nannetti in the chair, expressed sympathy with William O'Brien, M.P., a lieutenant of Parnell and a leader in the agrarian Plan of Campaign, who was suffering in Clonmel jail "the cruel, barbarous and tyrannical treatment of minions of the Chief Jailer of Ireland."[23] Neu-

20. *F.J.*, 8 Jan. 1894. The lathmaker (Best) held that it was a political question as it was part of the Newcastle program of the Liberal Party.

21. D.T.C. minutes, 14 Aug. 1899.

22. *F.J.*, 26 Nov. 1888.

23. *F.J.*, 4 Feb. 1889. The "Chief Jailer" was Arthur Balfour, Irish chief secretary. The motion by implication took the Liberal side in British politics; it prayed that the day "may be not far distant when our fellow toilers of England, Scotland and Wales may be afforded that opportunity which they so much desire of hurling from power a party and men so devoid of the commonest instincts of humanity, and whose semi-maniacal governing gyrations have assumed the character of 'administrative blackguardism' and 'street ruffianism.'"

trality during the years of the Parnellite split did not prevent the council from joining in amnesty demonstrations for political prisoners in the 1890s,[24] or in the various celebrations of the 1798 centenary.[25]

The indeterminate nature of the council's politics is admirably illustrated by John Simmons, who was its secretary, except for one year, from its formation in 1886 until 1917. Born in Carlow in 1852, he was apprenticed as a carpenter at the age of fifteen and came to Dublin when he was twenty-two. He claimed to have been a Fenian, "an old '67 man," but he was no intransigent; he approached the lord lieutenant in 1882 on behalf of the Dublin Workingmen's Club in order to get his assistance in establishing technical schools, and later was the secretary of the Dublin Conciliation Board and a member of a technical schools board and public library committee. As his council's representative he attended the British T.U.C. between 1888 and 1894 and several congresses of the Labour Electoral Association; in the meantime he became a member of an amalgamated union when his local society joined the A.S.C.J. He was in his early forties, a man of about middle height, with a greying beard and of a gentle appearance when he first contested a corporation election.[26] His mild disposition enabled him to act as peacemaker in council disputes and won him the regard of delegates. Unlike some others of his generation, he lacked personal ambition and continued to serve the council when under James Larkin's leadership it championed the cause of the unskilled. He resigned because of ill health in 1917 and the council rewarded him with a pension.[27]

Nationalist sentiments did not prevent the council from approving a Unionist considered to be well disposed to labor. On the suggestion of W. J. Leahy, delegates supported Sir Robert Sexton in 1896 for the lord mayoralty of Dublin. When Leahy changed his mind after they had publicly committed themselves, they were so incensed that they refused to consider him as a labor representative and did not take him back into favor for some years.[28] John Simmons and Patrick Shelley proposed Sexton again in 1898, Simmons citing his support for artisans' exhibitions and technical schools and describing him as "a good employer and a friend of labour." The motion was carried in spite of two dissentients who objected that Sexton did not "voice the national

24. D.T.C. minutes, 1 Apr. 1895, 18 Jan., 26 Apr. 1897.
25. Ibid., 14 Sept. 1897, 18 July, 8, 29 Aug. 1898, 5 June, 31 July 1899.
26. I.T.U.C., *Report, Third Congress,* contains a photograph and short biography of Simmons.
27. D.T.C. executive committee minutes, 15 Feb. 1917; D.T.C. minutes, 17 Feb. 1917. Simmons had been ill for some years and had offered his resignation in 1915.
28. D.T.C. minutes, 7 Dec. 1896.

sentiment with regard to self-government for Ireland."[29] A few weeks later Simmons had to admit Sexton's lack of national feeling in refusing the use of the Mansion House to the Wolfe Tone Memorial Committee, but he defended the council's previous endorsement on the grounds that they (the council) were nonpolitical.[30] Sir Horace Plunkett, the pioneer of agricultural cooperation in Ireland and a moderate Unionist M.P., was also warmly regarded. One delegate considered that he might be relied on for support in labor matters and on a later occasion E. L. Richardson and George Leahy sponsored a motion that spoke of "his whole-hearted concern for the material interests of Ireland."[31] Delegates who were members of the Irish Socialist Republican Party did not share the council's enthusiasm and disapproved of too fulsome an attitude toward public figures and employers. E. W. Stewart dissented from the Plunkett resolution as a consequence. The lavish hospitality that marked the Dublin (1900) congress was the special pride of W. J. Leahy, chairman of the reception committee, but when a motion was moved thanking the lord mayor (Sir Thomas Pile), W. McLoughlin submitted an amendment censuring "the action of the reception committee in soliciting favours from employers" and considering "such actions humiliating and uncalled for."[32]

In accord with the moderate opinions of delegates, moderate except when their craft privileges were in question, the council frequently approached prominent citizens, ecclesiastical and lay, on trades disputes. The Catholic archbishop of Dublin (W. J. Walsh) was sought as a last court of appeal; he was asked to intervene in the building strikes of 1889 and 1896—the second had lasted four months—and was duly thanked for his mediation.[33] Nine years later he was asked to arbitrate in a bricklayers' strike, but was prepared only to act his former part of conciliator.[34] A month later E. L. Richardson suggested the Church of Ireland archbishop (J. R. Peacocke) as arbitrator, but after a long discussion Richardson thought it wise to withdraw his motion.[35]

William Martin Murphy, the one-time nationalist M.P. and leading Dublin businessman with interests in two continents, was also highly regarded. John Ward, the president of the Metropolitan House Painters' Trade Union and an expresident of the council, urged support for him when he was a candidate for a Dublin constituency in 1892, and spoke of his "great services to my trade. . . . I have never met so earnest an advocate of the painters' rights as Mr. Murphy, and, moreover, what

29. Ibid., 20 June 1898.　　　　　　30. Ibid., 4 July 1898.
31. Ibid., 2 June 1902, 23 Feb. 1903.
32. Ibid., 18 June 1900. The amendment received only two votes.
33. Ibid., 31 Aug. 1896.
34. Ibid., 6 Mar. 1905.
35. Ibid., 3 Apr. 1905.

he preaches in public he practises in public."[36] Good relations between
the skilled unionists and Murphy continued; he provided hospitality
for the delegates to the first Irish T.U.C. in 1894 and in 1899 granted,
as chairman of the Dublin United Tramways Company, a most satisfactory interview to John Simmons. He was tendered the marked thanks
of the council, on the motion of an A.S.E. delegate, for the manner in
which he had acted in the interests of the engineers.[37] Two years later
Simmons had again occasion to speak of a favorable reception by Murphy and other directors when he sought the provision of early workmen's trams at cheap rates. Though some delegates were not prepared at
that stage to thank Murphy, cheap fares were granted shortly afterwards.[38] The tramwaymen had less cause to be pleased with Murphy,
who consistently refused to recognize their union or grant them a nine-
hour working day. In 1890 the council had assisted the men in forming
a union, which collapsed in 1897 without having secured any real
concessions from the company. Some years later it was refounded, and
the men again brought their case to the council, which on this occasion
merely referred it back to the union.[39] It is significant that the next
attack in the council on the tramways company was not concerned with
working conditions affecting the unskilled but with the importation of
tramways from England. F. Farrell, a coachmakers' delegate, protested
that there were capable tradesmen idle during the winter and spring
and added that "as almost the entire earnings of this company are
derived from the working classes, we consider their action a gross
injustice to the people by whom they live and thrive."[40] The motion
was passed, but only after George Leahy had deprecated what he considered were personal attacks on Murphy.

Labor in the Dublin Corporation

The attempts of the Dublin Trades Council to form a Labour Electoral
Association and send a distinctive labor group to the city council met
with a very moderate success. Of the number of "labour" candidates
elected in January 1899, only E. L. Richardson might be considered
independent of party affiliation, though he had close relations with
official nationalist councillors. William Doyle, who visited the council
in December 1898 (he was described as the "Labour candidate for the
Rotunda ward"), ran with three other nationalists, including Nan-

36. *F.J.,* 4 July 1892.
37. D.T.C. minutes, 25 Sept. 1899.   38. Ibid., 23 Sept., 7 Oct. 1901.
39. The tramwaymen's case was presented to the Cork (1902) congress of the
I.T.U.C. by W. J. Leahy. Eleven years later Leahy adopted a very different attitude
during the 1913 dispute, when he praised Murphy and attacked Larkin.
40. D.T.C. minutes, 11 June 1906.

netti, and won a seat as alderman.[41] In June 1899 he appeared as a delegate of an A.S.C.J. branch, was elected to the executive committee at the same meeting, and became vice-president in August.[42] W. J. Leahy was the only other member of the "Dublin Labour Party" who could be counted as a member of the trades council, though his attendance as a delegate was fitful.[43]

The semblance of unity possessed by the group before the election was soon lost. Connolly, writing in the *Workers' Republic* nine months later, was severe: "All of them hold the same political and social beliefs as the remainder of the municipal council—believe equally with them in the capitalist system, and that rent, profit and interest are the necessary and inevitable pillars of society. . . . From the entry of the Labour Party into the municipal council to the present day their course has been marked by dissension, squabbling and recrimination. No single important move in the interest of the worker was even mooted, the most solemn pledges were incontinently broken, and where the workers looked for inspiration and leadership, they have received nothing but discouragement and disgust."[44] In the same article he described a contest for the position of lord mayor, in which Alderman Patrick Dowd was the "labour" candidate, not as a fight between capital and labor, but as "a sordid scramble between two sets of political wirepullers, both equally contemptible," and confessed to having been seriously disappointed in the labor men elected under the auspices of the Labour Electoral Association.[45]

Arthur Griffith, who had welcomed the return of the labor candidates in the hope that they would clear up corruption, turned in disgust from them and referred in 1901 to the group as "the so-called Labour Party, which having made itself the tool of the Pile[46]-clique and the whiskey ring in turn in the council chamber, has earned for itself the contempt and laughter of men who looked to it once with hope

41. Ibid., 5 Dec. 1898; *F.J.*, 18 Jan. 1899.

42. D.T.C. minutes, 19 June, 14 Aug. 1899. When Doyle resigned from the corporation in 1913 the *Freeman's Journal* (31 May 1913) described him as the last of "the original Dublin Labour Party in the corporation." The other members were given as J. P. Nannetti, Patrick Dowd, E. L. Richardson, Joseph Clarke, W. J. Leahy, Michael Fitzpatrick, and A. J. Lord.

43. After a long absence he reapppeared in March 1899 as a delegate of his local union, the Regular Society of Coopers (D.T.C. minutes, 13 Mar. 1899).

44. D. Ryan, ed., *The Workers' Republic*, pp. 51–52.

45. Dowd was one of the candidates endorsed by the L.E.A., the others being George Leahy, E. L. Richardson, Joseph Clarke, John Simmons, Michael Canty, William Doyle, Alexander Blaine, John Gibbons, and Edward Fleming (*F.J.*, 13 Jan. 1899).

46. Alderman Sir Thomas Pile, Dowd's rival and a very moderate nationalist.

as the party of nationalism, progress and corruption-killing in the corporation.[47]

In September 1899 the trades council considered a Labour Electoral Association resolution calling for an investigation into charges of bribery made against corporation labor members. It was supported by Aldermen Doyle and Dowd and carried easily, an amendment expressing confidence in the members being rejected.[48] The investigation settled nothing, and until its demise the L.E.A. was an occasion of wrangling and bitterness. When it refused to endorse E. L. Richardson the trades council chairman proposed its repudiation. His motion, moderated by the peace-loving Simmons, was carried by 17 votes to 15. A recount was demanded and refused. Delegates protested that the council's time was being wasted "on matters not affecting labour—not an item on the agenda had been taken up." The meeting ended in disorder.[49] In 1902 and 1903[50] efforts were made to patch up matters, but the L.E.A. was finally repudiated by the council, which decided in August 1903 to set up a new organization.[51]

The council's executive committee decided that the new body, if the council were to recognize it, should consist of at least twenty societies with an aggregate membership of five thousand.[52] The Labour Representation Committee, a name borrowed like that of its predecessor from the English organization, was however, immediately assailed by William Field, M.P., and a number of United Irish League councillors that included Joseph Clarke, who had been endorsed by the L.E.A. in 1899. When E. L. Richardson, as president of the trades council, submitted the scheme to the council for approval in November 1903, he complained of the grossly malicious attacks on it and on himself. The attackers, whom he described as "moral assassins and unfit for public life," had gone so far as to interfere with his means of livelihood. E. W. Stewart, anticipating Larkin's later denunciations of the local bosses of the United Irish League, dismissed the arguments of the attackers as absurd and their nationality as sham—"they had no more nationality than a cat." The attacks were condemned and the L.R.C. approved, though George Leahy declared his opposition on the grounds that the breach in the labor ranks would be widened, and P. T.

47. *United Irishman,* 7 Sept. 1901, quoted in Clarkson, p. 257.
48. D.T.C. minutes, 25 Sept. 1899.
49. Ibid., 17 Dec. 1900. The supporters of the repudiation included E. W. Stewart and W. McLoughlin; the most prominent of the L.E.A. defenders was Alderman Doyle.
50. Ibid., 1 Oct., 20 Oct. 1902. 4 May 1903.
51. Ibid., 24 Aug. 1903.
52. D.T.C. executive committee minutes, 8 Oct. 1903.

Daly regretted that he could not vote for the motion, no doubt because of his Sinn Féin sympathies.[53]

The new model was no more effective than the old. P. T. Daly, elected a councillor in 1903, dissociated himself from the group in 1904.[54] The conduct of some of the men endorsed as labor candidates by the council finally alarmed E. L. Richardson, who wished to protect the council's good name; he carried a motion early in 1906 instructing the executive committee to formulate rules that would make endorsement less automatic.[55] At the end of the same year a long debate took place on the subject. J. Lumsden, a plasterer, in proposing his motion, said that he was afraid it was "the political and not the trade union ticket" that appealed to the workers of Dublin.[56] The motion instructed the executive committee to call a delegate meeting of all trades and labor societies in Dublin to establish a Labour Representation Committee and secure direct labor representation on the public boards of the city. A suggestion that the association should be established on the lines of the English organization, made by W. McLoughlin, provoked Michael Canty to exclaim that the trades of Dublin were capable of minding their own business without the interference of Englishmen in their affairs. Simmons defended the English L.R.C., saying that it was composed of good trade unionists in sympathy with Ireland. P. T. Daly pointed out that he had had to dissociate himself from some of the men put forward under the first regime and that he would have to consider his position if the resolution were passed. Lumsden quieted some fears by denying that he wished affiliation with the English L.R.C. and the motion was passed with one dissentient.[57]

The formation of the organization was delayed for some months. Finally Lumsden, now president of the council, moved that the secretary call a meeting of trades and labor bodies in June 1907 "to discover whether it is possible to form an L.R.C. in Dublin."[58] The L.R.C. was formed, but as there had been no radical change in the personnel of the corporation labor group its effectiveness was limited.

Griffith, writing in January 1903 before the municipal elections, lashed both the United Irish League ("an agency of the worst description for demoralisation") and "the so-called Labour Party":

53. D.T.C. minutes, 16 Nov. 1903.
54. Ibid., 5 Sept. 1904. Daly, who as chairman of the meeting had to put a motion inviting the Labour Party in the corporation to sympathize with and support the corporation laborers, whose grievances were ignored, said he had "separated himself from the previous Labour Party, as constituted," but that the workmen would have his full support.
55. Ibid., 5 Feb. 1906.   56. Ibid., 3 Dec. 1906.
57. Ibid., 3 Dec. 1906.   58. Ibid., 27 May 1907.

We observed the Labour Party on Christmas Day going to Mass at the Pro-Cathedral in state. It wore an unctuous smile, a London tall silk hat and kid gloves, a Leeds suit and Nottingham boots, and leaned on the arm of the Publican. . . . The publican, the slum-owner, the loyal-address shoneen,[59] the bogus labour man, are in the corporation, and control it only because they have been voted there by the voters whom little knots of knaves in every ward drive like sheep to the polls.[60]

Griffith's description of the social aspirations of these labor representatives is in keeping with their conduct even within trade union bodies. W. J. Leahy, as has been already noted, solicited funds from Dublin employers for the 1900 congress banquet. Alderman Doyle presented "a handsome gold locket and pendant" to George Leahy as president of the Irish T.U.C. and Dublin Trades Council, as well as the customary address.[61] Most of the labor group identified themselves with their fellow corporators and rose out of their class rather than with it. Patrick Dowd did so as early as 1895, when he retired from the treasurership of the trades council in order to set up in business on his own; on his departure he received a chain, an inscribed medallion and an address.[62] In 1913 William Doyle laid down his aldermanship because of the pressure of his own growing business,[63] and early in the following year W. J. Leahy, whom the Dublin business community had elevated to the presidency of the Court of Conscience (a quasi-judicial municipal office), denounced Larkin to the Dublin Mercantile Association.[64]

The positive achievements of these labor representatives in the corporation were slight. Alderman Doyle claimed to have been the moving spirit in reviving shipbuilding at the North Wall yard, a project backed by the trades council, which persuaded the corporation to initiate it.[65] Richardson, the member of the group least entangled with nationalist municipal politics, attended to the grievances of corporation employees, for whom he secured holidays ("four full and free days") in 1898.[66] But the first Dublin Labour Party as a whole was in no danger of being mistaken for a group of municipal reformers.

The high proportion of its population suffering from unemployment and low wages gave Dublin an unenviable reputation, and its housing

59. "Shoneen" (Irish *seoinín* = little John), a term of contempt for the Irishman who apes English manners, attitudes, and pastimes.
60. *United Irishman,* 3 Jan. 1903, quoted in Clarkson, p. 258.
61. D.T.C. minutes, 27 Aug. 1900.   62. *F.J.,* 5 Mar. 1895.
63. *F.J.,* 31 May 1913.   64. *Irish Independent,* 18 Feb. 1914.
65. *F.J.* and D.T.C. minutes, 11 Feb., 7 Oct. 1901. Simmons said at the October meeting that William Martin Murphy should be included in the vote of thanks as he had suggested that a Clyde firm be approached.
66. D.T.C. minutes, 29 Aug. 1898.

conditions made it notorious. The most spectacular Dublin slums consisted of areas once inhabited by prosperous citizens who had moved to the suburbs and adjoining townships as the older portions of the city decayed or became unfashionable. Within a few minutes' walk of O'Connell Street, the main thoroughfare, lay streets of tall tenement houses whose lingering elements of visual grace were mocked by smashed fanlights and windows, broken or missing doors, peeling halls, and a general air of decay. For the slum dwellers there was the all-pervading stench of poverty that even the passerby could not escape—the smell of overcrowded, unwashed humanity reinforced at intervals by the odor of human urine and excrement. In 1901 the percentage of the population living five or more to a room was 10.61, double the figure for Glasgow, itself notorious for such districts as the Gorbals.[67] Of the 59,263 families resident in Dublin, 21,429 or 36.7 percent of the total had each but a single room, and of these one-room families 573 consisted of eight or more persons.[68] The standard of sanitation can be judged by the fact that though the number of tenement houses fell from 6,195 in 1903[69] to 5,322 in 1914, there were in the latter year 1,161 that had only one water closet for 20 or more people.[70]

The Irish rural laborer had fared better in the matter of rehousing than his urban counterpart. By March 1901 loans granted under various Labourers' Acts amounted to £2,051,374, whereas only £438,550 11s. had been advanced under the Housing of the Working Classes Act (1890).[71] In Dublin the corporation had built 375 houses, but most of the low-rent housing schemes had been carried out by companies set up for the purpose.[72] The Dublin Artizans' Dwellings Company, which declared a dividend of 5 percent in 1900 and placed over £7,000 in a reserve fund, had built 1,800 and other companies between 200 and 300.[73] But, apart from the inadequate numbers, such schemes did not

67. R. E. Matheson, "Housing of the People in Ireland during 1841–1901," in *Journal of the Statistical and Social Inquiry Society of Ireland,* xi. 211 (June 1903). In future references to the *Journal* the title will be abbreviated to *Stat. Soc. Ire. Jn.*

68. Matheson, "Housing of the People," p. 208.

69. Sir C. A. Cameron (Dublin city medical superintendent), *How the Poor Live* (Dublin, 1904), p. 7.

70. *Report of the Departmental Committee of Inquiry into the Housing of the Dublin Working Classes,* quoted in James Connolly, *Labour in Ireland* (Dublin, 1922), p. 339.

71. *Twenty-ninth Annual Report of the Local Government Board for Ireland for the Year Ending 31 March 1901,* pp. xxxii, xxxiv, [Cd. 1259] H.C. 1902.

72. Charles Eason, Jr, "The Tenement Houses of Dublin," in *Stat. Soc. Ire. Jn.,* x. 385 (1899).

73. Cameron, *How the Poor Live,* p. 6; Eason, Jr., "The Tenement Houses of Dublin," p. 385; Charles Dawson, "The Housing of the People, with Special Reference to Dublin," in *Stat. Soc. Ire. Jn.,* xi. 48 (1901).

deal with the real problem, for the rents charged were between 4s. and 5s. a week, far too high for the many families with incomes of 15s. a week or less. The extent of poverty in the city can be gauged by the 2,866,084 pawnbrokers' tickets issued in a single year; they represented £547,453 in loans, usually on clothing, bedding, or other small items pledged on Monday or Tuesday and redeemed the following Saturday.[74] The many who lived a hand-to-mouth existence could pay no more than 2s. 6d. a week, the average rent in tenement areas at this period.[75] Slum clearance could be enormously expensive, thanks to the exorbitant demands of ground landlords; a clearance scheme in one area (Brides Alley) cost the corporation nearly £12,000 an acre.[76] Vested interests were strong in slum property, for there was often a chain of sublandlords between the lodger and the ultimate owner,[77] with a consequent encouragement of rack-renting and a discouragement of any expenditure on repairs.

The wretched housing conditions in the city did not, it would appear, alarm the corporation labor group, and it was left to P. T. Daly to call for action from the trades council. He appeared as a Dublin Typographical Provident Society delegate for the first time in January 1902 and at the next meeting moved a long resolution calling for the "taxation of ground and land values, the rating of empty houses, the establishment of fair rents tribunals (accessible to tenant roomkeepers as well as householders), fixity of tenure while obeying the tribunal, the compulsory regulation of tenement houses, the amendment of the act to allow municipal authorities to advance the entire purchase money on security of title and the compulsory sale on a valuation by a valuer appointed by the borough authority."[78] The motion was supported by George Leahy, James Connolly, and the president (Alderman William Doyle), and passed and sent to Irish M.P.s, a number of whom acknowledged it. The collapse of a tenement house in Townshend Street later in the year, accompanied by loss of life,[79] roused J. Lumsden, a plasterer, to condemn members of the corporation who were the owners of tenements and responsible for their condition. Wishing to prevent "these house jobbers" from entering the corporation, he moved a motion condemning the inadequate supervision of tenement property and

74. Cameron, *How the Poor Live*, pp. 3–4.
75. Ibid., pp. 8–9.
76. Dawson, "The Housing of the People," p. 48.
77. Eason, "The Tenement Houses of Dublin," pp. 394–5.
78. D.T.C. minutes, 27 Jan. 1902.
79. At the inquest evidence was given that an officer of the sanitary department of the corporation had served notice that the house was dangerous, but that a member of the city engineer's staff had objected (*B.N.-L.*, 11 Oct. 1902).

impressing on the labor group the necessity of agitating for proper supervision by competent tradesmen. The motion was supported by Richardson and sent to the lord mayor and the labor group.[80]

Griffith seized the opportunity presented by the labor group's inactivity to attack E. L. Richardson when he was a candidate for the Inns Quay ward in January 1903. He described him as the best candidate in the field for ability and common sense, but said that though he had represented the ward for two years[81] he had "never bothered his head about the slums surrounding that great institution, the Dublin Trades Hall, Capel Street."[82] Stung by Griffith's sarcasm, Richardson, trades council president for 1903, introduced two months later a lengthy report from the executive committee. The municipal authorities were to be approached to hasten building schemes, and a circular was to be issued to trades councils and other bodies in Ireland asking that proposals be forwarded to the prime minister and Irish M.P.s. The executive committee had been in communication with D. D. Sheehan, an Irish M.P. who had taken a special interest in rural housing, and who would move a private bill which the council would ask Dublin M.P.s to support. The council would also affiliate to the National Workmen's Housing Council, which had a bill before the House of Commons in charge of another Irish M.P., Dr. Macnamara. Finally, the council's delegate would move a housing motion at the Newry congress of the Irish T.U.C. The motion to approve the report was seconded by Lumsden and passed. The same meeting adopted other housing motions: one demanded that the corporation use its powers under existing acts to build new houses, prevent the creation of new tenements, and restrict the activities of jerry builders, while another repeated Daly's earlier resolution.[83]

Richardson continued to urge housing reforms,[84] but the caliber of the corporation members made it impossible for him to achieve any worthwhile results. The 1906 council president had to report that at a conference convened by the council with the object of promoting a housing bill in the next parliamentary session, only thirty-five corporation members had attended, though eighty circulars had been sent

80. D.T.C. minutes, 20 Oct. 1902.

81. In fact, he had served four years, since he had been first elected for the ward in 1899. Previously, from 1896, he had represented the Mountjoy ward.

82. *United Irishman,* 17 Jan. 1903, quoted in Clarkson, pp. 257–58.

83. D.T.C. minutes, 23 Mar. 1903.

84. He announced in August 1903 that the lord mayor had promised to convene a conference to urge the Irish chief secretary (George Wyndham) to have Ireland included in a housing bill (ibid., 10 Aug. 1903).

out.[85] Slum property in Dublin was safe, protected by a guard of publicans, house agents, and gombeen men in the corporation.[86]

A number of trades council members were also elected as poor law guardians during the period. Two at least, J. Chambers, a saddler and ex-president of the council, and George Leahy, did useful and honest work. In 1902, after sustained pressure, they persuaded the guardians of the North Dublin Union and the governors of the Richmond Asylum to make their workmen pensionable; the South Dublin Union followed suit when a similar resolution was submitted.[87] Bribery, "testimonials" from grateful workmen, and other forms of corrupton were common, however, and it is evident that some labor representatives succumbed. The practice of receiving "testimonials," in fact, was one of the reasons for the discredit that overtook the first "Dublin Labour Party," and at a much later date (1919) was the immediate cause of a disastrous split in the trades council itself.[88]

85. Ibid., 26 Nov. 1906.
86. The departmental committee's housing inquiry report of 1914 (Connelly, *Labour in Ireland*, pp. 330–40) revealed that fifteen members of the corporation owned slum property, and that three of them were receiving rebates of taxes to which they were not entitled.
87. D.T.C. minutes, 10, 24 Feb. 1902.
88. A circular letter, dated 24 May 1919 and signed by the officers and committee of the Dublin Trades Council, was addressed to "the officers and members of all affiliated unions." Before dealing with the matter in dispute (a "testimonial" to a labor poor law guardian) it rehearsed the history of labor representation in Dublin following the Local Government (Ireland) Act, 1898:

On that occasion, thanks to the awakening intelligence of the Irish workers, labour candidates were elected in large numbers in many parts of Ireland, and in Dublin no less than one-fifth of the Dublin Corporation was returned on the labour programme, pledged to sit, act and vote as an independent party. It soon became evident, however, that these men were utterly unfitted to maintain an independent, incorruptible party. They became involved in the intrigues and jobbery of the dominant political factions, and vied with the men they were elected to fight in getting jobs for their friends and relations, promoting testimonials to themselves and feathering their nests generally. As a result the workers became thoroughly disgusted with labour representation, the desire for an independent party of labour was killed, and the movement as a whole suffered through the discredit and dishonour of those it had elected. And so ended the first Dublin Labour Party, "unwept, unhonoured and unsung," and for almost a generation the Dublin workers lost faith in labour representation.

Given the number of labor candidates sponsored by nationalist organizations and the accommodating attitude of the trades council at that time, it may be questioned whether any binding pledge was exacted. The proportion elected also seems unduly high. But there can be little quarrel with the general description of the representatives castigated. I am indebted to the late William O'Brien for a copy of the circular, part of which is printed in Clarkson, p. 206, n. 2.

Public representatives, especially those in local government, are notoriously difficult to keep in line when strong organization is absent. The Dublin Trades Council did not exercise the same discipline over its representatives that the Belfast Trades Council did, nor shoulder the same financial burden in elections. It did, however, make a token grant of three pounds, at least from 1903, to approved candidates,[89] and ended the practice only when the formation of a new Labour Representation Committee was decided upon in 1906.[90] Broken time was also paid by the council, but if the public representative attended to protect the interests of a particular craft the trade union concerned was asked to pay the expenses involved.[91]

Cultural Nationalism

As Parnell's body was being lowered into the grave, Maud Gonne told Yeats, a shooting star flashed across the October sky and burnt out. It was an apt symbol of the fall of nationalist hopes, reduced to dust and ashes in the strife that followed. To the original feud between pro- and anti-Parnellites was added a struggle for power among the anti-Parnellite majority, until Archbishop Croke was driven to declare in 1895 that Home Rule was unattainable in measurable time because of the factitious behavior of Irish politicians.[92]

Yet these years of general nationalist humiliation after 1891 were also years of reconstruction. In November 1892 Douglas Hyde addressed the Irish National Literary Society. His theme was the necessity for de-anglicizing Ireland: "we have lost the notes of nationality, our language and customs. . . . we find ourselves despoiled of the bricks of nationality. . . . we must now set to, to bake new ones, if we can."[93] The task was undertaken by the Gaelic League, founded in July 1893 with Hyde as president. Two rules set out in the first annual report stated that the work of the society was to maintain Irish as a living language and banned political or religious controversy; they were followed by a declaration that these were fundamental rules that could not

89. P. T. Daly was grantd £3 towards his election expenses (D.T.C. excutive minutes, 13 Aug. 1903). The grant was later increased to £3 3s. (D.T.C. minutes, 15 May 1905).

90. D.T.C. executive minutes, 20 Dec. 1906; D.T.C. minutes, 7 Jan. 1907.

91. D.T.C. executive minutes, 10 Dec. 1903, 26 Jan. 1905 and passim. When work was suspended because bad weather or some other cause made it impossible, the employee was paid for the broken time.

92. *F.J.*, 13 Feb. 1895.

93. *The Revival of Irish and Other Addresses*, pp. 118–29, in Edmund Curtis and R. B. McDowell, *Irish Historical Documents*, pp. 310, 313.

be altered or abolished.[94] The members included moderate Unionists as well as nationalists during the period when its leaders were not overtly political. Branches were started all over Ireland and the organization was extended to Irish exiles in Great Britain; by March 1902 it had a total of 441 affiliated branches.[95] In 1905 Hyde went to North America and returned early in 1906 with £10,000 he had raised for the League's work. Irish received only lukewarm approval in the early years of the Gaelic League—the Catholic hierarchy and Maynooth in particular offering resistance—but it finally secured official recognition when in 1910 the senate of the National University of Ireland by majority vote made it a compulsory subject for matriculation.[96]

In addition to assisting local branches to conduct Irish classes, the League staged a yearly Oireachtas, or literary festival, encouraged Irish dancing and music, and promoted social activities that would bring together enthusiasts for the language. The League organizer traveling around the countryside on a bicycle was a familiar sight, engaged in making conscious what was almost a collective unconscious. Even sport and athletics did not escape the net of nationality, for the Gaelic Athletic Association, founded in 1884, revived, codified, and popularized the ancient games of hurling, handball, and Gaelic football. Nor was the growth of cultural nationalism confined to the Irish language. W. B. Yeats was the moving spirit in the Irish Literary Theatre, the precursor of the Abbey Theatre, and though most of its productions were in English, the distinctive atmosphere was Irish. Yeats took a part in the organization of '98 centenary celebrations and wrote *Cathleen Ni Houlihan* under their influence.[97] Its glorification of the 1798 rising prompted him in old age to ask himself:

94. "Is buin-riaghlacha an dá riaghail so thuas agus ní dleaghthach a n-athrughadh ná a gcur ar gcúl" (J. Carty, *Bibliography of Irish History, 1870–1911*, p. 272).

95. Carty, *Bibliography*, p. xvii.

96. The bishops issued a statement that in their opinion it would not be right to make Irish a compulsory subject in matriculation, as it would hinder the progress of the university by antagonizing those who did not know Irish or were unwilling to learn it. Griffith commented: "We are greatly grieved that once again the Catholic Church of Ireland has taken the wrong side" (Sinn Féin, 23 Jan. 1909, quoted in Seán Ó Lúing, *Art Ó Gríofa*, pp. 194–5). While some Catholic clergy supported the revival of Irish, or even compiled primers, dictionaries, and grammars in the language (the Irish Christian Brothers produced a widely used grammar), others, especially among the higher clergy, were unenthusiastic or hostile. Some remembered the use made by Protestant evangelicals of tracts and bibles in Irish during the mid-nineteenth century in the Gaelic-speaking areas of western Ireland; some saw English as a key to social and economic advancement for their flock and yet others saw it as the means by which Irish Catholics could assist in the reconversion of Great Britain.

97. *Cathleen Ni Houlihan* was produced in 1902. Yeats was for a time a member, though an inactive one, of the Irish Republican Brotherhood.

> Did that play of mine send out
> Certain men the English shot?[98]

Cultural nationalism was easily transformed into a more political form. When the divided nationalists were reunited in 1900, new rules were framed governing the conventions that selected parliamentary candidates. Among those bodies entitled to be represented at the conventions were branches of such organizations as the National Literary Society and the Gaelic Athletic Association. Some Gaelic League organizers doubled as political recruiting agents and Douglas Hyde finally resigned as president in 1915 because he considered that the League had violated a fundamental rule by abandoning its original political neutrality. In 1903 Padraic Pearse was appointed the editor of the League's official journal, *An Claidheamh Solais* (The Sword of Light). When in the next decade its editor, like a number of its readers, took up the sword in earnest, the journal's name seemed to betoken the transition from cultural to physical force nationalism.[99] In turn the Gaelic Athletic Association promoted more than athletic pastimes, not a few of its members graduating from physical culture to physical force by joining the ranks of the Irish Republican Brotherhood.

Sinn Féin

The significance of such movements in the slow development of new political attitudes may be difficult to assess, but a clear line of descent can be traced in the case of the societies to which Arthur Griffith and his colleagues belonged. Griffith returned from South Africa in October 1898, after a stay of less than two years, where he had worked for a time as a compositor (he was a member of the Dublin Typographical Provident Society). He then became, on the suggestion of his friend William Rooney, the editor of the new nationalist–separatist weekly, the *United Irishman*. The first issue appeared on 4 March 1899. In 1900 a new organization came into being, Cumann na nGaedhael, the result of a fusion of several literary–political clubs of which the chief was Rooney's Celtic Literary Society, a Parnellite offshoot of an earlier society. It held its convention in November of that year; among those present was P. T. Daly. While the objectives of Cumann na nGaedhael resembled those of the Gaelic League, they also included political aims, the most important being the "nationalising" of all public boards.[100]

98. From *The Man and the Echo* (W. B. Yeats, *Collected Poems*, p. 393), London, 1950.

99. *An Claidheamh Solais* (*The Sword of Light*) was first issued on St Patrick's Day, 1899.

100. Other objectives were: the publication of information about the natural re-

When Queen Victoria visited Dublin in March 1900, she was presented by the lord mayor (Alderman Thomas Pile) with a loyal address from the Dublin corporation, but when Kind Edward VII came three years later he did not receive one, for the proposal had been defeated by three votes after an angry scene in the council chamber. Public agitation against the proposal had been carried on for some months by a new body, the National Council, which was already in existence in May, a few months before the royal visit. Its constitution, adopted in August, stated that the National Council "consisted only of members opposed to the British government of Ireland."[101] Arthur Griffith was once again the begetter.

The new movement developed rapidly for some years after 1903. In 1904 Griffith wrote a series of articles entitled "The Resurrection of Hungary" in his paper the *United Irishman* and had them published in book form in the same year; twenty thousand copies were sold in three months.[102] He proposed that Ireland apply Hungarian methods, refuse to send members to Westminster as Hungary refused to be represented in the imperial parliament in Vienna, and by the summoning of a "Council of Three Hundred," composed of abstentionist members from Westminster as well as local government representatives, create an Irish parliament. Taking his stand on the Renunciation Act of 1783, he contended that the Act of Union of 1800 was invalid and called for the restoration of the constitution of 1782. The "Green Hungarian Band," as the National Council was derisively called by its opponents, endorsed *The Resurrection of Hungary*.[103]

The National Council held its first convention on 28 November 1905—a date usually regarded as marking the foundation of Sinn Féin. A new constitution was adopted, with provision for starting branches in every electoral division, and a committee elected. In the public session Griffith delivered a lecture, later published as *Sinn Féin Policy*, which was approved as the program of the movement. It called for the Council of the Three Hundred as an embryo parliament,[104] the dis-

---

sources of Ireland; support for Irish industries; the study and teaching of Irish history, language, music and arts; the initiation and execution of an Irish foreign policy (Seán Ó Lúing, *Art Ó Gríofa,* p. 106).

101. *United Irishman,* 8 Aug. 1903, in R. P. Davis, The Rise of Sinn Féin, p. 22.

102. Ó Lúing, *Ó Gríofa,* p. 125.

103. Ibid., chap. 9 and p. 131.

104. Griffith dropped his earlier scheme for the inclusion of abstentionist members of the British parliament. The first resolution passed at the convention asked the general council of county councils to act as a *de facto* parliament: "That the general council of county councils presents the nucleus of a national authority, and we urge upon it to extend the scope of its deliberations and action; to take within its purview

placement of British by national law courts, the creation of an Irish bank and stock exchange and an Irish civil service, and the appointment of consular agents abroad to protect Irish commercial interests. Griffith adopted wholeheartedly the protectionist ideas of the nationalist German economist Friedrich List, whose book he had read in Samson Lloyd's translation, *The National System of Political Economy*. Though List's theories presupposed an economy sufficiently large to be well-nigh self-sufficient (he visualized an economic *Grossdeutschland* that included the Low Countries), Griffith hailed them as the means by which Irish industry would recover and even exceed its former glories.[105]

P. T. Daly, who had retained his active membership of the movement from the founding of Cumann na nGaedhael, was present at the convention and made a statement that showed that there were those for whom nonviolent resistance was a temporary expedient: "We [sic] believed in passive resistance until by active resistance they could end the foreign government of Ireland (cheers)."[106] Daly continued to play a prominent part and was elected to the resident executive of the National Council for the five years from 1906 to 1910.[107]

By 1906 there were three organizations pursuing much the same program: Cumann na nGaedhael dating from 1900, the National Council from 1903, and the Dungannon Club, founded in Belfast by Bulmer Hobson and Denis McCullough in 1905. At a meeting in Dundalk in April 1907 Cumann na nGaedhael and the Dungannon Club were united to form the Sinn Féin League with Daly as president.[108] There was friction between the League and the National Council, though Daly publicly denied this, for the Sinn Féin Leaguers were strongly separatist and Griffith, in the opinion of P. S. O'Hegarty, did not want any of them in the National Council: "Griffith's platform is a platform . . . which excludes the separatist."[109] The Sinn Féin League had little time for the constitution of 1782 and the Renunciation Act, for many of its members were simply physical force men biding their time. Nonetheless the two organizations were united under the name of

every question of national interest and to formulate lines of procedure for the nation." *United Irishman*, 9 Dec. 1905, in Curtis and McDowell, eds., *Irish Historical Documents*, p. 314.

105. A summary is given in Ó Lúing, Ó Gríofa, pp. 135–9.

106. *United Irishman*, 9 Dec. 1905, quoted in Davis, Rise of Sinn Féin, app. VI.

107. *Sinn Féin*, 8 Sept. 1906, 7 Sept. 1907, 22 Aug. 1908, 28 Aug. 1909, 8 Oct. 1910. Daly was a member of the I.R.B.   108. Davis, Rise of Sinn Féin, p. 44.

109. Its first objective was the regaining of sovereign independence of Ireland. See letters of Bulmer Hobson (23 Aug. 1906) and P. S. O'Hegarty (11 Apr. 1907) to George Gavin Duffy in Ó Lúing, *Ó Gríofa*, pp. 141–2.

Sinn Féin when P. T. Daly carried a motion to that effect at the August 1907 convention of the National Council.[110] In the previous year the *United Irishman,* bankrupted by a libel action, had ceased publication, and its place was taken three weeks later by *Sinn Féin.*[111]

The appearance of Daly as a delegate at the Dublin Trades Council in January 1902 was followed by an increase in the council's interest in the language movement. Some delegates signed their names in Irish and the council received a deputation from the Gaelic League appealing for financial support and general approval from the trade unions. Approval was granted ("it would give an impetus to Irish manufacture") and the council was represented with its banner in an Irish-language demonstration in March.[112] The following year the same procedure was followed, with the council officers taking part in a preliminary organizing meeting.[113] Participation in language demonstrations became an annual event; council delegates attended an industrial conference[114] arranged by the Gaelic League, and when An Craoibhín Aoibhinn (Hyde) departed on his American tour in 1905, they presented him with a resolution of support and a suitable address.[115]

In 1891 the vice-president of the Glasgow Trades Council had accused the Dublin council of having an unholy alliance with the city's publicans, but by 1905 that accusation could no longer be made. George Leahy had always been an ardent temperance advocate; now he was supported by a number of the new delegates, especially those associated with Sinn Féin, who believed in the slogan, "Ireland sober, Ireland free." By 1905 the council as a body was committed to the temperance movement, for in that year its executive committee marched in the annual demonstration and in the following year had the Ireland's Own band accompany them in their tribute to Father Mathew, the nineteenth-century Irish apostle of temperance.[116] In 1906 Leahy had the council endorse a resolution of the Workmen's Temperance Association regretting the refusal of the Licensed Vintners' Association to close on St. Patrick's Day and calling on all workers to refuse to enter any public houses that did open. They had already pledged themselves the previous year to abstain from drink on Tem-

110. Davis, Rise of Sinn Féin, p. 49; Ó Lúing, *Ó Gríofa,* p. 143.

111. The last issue of the *United Irishman* appeared on 14 Apr. 1906, the first of *Sinn Féin* on 5 May. See Ó Lúing, *Ó Gríofa,* pp. 157–8, for the interesting libel action that reflects Griffith's integrity and freedom from sectarian prejudices.

112. D.T.C. minutes, 10 Feb., 10 Mar. 1902.

113. Ibid., 9 Feb. 1903.   114. Ibid., 23 Jan. 1905.

115. Ibid., 30 Oct., 13 Nov. 1905. It became customary for Gaelic League members to assume Gaelic pen names. An Craoibhín Aoibhinn (The Pleasant Little Branch) was Douglas Hyde.

116. D.T.C. executive minutes, 5 Oct. 1905; D.T.C. minutes, 1 Oct. 1906.

perance Day.[117] Also in 1906 the council sent a deputation of five (the officers and P. T. Daly) to the annual conference of the Workmen's Temperance Association and continued to do so in later years.[118] When Larkin settled in Dublin in 1907 he was to find a council already sympathetic at least to his views on alcohol.

Trade Union Nationalism

We have noticed the success of a number of British skilled unions in enrolling Irish workers in Dublin, as in the rest of Ireland, during the second half of the nineteenth century. There was, however, a decided resistance to amalgamation on the part of a number of local unions, the most unyielding being the Dublin Typographical Society and the Metropolitan House Painters' Trade Union, which had some nine hundred and six hundred members respectively in the 1890s. Their success in repelling the attacks of British unions was made possible by their strongly entrenched positions in the city, where they virtually controlled entry into the better-paid jobs in their trades. But a distinction must be drawn between a resistance to amalgamation arising from local loyalties or exclusive privileges and an opposition springing from a conscious nationalism, though in practice one might lead to the other. The prolonged resistance of the Cork and Belfast painters, who succumbed to amalgamation only in 1905 and 1908, was of the first kind, whereas that of the Dublin printers and painters was transformed during the opening years of the twentieth century into an aggressively nationalist opposition. The growing nationalist sentiment in the Dublin Trades Council during those years was evident even in minor matters; in 1902, for instance, P. T. Daly (Dublin Typographical Society) and C. Comiskey (Metropolitan Painters) began the practice of signing their names in Irish, a practice followed by such delegates as Peadar Macken and James Buggy when they began to attend in 1904.[119] As members of Sinn Féin, or sympathizers with it and its Irish-Ireland aims, they supported local societies and encouraged their expansion on the grounds that Irish workers should be organized in Irish unions. It was this group which carried a resolution in favor of an Irish federation of trade unions during Daly's presidency of the council in 1905.

As early as 1900 members of amalgamated unions felt the need to defend their organizations against charges that they were puppets of their English headquarters. During a lockout in the Dublin tailoring

117. D.T.C. minutes, 5 Mar., 1 Oct. 1906.
118. Ibid., 3 Apr. 1906, 8 July 1907.
119. Ibid., 7 Apr. 1902, 19 Sept. 1904 and passim.

trade W. McLoughlin took pains to make clear the local origin of the dispute and invoked the assistance of McCarron of Derry, an executive member of the Amalgamated Society of Tailors, who in a lengthy address to the council denied that the Dublin A.S.T. branch was under English influence.[120] In the printing trade the existence in Dublin of Typographical Association branches as well as of the Dublin Typographical Provident Society (D.T.P.S.) led to serious friction in 1905, when neither society would recognize the other's membership cards.[121] A motion condemning printing and bookbinding firms for importing workers when competent local members were available was used by one of its supporters, James Buggy, to attack the principle of amalgamation. W. McLoughlin and E. W. Stewart replied as members of amalgamated unions, but Daly took the side of his own union, the D.T.P.S., and declared the motion carried.[122]

The advocates of Irish unions received reinforcements in 1905 when the Irish Drapers' Assistants (I.D.A.) affiliated to the council. The union, which had been formed in 1901, had almost two thousand members in 1903.[123] Its leader, M. J. O'Lehane, was present at a council meeting in September 1902, but an application for affiliation was not made until 1905, possibly because a branch of the National Amalgamated Union of Shop Assistants, Warehousemen and Clerks (N.A.U.S.A.W.C.) was already affiliated. E. W. Stewart, who had received the congratulations of the council in 1904 on his appointment as Irish organizer of the N.A.U.S.A.W.C.,[124] opposed the acceptance of two temporary delegates of the I.D.A. When Daly overruled his objection he complained of O'Lehane's refusal to honor a resolution on reciprocal trade unionism passed at the Wexford (1905) congress of the Irish T.U.C.[125] The dispute dragged on for some months and was the subject of an inquiry by the executive committee; in the end agreement was reached and the two unions cooperated on matters affecting their members' interests.[126] But the Irish Drapers' Assistants was the stronger body; it sent six delegates to the council shortly after its affiliation, and as O'Lehane's influence grew Stewart's weakened.[127]

During the first decade of its existence Sinn Féin was for all practical

120. D.T.C. minutes, 7 May 1900.

121. See Musson, *The Typographical Association*, pp. 240–41, for an account of the relationship between the two unions.

122. D.T.C. minutes, 21 Aug. 1905.

123. *Report by the Chief Labour Correspondent of the Board of Trade on Trade Unions, 1905–7*, pp. 858–9 [Cd. 4651], H.C. 1909, lxxxix.

124. D.T.C. minutes, 19 Sept. 1904.   125. Ibid., 4 Sept. 1905.

126. Ibid., 18 Sept., 16, 30 Oct. 1905; 2 Apr. 1906.

127. Ibid., 2 Oct. 1905.

purposes a Dublin organization and its influence in other trades councils was negligible. Even in the Dublin Trades Council its adherents were few, but they carried a greater weight than their number might suggest, because they usually acted as a group and they had at least two members who were councillors in the Dublin Corporation—Daly from September 1903 and O'Lehane from April 1906. Daly had been returned at the head of the poll in his ward in 1903 and when he was being endorsed by the trades council for the 1906 election, he was praised for his "unceasing attention and able advocacy" of labor claims. A committee from the council was set up to work in conjunction with Daly's own committee, but it was not necessary, for he was returned unopposed.[128] The council congratualted O'Lehane on a similar result, E. W. Stewart seconding the motion.[129] A year earlier it had endorsed Peadar Macken's candidature on the motion of Daly, his fellow Sinn Féiner.[130] Macken was to be elected vice-president of the council in 1916, but before he could take office he was killed in the Easter rising.

The Council and British Politics

The council's attitude toward British labor politicians and their allies was in general favorable and on occasions enthusiastic. The efforts of Sir Charles Dilke on behalf of trade unionists were warmly appreciated, and when his wife, Emilie Francis Dilke, died in 1904 the motion of condolence described her as "one of the best friends of the workers, especially the women workers of these countries" and her husband as "the earnest friend of the workers."[131] The council also expressed pleasure at Arthur Henderson's "brilliant victory" in the Barnard's Castle by-election of 1903 and at Walter Hudson's selection as a parliamentary candidate for Newcastle-on-Tyne, considering it a compliment to the council of which Hudson was a member.[132] At the same meeting they rejoiced in the selection of William Walker, then chairman of the parlimentary committee of the Irish T.U.C., as candidate for an Irish constituency, "as we believe that if elected he will be a distinct addition to the Labour Party in the House of Commons, and a strenuous advocate of labour interests." The council cooperated heartily in the agita-

128. Ibid., 27 Nov. 1905, 8 Jan. 1906.
129. Ibid., 2 Apr. 1906.
130. D.T.C. executive minutes, 5 Jan. 1905; D.T.C. minutes, 9 Jan. 1905.
131. D.T.C. minutes, 31 Oct. 1904. Dilke's involvement in a divorce case (1885–86) cost him his cabinet post and parliamentary seat. He reentered parliament in 1892 and remained an M.P. until his death in 1911. His second wife, who shared his interest in labor conditions, joined the Women's Trade Union League and attended the British T.U.C. for some twenty years until she died.
132. Ibid., 5 Oct. 1903.

tion for a new Trades Disputes bill and were joint sponsors with the Irish and British T.U.C.s of a meeting on the subject, addressed by James Sexton, secretary of the N.U.D.L., and presided over by the lord mayor of Dublin.[133]

The British labor successes in 1906 impressed the council's delegates. Simmons moved an enthusiastic motion "That this Trades Council desires to congratulate the Great Democracy of Great Britain on its Great Triumph in the cause of labour, by its return to parliament of a splendid force of Uncompromising advocates of Trade Unionism. . . ."[134] The motion also took special note of Hudson's "triumphal return," and was seconded by J. Lumsden, a plasterer normally critical of things British, and supported by an Irish Drapers' Assistants delegate. The new executive committee, though containing a number of Sinn Féin members and sympathizers, were moved to order one hundred copies of the Labour Representation Committee conference report, an order repeated the following year.[135] In January 1905 the council had accepted the offer from Ruskin College of a scholarship for a delegate, and unanimously selected Peadar Macken.[136] When Walter Hudson left Ireland he was presented with a "handsomely illuminated address" and the council listened attentively to his account of the British Labour Party's work in parliament.[137] But even British labor successes were not sufficient to induce the council to follow Belfast's example and affiliate to the Labour Representation Committee.

The council's self-denying ordinance on politics was observed during the Boer War in that no motion was passed approving or disapproving British actions in South Africa. Some delegates, however, managed to express their sentiments indirectly. A resolution from the Blackburn (England) Trades Council asked for state assistance to be granted to those dependent on charity through the accidents of war, and its endorsement was moved by Simmons. A coachmakers' delegate described the resolution as a piece of impertinence and another moved that the letter be marked *read* on the grounds that politics should not be introduced. The resolution was nonetheless adopted by a large majority.[138] Echoes of the war were heard in another resolution passed by the

133. D.T.C. executive minutes, 20, 22 Oct. 1904.

134. D.T.C. minutes, 23 Jan. 1905.

135. D.T.C. executive minutes, 8 Mar. 1906, 31 Jan. 1907. It had ignored L.R.C. circulars in 1904 (8 Sept. 1904).

136. D.T.C. minutes, 23 Jan. 1905. There is no evidence in the college records that Macken attended Ruskin College, Oxford. The college, founded in 1899, offered courses, principally in politics and economics, to working-class students selected by various labor organizations (Brian Simon, *Education and the Labour Movement,* p. 311).

137. Ibid., 20 Aug. 1906, 21 Jan. 1907. There was but one dissentient from the proposal to offer Hudson an address.

138. Ibid., 29 Jan. 1900.

council condemning Sir George White, then governor of Gibraltar but previously in charge of the defense of Ladysmith, for employing naval and military personnel to load ships and break a strike of coal porters. Stewart, who moved the motion, described White's action as "a piece of unscrupulous tyranny . . . upon unarmed workmen," saying that White would not dare to use such methods with "the armed peasantry of South Africa."[139] The council also joined in condemning the employment of indentured Chinese labor in South African mines. A letter from the Capetown Trades Council on the matter resulted in Simmons moving a motion that was sent to the chairman of the Irish parliamentary party and Colonel Saunderson, the leader of the Irish Unionist M.P.s. Motions passed by British labor organizations about Chinese labor were less the result of humanitarianism than of a desire to ensure that British workers in South Africa should not be undercut in the labor market, and the Dublin Trades Council's resolution sprang from a similar desire: "believing that our own countrymen who are located there will be vitally affected, we call upon our representatives in the House of Commons to protest against the importation of these hordes of barbarians to the detriment of legitimate workers.[140]

The Council and Socialism

If, despite its admiration for the parliamentary successes of British labor, the council was not moved to follow the example of Belfast and affiliate to the Labour Representation Committee or its successor, the British Labour Party, it was even less ready to have dealings with such British socialist organizations as the Independent Labour Party. Nor did it take notice of indigenous socialist bodies. After prolonged negotiations the divided factions of the Irish Socialist Republican Party had united in March 1904 under the name of the Socialist Party of Ireland (S.P.I.), but, though they had agreed to the merger, a number of those who had been members before the split in 1903 drifted away or became inactive. Some of these, of whom E. W. Stewart was one, were delegates to the council. Stewart retained his formal membership of the S.P.I. after his appointment as Irish organizer of the National Union of Shop Assistants in August 1904, but three months later he took a step that showed that he had renounced his earlier commitment to revolutionary socialism; he proposed that the council endorse the candidature

139. Ibid., 25 Aug. 1902. Sir George White, born in County Antrim, had a long career in colonial wars in India, Burma, and South Africa. His son, Captain Jack White, took the workers' side in the Dublin 1913 lockout and helped to train the Irish Citizen Army.

140. Ibid., 10 Jan. 1904.

of J. P. Nannetti for a seat on the Dublin Corporation, though in earlier days he had denounced Nannetti as a creature of the corrupt nationalist ward bosses. The S.P.I. expelled Stewart and another veteran of the I.S.R.P., W. McLoughlin, who had kept silent when the endorsement was carried unanimously.[141] In the following February the council received a letter from the S.P.I. suggesting that Labour Day be celebrated, but on McLoughlin's motion it was referred to the executive committee and no more was heard of it.[142] Nearly two years later, in November 1906, P. Murphy wrote to the executive for permission to refer to socialism for trade unionists, only to have his request refused.[143] Yet within a year a branch of the Independent Labour Party had been formed in Dublin on the initiative of James Larkin and its chairman and treasurer were Lumsden and McLoughlin, president and vice-president respectively of the Dublin Trades Council.[144]

The Dublin labor movement, as represented by its trades council, had obviously made little progress since its first group of representatives entered the Dublin Corporation in 1899. The experiences of those early years were, however, not without effect, for the old procedure, whereby the council automatically endorsed almost any "labour" candidate, had been discredited. Successive attempts to form a labor representation committee were evidence that the council realized the need for discipline. By 1907 it was clear that the council willed the end but lacked the means—a dominant group to gain control by arousing support for its own policy. Sinn Féin had tried to be such a group but failed, for its efforts were piecemeal and spasmodic. But the council was no longer complacent, and the conjunction of new times and socialist leaders was to make it, in a few years, accept a militant program.

141. W. O'Brien to James Connolly, Dec. 1907 [O'Brien Collection, MS 13908 (3)]. When E. L. Richardson moved a motion in October 1900 congratulating the working men of Dublin on the return of J. P. Nannetti as M.P. for the College Green division, Stewart and McLoughlin dissented on the grounds that Nannetti was a political (i.e., nationalist) and not a labor member (D.T.C. minutes, 8 Oct. 1900).

142. D.T.C. minutes, 6 Feb. 1905. The minutes do not make it clear that "the Socialist Party" was the S.P.I. Possibly it was the rather shadowy Dublin Socialist Society. In a letter (4 Feb. 1904) to the secretary of the I.S.R.P., Daniel O'Brien, then secretary of the Socialist Labour Party of Ireland, urged the necessity of an early reunion as "these freaks" (the Dublin Socialist Society) were profiting by the former labors of I.S.R.P./S.L.P.I. members and, by their addiction to palliatives and neglect of the teaching of revolutionary socialism, constituted "a serious danger to the genuine Irish socialist movement and principles of international socialism generally" [O'Brien Collection, MS 13915 (2)].

143. D.T.C. executive minutes, 8 Nov. 1906. P. Murphy may have been the mail cart drivers' delegate of that name.

144. W. O'Brien to James Connolly, Dec. 1907 [O'Brien Collection, MS 13908 (3)].

Belfast

The Politics of Labor

"An elysium for the working man" was the description of Belfast that its lord mayor gave to the delegates attending the 1898 congress of the Irish T.U.C. He buttressed his hyperbole by citing the large volume of employment given by the shipyards and the "most comfortable" houses obtainable at rents of 3*s.* to 5*s.* weekly.[1] He did not spoil the fair prospect by a recital of the low wages of unskilled male labor or of conditions affecting women and juveniles in the linen industry, nor did he mention the sanitary state of the city revealed by a recent inquiry; in particular he did not refer to the sectarian animosities that divided the working class. Yet in a sense his exaggeration was understandable, for wage rates were somewhat higher in Belfast than in Dublin, unemployment lower, and housing superior (especially after the end of the century when water closets displaced dry privies). Belfast was an Irish Manchester and Glasgow combined, and though its labor force paid a heavy toll in accidents and industrial diseases,[2] it was comparatively

1. I.T.U.C., *Report, Fifth Congress,* p. 21.
2. The most dangerous occupation was shipbuilding, with 12 fatal accidents in 1905 and 1906. Dock work and work involving the use of lifting machinery came next (5 and 6 in 1905, 5 and 1 in 1906). Accidents caused by textile machinery were another important category in the industrial fatality totals of 25 and 31 for 1905 and 1906 [*Report of the Chief Inspector of Factories for 1905,* p. 195, [Cd. 3030] H.C. 1906; *Report . . . for 1906,* p. 156, [Cd. 3586] H.C. 1907]. The area covered by the Belfast factory district was altered several times, with consequent changes of name (North Ireland, Ulster). At its minimum it consisted of Belfast and its environs; at its maximum it included most of the area later known as Northern Ireland. Factory inspectors from the 1890s onward complained principally of the unhealthy conditions in the linen industry, where 12 years of work killed female carders and 16.8 years, male hacklers (*Report . . . for 1893,* p. 9, [c. 7368] H.C. 1893–4), of the neglect of safety precautions, of the repeated violations, especially in country districts, of the Truck Acts and the regulations governing the employment of women and juveniles, and of the frequency with which magistrates refused to convict offending employers or contented themselves with the infliction of derisory fines and costs. See also J. W. Boyle, "Indus-

free of economic pressure to emigrate. Trade union spokesmen, as well as employers and political leaders, boasted of their citizenship of the industrial capital of Ireland and took pride in its manufactures, however militant they might be during strikes or lockouts.

Local Manufactures and Fair Wages

The relative superiority of Belfast to Dublin as an employment center meant that its trades council spent far less time in protests against outside competition. The council nonetheless, in its earlier years, complained of work that could be done locally being carried out in England; in 1892 one of the questions put to municipal candidates asked that corporation contracts be given to local manufacturers.[3] Ten years later candidates were again asked much the same question, for it seemed likely that the furnishings of the new city hall would be imported, and labour councillors were for some years energetic in preventing or protesting subcontracts with outside firms. Edward McInnes, in other matters an impeccable Unionist, was positively an Anglophobe on the subject of cross-channel contracts. When the manager of the Belfast tramways system proposed ordering the new electric trams from England, McInnes denounced the suggestion, saying that "with a contractor from across the water they inevitably brought in a large floating population . . . and a good proportion of them would remain, as in Newcastle-on-Tyne, causing overcrowding, sickness and disease, and being a tax upon the poor-rate."[4] McInnes, as the organizer of general laborers, had no wish to have his task made more difficult by the introduction of more unorganized men into a city where unskilled unions had made little progress.[5] Skilled unions were less concerned, for they were aware that much of their own work was exported and that they could not logically protest at some imports. In addition, Belfast had no large number of dying handicraft industries to protect and, though a delegate of the Horseshoers said that his society was opposed

---

trial conditions in the twentieth century," in T. W. Moody and J. C. Beckett, eds., *Ulster since 1800: A Social Survey.*

3. B.T.C. minutes, 8 Apr., 28 Oct. 1892. A delegate pointed out that the executive committees of the two societies concerned in the April complaint (bootmakers and printers) had the printing for local branches done in England.

4. Ibid., 17 Sept., 1904. Newcastle-on-Tyne was the headquarters of his union, the National Amalgamated Union of Labour.

5. In 1893 a delegate of the N.A.U.L. said that about 16,000 laborers in the city were in great need of organization (B.T.C. minutes, 27 Oct. 1893). For the disintegration of the Belfast branches of the National Union of Dock Labourers and the Gasworkers at this time, see chap. 5.

to the introduction of electric tramcars, which would throw twenty members out of employment, the council was rarely moved to more than a passive sympathy.

Fair wages aroused more interest, but the relatively buoyant state of such occupations as the building trade protected craftsmen, if not laborers, against low wages. Occasional protests had to be made, but there were few of the denunciations so frequent in Dublin. A building trade delegate reported at one executive committee meeting that non-union labor was being used in the construction of a church; he had interviewed the churchwardens, but they had pointed out that the contract had been given to the contractor unreservedly, so no further action was taken.[6] In 1904 a delegate complained that the plastering of a Masonic hall in Ballymacarrett was being done by unfair labor, but this revelation, which would have caused anger in Dublin, was the subject of a brief and inconclusive discussion only.[7]

Government and municipal rather than private contracts caused greater concern. In 1899 William Walker was severely criticized by several delegates, including McManus, for not being sufficiently active in pressing the Belfast Board of Poor Law Guardians to adopt a fair wages clause. He defended himself by saying that he could do more by working quietly than by talking about it, in view of the difficulty in getting support from nonlabor guardians.[8] In the following year he was elected secretary of the council and wrote in that capacity to the War Office to complain that a government contract for metal castings had been subcontracted to unfair shops. Walker was dismissed by his employers, the Clonard Foundry, and was paid victimization wages for six months until his election as organizing delegate for his union, the Amalgamated Society of Carpenters and Joiners.[9] Another violation involved an admiralty contract for shot bags, normally made by sailmakers, whose recognized wages were 32s. per week. A local firm employed cheap labor and paid wages ranging from 9s. to 25s. The council sent a deputation to the Secretary of the Admiralty, H. O. Arnold-Forster, who was at that time the Member for West Belfast. His reply to the council caused great anger, for he considered that the clause was not violated if the men were willing to receive low wages. McInnes said that "a man of that type was incapable of representing any constituency of workers like those who made up Belfast" and urged that it was the trades council's duty to see that the Belfast M.P.s, with

6. B.T.C. executive minutes, 17 Aug. 1900.
7. B.T.C. minutes, 16 Jan. 1904.   8. Ibid., 25 July, 12 Aug. 1899.
9. B.T.C. executive minutes, 8 Aug. 1900, 2, 18 Jan. 1901; B.T.C. minutes, 6 June 1901.

the exception of T. H. Sloan, were called to account.[10] The unsympathetic attitude of Unionist M.P.s provided the council with a further incentive to contest parliamentary seats.

A fair wages clause in government contracts had been, in theory at least, obligatory since 1891 when a House of Commons resolution was passed to that effect, but a similar clause for local government work was permissive. Irish municipal and county councils were slow to agree to such a clause, and it was a marked triumph for the Belfast Trades Council that the city council adopted the proviso in 1903; a telegram despatched the same day by Councillor Robert Gageby reached Newry during the Irish T.U.C. dinner and was the occasion of further rejoicing.[11] The parliamentary committee of the congress was stimulated to fresh efforts and was able to announce in 1905 that the General Council of County Councils of Ireland had passed unanimously a resolution in favor of the inclusion of the clause in all contracts accepted by its constituent bodies.[12] But labor organizations, whether T.U.C. or trades councils, had to exercise constant vigilance to have the clause enforced or its application widened, and it normally formed one of the subjects raised in interviews or correspondence with government officials.

Social Assistance and Labor Journalism

The Dublin Trades Council during the early years of the twentieth century took a part in the temperance and Gaelic language movements in addition to sending representatives to ceremonies commemorating the patriot dead. The Belfast council shunned such activities, and while individual members might speak at temperance meetings they did not attend as representatives. On the other hand the council, almost from its foundation, assisted in the yearly collections for the Royal (later the Royal Victoria) and Mater Infirmorum hospitals.[13] Both hospitals had workingmen's committees that arranged for small levies to be collected regularly by some of the principal firms from their employees' pay. In return contributors had priority in the allocation of hospital beds.

Trades councils constantly received appeals on behalf of men locked out or on strike, or for the families of prominent trade unionists when

10. B.T.C. minutes, 15 Nov. 1902, 5 Feb. 1903; B.T.C. executive minutes, 29 Jan. 1903.
    11. I.T.U.C., *Report, Tenth Congress,* p. 45.
    12. I.T.U.C., *Report, Twelfth Congress,* p. 25.
    13. R. Marshall, *Fifty Years on the Grosvenor Road,* pp. 100–102; B.T.C. minutes, May 1886 and passim.

the breadwinner died, or, less frequently, for the relief of general distress. The Belfast council at one meeting in 1891 reported three appeals: for striking railway servants in Scotland, for pottery workers at Doulton's (London), and from the local committee of the Irish Distress Fund.[14] Occasionally a contribution might be made from the council's own meager resources, but normally the appeal was endorsed and sheets circulated among the affiliated trade unions. For the Cardiff dock strike in 1891 the council raised over ninety pounds in answer to Havelock Wilson's circular.[15] It also assisted the weaker local societies or helped to cover the initial expenses of organizing laborers' and women's unions.

In 1899 the trades council secured representation for the first time on the Belfast Board of Guardians when William Walker was elected to it. From 1899 until 1910 the council provided a Christmas treat, and occasionally a summer excursion, for children and old people in the city's workhouse.[16] Like their Dublin confreres the Belfast labor guardians took an active interest in poor law matters and gave evidence to the vice-regal commission, which had its report published in 1906.

It was during the 1890s that the council made a first attempt to venture into labor journalism. In November 1895 the vice-president, Richard Wortley, proposed that a monthly paper be published, with the stipulation that it should "avoid all party politics, and . . . be run purely in the interests of labour by the Belfast United Trades and Labour Council."[17] He estimated that five hundred pounds would be needed, but declared that it would be a shame if the thirteen thousand trade unionists affiliated to the council did not launch such a journal and make it a success. It appeared under the name of the *Belfast Citizen*, with Alexander Taylor as editor,[18] but by March 1898 it needed a subsidy of three pounds a month and it seems to have ceased publication during the same year.[19] No copies appear to be extant.

Renewed labor activity after the Boer War resulted in another paper, the *Belfast Labour Chronicle*, published jointly by the executive committee of the council and the Labour Representation Committee.[20] Its first number appeared in October 1904, and bore the motto "Labour con-

14. B.T.C. minutes, 24 Jan. 1891.

15. Ibid., 28 Feb., 7, 28 Mar. 1891. By July 1900, 3,001 had been subscribed through the council for the *Quinn v. Leathem* case (*N.W.*, 28 July 1900).

16. B.T.C. account book, passim; minutes, 30 Dec. 1899.

17. B.T.C. minutes, 7 Nov. 1895.

18. The photograph of Taylor in the report of the 1898 (Belfast) I.T.U.C. congress has a caption describing him as editor.

19. B.T.C. minutes, 28 Mar. 1898.   20. Ibid., 17 Sept. 1904.

quers all things";[21] it cost one halfpenny. The early issues, consisting of four pages and published once a month, devoted much of their space to corporation affairs. John Murphy seems to have been the editor, but Walker was a constant, and probably the principal, contributor. With the approach of the North Belfast by-election (September 1905) the paper was doubled in size and published weekly. A notice in November claimed that the demand for "the only Labour weekly in Ireland" had become so great that the printing order had been increased by two thousand. "We are pleased to say that we have secured a very large circulation and the journal has now become an excellent medium for business men's advertisements. We want to make the *Chronicle* a thoroughly self-supporting weekly."[22]

With the exception of one issue, the printing was carried out by John Adams, a Belfast printer. The excepted number was printed in Bangor, and the transfer led to charges during the 1905 election that this was done because printing workers' wages were lower there than in Belfast. Walker convincingly rebutted the allegations by showing that printers' wages were the same in Bangor as in Belfast; he added, rather weakly, that Adams had been overburdened with work but that the paper would be printed by him in future.[23] Whatever the relations may have been at that time between the paper's publishers and their printer, they were complicated in December by the appearance in the *Chronicle* of an unsigned article attacking Sir Daniel Dixon, the lord mayor of Belfast and Walker's election opponent. Walker acknowledged authorship of the article but for various reasons could not appear in the subsequent libel action successfully taken by Dixon against Adams.[24] Walker considered that he had been badly treated by Adams and refused to write for the paper, which was nevertheless carried on by Murphy and others.[25] But the *Chronicle* did not pay its way in spite of efforts by the trades council and the Labour Representation Committee,[26] and in all probability it ceased publication in the second half of 1906. The council owed over sixty pounds to Adams on the paper's account in January 1907 and had to spread repayment over several years.[27]

21. Clarkson, p. 489, is incorrect in stating that it was published during 1903–5.
22. *Belfast Labour Chronicle*, 4 Nov. 1905.
23. *Belfast Evening Telegraph*, 6, 8 Sept. 1905.
24. An appeal against the verdict in the High Court (Dublin) was lost (*B.N.-L.*, 27 Jan. 1906).
25. B.T.C. minutes, 7 June 1906.
26. B.T.C. minutes, 17 Mar. 1906. A joint meeting of both bodies was held to deal with the position of the paper.
27. B.T.C. account book, liabilities folowing on statement of accounts for quarter

The extant issues[28] show that the *Chronicle* was concerned chiefly with municipal affairs and personalities, treated with a freedom not altogether unwarranted if some of the charges of corruption were well founded. It also printed statements issued by the L.R.C. headquarters in London, sympathetically supported the campaign in England and Wales carried on by nonconformists against the English education act of 1902, which gave some aid to denominational education, and reported the resistance to compulsory smallpox vaccination. On Irish affairs it was uncompromisingly anti-Home Rule and was obsessed with the fear of Catholic clerical domination.

Labor in the Belfast Corporation

Belfast provided the first Irish parliamentary labor candidate and was also the first Irish city to have a trades council following consciously a political labor policy. The life of the I.L.P. branch in the 1890s had been short and its activities considered with disfavor by the council, but some of the I.L.P. members were also able and hardworking delegates who gradually managed to influence and finally to dominate that body. The hard core of old unionists had been eliminated as early as 1894, when the president, Samuel Monro, and vice-president, Joseph Mitchell, had resigned because they objected to the way in which council delegates to the Norwich congress of the British T.U.C. had been selected and considered that laborers were overrepresented on the council itself. When Taylor reported his interview with them, a heated discussion took place and a motion to accept their resignation was carried by a single vote (28 to 27).[29] Monro later set up in business on his own and did some of the council's printing,[30] while the ironfounder Mitchell seems to have severed all connections with it.

Most of the councillors elected in 1897 were moderate trade unionists, even if they were not as conservative as Samuel Monro. But the tide was running against moderation. The Clyde-Belfast engineering strike of 1895–96 ended in the Belfast members being forced back to work by the decision of the Amalgamated Society of Engineers execu-

---

ending 7 Jan. 1907. Interest was charged on the debt, which was still being paid off in 1911 (statement of accounts for quarter ending 6 Oct. 1911).

28. The issues available seem to be: in 1904 no. 1 (Oct.); in 1905 nos. 12–14 (Sept.), 15, 17, (Oct.), 19, 21 (Nov.), 24 (Dec.).

29. B.T.C. minutes, 29 Aug. 1894.

30. Monro did job-printing for the council (B.T.C. account book, statement of accounts for quarters ending 4 Apr. 1907 and 2 Apr. 1909). McManus had earlier raised the question of giving printing work to Monro (B.T.C. minutes, 6 Oct. 1904).

tive not to continue contingent benefits, and the resultant dissatisfaction led to the election of more militant A.S.E. leaders.[31] During the strike about two thousand engineering laborers were locked out, and on the newly formed Ulster Conciliation Board appeals to the employers to intervene in the dispute were useless, so that the trades council had to content itself with condemning the lord mayor of Belfast and the chairman of the Belfast Water Board, both employer members.[32] The 1897 engineering strike was a further incitement to militancy and materially assisted the trade union candidates in their election. In April 1900 the refusal of the employers to grant a wages advance and a reduction in working hours led to a year-long strike by carpenters,[33] though the South African war was still raging. The trades council's executive committee helped to stage a demonstration in September of the same year.[34] There was, however, no political significance in the procession, for it was accompanied by the Cromwell, Kane Memorial, Ballymacerrett Conservative, and G. W. Wolff flute bands. The *Belfast News-Letter* commented favorably: "The display of Union Jacks and other loyal flags was an exceedingly creditable one, and it was noticeable that the music played by the bands was confined to loyal or patriotic airs."[35] In spite of this pleasing display, the Belfast employers did not hesitate to import nonunion joiners, and when the dispute finally went to arbitration seven months later, the men gained no advance in wages.

In 1899 John Murphy was elected president and William Walker assistant secretary of the council. In the following year Walker became secretary and in 1902 succeeded Murphy, who had retained the presidency in the intervening years. Walker's vote was more than five times that of his nearest rival and was a measure of the ascendancy he had obtained and was to hold for almost the entire decade.[36]

William Walker was born 18 March 1870 in Belfast, the son of Francis Walker, a boilermaker, and served his apprenticeship as a joiner in Harland and Wolff's shipyard, where he assisted in the organizing of the platers' helpers.[37] In 1893 he was a delegate of the Amalgamated Society of Carpenters and Joiners to the Belfast Trades Council, which

31. For an account of this strike see Jeffreys, *The Story of the Engineers*, pp. 140–41.

32. B.T.C. minutes, 24 Oct., 14, 22 Nov. 1895.

33. See Higenbotham, *Our Society's History*, p. 169.

34. B.T.C. minutes, 21 Sept. 1900.   35. *B.N.-L.*, 29 Sept. 1900.

36. B.T.C. minutes, 28 Jan. 1899, 28 Jan. 1900, 12 Jan. 1901, 19 Jan. 1902.

37. The sources used for the early years of Walker's career are R. McClung, Reminiscences, McClung papers, pp. 7–8, Higenbotham, *Our Society's History*, pp. 280–81, and an interview with Walker's widow (May 1962). Higenbotham is incorrect in some details.

elected him to an organization and propaganda subcommittee.[38] When the British T.U.C. met in Belfast in the same year, advantage was taken of the presence of trade union leaders to repeat earlier attempts to organize women linen workers, and Walker made arrangements for a large meeting in the Ulster Hall, where the speakers included Lady Dilke, Miss M. E. Abraham, Keir Hardie, and Ben Tillet.[39] Walker acted as secretary of the new union for several months, but handed over the position to a woman organizer after some criticism of his work.[40]

In 1893 Walker was only twenty-three years of age, but his energy and self-confidence quickly brought him to the front. His youthful looks, set off by artistically long hair, a bohemian tie, and a soft black hat, together with a fluent and aggressive style of speech, made him a favorite orator at the Custom House steps as long as the I.L.P. held meetings there.[41] In 1894 he attended the first congress of the Irish T.U.C. as one of the Belfast Trades Council delegates, and at the banquet was the northern representative who spoke to the toast "The Labour Cause," being chosen in preference to veterans such as Richard Sheldon. After working as a joiner in building and textile machinery firms, he was elected in 1901 as district delegate of his union, the Amalgamated Society of Carpenters and Joiners.[42] The position was a full-time one, but the holder had to seek reelection at the end of each three-year term. Walker served his members well and remained their official until he resigned in 1912 to become a representative of the commissioners appointed under the National Insurance Act.[43] After his death, one of the Belfast branches of his union was named after him.[44]

Appointment as a full-time trade union official greatly enhanced Walker's standing. He resigned from the secretaryship of the trades council when he became an A.S.C.J. official, but was elected president

38. B.T.C. minutes, 4 Mar. 1893.

39. McClung, p. 7; *B.N.-L.*, 9 Sept. 1893. Previous efforts had been made in 1890 and 1891. The first meeting was addressed by Misses Florence Routledge and M. E. Abraham of the Women's Trade Union and Provident League. A Women's Society of Spinners, Preparers and Reelers was formed, but went out of existence in 1891 (B.T.C. minutes, 27 Sept., 10 Oct., 1890, 10 Apr. 1891, and passim).

40. The report of a special committee of the Belfast Trades Council (minutes, 3 Aug. 1894) held that the charges made by a delegate of the Textile Operatives Society of Ireland, the new union, were justified and that the organization needed improvement; the report was adopted by a large majority. Some months later (minutes, 18 Oct. 1894) Walker reported that the membership, 750 at the beginning of the year, had fallen to 250. A motion that a woman organizer be appointed, and that the council and affiliated unions renew financial help, was carried unanimously.

41. McClung, p. 8.   42. B.T.C. minutes, 6 June 1901.

43. Minutes of the managing committee (Belfast district) of the A.S.C.J., 6 Jan. 1912.

44. He died 23 Nov. 1918 (*B.N.-L.*, 25 Nov. 1918).

at the first opportunity, in January 1902. It was in this year that he carried unanimously a motion for the affiliation of the council to the Labour Representation Committee and established himself as the political mentor and director of the Belfast labor movement.

The return of labor representatives to the Belfast corporation was a cherished ambition of the trades council. After the 1901 election it was left with four on the city council (William Liddell, Robert Gageby, Murray Davis, and Edward McInnes) and made a serious effort to increase this number in January 1902. Of the sitting councillors only Liddell had to stand 'for reelection, and when he was given an unopposed return the trades council was left free to concentrate on its two other candidates, William Walker in Pottinger ward and John Murphy in Victoria.[45] The executive committee was unable to have the services of the City Brass Band as it had decided not to take part in any political, religious, or election meetings; instead, two pipers were engaged at 7s. 6d. for a parade. For polling day, twenty-four personation agents were hired at 6s. each.[46] But the council had to be content with a moral victory only, for Walker was beaten more than two to one by a Conservative candidate in his ward.[47] In an inquest on the results, Walker declared that the fights had been the first on purely trade lines and principles, and that the nine hundred labor votes had been secured against powerful Conservative and Catholic associations with money and influence at their disposal. Another delegate once again deplored "the introduction of a religious element," which, he declared, robbed them of a certain victory in Pottinger.[48]

The death of Murray Davis in the same month left a vacancy in that ward.[49] There was a difference of opinion on the advisability of fighting it. Hugh McManus spoke bitterly of the difficulties facing labor candidates: "in his experience he had not been in any local election where the bogey of religion was not raised and flaunted in our faces.[50] The execu-

45. *B.N.-L.*, 7 Jan. 1902.

46. B.T.C. executive minutes, 9 Jan. 1902.

47. *B.N.-L.*, 16 Jan. 1902. The *Belfast News-Letter* editorial expressed satisfaction at the defeat of Walker and Murphy, whom it contrasted unfavorably as labor socialists with the respectable labor councillors, e.g., Gageby and Davis. It also labeled Murphy pro-Boer.

48. B.T.C. minutes, 19 Jan. 1902.

49. Davis died 19 January at the age of forty-eight. He was a member of two Masonic lodges and had been secretary of the Belfast Bakers' Society for thirteen years (obituary and death notices, *B.N.-L.*, 20, 21 Jan. 1902). His full name, Samuel McMurray Davis, was usually shortened to Murray Davis.

50. B.T.C. minutes, 24 Jan. 1902. McManus was Irish organizer (1894–1910) of the Typographical Association (Musson, *The Typographical Association*, pp. 112, 127). He was himself a Catholic (interview with Daniel McDevitt).

tive committee decided that the candidate should be Samuel McCormick, who was a member of Murray Davis's union, the Belfast Bakers' Society. McCormick reported that he had been offered fifteen pounds by an individual to withdraw from the election. He refused to do so, but was defeated.[51] During the campaign he had written to the Belfast Conservative Association asking that the seat be left open to him, an action that produced an angry but inconclusive discussion in the trades council.[52]

There were no labor candidates in the annual elections of January 1903, when as usual fifteen councillors' seats were filled.[53] In 1904 the trades council put up three candidates, Samuel McCormick, William Walker, and Alexander Boyd. McCormick on this occasion was given an unopposed return, Walker had a narrow victory, and Boyd a narrow defeat.[54] But Gageby did not contest his seat and the net result was a total of four labor councillors, as in 1901. In the same month the trades council was informed that Liddell would not complete his term as city councillor and that his seat would be declared vacant in June.[55] In the by-election, the seat was won by Boyd, whose prominence in the new Independent Orange Order gained him support.[56] The victory was welcome, but the total remained the same.

The election results of January 1904 had been declared on 16 January, the date of the trades council meeting. When Walker entered the hall that evening he was given a rapturous reception and the ordinary business of the council was suspended in favor of exultant speeches by the labor councillors and congratulatory resolutions.[57] Enthusiasm, however, was not confined to Belfast; one result of Walker's success was his appointment as president of the 1904 Irish T.U.C., to be held in Kilkenny, for the secretary of the Kilkenny Trades Council wrote

51. The Belfast Conservative Association candidate beat him by 79 votes in a total poll of 2,734. In reply to the B.T.C.'s statement that Murray Davis's seat should be filled by another labor man, the B.C.A. retorted that Walker had opposed their nominee in Pottinger. Dawson, the victor, promised to "follow in the footsteps of the late Mr. McMurray Davis, who was an honorable and straightforward gentleman, and a personal friend of his own" (B.N.-L., 25 Feb. 1902).

52. B.T.C. minutes, 6 Mar. 1902.

53. The Belfast City Council consisted of fifteen alderman and forty-five councillors elected by fifteen wards. Councillors held their seats for three years, fifteen (one in every ward) retiring each January. Aldermen held their seats for six years. In 1904 eight retired, leaving the remaining seven to hold office until 1907 (B.N.-L., 16 Jan. 1904).

54. In Duncairn Walker won by 58 in a total poll of 2884, while in Cromac Boyd lost by 85 out of 2,139 (B.N.-L., 16 Jan. 1904).

55. B.T.C. minutes, 26 Jan. 1904.

56. B.N.-L., 22 July 1904. Boyd had a majority of 239 in a total poll of 1895.

57. B.T.C. minutes, 16 Jan. 1904.

immediately to say that they were waiving the traditional right to have a local man as congress president so that he might preside.[58] Walker's election gave the labor group in the corporation a leader of energy and determination, and hopes for greatly increased representation were high.

The 1905 elections raised the number of labor councillors by one. Henry Howard, the district delegate of the Boilermakers' Society, won comfortably in Pottinger. Boyd retained the seat he had won six months earlier and John Murphy came within 120 votes of gaining a seat in Court ward.[59] The council for the first time contested a seat in Falls, but the candidate, Daniel McDevitt, could make little impression on the electorate, which in that ward was still absorbed in the bitter fight between rival nationalist factions.[60] McDevitt's failure was not unexpected, and the contest was undertaken principally for propaganda purposes. The council had further ill-luck, however, in the loss of Edward McInnes, who had been one of its original councillors, for he had a mental breakdown.[61]

The council's efforts in the 1905 election left it in debt,[62] and an appeal for subscriptions brought in so little that only two candidates went forward in 1906. Both were unsuccessful.[63] Finances, however, improved during the year, stimulated by the British Labour Party's successes and Walker's own parliamentary contests. In 1907 the council made its greatest attempt since 1897 to elect municipal representatives and put seven candidates in the field. All were defeated, including Walker, who did not defend his councillor's seat in Duncairn but stood for the aldermanship of another ward. Only the three labor councillors who had not to vacate their seats were left—Boyd, Howard, and McCormick. The *Northern Whig* commented with satisfaction on the defeat of "the Trades Council party," and pointed out that in reality its only representative was Boyd, as neither of the other two "acknowledge allegiance to its authority."[64]

58. *B.N.-L.*, 8 Jan. 1904.   59. *B.N.-L.*, 17 Jan. 1905.

60. McDevitt attributed his small poll (he came last with 487 votes in a three-cornered contest won by James Macken with 1516 votes) to the fact that the victor had long been a member of the trades council (*Northern Star*, 21 Jan. 1905).

61. Interview with Daniel McDevitt. In April 1906, G. Greig, a Scotsman who succeeded McInnes as N.A.U.L. organizer, informed the council that the McInnes family were in distress and arrangements were made to raise funds to relieve them (B.T.C. minutes, 5 Apr. 1906).

62. B.T.C. minutes, 6 Apr. 1905.   63. *N.W.*, 16 Jan. 1906.

64. *N.W.*, 16 Jan. 1907. The report is inaccurate in that it gives Gageby and Howard as labor councillors no longer under the control of the trades council. Gageby did not return to the corporation until January 1908. It is clear that McCormick was meant.

The 1907 defeat was a severe setback to the council's ambitions, though delegates did their best to explain away the results. The chairman, W. J. Murray, attributed the defeat to the combined action of the "Conservative Association, the Citizens' Association, the Christian Civic Union, the Roman Catholic Defence Association and the Licensed Vintners' and Grocers' Association," and alleged that these bodies had spent between £10,000 and £20,000 on the elections as against the trades council's £200.[65] One candidate, W. Hayes, speaking of his own election fight, said that "to have polled close on a 1,000 votes was a thing of which no man need to be ashamed, and that without the aid of any drink and cigars. It was money that lost the election." The chairman drew comfort from the total labor vote, which he said was greater than in any year since 1897, but he overlooked or neglected to point out that the number of labor candidates was also greater and that their opponents had done better. For a few years the council continued to put up candidates in appreciable numbers, but with negligible success. It was not until January 1920 that a sizable bloc of labor representatives were returned, and then under the more favorable voting system of proportional representation.

The fortunes of labor in the government of the two major Irish cities up to 1907 invite comparison. There was greater cohesion in the Belfast labor group, which, unlike the loosely associated Dublin corporators, had been elected in 1897 as distinctive trade union candidates free of commitments to other parties. They had taken their duties seriously and had held quarterly meetings in which they reported to the electors and trade unionists.[66] When their request for evening sittings of the city council was refused, they attended the daytime meetings, though those councillors who were not full-time trade union officials were inadequately compensated for lost time. A chronic shortage of money handicapped the trades council both in maintaining public representation and financing candidates.

The greatest number of labor councillors at any one time was six, a small minority of the full council of sixty. Most of the original councillors were of the "pure labour" variety and did not earn the hostility of their opponents. Walker and Murphy took a clearer political line, were dubbed "labour-socialist," and met with greater opposition; it became fashionable for the Unionist press from 1902 onward to regret the political attitude of the newer labor candidates, whom they contrasted unfavorably with the moderate older representatives.

65. N.W., 21 Jan. 1907.
66. Lengthy reports of one such meeting were given in B.N.-L., N.W., 27 Apr. 1898, and B.T.C. minutes, 26 Apr. 1898.

The financial weakness of the Belfast Trades Council was an important factor, but not the only one, in the lack of labor success. Death and forced retirements, as in the cases of Taylor, Davis, Bowman, and McInnes,[67] reduced the number of actual and potential councillors. When Walker entered the corporation six years after the first labor councillors had been elected, the team he led was small and its discipline lax. Some trade union candidates detracted from the appearance of unanimity by running as independents.[68] Such councillors as Howard and McCormick were representatives of their unions; Howard's selection had in the first instance been made by his own society, which then decided to ask for the council's endorsement.[69]

Candidates did not hesitate to have nonlabor speakers on their platforms, understandably so in a period when there was no political rank-and-file organization with a well-defined program and constitution. But such a practice caused friction, as when Walker denounced Murray Davis for having as one of his speakers in January 1901 a member of the corporation who employed nonunion labor.[70] Walker himself, however, sought a greater freedom of action in local government elections than might have been expected from the champion of independent labor representation. At the inaugural conference[71] of the Belfast branch of the Labour Representation Committee in 1903, he was successful in removing the words "local government bodies" from a resolution requiring L.R.C. candidates to adhere strictly to a party pledge—"it would offend people they did not want to offend at an election." Walker had been bitterly disappointed by his defeat in 1902 and was evidently determined to win in 1904. His success in that year no doubt confirmed him in the wisdom of his policy, but in the long run it made effective discipline impossible.

67. Taylor had to withdraw from the 1901 election when it was discovered that he was connected with a contractor to the Belfast corporation (B.T.C. minutes, 12 Jan. 1901). While Bowman did not fight his seat in the same election he would have been an obvious future candidate had he not been disqualified after September 1901 as a superintendent of corporation baths.

68. John Spence, an A.S.E. member, was refused endorsement but fought several elections unsuccessfully as an "industrial" candidate (B.N.-L., 16 Jan. 1904, 17 Jan. 1905; N.W., 16 Jan. 1906). J. Mercer, a former delegate, offered himself as a candidate "in the labour interest" for Shankill ward, but his letter was marked *read* (B.T.C. minutes, 2 Nov. 1905).

69. B.T.C. minutes, 6 Oct. 1904. The selection of candidates was normally carried out by the Belfast Trades Council. The procedure in Howard's case was exceptional and resembled that of the Dublin Trades Council. The unsatisfactory results of subsequent endorsement have already been described in the case of Dublin.

70. Ibid., 12 Jan. 1901.

71. N.W., 2, 29 June 1903. The unfinished business of the first day's meeting (30 May) was adjourned until 27 June. Walker's amendment was carried 28 to 16.

Some councillors were inclined to side with the Belfast corporation and its officials against the city's employees. The Municipal Employees' Association complained to the executive committee in 1901 that for two years Murray Davis had been hostile to the interests of their members and submitted a detailed list of grievances.[72] Davis would not attend a meeting to discuss the matter, but wrote that the employees had no grievance and that "he wasn't going to be bounced."[73] The dispute continued for some months and ended only with Murray Davis's death.

In 1904 the Belfast corporation set about acquiring the privately owned tramways system. The Belfast Trades Council approved of the project but objected to the omission and inclusion of certain clauses in the parliamentary bill. The council was very active in pressing objections, and despatched a deputation consisting of Walker, McInnes, and the secretary (John Murphy) to London, where they interviewed some of the Irish nationalist M.P.s and secured certain concessions.[74] But within a week a bitter quarrel broke out over the retention by the corporation of Andrew Nance, who had been manager of the private system. A motion objecting to the appointment of Nance was moved by Murphy and supported by Walker and Boyd (now councillors), but opposed by McInnes. Boyd wished to know if McInnes had changed his views after a personal interview with Nance and Murphy said that he (McInnes) "left himself open to the gravest suspicion of every honest man in the room." Though McInnes characterized Murphy's statement as "untrue, cowardly and unfair," the chairman sided with Murphy and the motion was carried by a majority of over two to one.[75] Much of the energy of the council was spent subsequently in fruitless attacks on Nance. Relations between McInnes and the other labor councillors deteriorated and impaired the work of the group in the corporation. The discovery of an agreement between McInnes and a company engaged in the reconstruction of the tramways system, by which McInnes' union was given sole organization rights, produced a final breach in 1905.[76]

72. B.T.C. executive minutes, 24 Oct. 1901. Davis was accused of opposing the granting of shirt money to stokers, waterproofs and emergency duty money to lamplighters, and "security" (i.e., the oldest men getting good work).
73. Ibid., 30 Oct. 1901.
74. Ibid., 12 May, 11 June, 4 Aug. 1904. They were successful in having clerkships in the transport department filled by competitive examination and securing guarantees about the completion of a section of the system.
75. B.T.C. minutes, 27 Aug. 1904.
76. The council records make no mention of the episode, though some obscure

When facing the electorate the labor councillors were in the embarrassing position of having had some of their program adopted before any of them entered the corporation. The principal public services—gas, water, and electricity—were municipally owned before 1900. The tramways system was taken over a few years later, but at best the trades council could claim only to have hastened its acquisition. Municipal housing had been a labor demand in 1897, but it did not attract public support. The city was growing rapidly, housing conditions by nineteenth century standards were tolerable, and rents were not excessive for the skilled worker in regular employment. Primary school education was poor and insufficient but, since schools were for the most part denominationally controlled, Walker's attempts to have new buildings provided and administered by the corporation were unsuccessful. Labor councillors therefore had to concentrate on defects in administration.

In 1903 Walker had defeated an attempt to strengthen discipline among the labor representatives, and his subsequent conduct weakened it still further. Three months after the failure in the January 1907 elections, W. J. Murray gave notice of a motion instructing the executive committee to draw up a reorganization scheme for the municipal labor group under four heads: (1) joint consultation, (2) a scheme to clear off the council's debt, (3) reconsideration of the municipal program, and (4) consideration of ward organization.[77] The council adopted it at a meeting in June,[78] but in the interval Alexander Boyd had incurred their displeasure[79] and they ceased to have an official representative. Boyd lost his seat in St. George's ward the following year.[80]

In addition to internal difficulties, the trades council had to contend

---

remarks in the *Belfast Labour Chronicle* (18 Nov. 1905) may refer to it. The following is a summary of the account given in a personal interview to the present writer by the late Daniel McDevitt:

> The American construction firm of White and Co. concluded privately with McInnes what may appropriately be described as a "sweetheart contract." Because of a puzzling discrepancy between hourly and weekly wages the B.T.C. sent Walker and McDevitt to interview the American manager. While waiting for him McDevitt picked up a volume lying on the table in the outer office and, with Walker's assistance, discovered that it contained the terms of an agreement whereby McInnes was given exclusive organization rights in return for concessions on wages. McInnes suffered a mental breakdown on the night the matter was reported to the trades council and was committed to an asylum.

77. B.T.C. minutes, 20 Apr. 1907.   78. Ibid., 6 June 1907.

79. They censured him for supporting John Murphy's opponent in a by-election in Dock ward.

80. Boyd, who had to face increased opposition from official Unionists and Orangemen to the Independent Orange Order of which he was a prominent member,

with a number of reformist organizations. Conservative and Liberal-Unionist associations lost ground, but bodies—such as the Belfast Protestant Association, the later formed Citizens' Association and the Christian Civic Union—drew off support that might have gone to a vigorous labor goup. Dissatisfaction with jobbery, corruption, and the state of public health led to the creation of the Citizens' Association early in 1905. The trades council had campaigned against corruption in municipal affairs; Walker had in particular attacked Sir Daniel Dixon, the lord mayor, for allegedly making large profits out of the sale to the corporation of recently purchased sloblands,[81] and labor speakers critized the abnormally high death rate in the city, sending delegates to a special public health conference summoned by the Citizens' Association.[82] But their efforts earned them no electoral dividends. In November 1906 the Citizens' Association held its second annual meeting and claimed that it had a membership of over one thousand as a result of its growth in twenty months. Its president appealed to the "better class of business men" to stand for the city council, and its secretary announced that the association intended to contest the next municipal election.[83]

Traditional Tory strength was reduced in January 1907, but the gains went to the new middle-class organization, which returned five councillors. Independents of various kinds, including independent labor and Sloanite[84] candidates, contributed to the defeat of the trades council. A slight consolation was afforded by the election in Smithfield ward of Michael McKeown, long associated with unskilled trade unionism and a former delegate to the Belfast Trades Council.[85] He was, however, returned as a United Irish League nominee, for the council did not on that occasion venture to fight in either Smithfield or Falls, where the clerical party received its death blow at the hands of the lay nationalist organization directed by Joseph Devlin.

---

was beaten by 507 votes in a total poll of 2,311. Drumming parties and bonfires celebrated his defeat (*B.E.T.*, 16 Jan. 1908).

81. *Belfast Labour Chronicle,* 9 Dec. 1905. Walker reprinted his article and used it in his second election fight against Sir Daniel Dixon (Jan. 1906). Dixon was successful in a libel action against John Adams, the printer. Delays on the part of the defendants, and a mistake in one of the sums mentioned in the article, prevented Walker from appearing in the case. The judge commented dryly on the article's alliterative headlines—"At It Again—Robbing the Ratepayers—Dodger Dan's Deal" (*B.N.-L.*, 27 Jan. 1906).

82. B.T.C. minutes, 3 May 1906.   83. *B.N.-L.*, 9 Nov. 1906.

84. For Sloan, see chap. 12, first section.

85. The council withdrew their candidate, McDevitt saying that McKeown was "a very good labour man" (B.T.C. minutes, 3 Jan. 1907).

The Labour Representation Committee in Belfast

Politics in the strict sense of involvement with either of the main English parties or with Irish nationalists or Unionists found no place in the Belfast Trades Council's deliberations or activities. Most of the delegates were Unionist in as far as they took it for granted that Ireland should remain part of the United Kingdom. When Richard Wortley presided over the Belfast (1898) congress of the Irish T.U.C., he offered the "delegates assembled from the four provinces of Ireland a *cead mille failthe* [sic] to the industrial and commercial capital of Ireland, "but his use of the traditional Gaelic welcome was no indication of nationalist views—the terms "Irish" and "British" were still compatible. The defeat of the second Home Rule bill (1893) and the disorganized state of Irish nationalist politics after Parnell's death assured a degree of tranquility during the long tenure of government by the Conservatives. The Irish question did not become a matter of serious public controversy until after the Liberal victory of 1906.

The trades council was silent on Boer War issues; the I.L.P. branch had collapsed and meetings at the "Steps" had ceased. The only entry in the council's executive committee minutes indicating its feelings is for November 1899—no seconder could be found when a delegate moved that Alex Taylor should represent the council on the lord mayor's Transvaal Refugee Fund.[86] The council contributed to the relief of Gibraltar laborers on strike against Sir George White, the governor,[87] but no delegate used the opportunity to denounce the South African war, as happened in the Dublin council.

In January 1904 the war was discussed in retrospect. J. Keown, a plasterer, introduced a motion protesting against the introduction of indentured Chinese labor on the Rand. His argument was a simple one—the war had cost the British public a large amount of blood and treasure; British labor should be employed "to relieve the urgent strain that England is suffering from at present, that of over-population, and compensate the nation for the great sacrifice made; that sacrifice was made mainly by the working classes of the Empire." The seconder of the motion argued that the war had been undertaken to secure the franchise for the British Uitlanders, but the effect of the Chinese labor ordinance would be to drive the white man out of South Africa. McDevitt considered that the problem of sweated labor in Belfast, rather than that of Chinese labor, should occupy the council's atten-

86. B.T.C. executive minutes, 4 Nov. 1899.
87. Ibid., 22 July 1902. No action was taken on an S.D.F. circular about the strike (B.T.C. minutes, 3 July 1902).

tion. A scriptural condemnation of the South African war came from a delegate who quoted from "an old book—"That whatsoever a man soweth that should he also reap." He thought that "by going to war with the Boers we had entered into one of the most unjust and cruel wars that had ever disgraced a nation, and we were now reaping our reward."[88] The motion was nonetheless carried, only three dissenting.

With the end of the South African war, political labor organization in Belfast revived. The Belfast Trades Council affiliated to the Labour Representation Committee in 1902[89] and in 1903 held a conference to start a Belfast branch of the L.R.C.[90] Most of the delegates came from trade unions, but the Belfast Co-operative Society, the I.L.P., the Clarion Fellowship, the Ethical Society, and the Ruskin Hall Educational League were also represented. The eagerness with which developments in the English labor movement were followed and imitated in Belfast accounts for the existence of the last three bodies.[91]

The conference was held on Saturday, 30 May. The tone had been set by a meeting of postal telegraph clerks addressed by Keir Hardie the previous day. At that meeting the clerks' grievances over wages had been discussed and a resolution passed protesting at the membership of the government committee appointed to consider the matter, a body selected by the Postmaster General that contained no workers' representatives. The meeting also adopted a resolution in favor of direct labor representation, and the speakers emphasized that without such representation no permanent and satisfactory settlement of labor

---

88. B.T.C. minutes, 26 Jan. 1904.   89. Ibid., 18 Oct. 1902.

90. The conference was held in two parts (30 May and 27 June).

91. The Ethical Society and the Clarion Fellowship in Belfast dated from 1897 and 1900 respectively. In 1902 the Clarion Fellowship had offered to assist the trades council in organizing meetings to press for the municipalization of the tramways (B.T.C. executive minutes, 12 Nov. 1902) and some months later was given permission to sell its literature at the postal clerks' meeting that preceded the conference (B.T.C. minutes, 18 Apr. 1903). The date of the reestablishment of the Belfast I.L.P., which was represented at the conference by its secretary, John Burns, is not certain. The I.L.P. annual reports from 1897 to 1902 make no mention of branches in Ireland. The Belfast branch is noted in the I.L.P. branch directory for 1903 and 1904, but it sent no delegates to I.L.P. conferences. In September 1907 three new branches were formed (McClung, Reminiscences, card 14) and from 1909 onward Belfast was represented at the annual conferences. The Ethical Society and the I.L.P. applied to be represented at the conference, as they were not automatically invited, whereas the Belfast Co-operative society was approached by a deputation to secure endorsement of the circular calling the conference and inviting appointment of delegates (B.T.C. minutes, 18 Apr. 1903, B.T.C. executive minutes, 24 Apr. 1903). The Belfast Co-operative Society did not have the intimate connection with the political labor movement that many English societies had, and its leading officials, at least in later years, tended for the most part to be Unionist and Orange in sympathy.

claims could be secured.[92] Two delegates were sent to the next day's conference.

The 112 delegates at the L.R.C. conference in Ye Old Castle Restaurant represented thirty-six amalgamated branches and local unions, as well as the political organizations already mentioned.[93] The A.S.C.J. sent twelve members, the biggest delegation, and the Belfast Trades Council, as joint sponsors with L.R.C. headquarters, represented by Hardie and MacDonald, came next with eleven. The need for labor to have a party of its own was reiterated by speaker after speaker, from Hardie and MacDonald downwards. Edward McInnes and James Dyson, a boilermaker, both proclaimed themselves "ardent" conservatives but were prepared to put their politics on one side in order to do their best "for direct parliamentary representation of labour." Alexander Taylor and Walker referred to Bowman's fight nearly twenty years earlier, Taylor saying that every man must now do his duty, as a small majority of the working-classs vote would have elected Bowman. Each of them moved resolutions that were passed. Taylor proposed support for labor representation in parliament and a pledge to advance the interests of the L.R.C. among trade unionists. Walker's resolution was more specific. It asked that the labor movement generally should unite in promoting labor candidates in favorable constituencies, "of which Belfast is one," and that such candidates, if returned, should "form one of, and loyally co-operate with a labour party in Parliament in advancing the interests of labour and that on all labour matters they shall act independently of other parties."

The conference was adjourned for a month, and when it reassembled the Belfast L.R.C. was finally constituted on the lines proposed by the executive committee of the Belfast Trades Council.[94] Trade union branches were entitled to two delegates per hundred members, with a maximum of five; the trades council itself had eleven, and the Belfast Co-operative Society, the I.L.P., and the Clarion Fellowship two each. The constitution provided for a president, vice-president, treasurer, and secretary, and an executive committee of twelve composed of six representatives of trade union branches, four of the trades council, and one each of the I.L.P. and the Belfast Co-operative Society. John Keown objected to the Clarion Fellowship being represented, saying that the L.R.C. might as well provide for the "Orange Society, the Conserva-

92. *Irish News*, 30 May 1903.

93. *I.N.*, 1 June 1903, which contains the fullest report, including a list of delegates. See also *B.N.-L.* and *B.E.T.* of same date and *N.W.*, 2 June.

94. This account of the adjourned conference is taken from reports in the *B.N.-L* and *N.W.*, 29 June 1903. Clarkson, p. 351, is wrong in stating that "in 1905 the Belfast Labour Party came into being."

tive Association and the Belfast Protestant Association," but his amendment to exclude the Clarion Fellowship was defeated after Murphy had declared amid applause that "as soon as the Orange Society falls into line with the general labour question we will be very happy to receive them."

The officers elected were all leading members of the trades council, so that the new body and the council were governed by an interlocking directorate.[95] The L.R.C. theoretically maintained a separate existence for three years and was useful in mobilizing extra support at election times. It was finally amalgamated in August 1906 with its parent body, the trades council,[96] no doubt to avoid duplication of effort; provision was made for separate balance sheets, but the same delegate could represent their societies on both bodies.[97] A curious discrepancy in membership came to light during a discussion of the details of the fusion. Some nine or ten branches of the A.S.C.J. were affiliated to the L.R.C., but only one to the trades council. The explanation is to be found in the bad relations between the council and Walker over an interunion dispute, and the latter's interest in the L.R.C. as an electoral machine.

The adjourned conference also passed Walker's resolution, which had been previously adopted at the meeting on 30 May, with some changes. Joseph Harris, a delegate of the Amalgamated Society of Upholsterers and a member of the trades council, moved to amend the resolution so that labor representatives on local government bodies would be subject to the same discipline as members of parliament[98] and would be unable to support nonlabor candidates without the consent of the L.R.C. Walker objected to the first part of the amendment, but Harris would not withdraw it; Walker, however, carried a further amendment deleting it.

The month between the two parts of the conference had been used to invite unions to suggest a constituency to be fought and to nominate candidates. John Murphy, now secretary of the L.R.C. as well as of the trades council, reported that there was practical unanimity among the

95. The officers were A. Taylor (president), E. McInnes (vice-president), John Whitla (treasurer), John Murphy (secretary), and Daniel McDevitt (assistant secretary).

96. B.T.C. minutes, 30 Aug. 1906. The Belfast L.R.C. had passed a motion for amalgamation (17 May 1906). A pencil draft of the L.R.C. minutes on a loose sheet in the B.T.C. minute book shows that the officers were still drawn from the B.T.C. in 1906.

97. B.T.C. minutes, 2 Aug. 1906.

98. I.e., that if returned they should "form one of, and loyally co-operate with a labour party in Parliament and *local government bodies*."

trade unions that North Belfast (the scene of Bowman's attempt in 1885) should be fought, but that the twenty branches submitting candidates' names were divided. Robert Gageby and William Walker had each received nine nominations, and Alexander Taylor and Alexander Bowman one each. The suggestion of one union that Walker should fight South Belfast was greeted with laughter, as it would have meant opposing both an official Unionist and Tom Sloan, the independent Unionist M.P. elected the previous year. North Belfast was the final choice and three months later the L.R.C. selected Walker to fight the seat, a decision ratified by the trades council.[99]

Belfast's affiliation to the L.R.C. headquarters in London continued to be the responsibility of the trades council. Hugh McManus and Thomas Hughes attended the 1903 conference at Newcastle-on-Tyne and reported encouragingly on the growth of the organization, for the 240 delegates present represented over 840,000 affiliated members, more than double the number affiliated at the previous conference.[100] The council attached importance to the L.R.C. and always selected its delegates from among its leading figures if they were not attending on behalf of their own unions. At Bradford (1904), the Belfast delegates invited the L.R.C. to hold the 1905 conference in their city, but Liverpool was chosen instead. At Liverpool, Belfast was selected "by a clear majority" as the meeting place for 1906.[101] At the same conference, Walker, present as an A.S.C.J. delegate, was elected to the standing orders committee for the following year and moved a motion of appreciation for MacDonald's work as secretary.[102] The general election of 1906 upset the conference arrangements, so that the conference itself had to be postponed and transferred to London, where John Murphy attended as the council's representative. Belfast finally received the L.R.C. under its new name of Labour Party in 1907 and had the satisfaction of hearing Walker as a principal speaker at a public meeting in the Ulster Hall. The council remained faithful in its affiliation to the British Labour Party and continued to send delegates to annual conferences until 1918.

99. B.T.C. minutes, 1 Oct., 7, 21 Nov. 1903. No L.R.C. minutes are extant, apart from the draft minutes of 17 May 1906, but the trades council minutes contain occasional letters and reports.

100. Ibid., 5 Mar. 1903.

101. Labour Representation Committee, Fifth Annual Report, 1905, p. 54.

102. Ibid., pp. 37, 57. Some amalgamated, and occasionally local, Belfast unions sent Irish delegates to L.R.C. and British Labour conferences, but even after 1906 they did not exceed a half-dozen, mainly from Belfast.

12

Belfast

The Walker Years

The Example of Sloan

In August 1902, T. H. Sloan, a semiskilled shipyard worker, was elected as an independent M.P. for South Belfast. In 1901, Arthur Trew, the founder of the Belfast Protestant Association (B.P.A.), had been sentenced to a year's imprisonment for disturbing a Corpus Christi procession in the city. During his detention Sloan filled Trew's position as Sunday orator at the Custom House steps and leader of the B.P.A. He attacked what he called the Ulster "deadheads," the official Conservative and Orange leaders, declaring that they slighted the Protestant workingman, opposed temperance reform, were unduly tender of ritualism in the Church of Ireland, and disregarded the menace of Rome. At the 12 July 1902 Orange demonstration he accused Colonel Saunderson, leader of the Irish Unionist M.P.s and Grand Master of Belfast, of opposing the inspection of convent laundries, an offense that earned him a two years' suspension from the Orange Order.

William Johnston of Ballykilbeg, M.P. for South Belfast, died 17 July 1902. Though in his later years he had made his peace with the Conservative leaders, he had maintained his earlier reputation of being the champion of Protestant working-class interests, and the B.P.A. determined to contest the seat with a candidate who would follow the same tradition. Trew emerged from prison on 18 July, but Sloan, who had established his ascendancy during Trew's enforced absence and had a strong following among the shipyard workers of Harland and Wolff, received the nomination.[1] The official Conservative and Liberal-Unionist candidate, C. W. Dunbar-Buller, found that he had exchanged the peaceful precincts of All Souls for the very unquiet streets and halls of Belfast. Sloan's followers wrecked his election meetings, and Sloan

---

1. Sloan used to hold evangelical meetings during the midday break. Trew supported Sloan during the election but quarrelled with him later and left the B.P.A.

himself described his unlucky opponent as fighting "Protestantism, Orangeism, total abstinence, trade unionism, and in a word he was fighting Protestant Belfast."[2] The electors of South Belfast gave Sloan an eight-hundred-vote majority.[3]

Sloan carried the Protestant working-class revolt into the ranks of the Orange Order with the assistance of Robert Lindsay Crawford, a member of the Grand Lodge of Dublin and editor of the *Irish Protestant*, a Dublin monthly (from 1904 a weekly) journal strongly low church in temper. In 1903 the two founded the Independent Orange Order, of which Crawford became the first Imperial Grand Master and policy-maker. Under his direction the new order gradually shed its more sectarian features and moved in the direction of a liberal, nonsectarian, strongly democratic nationalism. The order gathered strength rapidly and for some years was a force to be reckoned with in Ulster politics.[4]

During his election campaign Sloan had the assistance of several members of the Belfast Trades Council, principally John Keown, a plasterer, and Alexander Boyd, who had succeeded Alexander Bowman as organizer of the Belfast Municipal Employees' Association, though the council as a whole refused to endorse him. He was the first working-class candidate to be successful in Belfast and his election was an invitation to others to challenge the Conservative and Liberal-Unionist Associations in the city. During a discussion on a motion to endorse Sloan, one delegate held out hopes that the A.S.C.J. might nominate Walker for the constituency, and though they were not realized, such hopes reflected the temper of the time.

Over a third of the delegates supported Sloan, though his sectarianism antagonized many and his claim to be a trade unionist was questioned—it was both asserted and denied that he was a member of the N.A.U.L. Joe Mitchell,[5] the council's assistant secretary, reminded delegates that during the January municipal election in Pottinger, where Walker had been defeated, Sloan and his "comic" man Galbraith denounced Walker all over the city. The strongest arguments on behalf of Sloan were that he was a workingman's candidate and that not to endorse him was to countenance his opponent, who was a landlord. To those who feared that Sloan might be too political (i.e., on the Irish

2. *N.W.*, 7 Aug. 1902.

3. Sloan 3795, Dunbar-Buller 2969, majority 826 (*B.N.-L.*, 19 Aug. 1902).

4. For a fuller account of the Belfast Protestant Association, the Independent Orange Order, and the careers of Tom Sloan and Lindsay Crawford, see J. W. Boyle, "The Belfast Protestant Association and the Independent Orange Order, 1901–10" in *I.H.S.*, xiii (Sept. 1962), pp. 117–52.

5. Joseph Mitchell, a bookbinders' delegate, should not be confused with Joseph Mitchell, an ironfounder, who was B.T.C. president (1886) and vice-president (1894) and resigned together with Samuel Monro.

question), his chief supporter in the debate, W. Nicholl, an iron-founder, declared that "as they were aware, any man going up for a constituency in Ireland must be the one thing or the other, Orange or Green." There was no direct reply to this contention, but one delegate, who declared himself a Protestant, considered Sloan's bigotry an insuperable barrier. "They must admit that the best members they in Ireland had in the House of Commons as regards the Labour cause were the Nationalists, and he did not see for a moment how Mr Sloan could go into the same lobby with those men when he was ridiculing them from one year's end to the other."[6] Had Sloan been less virulent in his sectarianism he would have had the council's official backing, for delegates were united in their desire to see Belfast return an M.P. sympathetic to labor.

The Belfast Protestant Association followed up their success in South Belfast by endeavoring to increase their membership. At the beginning of October they wrote to the trades council asking for the names of secretaries and delegates of affiliated unions. The motion to mark the letter *read* was carried, but only after the defeat of an amendment to authorize the sending of the names requested.[7] A more positive reply to the B.P.A. challenge came a fortnight later when the council unanimously decided to affiliate to the L.R.C., a delegate asserting that they could win East Belfast.[8] The council was committed as a body to fight elections when its representatives to the Newcastle conference (February 1903) of the L.R.C. were instructed to invite speakers from headquarters to address the council on contesting one or more Belfast seats at the next general election.[9] Walker's comment, that local M.P.s would be more amenable to reason if they believed that they would be opposed, was an indirect tribute to Sloan's success. Sloan had owed his victory to more than mere sectarian prejudice; he had appealed to the latent resentment that working-class Protestants nourished for the landed gentry, manufacturers, and lawyers who were their political leaders but who ignored their economic grievances. Nor were delegates unaware that in the House of Commons Sloan voted consistently for social reforms and that his parliamentary record in this respect made him a labor M.P. in all but name.[10]

6. B.T.C. minutes, 7 Aug. 1902. 7. Ibid., 2 Oct. 1902.
8. Ibid., 18 Oct. 1902.
9. Ibid., 5 Feb. 1903. This paragraph in the minutes is headed "Institution of the Belfast L.R.C."
10. Before the introduction, in 1911, of parliamentary salaries, and in the absence of a private income, Sloan was in the financial position of Keir Hardie (and some nationalist members). Sloan was paid £3, later £6 a week, initially by the B.P.A. and subsequently (from the autumn of 1903) by the Independent Orange Order (I.O.O.) (interviews in 1962 with Robert Matchett, born 1871, a former member of the Grand

The choice by the Belfast L.R.C. and the trades council of Walker as the candidate for North Belfast was made toward the end of 1903. During the following year Walker's prestige grew as he won a city council seat in Duncairn ward, was reelected district delegate of his union, and presided over the Kilkenny congress of the Irish T.U.C. In January 1905 the trades council elected him president once again, this time unopposed. Such distinctions were gratifying, but they did not make any direct contribution to the election expenses to be faced. In April, however, John Murphy announced that Walker had been one of the parliamentary candidates chosen by the A.S.C.J. to run under L.R.C. auspices, a decision that meant he would be financed by his society.[11] The general council of the A.S.C.J. had in 1904 proposed a scheme, later accepted by the rank and file, by which three members should be selected to contest suitable parliamentary constituencies. Election costs and a parliamentary salary of 250 pounds per annum plus traveling expenses were to be raised by an annual levy of one shilling per member.[12] Murphy also pointed out that Walker had headed the list in each of the two ballots held by the union. The motion of congratulation he moved was passed unanimously, and he announced that arrangements would be made for a series of meetings in the constituency with Arthur Henderson, an M.P. since 1903, as principal speaker. Walker, replying to the congratulations offered, felt that he had "surpassed himself" even in getting into the first three, "as unfortunately it seemed to be a canon of the amalgamated unions that 'Irishmen need not apply,' but in this instance they had excelled themselves—out of 62,000 votes he had obtained 16,333."[13] He added that his election would be the first contest in Belfast where labor and capital would meet on an equal financial basis, a remark appreciated by a council always handicapped in fighting wealthier opponents.

Walker at this time was the most prominent figure in the Irish labor movement. The Dublin Trades Council in 1903 and the Irish T.U.C. over which he had presided in 1904 had rejoiced at his candidature, and hopes were heightened when he was adopted by an amalgamated union, for it was proof of his standing in the British trade union world. But entire harmony did not prevail within the Belfast Trades Council. A cabinetmaker delegate, speaking to the congratulatory motion on

---

Lodge of Independents, and W. J. Alexander, secretary of the Belfast County Lodge of Independents). It is probable that Sloan also received some financial help, at least during his early years as an M.P., from the Irish Temperance League.

11. B.T.C. minutes, 6 Apr. 1905.
12. Higenbotham, *Our Society's History,* p. 274.
13. B.T.C. minutes, 6 Apr. 1905.

Walker's success in the A.S.C.J. ballots, hoped that he (Walker) would fight as hard for North Belfast as he had for the joiners.[14] The reference was to a demarcation dispute between the two unions. The disagreement had been discussed at a meeting[15] of the trades council a month earlier and a resolution passed that a joint committee of the unions and the council should deal with it. Walker adopted an uncompromising attitude, ignored the suggestion of a joint committee, and declared that the dispute was not a suitable one to be dealt with by the council.[16] The cabinetmakers complained several times about Walker's statements on the issue, and the council, at a particularly acrimonious meeting in July 1905, recommended that an agreement like that operating in other towns be adopted in Belfast and requested a reply within three months. Though the recommendation had been carried by a two-to-one majority, Walker refused to accept it and resigned his presidency of the trades council.[17]

Walker's decision was embarrassing to the council. Some delegates wished to send a deputation asking him to reconsider his resignation—"it would be a great loss to the trades union movement"—but the secretary (John Murphy), normally a stout supporter of Walker, said that it would be useless. He feared that demarcation questions would be decided by the courts "to the discredit and discomforture of trade unionism" if strong unions were to crush small ones and refuse to accept arbitration within the movement. W. J. ("Skin") Murray, a boilermaker, expressed the opinion of various trades when he said that Walker had resigned because the council had reversed an earlier ruling of his. The motion to send a deputation was defeated and Walker's resignation accepted "with regret."[18]

Though the cabinetmakers assented to the council's demarcation scheme within the stipulated time,[19] the A.S.C.J. made no reply. The dispute dragged on into 1906 and was aired again at a council meeting in March. The cabinetmaker delegates were understandably irritated, for they had kept silent for six months in order not to embarrass Walker

14. Ibid., loc cit.   15. Ibid., 9 Mar. 1905.
16. Ibid., 18 Mar., 15 Apr. 1905.
17. Ibid., 20 July, 3 Aug. 1905. Walker also announced that he had given notice of motion in his society (A.S.C.J.) that it withdraw from the trades council and that he placed his poor law and city council seats at the council's disposal. A linendraper delegate (Bloomer) said that "Councillor Walker could not bear to hear any of the delegates give an opinion on the matter contrary to his own without interrupting and disagreeing with them" (N.W., 4 Aug. 1905). Walker did not carry out his threat to have the A.S.C.J. disaffiliate, and his offer to resign from his public offices was not accepted.
18. Ibid., 3 Aug. 1905.   19. Ibid., 5 Oct. 1905.

during his election fights in September 1905 and January 1906; indeed they had not opposed Walker's reelection as president at the beginning of the year. Their motion to condemn the joiners for not putting the demarcation scheme into force was carried, but it was a hollow victory, for a further motion to allow the matter to drop was passed after the council's powerlessness to enforce the decision had been pointed out.[20]

Disagreements between the two closely related trades over the allocation of work were common enough, and they ceased only when the two unions concerned, the Amalgamated Union of Cabinetmakers and the A.S.C.J., were united in 1918.[21] The dispute was, however, not an isolated event, for during 1906 Walker was involved in further quarrels. In June he accused the secretary, John Murphy, of neglecting his duties by attending the Irish T.U.C. instead of staying to deal with a dispute in the linen industry. The secretary in turn asked Walker why he furnished reports to the *Ulster Guardian* when there was a labor paper, the *Belfast Labour Chronicle,* in existence, to which Walker replied that he would never write a line for it while it was printed by John Adams, "who had betrayed them over it." The secretary was defended by other delegates and the executive report, on which most of the discussion had taken place, was adopted.[22]

A month later, as a sequel to the linen industry dispute, W. J. Murray gave notice of a censure motion on Walker. Though he later withdrew it, A.S.E. delegates complained of Walker's action in a demarcation quarrel between their own society and the A.S.C.J. They alleged that he had secured the dismissal of one of their members by reporting the dispute to Alexander Carlisle, the general superintendent of Harland and Wolff's shipyard, instead of first taking it up with the A.S.E. district committee.[23] The subject was debated at a later meeting when Walker was present. Walker denied that he had mentioned any names, saying that the man had been dismissed with other fitters and if similar circumstances arose he would act again in the same way. He refused Murray's invitation to admit that mistakes had been made on both sides. Appeals for peace induced the mover of a censure motion to withdraw and its seconder put forward a modified version. In the end, after a vote in which most of the delegates took no part, the motion was defeated.[24]

20. Ibid., 1 Mar. 1906. The dispute arose over the making of show cases, which the cabinetmakers claimed was done by their members in England and Scotland.

21. Higenbotham, *Our Society's History,* pp. 212–13.

22. B.T.C. minutes, 7 June 1906.   23. Ibid., 5 July 1906.

24. Ibid., 6 Sept. 1906.

The 1905 Election

The year 1905, the last of some nine years of Conservative and Unionist rule, was an eventful one in Irish, and notably in Ulster, politics. In August 1904, Lord Dunraven, the president of the Irish Reform Association, which consisted of a group of moderate Unionist landlords whose cooperation had made possible the 1903 Land Act,[25] drafted proposals for the devolution of certain powers to an Irish financial council and to a statutory body of a partly representative nature.[26] The devolution scheme was made public in September, but despite its restricted scope it provoked a strong reaction from Irish, and particularly from Ulster, Unionists, who saw it as a Home Rule wolf in sheep's clothing. The proposals came to nothing, but the political storm that followed forced the resignation of the Irish chief secretary, George Wyndham, whose under secretary, Sir Antony MacDonnell, had helped to draft them. Ulster Unionists, suspicious of the ability and of the determination of their southern colleagues to resist Home Rule, formed their own council in December. In March 1905 it held its first public meeting and was henceforward known as the Ulster Unionist Council. When a serious Home Rule crisis developed in 1911, it stood ready to assume the powers of a provisional Ulster Unionist government; in the meantime it served as the rallying point for Ulster, as distinct from Irish, Unionism.

A further event of special interest in Ulster politics was the appearance of the Magheramorne manifesto,[27] drafted by Lindsay Crawford and adopted by the Independent Orange Order on 13 July 1905. This

25. The act enabled Irish tenants to buy their holdings with government-financed loans repayable over a term of years.

26. The proposals were in brief: (1) a financial council to administer Irish expenditure; (2) the council to consist of the Lord Lieutenant as president with twelve elected and twelve nominated members, one of whom would be the Chief Secretary; (3) methods by which Irish revenue might be raised; (4) a statutory body to deal with certain Irish business of a parliamentary nature, the body to consist of Irish representative peers, the Irish members of parliament, and members of the financial council past and present. For a detailed account of the origin and fate of the proposals see F. S. L. Lyons, "The Irish Unionist Party and the Devolution Crisis of 1904–5," in *I.H.S.*, vi. 1–22.

27. The manifesto was printed in full in the *Northern Whig* and the *Irish News*, 14 July 1905, in the *Irish Protestant*, 22 July 1905, and in pamphlet form. It derived its name from the place, Magheramorne, Co. Antrim, where the Independent Orange demonstration was held. As the "Twelfth" fell on a Sunday, Orange demonstrations were held on the following day. For details of the origin and reception of the manifesto see Boyle, "The Belfast Protestant Association and the Independent Orange Order," *I.H.S.*, xiii. 117–52.

remarkable document attacked clericalism and sectarianism of all kinds in Irish politics, demanded that clerical control of education be abolished, and called for compulsory land purchase to hasten the transfer of holdings to tenant farmers and for the support of the claims of town tenants. It condemned Dublin Castle government and the two major English political parties as playing off "Irish Protestants and Nationalists against each other to the prejudice of our country." It rejected the Dunraven devolution proposals as undemocratic on the grounds that the councils they envisaged relied too much on nomination instead of election, but it said nothing about the Act of Union. Instead its conclusion declared that Ireland needed "a patriotic party with a sound constructive policy that will devote itself to the task of freeing the country from the domination of impracticable creeds and organised tyrannies and to securing the urgent and legitimate redress of her many grievances."

The Unionist press immediately denounced the manifesto as a devolutionist document, singling out for special condemnation the phrase "Unionism is likewise a discredited creed." Though there were a number of defections,[28] and some wavering on the part of Tom Sloan, Crawford was able to hold the order behind the manifesto, and he and Sloan continued to work together for the rest of the year.

While the repercussions of the devolution proposals were still being felt, and Unionists were sounding the alarm over the Magheramorne manifesto, Walker was faced with his first parliamentary contest. Sir James Hazlett, the sitting member for North Belfast, died in August 1905 and a by-election ensued. The Belfast Trades Council held a special meeting, repudiated the suggestion of a section of the Belfast press that the demarcation dispute would affect the council's support for Walker, and passed a unanimous resolution endorsing him.[29] The Conservative candidate was a local timber merchant, Sir Daniel Dixon, lord mayor of Belfast, and a constant target for Walker's attacks in corporation affairs.

The labor candidate's campaign was vigorous and thorough. L.R.C. headquarters supplied Ramsay MacDonald as election agent and Arthur Henderson as principal visiting speaker. In spite of Conservative posters denouncing MacDonald as pro-Boer and a Home Ruler, and attacks on Henderson as a nationalist ally, labor meetings were held successfully in every part of the constituency. A dinner-hour audience

28. One of the defectors was John Keown, the B.T.C. plasterers' delegate who had chaired an election meeting for Sloan. Alexander Boyd, on the other hand, continued to support both the B.P.A. and the I.O.O.

29. B.T.C. minutes, 22 Aug. 1905.

at Workman and Clark's shipyard listened attentively even to Ramsay MacDonald,[30] though many shipyard workers were by tradition violently Orange and Unionist. In a preelection address Walker had announced himself as a Unionist in politics who desired "to cooperate with any section of parliament on social questions."[31] At one meeting he made a strong appeal for support to the Protestant working class when he announced that the contest was unique since members of both the new and the old Orange orders were on his brake. He refused however to rely on "any party, section, or religious bigotry. Catholics and Protestants, though not agreeing on certain grounds, should agree on others when it was a question of the Workman's Compensation Act, the amendment of the Factories Act, and an Old Age Pension scheme."[32]

The enthusiasm shown for Walker throughout the constituency alarmed the Belfast Conservative press, which feared in North Belfast a repetition of the defeat suffered earlier in the 1902 by-election in South Belfast. The speakers at Dixon's inaugural meeting, held in Clifton Street Orange Hall, were shouted down by a combination of Sloanites and Walkerites and a melee broke out in which, as Devlin's paper, the *Northern Star,* joyfully put it, "the furniture and fittings of the hall suffered sadly."[33] The alliance between labor and dissident Unionist supporters was further emphasized by the presence on Walker's platform of such men as Alexander Boyd of the Independent Orange Order. Boyd during these weeks was also speaking with Sloan on behalf of Richard Braithwaite, the secretary of the Belfast Protestant Association, in a municipal election against Lord Shaftesbury.[34] Walker himself at one of his own meetings adopted Sloan's language and sentiments, saying that "as soon as they sent men to the House of Commons who had a strong love for their fellows they would smash the deadheads of Ulster, and remove the objections the labourers of England had to the Ulster Unionist Party."[35]

The South Belfast by-election of 1902 had taken place at a time when Home Rule was a dormant issue, but the devolution proposals and the Magheramorne manifesto aroused suspicions that prompted

30. McClung, Reminiscences, pp. 12–13.

31. *N.W.,* 24 Aug. 1905.   32. *N.W.,* 6 Sept. 1905.

33. *Northern Star,* 9 Sept. 1905. McClung estimated that some sixty percent of the audience were Walkerites and Sloanites. The chairman, a linen manufacturer named Sir William Ewart, opened by saying, "Ladies and gentlemen, this is a splendid meeting and I only wish some of the Walkerites were here." A joiner spoke up, "Man, we are all here," whereupon pandemonium broke out and continued until the meeting ended. Subsequent meetings were heavily stewarded and potential interrupters refused admission (McClung, p. 12).

34. *N.W.,* 9 Sept. 1905.   35. *N.W.,* 6 Sept. 1905.

official Unionism to question the *bona fides* of Walker and of dissident Unionist candidates. The principal Unionist newspapers carried editorials and the usual anonymous letters signed "A Protestant" or "Shipyard Worker," questioning the labor candidate's loyalty in view of his association with Henderson and MacDonald. One Unionist speaker made the charge that when Walker presided at the Irish T.U.C. dinner in Kilkenny, no toast of "The King" was given, but instead "Ireland a Nation."[36] Walker redoubled his assurances, excusing English labor support for Home Rule on the grounds that every Irish Unionist member of parliament, with the exception of the independent Sloan, had voted against an eight hours' bill for miners, but asserting that if they returned to the House of Commons a man who "was a Unionist, plus a labour representative, they would be striking the greatest blow that could be struck against the maintenance of Home Rule opinion in England."[37] This assertion was greeted with cheers, as was also a categorical statement that if returned he would vote against Home Rule. Even MacDonald assured the audience that Walker, as an M.P., would be free to vote as he pleased on the issue and would not be subjected to any pressure: "In this contest there was no question of Home Rule, because Mr Walker was perfectly sound from their point of view."

Though the Belfast press, with the exception of the nationalist *Irish News,* sided with Dixon and gave little coverage to Walker's campaign, the Unionists were increasingly apprehensive of the outcome as polling day, Thursday, 14 September, approached. The labor attack on Dixon and his supporters was extremely damaging. Dixon's record in the allocation of municipal contracts, which included the purchase of tramwaymen's clothing from a London sweatshop, and in the sale to the corporation of land owned by him, was fully exposed at Walker's large and numerous meetings, as was his constant opposition to fair wages for corporation employees and to reforms in housing and education.[38]

36. *N.W.,* 6 Sept. 1905. According to John Murphy, who was present with Walker at Kilkenny, no northern delegate had seen the toast list before the dinner began. On Murphy's suggestion, E. L. Richardson, secretary of the parliamentary committee of the Irish T.U.C., conferred with the chairman, Councillor McCarthy of the Kilkenny Trades Council. McCarthy spoke to the toast's proposer, who made no statement "which could give offence to the most loyal man in Ireland. Some of the Ulster representatives present, thinking no evil, honoured the toast, but Mr Walker and I kept our seats" (open letter of Murphy to Ramsay MacDonald, *Belfast Labour Chronicle,* 12 Sept. 1905).

37. *N.W.,* 7 Sept. 1905.

38. The London firm Hyman Lotery paid 6*d.* per jacket to outworkers making boys' reefer jackets; a mother and daughter by working fourteen hours a day were able to earn only 4*s.* per day. Boys' suits were paid for at the rate of 5½*d.* per suit (*Truth,* 12 Apr. 1900, quoted in *Belfast Labour Chronicle,* 23 Sept. 1905). Dixon's sale of land to

One speaker, indignant at a Conservative's belittling of Walker's nominators, retorted that at least it was not they who had turned Carrick House into a brothel, while a *Chronicle* editorial referred to Dixon as a man who "has but narrowly escaped 'the stench of the Divorce Court.'"[39]

In spite of large numbers of paid canvassers, of bribes and of intimidation,[40] prospects of an official Unionist victory grew dimmer as Walker continued to win more Protestant workers. There remained the Catholic voters in the constituency, estimated at about one thousand. The *Irish News* was not unsympathetic to the labor candidate and Joseph Devlin's weekly *Northern Star* gave him qualified encouragement: "The Nationalist vote might just make all the difference in the case of a close contest, and as Mr Walker, the Independent Orange Candidate, professes Labour sympathies, he is certain to attract a large element of support. The issue will be decidedly interesting."[41] An official Unionist candidate could scarcely expect to attract even a sizable minority of nationalist votes; at best he might hope that they would not be cast for either candidate. Dixon took some care to avoid extreme sectarian statements in his election address, had it published in the nationalist press (it appeared twice in the *Northern Star*), and gave prominence to his support for the reform of the poor law system, the provision of old age pensions, and the improvement of workmen's compensation acts.[42] He declared his opposition to the establishment or endowment of any sectarian university in Ireland,[43] and called for a shortening of drinking hours. The lord mayor was himself no total abstainer, but he was regarded with amused tolerance by many, who preferred his free-and-easy manners (he had started life as a joiner in

---

the corporation included the site of Dundonald cemetery and some sloblands for sewage purification works.

39. *Belfast Labour Chronicle*, 12, 23 Sept. 1905. Carrick House was a municipal common lodging house, the subject of an earlier scandal involving Unionist councillors. Sir Daniel Dixon's misadventures figured in satirical verses and election songs, replete with references to "Daniel in the Lyons' den"—the Lyons were near neighbors of Sir Daniel.

40. Ibid., 23 Sept. 1905. The local report to the A.S.C.J. headquarters stated that "so patent was the corruption even to the man in the street that eight days before the election Mr J. Ramsay MacDonald . . . advised doing no more fighting but to permit matters to run their course and then claim the seat on petition" (Higenbotham, *Our Society's History*, p. 230).

41. "The Week at Home," *Northern Star*, 2 Sept. 1905.

42. Text in *N.W.*, 30 Aug., *Northern Star*, 2, 9, Sept. 1905.

43. The reference is to the Catholic demand for state assistance to the Catholic University in Dublin, of which John Henry Newman had been rector.

Ballycastle, County Antrim) to the frock-coated virtue of some of his predecessors. Nor was he unique in making money from selling property to the corporation, for councillors frequently bought and sold land on the outskirts of the growing city.

The Belfast Protestant Association, though it had been rebuffed some years earlier by the Belfast Trades Council, was determined to intervene in the election. Its secretary Richard Braithwaite, armed with a series of questions drawn up by the council of the Imperial Protestant Federation, interrupted his own municipal campaign against Lord Shaftesbury to demand answers from both candidates. The fourteen questions, some of them in the Maria Monk tradition, would antagonize Catholic voters if answered in the affirmative. Braithwaite made numerous attempts to interview Sir Daniel Dixon, but Dixon's agent used delaying tactics and at last insisted that Walker must be approached first, since Sir Daniel's Protestant and loyalist *bona fides* was beyond suspicion. Walker in turn evaded Braithwaite for some time until finally the B.P.A. secretary encountered him alone a week before polling day, 14 September. Pressed hard and fearful of losing Sloanite votes, Walker, without consulting his election committee, answered the questions to the satisfaction of the B.P.A.[44] He committed himself to the retention of the sovereign's accession declaration against transubstantiation[45] (which described "the sacrifice of the mass" as "superstitious and idolatrous"); to the continued exclusion of Roman Catholics from the offices of Lord High Chancellor and Lord Lieutenant of Ireland; and, in answer to a question as to his willingness, in all things, to place the interests of Protestantism before those of the political party to which he was attached, to the statement that "Protestantism means protesting against superstition, hence true Protestantism is synonymous with labour."

When Ramsay MacDonald and the election committee were presented with Walker's answers there was consternation in Tudor Place, the labor headquarters. The general opinion was that the one thousand Catholic votes had been lost. MacDonald's first reaction was to throw up his position as agent, but he was persuaded to stay. The B.P.A. then approached Dixon's agent, who affected to disbelieve their claim that Walker had answered the questions. When he was shown Walker's

44. Interviews with Daniel McDevitt, George Scanlin, and William Boyd. The questions, and Walker's answers, are given in Appendix 7.

45. Text in Sir C. G. Robertson, ed., *Select Statutes, Cases and Documents* 8th ed., London, 1947, pp. 137–38. A bill to modify the declaration was introduced into parliament in 1901, but was not proceeded with. The declaration was finally modified by the Accession Declaration Act, 3 Aug. 1910 (1. Geo. V. c. 29).

replies, he turned the B.P.A. officials out, prepared handbills containing the questions and answers, and had them circulated at a Holy Family confraternity meeting shortly before polling day.[46]

The B.P.A. document was printed in Lindsay Crawford's paper, the *Irish Protestant,* on Saturday, 9 September, and in the *Northern Whig* on the following Monday. On Monday evening the Belfast executive of the United Irish league held a private meeting to consider the North Belfast election. No statement was issued, but opinion was divided on the disposition of the nationalist vote, according to the *Whig* correspondent, who hopefully believed that it would go to Dixon.[47]

Though the Catholic vote was doubtful, Walker's supporters were in good heart. They had made a thorough canvass of the constituency and had been favorably received by all but the most intransigent Conservative supporters.[48] On polling day the display of blue and white favors and the stream of voters to labor tally rooms promised victory. But Dixon's pink favors were worn by over one thousand paid canvassers, 725 vehicles carried his voters to the polls and Unionist out-voters had their expenses and first-class fares paid.[49] Unionist election expenses, according to the not unbiased *Belfast Labour Chronicle,* were "six or seven times" the thousand pounds they should have been. To his followers outside the city hall Walker promised that he would be at the head of the poll at the general election:[50] he had been defeated by less than 500 votes.

The high expectation of success and the mixture of anger and disappointment at the result among Walker's supporters found expression in the editorial of the *Belfast Labour Chronicle.* Headed "A Discredited City," it asserted that Dixon's return could be explained only on the assumption that "a great many of the voters in the division are either invincibly ignorant or hopelessly corrupt." Dixon was "a wealthy and ignorant old dotard" in whose election "every dodge incident to parlia-

46. The fullest account of the entire episode was supplied by McDevitt, who was at the center of the election campaign. Confirmatory evidence of some details came from Scanlin, Boyd, and R. R. Campbell, son of D. R. Campbell. I have been unable to trace the handbills in question, but see John Gray, *City in Revolt,* pp. 37–8.

47. *N.W.,* 11, 12 Sept. 1905.

48. McClung, pp. 13–14, tells of canvassing an elector who would have made an admirable senator under Caligula. "Logan and I called on a man in Foyle Street, and we suggested that he should vote for the best man (Walker) irrespective of parties, but he replied that he was a party man and would vote for an ass if the Conservative Party instructed him to do so." Another voter was more discriminating, if equally impratical, for he announced that he would vote for "King Billy," i.e., William of Orange.

49. Local report to A.S.C.J. headquarters (Higenbotham, p. 280).

50. *N.W.,* 16 Sept. 1905. Dixon had a majority of 474 in a total poll of 8,406.

mentary elections in the days of pocket boroughs were [sic] resorted to without scruple or shame." The writer was confident that an election petition would unseat Sir Daniel, but the cost would be £1000 to £1500, "about double the sum spent by the Labour Party" in the election, and there was no guarantee that Walker would not have to fight the seat a second time. The editorial contrasted Walker's "unsullied reputation in private life" and his record of public service with the sullied reputation and reactionary career of Dixon, "this foe of the people." It added that Walker believed in the "Union between Great Britain and Ireland and," with a glance at Dixon's private life, "in the union between one man and one wife, in spirit and fidelity." It made no reference to the B.P.A. questions, nor did it attempt an analysis of voting figures. It ended with the assertion, "Next time we will win."[51]

The North Belfast election had been followed closely in England. Some days after the declaration of the poll, Pete Curran, the I.L.P. and Gasworkers' Union veteran and an original executive committee member of the L.R.C., wrote to the *Daily News* protesting at Walker's description of himself as a "Unionist in politics" on the grounds that he had violated the L.R.C. constitution. He contended that Walker was in the same category as a candidate describing himself as a Liberal or Conservative, and defended his own Home Rule opinions by arguing that self-government for Ireland was "essentially a labour question," because the country's industrial resources would never be developed until the Home Rule question was settled once and for all.[52]

The executive committee of the A.S.R.S. supported Curran's objection and requested the L.R.C. to explain their endorsement of Walker as a "Labour Unionist" candidate. Walker, however, did not lack defenders. Among the writers to the *Daily News* was T.R.J. of Belfast, who argued that "the workmen who have been weaned from Conservatism in favour of Independent Labour representation are expected by Mr Curran to support without question the Liberal Party's proposal known as Home Rule."[53] The *Chronicle* in the same issue announced that the L.R.C. executive committee had "come to the sensible finding that Mr Walker had stood as a labour candidate only" and remarked that Curran might never have written his letter if he had not been a candidate for Jarrow, where there was a strong Irish nationalist vote.

The *Daily News* controversy was repeated in the Belfast Trades Council. One meeting was abandoned after an excited delegate had

51. *Belfast Labour Chronicle*, 23 Sept. 1905.
52. Quoted in *Belfast Labour Chronicle*, 25 Sept. 1905.
53. Ibid., 30 Sept. 1905. T. R. J. was Thomas R. Johnson, later a leading supporter of Home Rule, president and secretary of the Irish T.U.C., and a leader of the Irish Labour Party in the Dáil.

declared that the Belfast press, "rotten to the core," was responsible for Walker's defeat, and when he had been ruled out of order, accused some delegates of being rotten trade unionists who, instead of voting for Walker on the day of the poll, had been running around looking for drink.[54] In October a calmer discussion took place on a circular from J. R. Clynes of Oldham, the trades councils' representative on the L.R.C. executive. Clynes's defense of Walker was a reply to an attack in the *Manchester Evening News*. A motion to mark the letter *read* was defeated in favor of an amendment to refer it to the executive committee, which could draw up a resolution and give its views on the matter to the next L.R.C. conference.[55]

The controversy over the "Unionist in politics" phrase was renewed on the arrival of a letter from the Rotherham Trades Council asking for the Belfast council's opinion. After a lengthy debate the closure was applied, and an amendment to give the decisions of the L.R.C. executive committee as the opinion of council carried against a motion to mark the letter *read*.[56] Later in the same month (November) John Murphy as secretary moved a resolution for the L.R.C. conference declaring that Walker had stood solely as a labor candidate; after some objections that it had not been discussed by the executive committee, it was carried by 18 votes to 12.[57] At the same meeting a stiff debate took place on a proposal to add the Irish nationalist to the Liberal and Conservative parties as banned organizations in the L.R.C. candidates' pledge. A delegate's pleas that the change would be disastrous to the Labour Party, as the nationalists were the best friends of labor in the House of Commons, were disregarded and the motion carried by 22 votes to 9. The balance was redressed when, on a 29-to-8 vote, the Unionist Party was also proscribed.

The general election of January 1906 caused the L.R.C. conference to be held in London instead of Belfast. By the casting vote of the chairman, Walker, the council decided to send one delegate, the secretary, to London. He was allowed at his discretion to drop the resolution affirming that Walker had stood as a labor candidate only.[58]

At the London conference John Murphy withdrew the resolution on Walker but moved the council's amendment to the party pledge.[59] He

54. B.T.C. minutes, 16 Sept. 1905.   55. Ibid., 21 Oct. 1905.
56. Ibid., 2 Nov. 1905.   57. Ibid., 18 Nov. 1905.
58. Ibid., 25 Jan., 1 Feb. 1906.
59. "Clause II. Object: To secure by united action the election to parliament of candidates promoted in the first instance by an affiliated society or societies in the constituency who undertake to form or join a distinct group in parliament, with its own whips and its own policy on labour questions, to abstain strictly from identifying themselves or promoting the interests of any section of the Liberal or Conservative parties, and not to oppose any other candidate recognized by this committee. All such

disclaimed any intention to bar cooperation, wishing merely to declare labor's independence: "They did not regard Home Rule in the North of Ireland as being a labour question."[60] Murphy was supported by Charles Darcus, the Belfast T.A. delegate, and by J. Jones, a Liverpool Irish stonemason. Jones, though he proclaimed himself a Home Ruler, "not only for Ireland, but for every other country," denounced labor "hobnobbing" with the Irish party, which he said contained some most reactionary men. James Sexton, the secretary of the N.U.D.L., countered by quoting the support given by the Irish nationalist M.P.s to the Trades Disputes bill and thought that they could leave it to the labor men "in the Irish party to work out the salvation of that party."

The last speakers were two Belfast delegates. Joseph Glennon (U.K. Society of Coachmakers) described the B.T.C.'s amendment as "absurd and ridiculous," more especially as the council by resolution had supported at least one nationalist candidate in Belfast at the general election.[61] Walker, present as an A.S.C.J. delegate, scouted the idea that the nationalist M.P.s were disinterested in traveling to London to vote for the Trades Disputes bill. Dozens of Liberals—and Tories—did the same. Support would be forthcoming in proportion to labor's independence. "They must remember that the bulk of the men from whom they must draw their recruits in Ulster and in Lancashire were Tories, but how were they going to do that if it could be said that the labour movement was open to an alliance with the Nationalist Party. That party had men in its ranks true on labour questions, and they wanted those men to come out of that party into their party—the Internationalist Party (cheers)."

The amendment was carried with only a few dissentients. On the following day Sexton moved a further amendment that L.R.C. candidates should not "include in their election addresses any expression of political faith other than that of the Labour Party." He would have withdrawn his amendment, he said bitterly, had it not been that on the previous evening one had been adopted" in order to accommodate the peculiar morals of Belfast." When a delegate asked if there were no peculiar morals at Liverpool as well,[62] he replied that they were bad

candidates shall pledge themselves to accept this constitution, to abide by the decisions of the group in carrying out the aim of this constitution, and to appear before their constituencies under the title of Labour candidates only" (L.R.C. Sixth Annual Report, p. 50).

60. The debate is given in the same L.R.C. report, pp. 50ff.

61. The reference is to the B.T.C. endorsement of Devlin discussed later in this chapter. In 1890 Glennon protested that the then B.T.C. secretary, F. C. Johnston, had compromised the council by acting as a Unionist lecturer in England.

62. The N.U.D.L. headquarters were at Liverpool, which, like Glasgow, had substantial numbers of Orange and Hibernian immigrants.

enough, but he drew the line at Belfast. He went on to complain that while Will Thorne was not endorsed at South West Ham because he was a socialist, Walker could proclaim himself a "Unionist in politics" and be "whitewashed by the Executive." But the conference was not prepared to reverse the previous day's decision and Sexton's amendment was lost.

There was curiously little comment on the B.P.A. questions in the trades council, though the explanation may be that any prolonged discussion of them might have disrupted the organization. Hugh McManus, speaking on the Rotherham Trades Council letter did, however, refer to them. Arguing that the L.R.C. had not the whole of the facts before them in making their decision, he gave it as his opinion that Walker should not have answered the questions, as they had no connection with labor.[63] The chairman ruled that the points raised by McManus were irrelevant, as the L.R.C. had been concerned solely with Walker's views on Home Rule. Comment of a more pungent kind came from outside. "Stargazer" in Devlin's *Northern Star* considered that Walker had been responsible for his own defeat.

Mr Walker might have counted on the Nationalist vote had he been a genuine labour candidate, professing merely Unionist proclivities, for, as between two Unionists the Nationalist Party ever supports the more tolerant and progressive of the two, especially if he happens to be a Labour candidate. But Mr Walker showed himself to be not only a violent Unionist, but a rabid bigot to boot.

In a word, Sir Daniel Dixon played his cards admirably, completely outwitting the Labour nominee. He refused to be badgered into signing the blasphemous declaration consisting of a series of questions put to him by the Belfast Protestant Association of bigoted guttersnipes.[64]

One further reference to the questions was made in the council. When it discussed Walker's renomination for the general election of 1906, Joseph Glennon opposed endorsement because he (Walker) "had entered into political and religious entanglements from which their candidates should be absolutely free. He had dragged himself through the party mire of the city up to the neck, and this would be laid at the door of trade unionism."[65] George Greig, a Scotsman and local organizer of the N.A.U.L. in succession to McInnes, pleaded for solidarity among trade unionists, saying that they should not fasten upon one mistake in a heated election campaign. His plea was accepted and Walker was endorsed by a vote of 36 to 2.

63. B.T.C. minutes, 2 Nov. 1905.   64. *Northern Star,* 23 Sept. 1905.
65. B.T.C. minutes, 16 Dec. 1905. Glennon was elected to the executive committee of the council in 1906 and 1907.

The Three-Leaved Shamrock

A triple alliance of Liberal, Labour, and Irish nationalist voters helped to determine the outcome of the general election of 1906 in Great Britain. A more tenuous alliance,[66] less public and with local variations, operated against the Unionists, especially in the north. In Belfast three of the four divisions were contested. Sloan defended his South Belfast seat, Walker again fought North Belfast, and Joseph Devlin, secretary of the United Irish League and National president of the Ancient Order of Hibernians, left his safe North Kilkenny seat in an attempt to win back West Belfast, which had been in Unionist hands since Thomas Sexton lost it in 1892.[67]

Walker was not the only candidate challenging the official Unionists in Belfast to have some disharmony in his camp. Sloan, though a signatory of the Magheramorne manifesto, had been apologetic and defensive in the face of Unionist press attacks on it, and it was some time before Lindsay Crawford was able to recall him to the straight path. But with the approach of the general election he deviated once more, this time going to the lengths of issuing a full recantation of anything in the manifesto that might be construed as "antagonistic to the settled policy of the Unionist Party in Ulster," promising loyal cooperation with the Ulster Unionist Party at Westminster and attending as a member of the platform party the Ulster Unionist Council's demonstration on 2 January 1906.[68] His apostasy was denounced by Colonel Hutcheson-Poe of the Irish Reform Association and by Crawford, who confirmed that a suggestion had been made to have the Independent Orange Order oppose him in South Belfast.[69] Official Unionist leaders had earlier promised Sloan a clear run if he removed Independent Orange opposition to their candidates elsewhere, but as he was unable to do so he found himself facing a Conservative and Unionist candidate, Lord Arthur Hill, in his own constituency. Fearful of losing left-wing Independent Orange, Labour, and nationalist votes, he hastily made a partial withdrawal of his recantation.[70]

Devlin was not threatened by dissensions among the nationalist

66. On reading this section the late Mr. Fred Carson, who was a youthful Labour supporter at that period, contended that the alliance amounted to no more than a fellow-feeling common to opponents of the official Unionists.

67. When, nine years after the Parnell split, the Irish parliamentary party was reunited in 1900 under John Redmond's leadership, the United Irish League became its organization in the constitutencies. The split in the Ancient Order of Hibernians, divided since 1884, was substantially healed in 1902 and Devlin was elected its leader two years later.

68. *B.N.-L.*, 1 Jan. 1906; *I.N.*, 3 Jan. 1906.

69. *I.N.*, 5, 8 Jan. 1906.   70. *B.N.-L.*, 9 Jan. 1906.

voters in West Belfast. On the national level unity had been restored in
1900,[71] while in West Belfast the war between the clerically dominated
Catholic Association and Devlin's lay organization, now the local section of the United Irish League, had ended in 1905 with the rout of the
former. His national secretaryship of the U.I.L. made him a key figure
in Irish politics, but his control of the Ancient Order of Hibernians
(A.O.H.) was of greater local importance. The A.O.H., the Catholic
equivalent of the Orange Order, flourished in the sectarian atmosphere
of Ulster. "Wee Joe," the affectionate nickname by which he was
known in the constituency where he had started his working life as a
barman, in a remarkably short time built a personal political machine
of great efficiency from the Belfast branches of the A.O.H.[72]

The sectarian nature of the A.O.H. did not prevent Devlin seeking
support from beyond its ranks. One of his meetings was addressed by
Hugh McManus and attended by Protestants as well as Catholics. Its
chairman, John Rooney, was so moved by the honor of presiding over a
mixed audience that he had recourse to a Patrician symbol: "He sin-
cerely hoped their efforts would result in the blending of Orange and
Green on Thursday next, and that it would be a three-leafed victory.
They had a shamrock with the name of Devlin on it, and he trusted that
next Friday morning it would bear three names—Devlin, Walker,
Sloan (three cheers)."[73]

The trinity was indeed endorsed by the Belfast Trades Council, but
not *en bloc*. The council had sent to candidates in several constituencies
a list of eighteen questions on their attitude toward trade union demands (the amendment of acts governing workmen's compensation,
industrial disputes, and an eight-hour working day) and toward
matters of more general interest (old age pensions, the Chinese labor
ordinance, housing, temperance and poor law reform, adult suffrage,
and payment of M.P.s).[74] In North Belfast Sir Daniel Dixon was not
troubled with the list, and Walker was formally endorsed. In South
Belfast little time was wasted. A motion expressing support for Sloan
had been moved in May 1905, when it seemed likely that he would be
opposed by Dr. Henry O'Neill, who had done much for public health

71. Nationalist Ulster was not affected by the expulsion of T. M. Healy in 1900 or
by the later departures of William O'Brien and some others, principally M.P.s from
Cork city and county.

72. See F. S. Lyons, *Ireland Since the Famine*, rev. ed., 1973, p. 262, and E. Larkin,
James Larkin, pp. 314–15.

73. *Northern Star*, 20 Jan. 1906. The meeting was held in the National Club, Berry
Street, on Sunday, 14 January. The badge consisted of a shamrock with a photograph of
Devlin in the middle (courtesy of John Jamison).

74. The questions are given in Appendix 8.

in Belfast. Opinion at that time had been divided among supporters of both candidates, and an amendment to defer consideration of the whole matter for two months had been carried by a margin of three votes. Both John Murphy and Joe Mitchell had objected that endorsement of Sloan would be inconsistent with the spirit of independent labor representation and with the nonsectarian nature of the trades council, "which was composed of delegates of different faiths"; Murphy, however, had added that "the council should not commit itself to the support of Mr Sloan unless they received something like an equivalent in the North."[75] In January 1906 Sloan's opponent, Lord Arthur Hill, did not reply to the council's questionnaire. Sloan answered yes to all the questions but two, and even on those he kept an "open mind."[76] The council unanimously decided to support him. No other course was possible in view of the support Walker had received from Sloan's followers in September 1905 and expected to receive again.

The situation in West Belfast was more complicated. The candidates were Captain J. R. Smiley, official Unionist, Joseph Devlin, nationalist, and J. A. M. (Alexander) Carlisle, independent Unionist. Carlisle was general superintendent, and his brother-in-law, William J. Pirrie, chairman of Harland and Wolff, the Queen's Island shipbuilding firm. Pirrie had been refused the Unionist nomination for South Belfast in 1902, and in revenge the two brothers-in-law, Carlisle openly and Pirrie more discreetly, had supported Sloan.[77] In the general election Pirrie was again refused the Unionist nomination, this time for West Belfast. He declared himself a Liberal and subscribed generously to Liberal election funds in both London and Belfast, receiving his reward in June 1906 by being elevated to the peerage. In West Belfast his instrument of revenge was his brother-in-law. When Francis Joseph Biggar (Protestant nationalist, solicitor, and amateur Irish historian) suggested to Carlisle that he should stand, he welcomed the opportunity to inflict further damage on the Unionists. West Belfast was a constituency where the electorate was almost evenly divided between nationalists and Unionists, and where the intervention of a third candidate could subtract the handful of votes needed to throw the election either way. Biggar acted as Carlisle's election agent and arranged the formalities for his shadowy campaign.[78]

75. B.T.C. minutes, 4 May 1905.   76. Ibid., 13 Jan. 1906.
77. *B.N.-L.*, 13 Aug. 1902, *N.W.*, 6 Aug., 8 Aug. 1902. For Pirrie's career see R. D. C. Black, "William James Pirrie," in Conor Cruise-O'Brien, *The Shaping of Modern Ireland*, pp. 174–84.
78. Biggar was sympathetic to such incipient Sinn Féin organizations as the Dungannon Club, founded by Bulmer Hobson and Denis McCullough, rather than to the parliamentary Irish nationalists. As Carlisle would have been mobbed he held no meetings; instead, Biggar arranged an enormous poster display and the "delivery" of a

All three candidates sent replies to the council's questionnaire. Smiley considered that his views on public questions were adequately represented in his election address and speeches. Alexander Carlisle's answer was also limited to a sentence, though an engagingly frank one: "If returned to parliament you may rest assured that my actions will not be against the interests of the working man or of the poor, and although you and many trade societies may have thought that I was on the wrong lines during the last quarter of a century, in the management of the men, I can assure you that anything I did was, in my opinion, for the best interests of the working man and the firm with which I was connected."[79]

Devlin replied fully to all eighteen questions and was able to show that he had already voted in favor of a number of them. In view of his dependence on the support of the licensed trade, his answer on temperance reform was ingenious: "I consider that the proper housing of the working classes is a real solution of the temperance question." His replies were so satisfactory that one delegate, James Dyson, while admitting himself "to be a strong Conservative," could not withhold his approval of such a "strong Labour programme."

The reactions of the delegates at the small meeting[80] revealed the political strains within the council. One delegate moved support for Smiley, but could find no seconder, for the Unionist candidate's reply was too chilly for all but the most ardent Conservatives. A motion of support for Devlin was then moved. An amendment to publish the replies and let the electors judge for themselves was ruled out of order because the circular to candidates promised a decision. A second amendment, to substitute Carlisle's name for Devlin's, resulted in a tie of 8 votes each, and it needed a further vote before Devlin won by 10 votes to 9.

In the 1906 general election a number of opposition candidates appeared in hitherto peaceful Unionist constituencies. They were dubbed "Russellites" by the Unionist press on the convenient, if not always accurate, ground that their politics were those of T. W. Russell, the member for South Tyrone. It was in this election that Russell made

certain number of votes (interview with Bulmer Hobson, who was in constant touch with Biggar at this period).

79. The replies of all candidates were considered at a special meeting (B.T.C. minutes, 13 Jan. 1906).

80. Many delegates were taking part in the trade union demonstration, a regular feature of Walker's elections, or working in the North Belfast constituency (letter of John Murphy to Carlisle, B.T.C. minutes, 13 Jan. and *I.N.*, 16 Jan. 1906). Attendances were normally much larger; e.g., at a meeting to consider the 1906 municipal elections at least 64 were present (B.T.C. minutes, 20 Jan. 1906).

his first appearance as an independent Unionist; he later became a Liberal Home Ruler. One independent, R. G. Glendinning, defeated the official Unionist, William Moore, in North Antrim, where the Independent Orange Order had attracted a larger following than the official organization.[81] Had it not been for an error in his nomination papers, Lindsay Crawford would have carried the attack as far as South County Dublin, where he proposed standing against the Unionist Walter Long, Irish Chief Secretary.[82] Seven "Russellite" candidates, as well as Russell himself, fought in the general election. All contested county seats: three in Antrim, two in Down, one in Londonderry, and one in Fermanagh. In North Tyrone a Liberal candidate, Sergeant Dodd, defeated his Unionist opponent.

In Belfast the anti-Unionist alliance consisted of nationalist, Labour, and independent Unionist forces. But it also extended beyond the city, more tenuous and less effective. The Belfast Trades Council sent its questionnaire to candidates in three neighboring constituencies, East Antrim and North and East Down. None of the official Unionist candidates deigned to reply and the answers of their "Russellite" opponents earned them the council's support.[83] All three were defeated, however. Though other constituencies were beyond the council's reach, the sympathies of at least the Independent Orange delegates were on the side of the "Russellites."[84]

In the second attempt to win North Belfast Walker did not repeat his gaffe of answering B.P.A. questions, nor does it appear that Sloan's henchmen were prepared to risk the loss of possible Labour or nationalist votes by asking them. In fact, Walker made an effort to regain lost ground by declaring at one of his meetings that "he was neither a bigoted Protestant nor a Roman Catholic; he was not ashamed of his Protestantism, but he was not a bigot, and he wanted to get every man equal rights."[85] The *Northern Star* in return made no reference to "bigoted guttersnipes"; instead it reported its founder's description of the three contests in Belfast as "a fight of the workers and toilers against

81. Sloan spoke in suport of Glendinning at election meetings and the Rev. D. D. Boyle, Grand Chaplain of the I.O.O., accompanied the candidate at the counting of the votes (*B.N.-L.*, 29 Jan. 1906). Independent Orange candidates tended to describe themselves as Independent Unionists.

82. *Northern Star*, 27 Jan. 1906.   83. B.T.C. minutes, 13 Jan. 1906.

84. Dr. S. R. Keightley in South Londonderry, denounced as an ex-Orangeman who had been only a year in the old order, appears to have joined the Independent Order. He was a member of the platform party both at the meeting addressed by Captain Shawe-Taylor of the Irish Reform Association in December 1904 (*Irish Protestant*, 24 Dec. 1904) and at a lecture by Lindsay Crawford on "Democracy and Nationalism" in November 1906 (*B.N.-L.*, 6 Nov. 1906).

85. *N.W.*, 4 Jan. 1906.

intrigues, political machines and confiscation."[86] In the same election speech Devlin promised that if Sloan and Walker were elected, "whatever differences I have with them—and the differences will be as vital in future on fundamental questions as before—I shall be glad to cooperate with them in everything that can appeal to the cause of labour."

Walker in his election address outlined a program covering the points submitted by the trades council to other candidates. He also included demands for financial reform to prevent Ireland being taxed beyond her capacity, for economy in government spending, and for the administration of primary, secondary, and technical education by popularly elected bodies. For the contentious phrase "a Unionist in politics" he substituted a no less explicit declaration: "As you are fully aware, *I am Firmly Opposed to Home Rule,* or to any measure tending to *weaken or impair* the legislative Union between Great Britain and Ireland."[87] The *Northern Whig,* in a review of prospects early in the campaign, affected to believe that Walker's statement represented a weakening of his Unionist convictions, that the change had been made in deference to the views of the L.R.C., and that it would lose him votes.[88] On this occasion there were no British Labour speakers to assist him, but he had good prospects of getting well-nigh a full nationalist vote, which had been divided in the previous election. The extent of the collaboration between labor and nationalists was disclosed two years later by Joseph Mitchell: he claimed that prominent United Irish League members had asked him to use his influence with Protestant working men to secure votes for Devlin and given him two hundred tickets to distribute on the Shankill Road, the major Protestant working-class district in West Belfast, for Devlin's Ulster Hall meeting. W. J. Murray added that he too had used his influence on Devlin's behalf.[89]

In the North Belfast by-election of September 1905 there had been a poll of 82 percent. At the general election the poll reached 84 percent on a new register containing 1,100 additional voters.[90] Walker, with substantial nationalist support, increased his vote by 650, but Sir

86. *Northern Star,* 20 Jan. 1906.

87. "Address of Councillor William Walker (Labour Candidate)," dated 1 Jan. 1906.

88. *N.W.,* 8 Jan. 1906.

89. *B.E.T.,* 13 Jan. 1908. These disclosures were made after Labour candidates and speakers had been pelted with rotten eggs and flour during municipal election meetings in Falls and Smithfield, wards with nationalist majorities. Walker, who was one of the speakers, commented, "If this is a sample of Home Rule, then God save us from it."

90. 1905 register: 10,232; 1906 register: 11,385 (*N.W.,* 18 Jan. 1906).

Daniel Dixon, sparing no efforts, financial or otherwise, pushed up his own by 467, winning with a reduced majority of 291.[91]

The Belfast Trades Council offered hearty congratulations to their chairman on his "vigorous and energetic fight . . . to rescue the parliamentary seat from the enemies of labour" and considered the "splendid poll indicative of a glorious victory on the next occasion."[92] Walker himself, in an interview published in the *Daily Mail,* attributed his defeat to the success of the Liberals in Engalnd. Their return to power had "brought Home Rule into the arena" and made Belfast voters all the more anxious to return official Unionists.[93] Walker's explanation was questionable, for it did not account for the defeat of the official Unionist in South Belfast. In spite of Dixon's reduced majority in 1906, the Labour candidate's real opportunity had come four months earlier when there had been a hasty assembling of the Unionist machine. It is possible that if Walker had then obtained a maximum nationalist vote, instead of losing a substantial portion of it by answering the B.P.A. questions, he would have fought the general election with the added prestige of being the sitting member.

To the bitterness of narrow defeat were added troubles arising from the aftermath of the contest. The council assumed financial responsibility for the legal costs that fell upon some of Walker's supporters involved in personation cases. It appealed to its affiliated unions for help, but received a dusty answer from those engaged in demarcation disputes with Walker.[94]

The other two leaves of the shamrock bore the names of Sloan and Devlin. The official Unionist campaign in Belfast had opened with a large demonstration on 2 January in the Ulster Hall, which was decorated with Union Jacks, banners, and mottoes bearing such legends as

---

91. Dixon: 4,907; Walker: 4,616; majority: 291 (*N.W., B.N.-L.,* 19 Jan. 1906).

92. B.T.C. minutes, 20 Jan. 1906.

93. Quoted in *N.W.,* 22 Jan. 1906. Voting did not take place on the same day in all constituencies. Many election results had already been declared before polling day in North Belfast, by which time a Liberal victory was not in doubt.

94. E.g., a postcard, postmarked 21 May 1906, from an A.S.E. branch secretary: "I am sorry to state that I have met with a very cold reception re subs. for personation cases owing to a little friction caused by an action of W.W. re demarcation of work between A.S.E. and A.S.C.J."

The trades council paid £17 10*s.* to Walker as a contribution to the expenses of the personation cases (Statement of account, 7 March 1906 to 5 June 1907, of the Belfast Labour Representation Committee in the account book of the Belfast Trades Council). It is not clear whether those involved had been guilty of personating, i.e., of voting in another person's name, or had wrongly accused others of the offense and thereby laid themselves open to an action for damages.

"One Crown, One Flag, One Parliament."[95] Though their leader had joined the platform party, admittedly at the rear, as part of his attempt to placate the Ulster Unionist Council, Sloan's followers showed scant respect for their surroundings, greeted warnings about the dangers of Home Rule with cries of "It's a bogey," "We've been gulled long enough," and interrupted the principal speakers continually.[96] Lord Arthur Hill, the official Unionist candidate in South Belfast, fared no better than his predecessor Dunbar-Buller and was defeated by the same margin of over 800 votes, which he said were cast by nationalists. Sloan's supporters sang "Derry's Walls" and cheered Alexander Boyd, who presided over the victory celebrations, when he said that the democracy of labor would have at least one representative in the House of Commons.[97]

Thanks to the intervention of Alexander Carlisle, adroit intrigue, and a first-class political machine, Devlin won back West Belfast for the nationalists by a majority of 16 votes in a total poll of 8,413.[98] Carlisle, who had polled 153 vital votes, was held responsible by the Unionists for the loss of the seat, and his effigy as a latter-day Lundy was borne in procession and burnt by Arthur Trew and his followers, who for good measure stoned the windows of the Independent Orange headquarters, formerly a synagogue, in Great Victoria Street.[99]

For the official Unionists the 1906 general election was a serious setback. Not only had some ten years of Conservative and Unionist rule been ended by the Liberal sweep in Great Britain, but even in Ulster the Unionists were in a minority, holding at best 15 seats against the 18 won by nationalists, Liberals, and independent Unionists. Even more ominous was the loss of the South and West constituencies in Belfast, the *Feste Burg* of Ulster Unionism. North Belfast, held by under 300

95. The demonstration had been arranged by the Ulster Unionist Council. The Ulster Hall had been the scene of a meeting during the campaign against the first Home Rule Bill in 1886. It was at that meeting that Lord Randolph Churchill had uttered the slogan, "Ulster will fight, and Ulster will be right." The 2 January demonstration is described at length in *B.N.-L.*, 3 Jan. 1906.

96. *Northern Star*, 6 Jan. 1906.

97. *N.W.*, 20 Jan. 1906. "Derry's Walls" is a popular Orange ballad containing the refrain, "We'll guard old Derry's walls."

98. Devlin: 4,138; Smiley: 4,122; Carlisle: 153; majority: 16 (*B.N.-L.*, 20 Jan. 1906).

99. *N.W.*, 20 Jan. 1906. Lundy, the faint-hearted governor of Derry, ordered the city's gates to be opened to the Jacobite troops besieging it in 1689. They were closed by apprentice boys and Lundy became the Orange prototype of traitor. Arthur Trew had quarrelled with Sloan shortly after the 1902 South Belfast by-election and had resumed an independent role. One of the official Unionist election posters showed Carlisle opening gates to allow Devlin and his followers to enter; it bore the inscription, "A Modern Lundy."

votes, might fall to a third assault by Labour. East Belfast was the only seat in which the Unionists had been given an unopposed return, but its heavily industrialized electorate promised to make it a second North Belfast. It was not surprising that, heartened by the election of some 54 Labour, "Lib-Lab," and other trade union M.P.s in Great Britain, Belfast Labour supporters expected that success in their own city would not be long delayed.

The Growth of Socialist Organizations

The activity generated by Walker's election fights was responsible for the birth of some new political organizations. During the autumn of 1905 a Labour club[100] was formed in Duncairn ward, which Walker represented on the Belfast city council. A month after the general election Walker's election committee leased the premises in Tudor Place that they had used as election headquarters, and founded the North Belfast Labour Club.[101] Its activities included two large meetings in Belfast, the first addressed by the British Labour M.P.s (G. H. Roberts, Philip Snowden and Ethel Snowden, Snowden's wife) and the second by Pete Curran.[102]

The labor clubs were primarily electoral bodies concentrated in the North Belfast parliamentary division and composed of election workers and followers of Walker. Two other organizations with aims of a more general propagandist nature were less involved in the political hurly-burly, the Belfast Ethical Society and the Clarion Fellowship.[103] Whether the Belfast I.L.P. branch represented at the inaugural meeting of the Belfast L.R.C. in 1903 was still in existence is questionable,

100. B.T.C. minutes, 21 Oct. 1905. A delegate asked if the council intended to put forward a candidate for Duncairn in the January 1906 municipal elections as "the new club there" wished to be informed of the council's plans.

101. McClung, Reminiscences, p. 17 and card 11. McClung implies that both clubs were founded at the same time and notes their period of existence as March 1906 to September 1907. He gives the North Belfast Labour Club's officers as Sam Irvine, chairman, J. Bush, vice-chairman, Joseph Mitchell, secretary, and Robert McClung (himself) as treasurer. Samuel Hazlitt listed the labor clubs at this period as Duncairn, North Belfast, and Greencastle, the last in the Belfast suburb of that name (interview with S. Hazlitt).

102. McClung, p. 17 and card 11; B.T.C. minutes, 6 Sept. 1906. Both meetings were held in the Y.M.C.A. hall, the first on 11 October. According to McClung, the hall, which holds some 2,000, was filled on both occasions, though admission cost sixpence per head. Other meetings were held in the provincial towns of Ballymena and Lisburn.

103. During the winters of 1905 and 1906 the indefatigable Knox and Gilliland ran lectures and discussions at the Ethical Society's meetings in a little hall in York Street, convenient to several working-class areas (McClung, p. 17).

since 1904 was the last year in which it was listed in the I.L.P. branch directory. A new society made its appearance in 1905, the Belfast Socialist Society. In a letter to the *Belfast Labour Chronicle* Thomas Johnson (T. R. Johnson) referred to the cry, "Beware of Socialism," raised by the press during Walker's first election, and invited those socialists willing to support "an active propaganda of their principles" to attend an organizing meeting.[104] The society was formed on 7 October with about seventy members, who elected the veteran Alexander Stewart[105] as chairman and T. R. Johnson as secretary.[106] After some time the members decided to conduct open-air propaganda and engaged a cross-channel speaker through an advertisement in Keir Hardie's paper, the *Labour Leader*. The "week's mission" consisted of six meetings at the Custom House steps, the first to be held there since labor speakers had been driven away by Arthur Trew's followers in the 1890s.[107] After this venture the "Steps" became once more a center for labor and socialist propaganda.

The regular meetings of the Belfast Socialist Society were held on Saturday evenings in a hall in Garfield Street, near the city center. A catholic selection of pamphlets was on sale, Henry George's *Progress and Poverty*, Robert Blatchford's *Britain for the British*, Ramsay MacDonald's *Socialism and Society, Fabian Essays,* and H. M. Hyndman's *Economics of Socialism.*[108] McClung records his impressions of the society's meetings as follows: "Looking back now after a lapse of years it seems to me that no matter what subject was under discussion, someone always managed to get in a speech about the class war."[109] Divergent reformist and Marxist views among the members caused the secession of a number led by Hugh Orr, who formed the Communist Club in 1908. During its short existence it met in a room in 109 Donegall Street, on the same floor as the Clarion Fellowship, and was soon absorbed by the older body. In turn the Clarion Fellowship became a purely social club.[110]

104. *Belfast Labour Chronicle*, 30 Sept. 1905.

105. Stewart had helped to found the Dublin Democratic Association in 1884 and had been a chairman of the first Belfast I.L.P.

106. *Belfast Labour Chronicle,* 7 Oct. 1905; McClung, p. 15. Other prominent members were W. J. Murray, Joseph Hayes, Joseph Evans, Harry Stockman, and James Baird. Walker was a member but rarely attended.

107. McClung, p. 16. The cross-channel speaker was Chapman.

108. Belfast Socialist Society pamphlet in the possession of the late T. R. Johnson, who stated in an interview with the present writer that the society profited by a Christian socialist current running at the time. The society ran a meeting in the Ulster Hall addressed by a Congregational minister, the Reverend R. T. Campbell, who was prominent in the English movement.

109. McClung, p. 15.

110. Interview with the late F. Carson. The brothers Hugh and William Orr, who were employed in the Post Office, corresponded with De Leon's Socialist Labor Party

In September 1907 three branches of the I.L.P. were formed in Belfast. The North Belfast and Duncairn Labour clubs were the nuclei of the corresponding I.L.P. branches and the Belfast Socialist Society became the Belfast Central I.L.P. Later branches were started in the parliamentary divisions of South and East Belfast. A federal council, with Tom Henderson as its first chairman, was elected and charged with joint propaganda work.[111]

North Belfast: Walker's Third Round

The year 1906 was marked by frequent quarrels between Walker and other members of the Belfast Trades Council. Walker did not stand for any office or for the executive committee at the beginning of 1907 and George Greig, the successor to Edward McInnes as Belfast N.A.U.L. organizer, was elected president. In January 1907, however, all the labor candidates were defeated in the municipal elections, and differences appeared less acute in face of the common disaster.

Further encouragement to unity came from the conference of the British Labour Party, held later in the same month and presided over by J. J. Stephenson, a member of the general executive council of the A.S.E. He was a Belfast man by birth and had been one of the I.L.P. pioneers in the city during the 1890s. Walker himself was elected to the executive of the British Labour Party[112] and spoke in company with Keir Hardie, David Shackleton, Arthur Henderson, and Ramsay Mac-

---

and sold its literature at the Belfast Socialist Society meetings. They also helped to organize Connolly's return from the United States in 1910.

111. McClung, p. 21; interview with Samuel Hazlitt. The I.L.P. federal council was formed at least as early as January 1908, when a lecture on "Land Values" was advertised under its auspices (*B.E.T.,* 18 Jan. 1908). Tom Henderson, a joiner in Workman Clark's shipyard, was expelled in July 1912 when socialists and Catholics were driven from their employment. He became one of the Clydeside M.P.s in the 1920s.

Clarkson's account of the Belfast Socialist Society is inaccurate in several respects. He suggests that, after the demise of the Belfast I.L.P. branch in the 1890s, "as the Belfast Socialist Party, the handful of propagandists lived on" (pp. 349–50). He seems to have confused Ernest Milligan's Belfast Socialist Society, which was in existence in 1898 and 1899, with the society of the same name founded by T. R. Johnson in 1905. On p. 213 he states "in 1905 the Belfast Socialist Party was carried over into the Independent Labour Party, over the protests of the Irish-Ireland elements." The merger did not take place until September 1907 and there were no protests from an "Irish-Ireland element" (interviews with F. Carson, William Boyd, J. Jamison, and T. R. Johnson).

112. (British) *Labour Party, Seventh Annual Report, (1907),* p. 59. Walker, who was present as an A.S.C.J. delegate, was elected to the trade union section of the executive committee.

Donald, all M.P.s, at a demonstration in the Ulster Hall, an honor that
gave much satisfaction to his admirers. Despite the municipal defeats a
week earlier he made a prediction as singular as it was optimistic when
proposing a vote of thanks to Hardie: The old hostility towards the
exponents of Socialism had passed away in Belfast, and in no city in the
empire could they witness such signs of progress. They were bigoted by
nature and disposition, and they carried into the new movement the
old instinct of keen antagonism to those opposed to them. It was
because of that instinct that he ventured to say that within the next ten
years Belfast would leave Bradford and other towns far behind in regard
to the type of men they sent, not only to the corporation, but to the
Imperial Parliament (applause).[113]

When Keir Hardie rose to reply the large audience stood and cheered
enthusiastically, waving hats and handkerchiefs. The veteran leader,
moved by the reception, declared that the meeting was a most remarkable one and recalled the hostility shown him on his first visit to
Belfast, when he was prevented from reaching the Custom House
steps. Echoing Walker's optimism if not his appreciation of Belfast
virtues, he declared that "political intolerance and religious bigotry
were going down before the Labour movement, and the people were
going back to the old religion—the religion of humanity."

The death of Sir Daniel Dixon in March provided the occasion for
testing the correctness of these pronouncements. Before the election a
new factor, or more accurately a new version of an old one, disturbed
the political situation. This was an offer by the Liberals, who now
possessed an absolute majority in the House of Commons, of a devolution scheme embodied in an Irish Council bill. Described frankly by Sir
Henry Campbell-Bannerman, the Liberal prime minister, as a "little,
modest, shy, humble effort to give administrative powers to the Irish
people,"[114] it fell far short of Home Rule demands, and though the
Irish leader, John Redmond, did not condemn the bill out of hand for
tactical reasons, he gave it a very cool reception on its appearance.

113. *N.W.*, 25 Jan. 1907.
114. J. A. Spender, *Life of Sir Henry Campbell-Bannerman*, ii. 339, quoted in
F. S. L. Lyons, *John Dillon*, p. 294. In the final version the Irish Council was to consist
of 107 members, 82 of them elected and the rest nominated, with the Chief Secretary
an *ex-officio* member. It was to control a number of Irish departments, those concerned
with local government, agriculture, education, public works, and the congested districts, and to have a special fund created out of the British exchequer. It was to be
subject to the veto powers of the Lord Lieutenant and ultimately to the control of
the British cabinet and parliament. See Lyons, *John Dillon*, pp. 289–98, and A. C.
Hepburn, "The Irish Council Bill and the Fall of Sir Antony MacDonnell in 1906–7,"
in *I.H.S.*, xvii (Sept. 1971).

Augustine Birrell, the Irish Chief Secretary, introduced the bill on
7 March, and though the proposed Irish Council was to have modest
powers indeed, it awakened memories of the Dunraven devolution
scheme of 1904–05 and revived Unionist fears. The government abandoned it after its rejection by a nationalist convention in May but it had
already served as a stimulus to Ulster Unionist energies.

When Dixon died Walker's supporters assumed that he would once
again contest North Belfast, but his first reaction was to refuse.[115]
When he accepted the nomination he did so reluctantly,[116] for his
failure in the January municipal elections to win the aldermanship of
Shankill ward, which had polled strongly for him in his second attempt
to win North Belfast, and the renewed Home Rule threat were unpromising portents. To support him the Belfast Trades Council summoned a special meeting of delegates and trade union officials. W. J.
Murray, who had himself quarrelled with Walker, appealed to the
meeting to sink all differences in the common effort and moved a
motion, seconded by Alexander Boyd, pledging assistance. The motion was carried without opposition and forty enrolled themselves as
election workers.[117]

Once again the A.S.C.J. assumed responsibility for election expenses, the L.R.C. undertaking to contribute one quarter of the total
amount.[118] Walker on this occasion had the help of a team of British
Labour M.P.s led by Keir Hardie.[119] The rise in the political temperature of Belfast made him all the more anxious to emphasize his opposition to Home Rule. Speaking in the Ulster Hall on 22 March with
Hardie and W. T. Wilson, he declared that he was "personally totally
opposed to a Parliament in Dublin," but qualified it by saying that he
was not afraid if there were such a parliament "the Roman Catholics in
his society would cut his throat."[120] Hardie assured the audience that
on questions "outside labour—such as Disestablishment, Home Rule

115. The *Northern Whig* stated on 15 March that Walker was unlikely to stand and
that his refusal had taken his sympathizers aback. His wife had died earlier in the
month after a long illness and the Belfast Trades Council had passed a vote of sympathy
with him (B.T.C. minutes, 7 Mar. 1907).

116. "He did not think he was saying too much when he informed that audience [at
an election meeting in the Ulster Hall] that his own personal inclinations were absolutely adverse to the fight" (*N.W.*, 23 Mar. 1907).

117. B.T.C. minutes, 21 Mar. 1907.   118. *N.W.*, 19 Mar. 1907.

119. Others were George N. Barnes, W. T. Wilson, G. H. Roberts, Arthur Henderson, Will Crooks, and Ramsey MacDonald. Councillor Alfred Gould of Hull also
took part in the campaign. Walker's membership of the executive committee of the
British Labour Party accounts for the large number of cross-channel speakers.

120. *N.W.*, 23 Mar. 1907.

and other kindred topics," each Labour Party member was free to vote as he pleased; unless he (Hardie) were converted, he would support a Home Rule bill and equally Walker could vote against it. Two other British M.P.s, George N. Barnes and W. T. Wilson, were more definite in their assurances a fortnight later, when both made light of Home Rule fears at an open-air meeting. Wilson denied that the Labour Party was committed to Home Rule and Barnes went so far as to say that the people of England and Scotland had made up their minds that Home Rule was unattainable.[121] The electorate was offered a further British Labour view on the constitutional question when Arthur Henderson spoke at a second Ulster Hall meeting of preserving "one unbroken imperial family" and restricting Home Rule to local matters.[122]

The Unionist candidate in the by-election was George S. Clark, a principal of the second Belfast shipbuilding firm, Workman, Clark. Like Sir Daniel Dixon he spent money lavishly on the election.[123] The *Northern Star's* account of the Unionist campaign was vivid if uncomplimentary: "The Old Gang are sparing no pains or expense. . . . Well equipped with the sinews of war, the North Division has been utterly overwhelmed with the output of flaring posters and gorgeous handbills." The children were not forgotten; tiny Union Jacks were distributed among them and they were instructed in the various Unionist committee rooms to shout "Vote for Clark. Down with the traitors!"[124] When Walker offered to debate publicly with his opponent, Clark refused and repeated in his reply earlier charges that the British Labour Party was under Irish nationalist influence.[125]

Though the anti-Home Rule card was the strongest in the Unionist pack, it was not the only one played. Walker endeavored to meet criticism of the "collectivist tone"[126] of the 1907 British Labour Party conference by citing the moderator of the Presbyterian General Assembly, who had urged the necessity of cooperation and brotherhood, in Walker's view qualities that constituted "the essence of socialism.[127] In the same speech he complained of the difficulty of knowing what a Unionist was. "Unionism seemed to be synonymous with Protestantism in the old days of 1886, but at present they found Orange

121. *N.W.*, 6 Apr. 1907.　　　　　122. *N.W.*, 16 Apr. 1907.

123. Comment by Mr. F. Carson: "A few weeks earlier [i.e., after the election] it was rumoured that Clark was enraged at the high cost of the election and vowed 'never again.' The fact that he did not stand again gave some semblance of truth to the rumour."

124. *Northern Star*, 20 Apr. 1907.　　　125. *N.W.*, 5 Apr. 1907.

126. *N.W.*, 19 Mar. 1907.　　　　　127. *N.W.*, 23 Mar. 1907.

lodges passing votes of confidence in Roman Catholic candidates for parliament."[128]

Neither criticism of the voting records of Unionist M.P.s nor opposition to the endowment of a Catholic university[129] were sufficient to win over Unionist electors. Ramsay MacDonald and Walker addressed a dinner-hour meeting at Workman, Clark's shipyard, but were unable to repeat their 1905 success. A boilermaker challenged the claim of a trade union official, John Hill, who had spoken at a previous meeting, to represent the executive committee of his society, and the following day held a shipyard meeting in support of Clark.[130]

Walker's campaign concluded with the customary demonstration organized by the Belfast Trades Council. The unions paraded through the city, bearing their banners and followed by a large but not altogether friendly crowd. Among the unions represented was the revived National Union of Dock Labourers led by its organizer, James Larkin, who had already begun the work that was to alter the basis and direction of Irish labor.[131] In a scuffle with a hostile section of the crowd the dockers' banner was torn, but the meeting place was reached without further incident.

Larkin was one of the speakers, and he denounced those responsible for the attack on his union's banner. He welcomed the announcement by the managements that both shipyards would be closed on polling day, for it would enable the men to vote for the Labour candidate. The time had come to strike a vote for trade unionism and their watchword should be "Walker, London."[132] Walker, conscious perhaps that he had

128. Walker's reference was to Denis Henry, K.C., a Catholic barrister who stood several times as a Unionist candidate in North Tyrone, a constituency held from 1895 by a Liberal relying on a combination of nationalist Catholic and Protestant Home Rule voters.

129. Much of the controversy over the reorganization of Irish university education between 1903 and 1908 centered on the desire of the Irish Catholic hierarchy to have the former Catholic University College, Dublin, subsidized out of public funds, and on the mainly Unionist opposition to it. Successive schemes, one by Lord Dunraven, were rejected by the various interested parties until 1908, when the Irish Universities Act was passed. Under it the University of Dublin (Trinity College) and the Presbyterian Magee College, Derry, remained independent; Queen's College, Belfast, became a separate university; and the remaining university colleges formed the National University of Ireland (see T. W. Moody and J. C. Beckett, *Queen's, Belfast*, i. 353–61, 381–91).

130. *N.W.*, 12, 13 Apr. 1907.

131. The Belfast branches of the N.U.D.L. had collapsed in 1893. Credentials in favor of Larkin and four other delegates of the N.U.D.L. were received by the trades council early in April (B.T.C. minutes, 4 Apr. 1907). Larkin had begun his organizing work in late January, when he attended the British Labour Party conference in Belfast.

132. *B.N.-L.*, 17 Apr. 1907.

neglected nationalist voters, made a final appeal to them, "not because they were Catholics, but because they were democrats." He alleged that the Unionists had been angling secretly for their votes and had published a leaflet "which stated that the persecution of the Church in France was due to men like himself (laughter)."[133]

On polling day an impressive number of Unionist election workers ensured the maximum vote for Clark, aided by a transport fleet that included about one hundred motor cars, an unusual sight at that time in Belfast.[134] When the poll was declared it showed a majority of over 1,800 for the Unionist candidate. He had raised Dixon's general election figure by 1,100, while Walker had dropped 400.[135]

The 1907 fight was Walker's last attempt to win a parliamentary seat in Belfast. His prominence in the British Labour party—he was elected to its executive four times between 1907 and 1911—earned him an invitation to contest the Scottish constituency of Leith Burghs. He stood against a Liberal and a Conservative in the first general election of 1910, but came in last.[136]

The dissensions during 1906 and election defeats in 1907 lessened Walker's importance in the Irish labor movement. In his native city he still commanded a strong personal following, fought in two municipal elections, and took part in the work of the local I.L.P. It was inevitable, however, that the loss of public office should reduce his influence, especially as he did not stand for any of the leading positions in the Belfast Trades Council. The work of the council was taken over by other

133. *N.W.*, 17 Apr. 1907. During elections extensive use was made of anonymous posters and handbills lacking dates and imprints. In an editorial entitled "Piggotry and the North Belfast Election," the *Irish News* of 17 April refers to a number in circulation, one of which, signed "By Order," contained the following sentence: "Socialism has pillaged France's Church, broken up our Holy Images with Military Force, and put to the Sword her Bishops and clergy." The editorial's title is a reference to Richard Pigott, the author of the forged Parnell letters published as authentic by *The Times* in 1887. Another pamphlet, in my possession, addressed to the Catholic electors of North Belfast, claims that "the Catholic Church is constitutionally Democratic," but that "Socialism . . . is mob law and spoliation" and "opposed to the commandments of God." "The Catholics of North Belfast cannot conscientiously vote for Mr Walker, the Socialist Candidate."

134. *N.W.*, 18 Apr. 1907.

135. Clark: 6,021; Walker: 4,194; majority: 1,827 (*B.N.-L.*, 18 Apr. 1907).

136. R. C. Munro-Ferguson (Lib.): 7,146; Sir Robert Cranston (Cons.): 4,540; W. Walker (Lab.): 2,724; majority: 2,606 (*B.N.-L.*, 22 Jan. 1910). Clarkson is incorrect in stating (p. 352) that Walker had accepted a government post and was therefore not available to contest North Belfast. He did not become a representative of the national insurance commissioners until 1912. According to William Boyd, Walker's decision to accept the Leith Burghs invitation was influenced by his belief that he had antagonized Catholics in North Belfast (interview with W. Boyd).

delegates, the most important being D. R. Campbell, an insurance official. By the end of the decade Walker was no longer the commanding figure he had been, and though the council by resolution supported him in Leith Burghs, his choice of a Scottish constituency indicated that the former Belfast labor leader had transferred his interest to the British movement.[137]

Walker and his supporters advocated a policy that combined the constitutional views of Ulster Unionism with the social aspirations of British labor. Several decades later it was taken up enthusiastically by the leaders of the Northern Ireland Labour Party when that party endorsed partition in 1949. Perhaps the most percipient judgement has been made by John Gray in his *City in Revolt,* that both groups failed in the attempt "to establish the validity of a tradition of labour democracy coexistent with a Protestant ethos which was primarily concerned with dominance."[138]

137. Walker was elected vice-chairman of the British Labour Party at the 1911 conference. It is true that he fought a municipal seat, unsuccessfully, in January 1911, but in his election address he described himself as "The People's Candidate." He made no mention of endorsement by any labor organization (the Belfast Trades Council had endorsed him on 5 January), stated that he had consented to contest the seat "at the request of large numbers of the electors" and devoted most of the address to his past record as a councillor and poor law guardian (election address dated 6 Jan. 1911).

138. John Gray, *City in Revolt,* p. 215.

13

Conclusion

In the last decade of the nineteenth century the population curves of Scotland and Ireland intersected at a point not far short of 4,500,000,[1] a coincidence that invites a brief comparison of the two countries in terms of demographic history and economic development. When the century opened Scotland had some 1,600,000 inhabitants, or 32 percent of the Irish population of 5,000,000.[2] Forty years later the ratio remained the same, even though the absolute numbers had increased, Scotland's to 2,620,00 and Ireland's to 8,175,000. The Great Famine of the 1840s marked the parting of the ways, for by savagely reversing the direction of the Irish curve, it precipitated the fall in Irish population numbers that continued, though at a generally decreasing pace in the later decades, into the twentieth century. In contrast the Scottish population continued to increase steadily until it equaled and then surpassed the declining Irish total.

The two populations differed not only in the matter of growth and decline, but also in their degree of urbanization. Although the losses during and subsequent to the Great Famine had been borne principally if not exclusively by the rural areas, Ireland at the end of the century was a country where less than a third of its inhabitants lived in urban areas, defined as towns with a population of over two thousand. In Scotland two-thirds were town-dwellers and Glasgow, its largest city, alone had more inhabitants than Belfast and Dublin combined. The extent to which the economy was industrialized during the nineteenth century was reflected indirectly in the territorial, and directly in the occupational, distribution of the Scottish population: the returns of the first (1907) census of production of the United Kingdom showed that Scottish industry employed almost 900,000 workers, nearly three times the Irish total, and that the value of its production was three

---

1. 1891: Ireland (4,705,000), Scotland (4,026,000); 1901: Ireland (4,459,000), Scotland (4,472,000). The figures are given to the nearest thousand.
2. These are estimates in the absence of satisfactory census returns.

times as great. But the difference between the industrial sectors of the two economies was not merely quantitative, for though Ireland had shipbuilding, engineering, and textile manufactures in the Lagan valley, it did not have the coal and other mineral deposits that had given rise to the Scottish extractive industries, and its work force did not include the miners who were an important element in the labor movement in Scotland and, indeed, in Great Britain as a whole.

The formation of a separate Irish T.U.C. in 1894 was followed three years later by a similar development in Scotland. In 1902 the Irish T.U.C. had about 70,000 affiliated members, a figure that did not undergo any marked change for the rest of the decade. In the same year the Scottish T.U.C. had 128,000 members after five years of existence.[3] Though Irish skilled workers were highly organized, in branches of British amalgamated unions or in long-established local societies, disparity in the total number of trade unionists was such that it accounted in a large measure for the slow growth of the Irish as compared with the Scottish T.U.C. England, with its greater population and massive industrial force, presented an even sharper contrast.

The late appearance of separate T.U.C.s in Ireland and Scotland should not obscure the fact that both countries made early contributions to working-class organization on a basis wider than that of a single trade. If Michael Austin's information given to the Webbs is to be accepted, a type of trades council appeared in Cork in the 1830s, and though it did not survive the decade it was reconstituted in 1868 and, after a lapse of some years, again in 1880. The Regular Trades' Association of Dublin, clearly a trades council in organization and functions, was formed in 1844. It seems to have foundered during the Great Famine, but was followed at the end of 1862 by the Dublin United Trades' Association, which lasted at least until 1877. And in 1864 the Dublin body endeavored to form an Irish T.U.C., or more accurately a federation of trades councils or their equivalents, abandoning the effort after 1865 but sending delegates to the first formal meeting of the British T.U.C. in 1868. In Great Britain the Scots were early in the field, forming the Glasgow Trades Council in 1858, two years before its London equivalent. Two of its officials, Alexander Campbell and George Newton, aided by Alexander MacDonald of the Scottish Miners, were responsible for calling a London delegate convention in 1864 to amend the Master and Servant law that in breach of contract cases made employers liable to civil, but workers to criminal, proceedings; they had the satisfaction of seeing the law substantially altered in 1867. The Scottish contribution was not confined to purely trade union

3. I.T.U.C., *Report, Ninth Congress*, p. 36.

organizations, for Alexander MacDonald was one of the first two "Lib-Lab" candidates (the other was Thomas Burt of the Northumbrian Miners) to be elected to parliament in 1874. And, at a later date, it was another Scot, Keir Hardie, who was the first representative of the I.L.P. to be returned, though for an English constituency. Even if we omit those emigrants whose careers belong mainly to English labor history—John Doherty, the cotton operatives' leader, is an outstanding example from the first half of the ninettenth century—trade unionists of the "Celtic fringe" made a contribution, remarkable in proportion to their numbers and at times of a pioneering character, to the evolution of the labor movement in the British Isles.

Had there been no political complications to hinder development, the small proportion of skilled workers in the Irish population would still have afforded but a narrow basis for the building of a strong national center at the end of the nineteenth century. Belfast and Dublin, with the doubtful addition of Cork, were the only Irish towns of importance, and their trades councils and delegates as a consequence dominated the Irish T.U.C. The agricultural population was a poor source of recruitment, composed for the most part of tenant farmers in the process of becoming peasant proprietors and of a steadily diminishing number of laborers. Scattered groups of rural workers, mainly laborers in country towns and surrounding districts, were enrolled in local trade and labor leagues, which rarely reached a membership of more than a hundred or endured more than a few years. Even in England agricultural unionism was weak, though the concentration of laborers on the larger English farms made organization easier. The various attempts to form Irish agricultural laborers' unions from the 1870s onward had all ended in failure.

There remained the urban semiskilled and unskilled, potentially the biggest force, but one as yet unharnessed by the trade union and political labor movement. Weak local unions had existed in a number of Irish towns before the great upsurge of the late 1880s in England. Three of the new unions—the National Union of Dock Labourers, the National Union of Gasworkers and General Labourers, and the National Amalgamated Union of Labour—spread to Ireland, where the first two initially made rapid gains. The employers' counteroffensive was but one of the factors that ended the unions' growth or even their existence. In Belfast, where employment prospects were brightest, the N.U.D.L. was disrupted by press attacks on Michael McKeown, its local organizer, for taking part in a Home Rule campaign in Scotland at a time when the second Irish Home Rule bill had aroused political passions in Ulster. The subsequent collapse of the Belfast branches of the Gasworkers left the slowly growing N.A.U.L. as the only general amalgamated union in the city, and though it survived its membership fell from a maximum of nearly 2,900 in 1897 to 1,600 in 1905.[4] In Dublin unemployment was heavy and in consequence general unions were especially vulnerable to employers' assaults. After early spectacular successes the Dublin Gasworkers disintegrated, in part because of the poaching activities of the Irish National Labour Union, formed in 1892. A federal organization with branches in Dublin and Cork, the I.N.L.U. also had a jurisdictional dispute with the N.U.D.L., and after 1900 broke up into its constituent parts; in turn the Dublin branches of the N.U.D.L. disappeared. The position was no better in Cork, Derry, or the smaller towns. A motion debated at the Limerick (1896) conference of the Irish T.U.C. instructed the incoming parliamentary committee to inquire into the wages of unskilled labor and the existing degree of organization, and to circulate a scheme for unionization three months before the 1897 congress to districts supplying information. Several delegates complained of the exodus from congress during the debate, but to no avail, for though the motion was passed it was not implemented.[5]

Three problems faced the leaders of the Irish working class in 1906: the organization of the unskilled, the "nationalisation" of trade unions, and political action. No systematic attempt had been made to deal with the first, either by the Irish T.U.C. or by the few trades councils.[6] Michael Canty's complaint at the 1906 congress that the skilled men had neglected the claims of the unskilled was substantially justified and was reflected both in the composition of the Irish congress and its parliamentary committee. As long as the Irish T.U.C. remained the preserve of the craft unions, it represented bodies almost smugly conservative in outlook and concerned with their sectional interests. The inclusion of the laborer confronted the leaders with the miseries of the most oppressed strata of the working class—the poorly paid general worker, the women and juveniles in sweated industries, and the mass of the unemployed, the last a category peculiarly numerous owing to the weakness of the Irish economy.

Whether the progress of amalgamated unions in Ireland should be halted—and indeed reversed—was debated for the first time at the 1906 congress. Despite occasional jurisdictional clashes between British and Irish unions, the question assumed importance only with the growth of Sinn Féin sentiment, which stood for the "nationalisation" of

4. *Belfast Labour Chronicle*, 9 Dec. 1905. Possibly an inflated figure. Seven branches were affiliated to the Belfast Trades Council on less than 1,000 members in 1906 (Dues book of the Belfast Trades Council, pp. 37–42, 81).

5. I.T.U.C., *Report, Third Congress*, p. 30.

6. Only six trades councils were affiliated in 1906.

all organizations in Ireland. Since not all Irish unions shared the outlook of delegates like P. T. Daly—the Belfast unions catering for linen
workers are an obvious example—and their membership was small,
they could make little headway against amalgamated unions when the
temperature of nationalist feelings was low. The sentiment nonetheless
existed and in a period of resurgent nationalism was capable of winning
support, especially if Irish branches considered that they were treated
as troublesome relations by their British headquarters.

For delegates like P. T. Daly, on the left wing of Sinn Féin, political
action required a distinctive Irish labor party controlled by and answerable to the Irish T.U.C. Though the congress lobbied M.P.s of
various parties, by the beginning of the new century it had come to
depend heavily on the Irish parliamentary party to represent an Irish
labor viewpoint at Westminster. The Irish party, which claimed to be
labor as well as nationalist on the basis of its parliamentary record and
its somewhat infrequent selection of the odd trade unionist as a candidate for a safe seat, thus established itself as the liberal element in a *de
facto* "Lib-Lab" relationship with congress.[7] These services, coupled
with the desire for self-government, were sufficient to retain the support of many delegates. But no formal alliance was possible, and the
presence of Belfast delegates with Unionist sympathies made the discussion of any question remotely connected with Home Rule a danger
to congress unity. It was safeguarded by leaving the responsibility for
political action to trades councils.

Belfast had made the first attempt to return a labor M.P. from
Ireland when Bowman stood in 1885, and it was the only trades council
to set up a distinctive political organization and contest parliamentary
seats in the first decade of the twentieth century. Speculation may be
permitted on what would have happened had Walker been successful in
1905. His reputation stood high with Irish trade unionists in 1904,
and his importance would have been enhanced after British labor successes in the general election of 1906. As the first independent labor

7. Michael Austin and E. Crean were elected in 1892 and 1895. Austin was
defeated and Crean reelected in 1900. Alderman W. Doyle proposed (D.T.C. minutes,
24 Sept. 1900), in view of Redmond's and Davitt's encouraging remarks on direct labor
representation, that the council forward the names of John Simmons and Councillor
J. P. Nannetti for selection. Simmons stated that he would not stand for a division of
Dublin. Nannetti, who had not been connected with the council for many years, and
had been elected as a national candidate to the Dublin Corporation, was chosen by a
nationalist convention. He was returned for the College Green division at the general
election. The trades council received no reply to their letter. See also C. Desmond
Greaves, *The Life and Times of James Connolly,* p. 103, where Simmon's name is mis-
printed as "Sims."

M.P. returned by an Irish constituency, his prestige and influence might have been sufficient, at least until political feeling on Home Rule grew high, to induce others to follow his example and support the Labour Representation Committee and its successor, the British Labour Party.

At both the 1904 and 1905 congresses, the Belfast Trades Council's resolution urging affiliation to the L.R.C. was carried. In the heated debate of 1906 it was rejected, though the congress acclaimed the British labor victories of the preceding January. The bitterness of some of the speeches in the debate was caused by Walker's conduct in the 1905 by-election, when he had answered the questions of the Belfast Protestant Association to that body's satisfaction. Support for the British Labour Party was forthcoming in later congresses but, as in 1904 and 1905, it was never more than formal and no trades council outside Belfast applied for affiliation.

The importance of the 1905 by-election lay neither in Walker's defeat, nor even in his opposition to Home Rule, but in the sectarian image which he, as an L.R.C. candidate, presented to the electorate. Despite his energy and ability he did the cause of independent labor representation in Ireland both immediate and long-term damage when he equated labor with Protestantism in one of his replies, an answer with anti-Catholic overtones. That it was not an isolated aberration was shown by his review of the Dungannon Club manifesto some weeks later in the *Belfast Labour Chronicle* of 7 October 1905.[8] The manifesto's proposal that trade unions in Ireland should be "nationalised" provoked the following comment:

What do our manifestants want? Do they suggest that the international principle of trade unionism should be dropped, and that Irish trade unionism should take refuge under the banner of nationalism, and the upas tree of Rome's priesthood?

His opposition to Home Rule was couched in the same language: "With some of the methods suggested by the manifesto we heartily agree, such as the nationalisation of our transit service, the promotion of home manufactures (short of boycotting), and the improvement of education; but all these things may be attained without handing Ireland over to the domination of the priesthood, and we can find no escape from the conclusion that such domination would be complete and irrevocable if Ireland's representation, as suggested by the mani-

8. Bulmer Hobson, the author of the manifesto, stated to the present writer that the review was written by Walker; his informant was at that time associated with the paper. Internal evidence also supports Walker's authorship.

festo, were withdrawn from the House of Commons to exercise sub-clerical functions in Dublin."

Walker's statements must be viewed against the background of Belfast's pattern of segregation, which, if fundamentally economic in origin, was complicated by social, political, religious, occupational, and territorial factors. A form of Protestant ascendancy was to be found even at a working-class level. Though the working poor included substantial numbers of Protestants as well as Catholics, the skilled trades were dominated by Protestants. For many, opposition to Home Rule arose from the fear that its coming would not only imperil those civil and religious liberties that they regarded as peculiarly British, but also undermine the social and economic status that they had hitherto enjoyed. The frequent riots that characterized the history of Belfast had encouraged ghetto-like concentrations of working-class Catholics in well-defined areas of the city,[9] and the creation of Falls and Smithfield municipal wards in turn fostered representation on a politico-sectarian basis. In a city filled with the memories of past dissensions, Walker's surrender to opportunism encouraged the illiberal elements in both camps and ensured that the Catholic votes he received would be negatively anti-Unionist. Though in later elections he denied that he was a bigot, he did not denounce the sectarianism that in times of crisis caused Belfast workers, even those organized in the labor movement, to split along the familiar Unionist-Protestant, nationalist-Catholic lines.

Belfast's efforts to return independent labor M.P.s were not imitated elsewhere in Ireland. Even at the local government level Dublin's attempts to establish a genuinely independent labor group were ineffective. Labor councillors in other towns were hardly distinguishable from those of the various nationalist groups. Socialism in Dublin, though as a tradition it reached back to Chartist days, was confined to small groups of individuals, the remnants of Connolly's Irish Socialist Republican Party.

James Larkin's arrival in Belfast early in 1907 had been preceded, and in a sense prepared for, by certain events of the previous year. The Liberal government, under pressure from Labour M.P.s, had passed the Trades Disputes Act. It canceled the accumulated decisions of "judge-made" law and restored the right of picketing, which Larkin was to use effectively in his first Irish strike. Lindsay Crawford had moved to the north at the end of the year. The *Ulster Guardian* under his editorship was to prove sympathetic to labor, and under the direction of its first

9. See Andrew Boyd, *Holy War in Belfast,* and Emrys Jones, *A Social Geography of Belfast,* pp. 187–204.

Grand Master (Crawford) the Independent Orange Order was to be an ally in times of crisis.[10] Joseph Devlin, conscious of his indebtedness to Protestant as well as Catholic working-class votes in 1906, would lend temporary aid. The Dublin Trades Council, though it still lacked direction, had been slowly changing in personnel; it was no longer the complacent body it had been at the beginning of the century, for among the delegates were future lieutenants of Larkin.

In the first year of his Irish career Larkin attended a conference of the British Labour Party, carried out his unprecedented organizing drive in the major Irish ports, affiliated branches of the National Union of Dock Labourers to the Belfast and Dublin Trades Councils, acted as a delegate to both bodies, and appeared at the fourteenth congress of the Irish T.U.C. held in Dublin. He shifted the center of interest from conference and committee rooms to the streets, the quays, and the docks. His daemonic energy roused disciples, and enemies, wherever he went. He was responsible for the Irish labor movement taking up the first of its outstanding tasks—the organization of the unskilled.[11] Once that had begun, the other problems the "nationalisation" of trade unions and the creation of a political party representing labor—could not be delayed indefinitely.

10. The *Ulster Guardian* was a weekly newspaper, the official organ of the Ulster Liberal Association, which was formed in April 1906 as a result of the Liberal victory in the 1906 general election. The first number under Crawford's editorship appeared in January 1906.

11. For the career of Larkin see Professor Emmet Larkin's outstanding biography, *James Larkin, 1876–1947*.

Appendices

Appendix 1

Trades Councils in Ireland, 1894 to 1898

	Founded	1894		1895		1896		1897		1898	
		Trade union	Membership	Trade union	Membership	Trade union	Membership	Trade union	Membership	Trade union	Membership
Belfast	1881	77	18,830	77	18,830	65	16,000	56	17,500	53	16,892
Cork	1880	21	1,072	22	1,199	19	2,090	24	2,000	25	1,520
Drogheda	1891	13	626	13[a]	626[a]	11	739	9	400	8	194
Dublin	1885	74	15,000	61	12,710	64	12,010	60	12,000	62	16,000
Kilkenny	1895	—	—	9	371	9	371	7	134	5	130
Limerick	1893	19	1,112	20	1,600	18	1,277	12	940	10	850
Londonderry[b]		11	500	[c]	[c]						
Newry[b]	1890	7	250	7	377	7	250	7	250	—	—
Waterford	1895	—	—	13	350	13	370	14	600	[c]	[c]

Source: *Report by the Chief Labour Correspondent of the Board of Trade on Trade Unions in 1898*, pp. 204–5, [C. 9443] xcii, 493.
[a] Figures for 1894, those for 1895 not being available.
[b] Figures incomplete.
[c] Dissolved 1898.

Appendix 2

The Early Years of the Cork Trades Council

There is some doubt about the founding year of the Cork Trades Council, which, like its Dublin counterpart, had predecessors. The report of the chief labor correspondent of the Board of Trade on trade unions in 1898 (see Appendix 1) gives the year as 1880, a date that would make it the oldest trades council in Ireland. In his evidence to the Royal Commission on Labour, John Henry Jolly stated, in answer to a question by Michael Austin, that he had been the president of the Cork Trades Council in 1880, 1881, and 1883 (*Royal Commission on Labour, Minutes of Evidence Before Group C*, p. 246, Q. 17, 117 [c. 6795-vi], H.C. 1892, xxxvi, pt. II). While the local press does not mention the Cork Trades Council by name, there are reports of the activities of "the Trades of Cork" in September and October 1880, when they organized a demonstration to greet Charles Stewart Parnell on his return from the United States (*Cork Examiner*, 28 Sept., 4 Oct. 1880).

' The following notes on Cork trade union history were made by the Webbs on the basis of information supplied by Michael Austin in the early 1890s (the sheet notes that Austin was then a member of the Royal Commission on Labour).

Trade unions were very strong in Cork from 1833 to 1837. They had formed a kind of trades council which in 1837 had over £2000 and a large library of books. It appears to have died out soon after 1837, however. (Monument in Shandon cemetery erected by the "United Trades of Cork" to the memory of their President.)

The council, reformed in 1868, lasted only a few years and then was broken up by internal political dissensions. Believes the same cause killed the previous one.

Reformed in 1881. Austin secretary. Continued since then as Trades and Labour Council (B.L.P.E.S., Webb papers on Trade Unions, Collection E, Section A, volume III, f. 45).

A short biography of Michael Austin in the *Trade Unionist* (20 June 1891) does not mention the founding of the council, but states that because of troubles (unspecified) in that body during 1883 a reorganization committee was appointed. Austin, a compositor then aged 28, was a member of the committee and was subsequently elected secretary of the reconstituted council; he retained the office until he resigned it in 1891.

In the later 1880s there were further troubles in the council. One of its prominent members was Eugene Crean, a carpenter, who was elected under nationalist auspices to the Cork City Council in 1887 and later to Westminster in 1892 as one of the two successful Labour-Nationalists candidates (the other was Michael Austin). During his presidency in 1888 he had a resolution passed, calling upon the lord mayor of Cork to summon a citizens' meeting in order to expel about three hundred Jewish pedlars from the city on the grounds that they were an injury to honest trade (*Justice*, 17 Mar. 1888). Though he was strongly condemned by the lord mayor himself, William O'Brien, M.P., Parnell, and Michael Davitt, among others, he refused to withdraw or explain his language, maintaining that only those connected with the Cork Trades Council had any right to question his opinion (*Justice*, 31 Mar. 1888).

Appendix 3

The North Belfast Election of 1885

Alexander Bowman, the first labor candidate to appear in Ireland, was about thirty years of age at the time of the election.[1] His photograph in the report of the Sligo congress (1901) of the Irish T.U.C. is of a handsome bearded man in his middle forties, with fine eyes and commanding appearance. He started work as a machine boy in a linen mill at the age of ten under the half-time system then prevailing, and in due course became a flaxdresser.[2] His election speeches and his presidential address at the Sligo congress are evidence that he belonged to the small class of workmen whose natural intelligence overcame the handicap of long hours of work and little formal education. McClung says that he "was not a declared socialist, but a class-conscious trade unionist and a widely-read man."[3]

J. D. Clarkson (*Labour and Nationalism in Ireland*, p. 349) states that Alexander Brown ran as a Liberal candidate with the backing of the Belfast Trades Council. Bowman was indeed a Liberal, a member of both the general council and executive committee of the Belfast Liberal Association,[4] but there is no evidence that he was endorsed by that association. The reports of his candidature stated that a deputation waited on him with a requisition, signed by between 400 and 500 votes, asking him to come forward as "the working man's candidate for the North Division of Belfast."[5] The meeting at which he was formally adopted passed a resolution pledging itself "to put forth its utmost efforts, financially and otherwise, to secure his return to the Imperial parliament as labour representative for the Northern division of Belfast."[6] While there is no direct contemporary proof of his endorsement by the Belfast Trades Council (the council minutes for the period are missing), the weight of available evidence is strongly in favor of it. The chairman of his adoption

1. *N.W.*, 31 Oct. 1885. At the time of his nomination Bowman was a draper's traveller (*B.N.-L.*, 25 Nov. 1885).

2. (Belfast) *Morning News*, 31 Oct. 1885. He gave these details in a speech at his first meeting.

3. McClung, Recollections of the Labour Movement in Belfast, p. 1.

4. *N.W.*, 20 May 1886. This is Bowman's own description of himself in a letter to Broadhurst. See also *B.N-L.*, 30 Jan. 1885.

5. *N.W.*, *Belfast Evening Telegraph*, (Belfast) *Morning News*, 10 Oct. 1885.

6. *B.N.-L.*, 31 Oct. 1885.

meeting was James Workman, a leading member of the council, the president (Joseph Mitchell) was his first nominator, and the assentors included other members.[7]

Bowman's appearance as a candidate was met by one Unionist paper with assumed incredulity ("Mr Bowman and his friends . . . are having a harmless little joke") and real anger (an "impertinence").[8] The local nationalist paper, shortly after the first announcement of Bowman's intention to fight the election, said it was understood that a barrister (Robert Dunlop, Q.C.) had withdrawn in order to leave the struggle between the Conservative William Ewart and Bowman, "who comes forward in the Liberal interest," and that a fund would be opened to defray his expenses, to which a leading Liberal (John Shaw Brown, J.P.) intended to subscribe handsomely.[9] A speaker at one of Ewart's meetings declared that Bowman had been put forward by parties who did not care to be identified with him and that one merchant had contributed £100 to his election fund.[10] There was no acknowledgement by Bowman or his supporters of any such backing; at his adoption meeting he accepted the nomination on the condition that his election expenses were found for him. He suggested to his audience that, as the sheriff's expenses[11] would be between £125 and £150, 3,000 workmen in the division contributing one shilling each would supply all their requirements. If this were done and he were returned to parliament he undertook to support himself there—"he could do much with tongue and pen."[12]

Bowman was insistent throughout his campaign on the nonparty nature of his candidature. He declared that the requisition asking him to stand had been signed by "almost 500 electors, Whig, Tory and Nationalist, without distinction of religious creed" and criticized both liberals and conservatives for joining together to emasculate the Employers' Liability Act.[13] When he read his election address at one of his meetings he emphasized that "at present almost forty candidates were seeking suffrages on purely workingmen's principles and would not permit themselves to be absorbed in any of the great political parties," and that he was "in favour of the formation of a labour party which should zealously attend to the origination and promotion of measures likely to promote the well-being of the working population."[14] His own program owed much to that of Chamberlain's "unauthorised" one; it also contained such details of purely trade union interest as the demand for shorter hours of labor and the appointment of additional factory inspectors from the working class. In addition he advocated arbitration to settle international disputes and the extension of the vote to women householders. To a question about General Gordon he replied that he had not come forward as a politician

7. *B.N.-L.*, 25 Nov. 1885.   8. *B.E.T.*, 31 Oct. 1885.

9. *M.N.*, 15 Oct. 1885.

10. *N.W.*, 25 Nov. 1885. An interrupter identified the merchant as John Shaw Brown, but the speaker was not prepared to confirm it—"it was only common report."

11. See Appendix 4.   12. *M.N.*, 31 Oct. 1885.

13. *N.W.*, 19 Nov. 1885.   14. *B.N.-L.*, 19 Nov. 1885.

and had no statement to make.[15] No such answer was possible on the first item on his program, the maintenance of the union; here he made a somewhat oracular statement which was to be copied, *mutatis mutandis,* by many of his successors in the Belfast labor movement: "our true strength and interest lay in hearty and honourable union with Great Britain, but as we could only have satisfactory and abiding union on the basis of justice, he should oppose every movement in the direction of injustice and wrong."[16]

The first Irish labor candidate's campaign was distinguished by the wrecking tactics which labor's opponents have so often employed. A schoolroom engaged by Bowman for a meeting was seized by Ewart supporters who repelled the would-be speakers, wrecked the room, and did not spare even the school harmonium.[17] A later ticketed meeting was more successful, but even here there was interruption, for a number of Ewart supporters gained entry by forged tickets, and a substitute chairman (B. Hobson)[18] had to be called upon, as the intended chairman was prevented from entering by hostile crowds.[19] Bowman's own house in Berlin Street was wrecked, he and his family escaping by the back. The temper of the times is recalled by Robert McClung: "The Pope and Home Rule for Ireland played a big part in the fight which took place. Bowman had no intention of handing North Belfast over to the Pope, although the Tories declared he would. . . . Among the working classes in 1885 there was a real dread of Home Rule. I can remember the stories being told in '85 and '86 to the effect that the Home Rulers had already ballotted for who would own the shipyards. I can remember being told that the man who came to our door and sold herrings and Lough Neagh pollen was to own and control Ewart's spinning mills as soon as the Home Rule bill became law."[20]

Bowman was supported by the local nationalists, whose paper, the *Morning News,* interpreted his statement about the working of the Union as implying that its operation had been conducted without a due regard for justice, and prophesied that if he were returned to parliament he would find there "a powerful party [i.e., the Irish Parliamentary Party] devoted to every item, or almost every item, in his circulated address."[21] Its support became absolute when Parnell issued his directive to the nationalists of Ulster: "Mr. Bowman is opposing Mr. Ewart, conservative, on purely labour lines, apart from any

15. Bowman had earlier in the year proposed the government's Egyptian policy as a subject for discussion in the Belfast Debating Society, of which he and William Curries were members. Currie was the leader of the anti-Home Rule deputation which interviewed "Lib-Lab" M.P.s in 1886. The Belfast Debating Society also discussed Henry George's doctrines (*B.N.-L.,* 27 Jan., 17 Feb. 1885).

16. *N.W., B.N.-L.,* 19 Nov. 1885.

17. *N.W., B.N.-L., M.N.,* 14 Nov. 885.

18. Probably Benjamin Hobson (father of Bulmer Hobson) who was on the committee of the Ulster Liberal Association (interview with Bulmer Hobson).

19. *B.N.-L., N.W.,* 19 Nov. 1885.

20. R. McClung, Recollections, p. 4. The ballot referred to was an ingenious fund-raising device invented by J. G. Biggar, nationalist M.P. for Cavan.

21. *M.N.,* 20 Nov. 1885.

political organisation, and he should have the thorough support of the Nationalist voters."[22] The *Northern Whig*, Liberal-Unionist in temper, offered ostentatiously disinterested support,[23] for which it was bitterly attacked by speakers at Ewart's meetings; it summed up on the eve of the poll as follows: "In the North Division they [the Liberals] will generally, with the Nationalists and Orangemen, unite in support of the workingmen's candidate Mr. Bowman, on non-partisan grounds."[24]

The two remaining papers, the *Belfast Evening Telegraph* and the *Belfast News-Letter*, were violently partisan, the first-named excusing the wrecking of Bowman's meeting and the schoolroom in which it was held by referring to the labor candidate's "Liberal and democratic" opinions, which local residents viewed with disfavor.[25] The Unionists attacked Bowman initially as a follower of Henry George and a radical, but as the campaign progressed Thomas Johnston,[26] forerunner of a prolific succession of Unionist workingmen, denounced him as a republican of the deepest dye,[27] and, heartened by Ewart's approval, announced at the final meeting that Bowman "was worse than a Home Ruler, as, to the speaker's own knowledge, he had said that he wished that the last thread binding England and Ireland were severed."[28]

The results of the 87 percent poll showed that in North Belfast at least, the thread held strong. Bowman secured a high proportion of the nationalist vote in the area,[29] but his share of the rest was small; he was defeated three to one.[30] The next labor candidate, William Walker, fighting twenty years later, was to be less ambiguous about Home Rule.

While it is probable that Bowman received some covert Liberal support he is best considered a radical-labor rather than a "Lib-Lab" candidate, despite his appearance as a Gladstonian Liberal in the Home Rule controversy in 1886. In the 1880s he was associated[31] with James Morrison Davidson, a radical journalist who was one of the five candidates of the Scottish Land Restoration League in the general election of 1885, and was then a Scottish nationalist as well as a land reformer—he later became a socialist.[32] Bowman himself claimed to be on the list of lecturers for the Social-Democratic Federa-

22. *M.N.*, *N.W.*, *F.J.*, 26 Nov. 1885.

23. *N.W.*, 2 Nov. 1885. "An electoral victory in the cause of labor will be far more permanently beneficial than an electoral victory in the cause of King William or Mr. Parnell."

24. *N.W.*, 25 Nov. 1885.   25. *B.E.T.*, 14 Nov. 1885.

26. A member of the Belfast Trades Council; he acted as chairman on a number of occasions in 1887 (B.T.C. minutes May–Nov., passim).

27. *B.N.-L.*, 12 Nov. 1885.   28. *N.W.*, 25 Nov. 1885.

29. "The Nationalists gave him their cordial support, in accordance with the terms of Mr Parnell's manifesto" (*M.N.*, 27 Nov. 1885). In 1886 the Parnellite candidate (J. Dempsey) in a straight fight polled 732 votes against Ewart's 4,522.

30. W. Ewart: 3,915; A. Bowman: 1,330; majority: 2,505 (*B.N.-L.*, 8 Nov. 1885).

31. Interview with Daniel McDevitt.

32. See G. D. H. Cole, *British Working-Class Politics*, p. 100.

tion from 1886 onward[33] and in his later activities seems to have parted company with the Liberals. In 1889 he left Belfast,[34] where employment must have been hard to find after his part in the 1886 Home Rule controversy, and worked as an agent for a vending machine company in Glasgow.[35] Here he took part in the single-tax movement, becoming president of the Henry George Institute and of the Scottish Land Restoration Federation; in the latter capacity he debated with J. Bruce Glasier of the Socialist League on the best method of solving the labor problem.[36] After a brief return to Belfast, he moved in 1891 to London for a period of some four years.[37] In the summer of 1894 he was an active member of the Brixton branch of the S.D.F., represented them in a debate with a temperance organizer and, in the local government elections, stood as one of the ten S.D.F. candidates in Walthamstow.[38] On his return to Belfast he resumed work as a flaxdresser, for his position as organizer and secretary of the Belfast Municipal Employees' Association was a spare-time one.[39] Until his appointment to a post under the Belfast Corporation in September 1901, his public activities, apart from a three-year term as a city councillor, were in trade union affairs.

There is little doubt that Bowman was the first independent parliamentary trade union candidate in Ireland. G. D. H. Cole omits him from his lists in *British Working-class Politics, 1832–1914,* though he has a better title to be included than such men as Davitt, Austin, Crean, and Joyce, while Clarkson, as already mentioned, classifies him as a Liberal with labor backing; both mistakes may have arisen from such a source as the *Constitutional Year Book for 1911* (quoted by Clarkson, p. 349), where he is listed as a Liberal.[40]

33. Interview with Daniel McDevitt.

34. Interview with his son, R. R. Bowman.

35. *Brotherhood,* 4 Jan. 1890; *Belfast Weekly Star,* 7 June 1890.

36. *Brotherhood,* 15 Mar. 1890; *Belfast Weekly Star,* 11 Oct. 1890, 11 Apr. 1891.

37. Interview with R. R. Bowman.

38. *Justice,* 16 June, 7 July, 8 Dec. 1894.

39. Interview with R. R. Bowman. The Belfast M.E.A. became a branch of the [British] Municipal Employees' Association in 1905.

40. N. Belfast, 1885: W. Ewart C. 3519, A. Bowman, L 1330 (*Constitutional Year Book for 1911,* p. 213).

Appendix 4

Returning Officers' Expenses at Parliamentary Elections

The demand that returning officers' expenses at parliamentary elections should be a public charge recurs constantly in labor programs up to 1918. These expenses were fixed by a series of nineteenth century statutes.

By S.48 of the Representation of the People (Ireland) Act, 1832 (2 & 3 Will. 4, C.88) the cost of polling booths and the payment of returning officers' deputies (two guineas per day) and poll clerks (one guinea per day) were to be shared equally by all the candidates in an election.

S.19 of the Representation of the People (Ireland) Act, 1850 (13 & 14 Vict., C.68) limited the cost of a polling booth to £3 if it were erected in a public building and to £5 if not in a public building. It reduced payments to deputies and poll clerks to £2 and £1 per day respectively.

The Ballot Act, 1872 (35 & 36 Vict., C.33) required, by S.8, the returning officer to provide the additional apparatus (e.g., ballot and nomination papers) for a secret ballot, and the expenses incurred were also to be shared equally among the candidates. S.17 of the Act, modifying its application to Ireland, limited by subsection (4) the returning officer's expenses to those actually and necessarily incurred by him and provided that they should not exceed the amounts allowed by statutes then in force in Ireland.

The 1872 act did not enable the returning officer to require a candidate to give security for these expenses before he was nominated, and in a case (*Davies v. Lord Kensington* 1874 L.R. 9 C.P. 720) where a candidate refused to give such security and the returning officer declared the opposing candidate elected, the election was set aside. This loophole was filled by S.3 of the Parliamentary Elections (Returning Officers) Act, 1875, which enabled the officer, if he thought fit, to require security for the charges under the Act. The maximum amount of security, specified in the third schedule of the Act, varied between counties and boroughs and according to the number of registered electors. It could be as low as £100 where the registered electors in a borough did not exceed 1,000, or as high as £1,000 where the registered electors in a county exceeded 30,000. If a candidate did not give or tender security he was to be deemed to have withdrawn.

S.2 of the Parliamentary Elections (Returning Officers) Act, 1885 (48 & 49 Vict., C.62), reduced the maximum amount of the security that could be required where the number of candidates did not exceed the number of vacancies. Instead of being variable (one-fifth of the maximum specified in the third schedule to the 1875 Act) the figure was fixed at £5.

The inter-war system, whereby a candidate at a British election deposited £150 to be forfeited if he did not poll one-eighth of the total vote, dates from the recommendation (para. 27) of the Speaker's Conference of 1917 on Electoral Reform (Cmd. 8463). The conference also (para. 25) recommended that "returning officers' charges should be paid by the State on a scale to be fixed by the Treasury." Accordingly, S.29 of the Representation of the People Act, 1918 (7 & 8 Geo. 5) provided that the returning officer was to be paid by the Treasury in accordance with a scale of maximum charges prescribed by it. Ss. 26 and 27 also provided for deposits and forfeiture.

Irish Trades Union Congress Finances, 1895 to 1906

Year	(Town)	Subscriptions			Delegates' fees			Total receipts			Parliamentary committee meetings			Balance		
		£	s.	d.	£	s.	d.	£	s.	d.	£	s.	d.	£	s.	d.
1895	(Cork)	57	10	0	54	5	0	111	15	0	38	9	9	43	16	4
1896	(Limerick)	21	0	0	38	10	0	108	6	4	36	10	1	40	14	5
1897	(Waterford)	36	9	7	38	5	0	123	9	8	36	18	1	49	10	4
1898	(Belfast)	39	14	3	41	10	0	130	14	7	41	17	0	32	14	11
1899	(Derry)	20	13	9	42	15	0	96	3	8	36	12	3	26	10	5
1900	(Dublin)	37	10	6	61	10	0	125	10	11	41	18	10	50	2	7
1901	(Sligo)	55	16	4	54	15	0	176	12	7	38	14	8	64	16	2
1902	(Cork)	45	10	0	71	5	0	193	0	4	45	3	9	60	3	1
1903	(Newry)	53	0	2	62	5	0	183	14	11	40	7	7	70	16	0
1904	(Kilkenny)	57	17	2	54	0	0	190	5	2	44	17	11	45[a]		
1905	(Wexford)	56	9	11	50	5	0	192	6	5	36	17	9	56	11	5
1906	(Athlone)	74[b]	4	8	52	10	0	190	10	1	38	10	6	82	6	9

Source: Annual Reports of the Irish Trades Union Congress.

[a] Approximate figure.

[b] A new standing order dealing with finance was carried at the Wexford (1905) congress (Report, Twelfth Congress, p. 50). Affiliation fees, payable on Irish membership, were on the following scale: 1d. per member up to 250; 250–500 £1.8s.4d.; 500–1,000 £1.10s.; £1 for each 1,000, or part thereof, after the first 1,000. Trades councils: £1 for each 5,000 or part thereof represented.

Appendix 6

Officers and Parliamentary Committee Members of the Irish Trades Union Congress, 1894 to 1906

From 1894 to 1902, with the exception of 1901, the president of the local trades council was elected president of congress; in 1903 and subsequent years the chairman of the parliamentary committee was invariably elected to preside at congress.* From 1918 onwards the president was elected at congress, became the chairman of the national executive, and was entitled to preside at the following year's congress.

The secretary was appointed on a yearly basis until 1906, when a new standing order declared him an ex-officio member of congress and of the parliamentary committee, and as such permanent as long as he gave satisfaction.

The chairman and treasurer of the parliamentary committee were elected by the committee itself.

Year and place of meeting	1. President 2. Treasurer 3. Secretary	Members of parliamentary committee
1894 Dublin	1. T. O'Connell (A.S.C.J.) Dublin 2. Patrick Dowd (Plumbers) Dublin 3. John Simmons (A.S.C.J.) Dublin	†H. McManus (T.A.) Belfast E. L. Richardson (D.T.P.S.) Dublin R. Sheldon (A.U. Cabinetmakers) Belfast J. H. Jolley (T.A.) Cork T. O'Connell (A.S.C.J.) Dublin J. Carter (Local Bakers) Drogheda J. A. Hennessy, Limerick R. P. O'Connor (T.A.) Limerick
1895 Cork	1. J. H. Jolley (T.A.) Cork 2. J. H. Jolley (T.A.) Cork 3. John Simmons (A.S.C.J.) Dublin	J. H. Jolley (T.A.) Cork †P. J. Tevenan (A.S.R.S.) Dublin P. Goulding (United Labourers of Ireland) Dublin Murray Davis (Irish Federal Union of Bakers) Belfast Thomas Gavin (Local Painters) Limerick James McCarron (A.S.T.) Derry

Year and place of meeting	1. President 2. Treasurer 3. Secretary	Members of parliamentary committee
		R. Sheldon (Amalgamated Union of Cabinet Makers)
1896 Limerick	1. James D'Alton (T.A.) Limerick 2. J. H. Jolley (T.A.) Cork 3. John Simmons (A.S.C.J.) Dublin	James McCarron (A.S.T.) Derry Alex. Taylor (Irish Linenlappers) Belfast Murray Davis (I.F.U. Bakers) Belfast J. H. Jolley (T.A.) Cork †P. J. Tevenan (A.S.R.S.) Dublin P. Golden (U. Lab. of I.) Dublin J. Fitzpatrick (A.S.C.J.) Dublin P. J. Leo (Amalgamated Society of Porkbutchers) Waterford
1897 Waterford	1. P. J. Leo (A.S. Porkbutchers) Waterford 2. P. J. Tevenan (A.S.R.S.) Dublin 3. John Simmons (A.S.C.J.) Dublin	†James McCarron (A.S.T.) Derry R. P. O'Connor (T.A.) Limerick P. J. Leo (A.S. Porkbutchers) Waterford P. J. Tevenan (A.S.R.S.) Dublin Murray Davis (I.F.U. Bakers) Belfast Joseph O'Brien (Op. Plasterers) Cork A. Taylor (Irish Linenlappers) Belfast J. Fitzpatrick (A.S.C.J.) Dublin
1898 Belfast	1. R. Wortley (A.S.T.) Belfast 2. P. J. Tevenan (A.S.R.S.) Dublin 3. John Simmons (A.S.C.J.) Dublin	†J. McCarron (A.S.T.) Derry A. Taylor (Irish Linenlappers) Belfast P. J. Tevenan (A.S.R.S.) Dublin A. Bowman (Flaxdressers, M.E.A.) Belfast R. P. O'Connor (T.A.) Limerick Murray Davis (I.F.U. Bakers) Belfast Joseph O'Brien (Op. Plasterers) Cork W. J. Leahy (Regular Society of Coopers) Dublin
1899 Derry	1. J. McCarron (A.S.T.) Derry 2. A. Taylor (Irish Linenlappers) Belfast 3. Hugh McManus (T.A.) Belfast	J. McCarron (A.S.T.) Derry A. Bowman (Flaxdressers) Belfast †W. J. Leahy (Reg. Soc. Coopers) Dublin A. Taylor (Irish Linenlappers) Belfast Patrick Cassidy (N.U.D.L.) Dublin James Chambers (Saddlers) Dublin John Simmons (A.S.C.J.) Dublin R. P. O'Connor (T.A.) Limerick
1900 Dublin	1. George Leahy (Operative Plasterers) Dublin	J. McCarron (A.S.T.) Derry A. Taylor (Irish Linenlappers) Belfast †A. Bowman (Flaxdressers) Belfast John Simmons (A.S.C.J.) Dublin

Year and place of meeting	1. President 2. Treasurer 3. Secretary	Members of parliamentary committee
	2. A. Taylor (Irish Linenlappers) Belfast 3. E. L. Richardson (D.T.P.S.)	James Chambers (Saddlers) Dublin John Gribbons (Bakers) Dublin Walter Hudson (A.S.R.S.) Dublin W. J. Leahy (Coopers) Dublin
1901 Sligo*	1. A. Bowman (Flaxdressers) Belfast 2. George Leahy (Operative Plas- terers) Dublin 3. E. L. Richardson (D.T.P.S.) Dublin	A. Bowman (Flaxdressers) Belfast George Leahy (Op. Plast.) Dublin John Simmons (A.S.C.J.) Dublin Walter Hudson (A.S.R.S.) Dublin W. J. Leahy (Coopers) Dublin James McCarron (A.S.T.) Derry †Hugh McManus (T.A.) Belfast William Liddell (Local Painters) Belfast
1902 Cork	1. W. Cave (Boot and Shoe- makers) Cork 2. George Leahy (Plasterers) Dublin 3. E. L. Richardson (D.T.P.S.) Dublin	W. Cave (Boot and Shoemakers) Cork James McCarron (A.S.T.) Derry W. J. Leahy (Coopers) Dublin George Leahy (Plasterers) Dublin W. Walker (A.S.C.J.) Belfast James Chambers (Saddlers) Dublin †Walter Hudson (A.S.R.S.) Dublin Hugh McManus (T.A.) Belfast
1903 Newry*	1. W. Hudson (A.S.R.S.) Dublin 2. George Leahy (Plasterers) Dublin 3. E. L. Richardson (D.T.P.S.) Dublin	George Leahy (Plasterers) Dublin W. Hudson (A.S.R.S.) Dublin J. McCarron (A.S.T.) Derry J. Chambers (Saddlers) Dublin H. McManus (T.A.) Belfast Stephen Dineen (Bakers) Limerick R. S. McNamara (Stonecutters) Cork †W. Walker (A.S.C.J.) Belfast
1904 Kilkenny*	1. W. Walker (A.S.C.J.) Belfast 2. E. W. Stewart (Shop Assistants) Dublin 3. E. L. Richardson (D.T.P.S.) Dublin	J. McCarron (A.S.T.) Derry S. Dineen (Bakers) Limerick H. McManus (T.A.) Belfast †J. Chambers (Saddlers) Dublin W. Walker (A.S.C.J.) Belfast W. Hudson (A.S.R.S.) Dublin G. Coates (Painters) Cork E. W. Stewart (Shop Assistants) Dublin

Year and place of meeting	1. President 2. Treasurer 3. Secretary	Members of parliamentary committee
1905 Wexford	1. J. Chambers (Saddlers) Dublin 2. E. W. Stewart (Shop Assistants) Dublin 3. E. L. Richardson (D.T.P.S.) Dublin	J. McCarron (A.S.T.) Derry J. Chambers (Saddlers) Dublin E. W. Stewart (Shop Assistants) Dublin P. T. Daly (D.T.P.S.) Dublin †S. Dineen (Bakers) Limerick W. Hudson (A.S.R.S.) Dublin George Leahy (Op. Plasterers) Dublin J. Simmons (A.S.C.J.) Dublin
1906 Athlone	1. Stephen Dineen (Bakers) Limerick 2. E. W. Stewart (Shop Assistants) Dublin 3. E. L. Richardson (D.T.P.S.) Dublin	†J. McCarron (A.S.T.) Derry John Murphy (T.A.) Belfast J. Chambers (Saddlers) Dublin W. Hudson (A.S.R.S.) Dublin E. W. Stewart (Shop Assistants) Dublin S. Dineen (Bakers) Limerick Michael Egan (U.K. Coachmakers) Cork George Greig (N.A.U.L.) Belfast

*There were no trades councils in Sligo (1901) or Newry (1903); in 1904 the Kilkenny Trades Council waived their right to provide the president of congress in favor of William Walker, chairman of the parliamentary committee elected at Newry.

† Chairman of the parliamentary committee.

Appendix 7

Questionnaire Submitted by the Belfast Protestant Association to Candidates in the North Belfast By-Election, and William Walker's Replies (1905)

1. Will you oppose every attempt to abolish, or otherwise alter, the Bill of Rights and the Act of Settlement, which require the sovereign of these realms to make the Statutory Declaration against Transubstantiation upon his accession to the throne?

Yes

2. Will you uphold the Parliamentary enactments which prohibit the Throne of Britain to a Roman Catholic or to a Protestant who has married an adherent to the Papal Communion?

Yes

3. Will you resist every effort to throw open the office of Lord High Chancellor and Lord Lieutenant of Ireland to Roman Catholics?

Yes

4. Will you labour for the enforcement of the Acts of Parliament which prohibit the residence of Jesuits and Roman Catholic monks in this Kingdom?

Yes; except when they are English born, and keep within the limits of Civil law.

5. Will you contend against every proposal to open diplomatic relations between the Vatican and the Court of St. James?

Yes

6. Will you resist every attack upon the legislative enactments provided by our forefathers as necessary safeguards against the political encroachments of the Papacy?

Yes

7. Will you strive to secure the periodical inspection of convents and monastic institutions; the liberation of such of their inmates as are forcibly detained; the compulsory registration of all deaths in such institutions and the suppression of all private burial grounds?

All convents and conventual institutions which harbour other than their proprietors should be officially inspected.

8. Will you make an effort to obtain a redistribution of Parliamentary seats for the purpose of diminishing the extravagant representation of Ireland, by means of which the Roman Catholic and Disloyal party has hindered the business of the House of Commons?

Yes, but no reduction in the aggregate of numbers.

9. Will you offer strenuous resistance to all demands for the expenditure of public money upon the establishment or endowment of a Roman Catholic University or College in Ireland?

Absolutely.

10. Will you try to procure the institution of a Parliamentary inquiry into the manner in which the public funds have been bestowed upon Roman Catholic institutions (particularly in Ireland) and the publication of full particulars of each endowment and grant, the amount of public money given in each case, and the object to which it has been applied?

All public grants should forthwith cease, and a return made of how previously the money had been spent.

11. Will you use your influence for the purpose of obtaining the abolition of the Bishop's veto; the substitution of deprivation for imprisonment in the case of ministers who fail to obey the law; and the emancipation of the Church of England from the condition of anarchy created by the systematic disloyalty of the Romanising clergy?

Absolutely opposed to Sacerdotalism.

12. Will you withstand every attempt to bring foward Home Rule for Ireland; or any measure or clause of a measure which would introduce Home Rule by a policy of 'devolution' or by the establishment in Ireland of a legislative body empowered to enact laws on purely Irish affairs?

I believe that only by the co-operation of the English workman can the Irish labourer be helped; hence I shall oppose Home Rule in any form.

13. Will you insist upon the fulfilment of the duty of His Majesty's Government to protect the King's Protestant subjects from the boycotting persecuting policy formulated by the Church of Rome, and carried into effect by the Catholic Association of Ireland, the United Irish League and other organisations?

The full power of the state should be used to secure the fullest civil and religious liberty.

14. Will you, in all things, place the interests of Protestantism before those of the political party to which you are attached?

Protestantism means protesting against superstition, hence true protestantism is synonymous with labour.

Sources: *Northern Whig,* 11 Sept. 1905; *Northern Star,* 23 Sept. 1905.

Appendix 8

Questionnaire Submitted by the Belfast Trades Council to Candidates in the General Election of 1906

1. Will you advocate and support the amendment of the Workmen's Compensation Act, so that it may include seamen and all others at present excluded from its provisions?

2. Will you vote for a Bill giving Old Age Pensions to all workmen over 60 years of age?

3. Will you advocate and support a measure for the taxation of urban land values?

4. Will you support a Bill to sanction peaceful picketing in Labour disputes?

5. Are you in favour of the immediate nationalisation of Irish railways?

6. Will you support a Bill for the taxation of mineral royalties?

7. Are you in favour of the abrogation of the Chinese labour ordinance?

8. Will you vote for an eight-hours' working day in all occupations when the labour is continuous?

9. Will you state briefly your views on housing, Poor-law and Temperance reform?

10. Will you support a bill for adult suffrage and a single franchise?

11. Are you in favour of the compulsory sale of estates by the Irish landlords?

12. Are you in favour of extending the powers of municipalities in trading matters?

13. Will you support the amendment of the Unemployed Workmen Act so as to give the community power to abolish unemployment?

14. Will you vote against Labour Bureaux being made use of in connection with Trades Disputes?

15. Will you oppose the imposition, under any pretext, of further taxes upon the food of the people?

16. Are you in favour of the Returning Officers' expenses (in Parliamentary elections) being paid out of the public rates?

17. Are you in favour of the payment of M.P.s?

18. Are you in favour of the assimilation of the Belfast Harbour Franchise to the municipal?

Source: B.T.C. minutes, 11 Jan. 1906.

Bibliography

NOTE. J. D. Clarkson's *Labour and Nationalism in Ireland* (New York, 1925) lists a substantial number of publications in Irish labor history before 1925. Some items of labor interest appearing before 1940 are included in J. Carty's *Bibliography of Irish History, 1870–1911* (Dublin, National Library of Ireland, 1940). The annual lists of "Writings in Irish History" in *Irish Historical Studies*, in the files of *Saothar* (the Irish Labour History Society's journal) and in the *Bulletin of the* [British] *Society for the Study of Labour History* may be consulted for more recent publications.

I. PRIMARY SOURCES

A. Published

1. Trade Union and Socialist Organizations—Reports and Documents

Amalgamated Society of Railway Servants. *Report and financial statement, 1887.*

[British] Trades Union Congress. *Annual reports 1869–.* The 1868 report is in manuscript. The name used in early reports is "United Trades Congress" or "Conference of Trade Unions."

Fabian Society. *Annual reports of the executive committee, 1892, 1895, 1898, 1899, 1900–1903.*

Independent Labour Party. *Reports of annual conferences, 1893, 1901, 1918.*

International Socialist Congress (Second International). *Cinquième congrès socialiste international tenu à Paris du 23 au 27 septembre 1900; Compte-rendu analytique officiel.* Paris, 1901.

Cinquième congrès socialiste international: Compte-rendue sténographique (non-officiel) de la version française. Cahiers de la Quinzaine, Paris, 1901.

International Working Men's Association (First International). *Documents of the First International.* 5 volumes (1864–72). Moscow, [1960?–].

Irish Locomotive Engineers' Trade Union. *Rules and regulations (1917).*

Irish Trades Union Congress. *Annual reports, 1895–.* No official report of the first congress (1894) was issued, but an extensive report will be found in the *Freeman's Journal*, 28, 30 April 1894. The file in the possession of the Irish Congress of Trade Unions (formerly the Irish T.U.C.) lacks the reports for 1895 and 1897. Through the courtesy of the late William O'Brien I was able to complete the file and add the agenda of the first congress and other material published by the Dublin Trades Council in 1894. I arranged for microfilm copies to be deposited in the National Library of Ireland, the library of Queen's University, and the Institut français d'Histoire sociale, Paris.

Labour Electoral Congress. *Annual reports of second (1889), third (1890), and fifth (1892) congresses.*

Labour Representation Committee (after 1906 the [British] Labour Party). *Annual conference reports 1901–.*

National Amalgamated Union of Labour (formerly Tyneside and National Labourers' Union). *Annual reports 1891–3* (includes quarterly report ending 1 July 1893) *1897–8, 1917.*

National Union of Dock Labourers. *Executive committee reports 1891–5, 1905, 1912.*

National Union of Gasworkers and General Labourers. *Reports 1892–4.*

Socialist League. *Report of third (1887) annual conference.*

Trade Union Congress (British). *Annual Reports 1869—.*

2. Parliamentary Papers and Other Official Publications

(These have, as far as possible, been grouped according to subject and arranged in chronological order.)

(a) Reports on combinations of workmen and trade unions

First Report from the Select Committee to inquire into the state of the law regarding Artizans and Machinery, H.C. 1824 (51).

Report from the Select Committee appointed to inquire into the effects of 5 Geo. 4, c. 95, in respect to the conduct of Workmen and others in the United Kingdom, and how far it may be necessary to repeal and amend the same Act, minutes of evidence, H.C. 1825 (437, 417).

First report from the Select Committee on Combinations of Workmen: minutes of evidence, H.C. 1837–8 (488), viii.

Second Report on Combinations of Workmen, H.C. 1837–8 (646), viii.

Eleventh and Final Report of the Commissioners to inquire into the Organisation and Rules of Trade Unions and other associations, [4124-1], H.C. 1868–9, xxxi.

Report of the Chief Registrar of Friendly Societies for the year 1895, 1896 (94), lxxviii.

Report of the Chief Registrar of Friendly Societies for the year 1899, 1900 (30–1), lxxxi.

(b) Reports on the condition of the poor, on wages and hours of labor and on industrial agreements:

Third Report from the Commissioners for inquiry into the Condition of the Poorer Classes in Ireland, Appendix C, Pts. I and II, H.C. 1836, xxx.

Statistical Tables and Reports on Trade Unions, 1886–1907. (Consistency is not maintained either in the titles or numbering of the reports.)

Statistical Tables and Reports on Trade Unions for 1886, [C. 5104], H.C. 1887.

Statistical Tables and Reports on Trade Unions for 1888, [C. 5808], H.C. 1889, lxxxiv, 156.

Statistical Tables and Reports on Trade Unions for 1891, [C. 6990], 1893–4, cii.

Abstract of Labour Statistics (Board of Trade) for the years 1899–1900, [Cd. 495], H.C. 1901, lxxxiii.

Eighth Annual Report of the Chief Labour Correspondent of the Board of Trade on Trade Unions for 1895, [C. 8232], H.C. 1896, xciii, 364–9.

Ninth Annual Report of the Chief Labour Correspondent of the Board of Trade on Trade Unions for 1896, [C. 8644], H.C. 1897, xcix.

Tenth Annual Report of the Chief Labour Correspondent of the Board of Trade on Trade Unions for 1897, [C. 9013], H.C. 1898, ciii.

Eleventh Annual Report of the Chief Labour Correspondent of the Board of Trade on Trade Unions for 1898, [C. 9443], H.C. 1899, xcii.

Report of the Chief Labour Correspondent of the Board of Trade on Trade Unions for the years 1902–4, [Cd. 2838], H.C. 1906, cxiii.

Report of the Chief Labour Correspondent of the Board of Trade on Trade Unions for the years 1905, 1906 and 1907, [Cd. 4651], H.C. 1909, lxxxix.

Report from the Select Committee on handloom weavers petitions: minutes of evidence, 1835 (341, 492), xiii.

Royal Commission on Labour: minutes of evidence before Group C [C. 6795–iv], H.C. 1892,
  xxxvi, Pt. II.
Royal Commission on Labour: The Agricultural Labourer, IV, Ireland, pt. iv [C. 6894–xxi],
  H.C. 1893–4, xxxvii.
Report on Wages and Earnings of Agricultural Labourers in the United Kingdom, 1898 [Cd.
  346], H.C. 1900, xcii.
Money Wages of indoor Domestic Servants [C. 9346], H.C. 1899, xciii.
Report on the Changes in Rates of Wages and Hours of Labour in the United Kingdom in 1902
  [Cd. 1562], H.C. 1903, lxvi.
Report of the Industrial Council on the Inquiry into Industrial Agreements: minutes of evidence
  [Cd. 6953], H.C. 1913, xxviii.

(c) Reports of factory inspectors:

Report of the Chief Inspector of Factories for 1893 [C. 7368], H.C. 1893–4, xxi.
Report of the Chief Inspector of Factories for 1905 [Cd. 3036], H.C. 1906, xv.
Report of the Chief Inspector of Factories for 1906 [Cd. 3586], H.C. 1907, x.

(d) Reports on health and housing:

Minutes of Evidence of the Special Committee appointed 1 August 1896 to consider and report
  upon the present death-rate of Belfast and the condition of the public health of the city. Belfast,
  n.d.
Twenty-ninth Annual Report of the Local Government Board of Ireland for the year ending 31
  March 1901 [Cd. 1259], H.C. 1902, xxvii; supplement [Cd. 1260], H.C. 1902,
  xxxvii.
Bailie, H. W., M.S.O.H. *Report on the Health of the County Borough of Belfast for the year*
  1906. Belfast, 1907.
Bailie, H. W., M.S.O.H. *Report on the Health of the County Borough of Belfast for the year*
  1907. Belfast, 1908.

(e) Census returns and reports on population, production, and trade:

Census of Population (Ireland), 1901, table xx, pp. 15–32 [Cd. 1123a], H.C. 1902,
  cxxvi.
Report on the Trade in Imports and Exports at Irish Ports during the year ending 31 October
  1904 [Cd. 3237], H.C. 1906, cxiv.
Report on the Trade in Imports and Exports at Irish Ports during the year ending 31 October
  1905 [Cd. 3631], H.C. 1907, lxxxi.
Final report on the Census of Production of the United Kingdom, 1907 [Cd. 6320], H.C.
  1912, cix.

(f) Hansard:

Parliamentary Debates, 3rd series, xi.

3. Newspapers and Periodicals

(a) Newspapers (daily, unless otherwise described):
Cork:
  Cork Examiner (nationalist)
  Cork Herald (nationalist)
Belfast:
  Belfast Evening Telegraph (unionist)
  Belfast News-Letter (conservative)
  Irish News (nationalist)

Morning News (nationalist, absorbed by the *Irish News* in 1892)

Northern Star and *Ulster Observer* (nationalist, weekly; started in 1897 by Joseph Devlin in opposition to the *Irish News,* which favored the Catholic Association)

Northern Whig (liberal, liberal-unionist after 1886)

Weekly Northern Whig (liberal-unionist)

Dublin:

Evening Mail (conservative)

Freemen's Journal (nationalist, Parnellite for some months after split, then anti-Parnellite until 1900)

Irish Daily Independent (nationalist, Parnellite until 1900; title later changed to *Irish Independent*)

Irish Daily Telegraph (conservative)

Irish Times (conservative)

Sinn Féin (Weekly)

London:

Daily Chronicle

Daily Telegraph

Standard

The Times

Manchester:

Manchester Guardian

(b) Miscellaneous periodicals (issued weekly, monthly or irregularly):

Ireland:

Belfast Labour Chronicle (Belfast Trades Council and L.R.C.)

Belfast Weekly Star ⎱ Christian Socialist
Brotherhood ⎰ ed. Rev. Bruce Wallace

The Guardian and Tradesman's Advocate (Dublin)

Irishman (advanced nationalist, proprietor Richard Pigott, 1865–79)

Irish Protestant (ed. R. Lindsay Crawford, 1901–06)

Irish Worker (published by Bernard Doyle, Dublin printer)

Labour Opposition (organ of North Belfast I.L.P., 1925–26)

Nation (nationalist)

Shan Van Vocht [The Poor Old Woman, i.e. Ireland] (republican, Belfast)

Ulster Guardian (from 1906 organ of the Ulster Liberal Association)

Workers' Republic (published by James Connolly)

Great Britain:

Commonweal (Socialist League)

Clarion (Robert Blatchford's weekly)

Justice (S.D.F.)

Railway Review (A.S.R.S. journal)

The Socialist (published by the S.D.F. Scottish Council, and initially printed on the I.S.R.P. press)

Trade Unionist (15 August 1891)

France:

L'Irlande Libre (republican)

Revue Socialiste

4. Correspondence, Diaries, Memoirs

Campbell, T. J. *Fifty Years of Ulster.* Belfast, 1941.

De Latocnaye. *Promenade d'un Français dans L'Irlande*. Dublin, 1797.

Drennan, William. *The Drennan Letters*. Edited by D. A. Chart. Belfast, 1931.

Lynch, Arthur. *My Life Story*. London, 1934.

Marx, Karl, and Engels, Frederick. *Selected Correspondence*. Edited by S. Ryazanskaya. 2nd ed., Moscow, 1965.

Mitchel, John. *Jail Journal*. Introduction by Arthur Griffith. Dublin, n.d.

O'Brien, William. *Forth the Banners Go*. Dublin, 1969.

Sheehan, D. D. *Ireland Since Parnell*. London, 1921.

Tone, Theobald Wolfe. *The Life of Theobald Wolfe Tone*. Edited by W. T. W. Tone. 2 vols. Washington, 1826. This consists of Tone's autobiography, journals, letters and writings, together with an account by his son of Tone's last expedition and death.

Wesley, John. *Journals*. Edited by N. Curnock. 8 vols. London, 1909–16.

5. Contributions to Labor and Socialist Periodicals

Connolly, James. *Labour in Ireland (Labour in Irish History; The Re-Conquest of Ireland)*. Introduction by Robert Lynd. Dublin, 1922.

———. *Socialism and Nationalism; A Selection from the Writings of James Connolly*. Edited by Desmond Ryan. Dublin, 1948.

———. *Labour and Easter Week; A Selection from the Writings of James Connolly*. Edited by Desmond Ryan. Dublin, 1951.

———. *The Workers' Republic; A Selection from the Writings of James Connolly*. Edited by Desmond Ryan. Dublin, 1951.

———. *James Connolly: Selected Political Writings*. Edited and introduced by Owen Dudley Edwards and Bernard Ransom. London, 1973.

Marx, Karl, and Engels, Frederick. *Ireland and the Irish Question*. Edited by R. Dixon, with an introduction by C. Desmond Greaves. Moscow, 1971. A collection of articles, letters, and manifestoes on Ireland, together with Engels's draft of a history of Ireland. Miscellaneous circulars, election addresses, and leaflets.

6. Records and Documents

Calendar of the Ancient Records of Dublin. Edited by J. T. Gilbert. Vols. ii, v, x. Dublin, 1889–1906.

Irish Historical Documents. Edited by Edmund Curtis and R. B. McDowell. London, 1943.

Select Statutes, Cases and Documents. Edited by Sir C. G. Robertson. 8th edition, London, 1947.

Irish Historical Statistics: Population, 1821–1971. Edited by W. E. Vaughan and A. J. Fitzpatrick. Dublin, 1978.

Parliamentary Election Results in Ireland, 1801–1922. Edited by B. M. Walker. Dublin, 1978.

7. Works of Reference

Belfast Directory, 1884, 1892.

Concise Dictionary of Irish Biography. John S. Crone, Dublin, 1928.

Constitutional Yearbook for 1911.

Debrett's House of Commons.

Labour Annual, 1896, 1897. Manchester and London.

Thom's Directory of the United Kingdom, 1892.

Who Was Who, 1897–1916.

B. Unpublished

1. Manuscript and Other Archival Material

Amalgamated Society of Carpenters and Joiners. Minutes of the managing committee of the Belfast district in the Belfast office of the Amalgamated Society of Woodworkers.

Amalgamated Society of Engineers. Monthly and annual reports of the Amalgamated Union of Engineering Workers in the head office, 110 Peckham Road, London.

Amalgamated Society of Lithographic Printers. Records in the head office, Senefeldia House, 137 Dickenson Road, Rusholme, Manchester.

Belfast Corporation. Minutes of the gas committee.

Belfast Trades Council. The following records exist for the period covered by this book:
—Minute books. Complete except for two periods: October 1881–October 1885, December 1895–September 1897. Until November 1891, when the press was admitted, the minute books constitute the only record of council meetings.
—Executive committee minutes, February 1899–April 1905.
—Account Book, 1899–.
—Dues Book, 1905–.
—Annual reports for 1891, 1892, 1893.
In 1984 Microform Ltd. (East Ardsley, Wakefield, West Yorkshire) published microfilms of the records of the Belfast and Dublin Trades Councils, with introductions, up to 1951. In this work I have used the originals.

Crawford collection. In the possession of Miss Morna E. Crawford, Boston, daughter of Robert Lindsay Crawford. It includes letters, press clippings, and other material relating to the Independent Orange Order and to Crawford's career. To Mrs. Kathleen Morwood I owe the good fortune of an introduction to Miss Crawford.

Dublin Corporation, minutes, 1 January 1893.

Dublin Trades Council. The following records exist for the period covered by this book:
—Minute books, 1894–January 1908.
—Executive committee minutes, 1903–7.

Howell collection. This large collection, housed in Bishopgate Institute, London, includes the minutes of the Reform League General Council and George Howell's letterbook, now available on microfilm, edited by Dr. Royden Harrison.

Irish Socialist Republican Party. Minute books in the National Library of Ireland.

Jung papers. Hermann Jung's papers in the International Institute of Social History (International Instituut voor Sociale Geschiedenis), Amsterdam, contain a few items of Irish interest.

Labour Representation League. The minutes of the General Council and some related correspondence are in the British Library of Political and Economic Science, London School of Economics.

McClung papers. These reminiscences of the Belfast Labor movement, now in my possession, consist of twenty-six pages covering events during 1885–1912 and twelve cards of notes for the years 1901–20. Robert McClung was an official of the Workers' Union and of the union that absorbed it, the Amalgamated Transport and General Workers' Union.

MacDonnell collection. This consists of press clippings, pamphlets, and a ten-page biography of J. P. MacDonnell dictated by his widow in 1908 to Miss Clara Commons. It is at present in the archives of the State Historical Society of Wisconsin.

Marx–Engels Nachlass. The Marx–Engels correspondence in the International Institute of Social History (International Instituut voor Sociale Geschiedenis), Amsterdam, includes letters written by MacDonnell and De Morgan after their arrival in England.

O'Brien collection. Of special interest to labor historians, this extensive collection of manuscript and printed material includes the Connolly correspondence. William O'Brien joined the Irish Socialist Republican Party in 1899. During his subsequent career in socialist and labor organization he amassed and preserved records that otherwise might have been lost. His collection is now in the National Library of Ireland.

Russell papers. The journals of Thomas Russell are in the Irish State Papers Office and the library of Trinity College, Dublin. My thanks are due to Dr. R. B. McDowell, who lent me his transcript of the manuscripts.

Webb collection. In the British Library of Political and Economic Science, London School of Economics.

2. Interviews

(Interviews with Robert McClung were carried out in the early 1940's and with others during the years 1957–62. I had additional interviews with Frederick Carson and Bulmer Hobson subsequent to 1962.)

R. R. Bowman, son of Alexander Bowman; William Boyd, retired official of the National Union of Vehicle Builders; R. H. Campbell, son of D. R. Campbell; Frederick Carson, younger contemporary of William Walker and participant in Belfast labor politics; Samuel Hazlett, younger contemporary of Alexander Bowman; D. R. Campbell and Robert McClung; Bulmer Hobson, a founder of the Dungannon Clubs and friend of Francis Joseph Biggar, later a leading member of Sinn Féin and the I.R.B.; Mrs. F. F. Patterson, sister of Bulmer Hobson; John Jamison, retired shipyard worker; Thomas R. Johnson, founder of the Belfast Socialist Society, later secretary of the Irish T.U.C.; Robert Matchett, member (1904–5) of the Imperial Grand Lodge of the Independent Orange Order, Daniel J. McDevitt, delegate to the Belfast Trades Council from the mid-1890s onward and active in Belfast labor politics; Seán McKeown, son of Michael McKeown; William O'Brien (see his collection above); George Scanlin, retired painter; Mrs. William Walker (née Adams), widow of William Walker.

II. SECONDARY SOURCES

A. General

Lee, Joseph. *The Modernisation of Irish Society*. Dublin, 1973.
Lyons, F. S. L. *Ireland since the Famine*. London, 1971; rev. ed. 1973.

B. Biographical

Bédarida, François. *Will Thorne*. Paris, 1987.
Black, R. D. C. "William James Pirrie." In Cruise-O'Brien, C. (ed.), *The Shaping of Modern Ireland*. London, 1960.
Boyle, J. W. "William Walker." In Boyle, J. W. (ed.), *Leaders and Workers*. Cork, 1965.
Greaves, C. Desmond. *The Life and Times of James Connolly*. London, 1961.
Larkin, Emmet. *James Larkin*. London, 1965.
Lyons, F. S. L. *John Dillon*. London, 1968.
Moody, T. W. *Davitt and Irish Revolution, 1846–82*. London, 1981.
———. "Michael Davitt." In Boyle, J. W. (ed.), *Leaders and Workers*. Cork, 1965.

Ó Gríofa, Art. Griffith, Arthur. O Luing, Seán. *Art Ó Gríofa* (Arthur Griffith; written in Irish). Dublin, 1953.

Mulvany, T. J. *The Life of James Gandon.* Dublin, 1846.

O'Neill, T. P. "James Fintan Lalor." In Boyle, J. W. (ed.), *Leaders and Workers.* Cork, 1965.

Ryan, Desmond. *The Fenian Chief* (James Stephens). Dublin, 1967.

Ryan, Desmond. *James Connolly, His Life, Work and Writings.* Dublin, 1924.

St. Clair, Silvester. *John De Morgan Sketches of the Life and Labours of Jno. De Morgan.* Leeds, 1880.

Thornley, D. A. *Isaac Butt and Home Rule.* London, 1964.

C. Studies of the labor movement

Alcock, G. W. *Fifty Years of Railway Trade Unionism.* London, 1922.

Bagwell, P. S. *The Railwaymen.* London, 1963.

Bealey, Frank. "Les travaillistes et la guerre des Boers." In *Le Mouvement Social,* no. 45 (Oct.–Dec. 1963).

Bealey, F. and Pelling, H. M. *Labour and Politics.* London, 1958.

Boyd, Andrew. *The Rise of the Irish Trade Unions.* Tralee, Ireland. 1972.

Boyle, J. W. "The Rural Labourer." In *Threshold,* iii, no. 1 (Spring, 1959).

———. "Le développement du mouvement ouvrier irlandais de 1880 à 1907." In *Le Mouvement Social,* no. 52 (Juill.–Sept. 1965).

———. "Ireland and the First International." In *Journal of British Studies,* XI, no. 2 (May 1972).

———. "A Marginal Figure: The Irish Rural Labourer." In Clark, S., and Donnelly, J. S., Jr. (eds.), *Irish Peasants: Violence and Political Unrest, 1780–1914.* Madison, Wisconsin, 1983.

———. "Irish Labor and the Rising." In *Eire-Ireland,* Fall, 1967.

Briggs, A. and Saville, John. *Essays in Labour History.* London, 1967.

Clarkson, J. D. *Labour and Nationalism in Ireland.* New York, 1925.

Cole, G. D. H. *British Working-Class Politics.* London, 1941.

Collins, H. and Abramsky, C. *Karl Marx and the British Labour Movement.* London, 1965.

Daly, Seán. *Ireland and the First International.* Cork, 1984.

D'Arcy, F. A. "The Artizans of Dublin and O'Connell, 1830–47." In *Irish Historical Studies,* xvii, no. 66 (1970).

———. "The Trade Unions of Dublin and the Attempted Revival of the Guilds." In *Journal of the Royal Society of Antiquaries of Ireland,* 101, Pt. 2 (1971).

Fitzpatrick, David. "The Disappearance of the Irish Agricultural Labourer, 1841–1912." In *Irish Economic and Social History,* vii (1980).

Frew, Edmund, and Katanka, Michael. *1868, The Year of the Unions.* London, 1968.

Gray, John. *City in Revolt: James Larkin and the Belfast Dock Strike of 1907.* Belfast, 1985.

Harrison, Royden. *Before the Socialists.* London, 1965.

Higenbotham, S. *Our Society's History.* Manchester, 1939.

Hobsbawm, E. J. "General Labour Unions in Britain, 1889–1914." In *Economic History Review,* 2nd series, I, nos. 2 and 3 (1949).

Horn, P. L. R. "The National Agricultural Labourers' Union in Ireland, 1873–9." In *Irish Historical Studies,* xvii, no. 67 (March 1971).

Jeffreys, J. B. *The Story of the Engineers.* London, 1945.

Kendall, Walters. *The Revolutionary Movement in Britain.* London, 1969.

Keogh, Dermot. "The 'New Unionism' in Ireland: The Dublin Coal Porters' Strike, 1890." *Capucin Annual*, 1975.

―――. *The Rise of the Irish Working Class. The Dublin Trade Union Movement and Labour Leadership, 1890–1914*. Belfast, 1982.

Kidd, A. T. *History of the Tinplate Workers', Sheet Metal Workers' and Braziers' Societies*. London, 1949.

McBriar, A. M. *Fabian Socialism and English Politics, 1884–1918*. Cambridge, 1962.

McCarthy, Charles. *Trade Unions in Ireland, 1894–1960*. Dublin, 1977.

McKillop, Norman. *The Lighted Flame*. London, Edinburgh. 1950.

Moody, T. W. "Michael Davitt and the British Labour Movement, 1882–1906." In *Transactions of the Royal Historical Society*, 5th series, iii (1953).

Musson, A. E. *The Typographical Association*. London, 1954.

O'Higgins, Rachel. "Irish Trade Unions and Politics, 1830–50." In *The Historical Journal*, iv, no. 2 (1961).

―――. "Irish Influence in the Chartist Movement." In *Past and Present*, no. 20 (1961).

Pease, E. R. *A History of the Fabian Society*. London, 1916.

Pelling, H. M. *The Origins of the Labour Party*. London, 1954.

―――. "The Knights of Labour in Britain, 1880–1901." In *Economic History Review*, 2nd series, ix, no. 2 (1956).

―――. *A History of Trade Unionism*. Harmondsworth, 1963.

Poirier, Philip E. *The Advent of the Labour Party*. London, 1958.

Roberts, B. C. *Trade Union Government and Administration in Great Britain*. London. 1956.

―――. *The Trades Union Congress*. London, 1958.

Ryan, W. P. *The Irish Labour Movement*. Dublin, 1919.

Saville, John. "Trade Unions and Free Labour: the Background to the Taff Vale Decision." In Briggs, A. and Saville, John, *Essays in Labour History*. London, 1967.

Shaffer, Gordon. *Light and Liberty*. Electrical Trades Union, Hayes, Bromley, Kent, 1952.

Simon, Brian. *Education and the Labour Movement*. London, 1965.

Swift, John. *History of the Dublin Bakers and Others*. Dublin, n.d.

Thompson, E. P. *The Making of the English Working Class*. Rev. ed., Harmondsworth, 1967.

Webb, Sidney and Beatrice. *The History of Trade Unionism* (rev. ed.). London, 1920.

D. Studies exclusive of the labor movement

Armstrong, D. L. "Social and Economic Conditions in the Belfast Linen Industry, 1850–1900." In *Irish Historical Studies*, vii, no. 28 (1951).

Armytage, W. H. G. *Heavens Below*. Toronto, 1961.

Boyd, Andrew. *Holy War in Belfast*. Tralee, Ireland, 1969.

Boyle, Elizabeth. *The Irish Flowerers*. Holywood (County Down) and Belfast, 1971.

Boyle, J. W. "Industrial Conditions in the Twentieth Century." In Moody, T. W., and Beckett, J. C., *Ulster since 1800: A Social Survey*. London, 1957.

―――. "The Belfast Protestant Association and the Independent Orange Order, 1901–10." In *Irish Historical Studies*, xiii, no. 50 (1962).

"A Fenian Protestant in Canada: Robert Lindsay Crawford." In *Canadian Historical Review*, lii, no. 2 (June 1971).

Cameron, Sir C. A. *How the Poor Live*. Dublin, 1904.

Comerford, R. V. *The Fenians in Context: Irish Politics and Society 1848–82.* Dublin; Atlantic City, New Jersey, 1985.

Connell, K. H. *Irish Peasant Society.* Oxford, 1968.

Conroy, J. C. *A History of Railways in Ireland.* London, 1928.

Coyne, W. P. (ed.). *Ireland, Agricultural and Industrial.* 2nd ed. Dublin, 1902.

Crotty, Raymond D. *Irish Agricultural Production: Its Volume and Structure.* Cork, 1966.

Cruise-O'Brien, Conor. *Parnell and his Party.* Oxford, 1957.

———. *The Shaping of Modern Ireland.* London, 1960.

Cullen, L. M. *An Economic History of Ireland since 1660.* New York, 1972.

———. (ed.). *The Formation of the Irish Economy.* Cork, 1969.

Curtis, L. P., Jr. *Anglo-Saxons and Celts.* Bridgeport, Connecticut, 1968.

Daly, Mary E. *Dublin, The Deposed Capital.* Cork, 1984.

Dawson, Charles. "The Housing of the People, with Special Reference to Dublin." In *Journal of the Statistical and Social Inquiry Society of Ireland,* xi, 48 (1901).

De Beaumont, Gustave. *L'Irlande, Sociale, Religieuse et Politique.* 5th ed., Paris, 1842.

Eason, Charles Jr. "The Tenement Houses of Dublin." *Journal of the Statistical and Social Inquiry Society of Ireland,* x, Pt. 79 (1899).

Gill, Conrad. *The Rise of the Irish Linen Industry.* London, 1925.

Green, E. R. R. *The Lagan Valley, 1800–50.* London, 1949.

Hepburn, A. C. "The Irish Council Bill and the Fall of Sir Anthony MacDonnell." *Irish Historical Studies,* xvii, no. 68 (1971).

Inglis, Brian. *The Freedom of the Press in Ireland, 1784–1841.* London, 1954.

Jacob, Rosamund. *The Rise of the United Irishmen.* London, 1937.

James, F. G. "Irish Smuggling in the Eighteenth Century." *Irish Historical Studies,* xii, no. 48 (1961).

Jones, Emrys. *A Social Geography of Belfast.* London, 1960.

Lee, Joseph. "Irish Agriculture." *Agricultural History Review,* xvii, Pt. I (1969).

Lipson, E. *The Economic History of England.* Vol. 1, The Middle Ages. 7th ed., London, 1937.

Lynch, P., and Vaizey, J. *Guinness's Brewery in the Irish Economy, 1759–1876.* Cambridge, 1960.

Lyons, F. S. L. *The Irish Parliamentary Party, 1890–1910.* London, 1951.

———. "The Irish Unionist Party and the Devolution Crisis of 1904–5." *Irish Historical Studies,* vi, no. 21 (1948).

———. *John Dillon.* London, 1968.

McCaffrey, L. J. "Irish Federalism in the 1870s, a Study in Conservative Nationalism." *Transactions of the American Philosophical Society,* new series, lii, Pt. 6 (1962).

McDowell, R. B. "The Personnel of the Dublin Society of United Irishmen, 1791–4." *Irish Historical Studies,* ii, no. 5 (1940).

———. "Ireland on the Eve of the Famine." In Edwards, R. D., and Williams, T. D. (eds.), *The Great Famine.* Dublin, 1956.

———. *Public Opinion and Government Policy in Ireland, 1801–1846.* London, 1952.

———. "The Consolidation of the Union." In Moody, T. W., and Beckett, J. C. (eds.), *Ulster since 1800: A Political and Economic Survey.* London, 1955.

Marshall, R. *Fifty Years on the Grosvenor Road.* Belfast, 1953.

Matheson, R. E. "The Housing of the People in Ireland during 1841–1901." *Journal of the Statistical and Social Inquiry Society of Ireland,* xi, Pt. 82 (1903).

Maxwell, Constantia. *Country and Town in Ireland under the Georges.* 2nd. ed., Dundalk, 1949.

———. *Dublin under the Georges.* London, 1936.

Monaghan, T. J. "The Rise and Fall of the Belfast Cotton Industry." *Irish Historical Studies,* iii, no. 9 (1942).

Moody, T. W., and Beckett, J. C. *Queen's, Belfast.* London, 1959.

Murray, A. E. *A History of the Commercial and Financial Relations between England and Ireland from the Period of the Restoration.* London, 1903.

Nowlan, K. B. *The Politics of Repeal.* London, 1965.

O'Brien, George. *The Economic History of Ireland in the Eighteenth Century.* Dublin, 1918.

————. *The Economic History of Ireland from the Union to the Famine.* London, 1921.

O'Donovan, J. *The Economic History of Livestock in Ireland.* Cork, 1940.

Riordan, E. J. *Modern Irish Industry and Trade.* London, 1920.

Savage, D. C. "The Origins of the Ulster Unionist Party, 1885–6." *Irish Historical Studies,* xii, no. 47 (1961).

Shadwell, A. *The Engineering Industry and the Crisis of 1922.* London, 1922.

Spiller, Gustav. *The Ethical Movement in Great Britain.* London, 1934.

Wall, Maureen. "The Rise of the Catholic Middle-class in Eighteenth-century Ireland." *Irish Historical Studies,* xi, no. 42 (1958).

Whyte, J. H. *The Independent Irish Party.* London, 1958.

Wittke, Carl. *The Irish in America.* New York, 1956.

E. Unpublished research theses

(Owing to the kindness of their authors I was able to consult, while still unpublished, the theses listed below.)

Davis, R. P. The Rise of Sinn Fein, 1891–1910. Thesis approved for the degree of M. Litt., T.C.D., 1958.

D'Arcy, F. A. Dublin Artizan Activity, Opinion and Organisation, 1820–50. Thesis approved for the degree of M.A., N.U.I., 1968.

Johnston, G. F. E. Irish Agricultural Labourers, 1881–1921. Thesis approved for Moderatorship, T.C.D., 1954.

Whitford, F. J. Joseph Devlin. Thesis approved for the degree of M.A., University of London, 1958.

Index